Southern Families Made America

Colonization, Revolution, and Expansion from Virginia Colony, to the Republic of Texas, to the Pacific, 1607 to 1848

A narrative-style history of the Southern people and their leaders as they expand and make productive a 2,400-mile span of America, beginning at Jamestown, Virginia Colony in 1607, proceeding westward to the Republic of Texas and concluding in 1848 at the Pacific Ocean.

Published by SouthernBooks

By Howard Ray White
(www.howardraywhite.com)

About Howard Ray White, the Author

Howard Ray White, 85, is the author of many histories about the South, including his first major work, the comprehensive four-volume series, *Bloodstains, an Epic History of the Politics that Produced and Sustained the American Civil War and the Political Reconstruction that Followed.* The four volumes are subtitled: *The Nation Builders*, *The Demagogues*, *The Bleeding*, and *Political Reconstruction and the Struggle for Healing.*

He is also co-founder of the Society of Independent Southern Historians, which joins together academic historians and non-academic historians in the pursuit of common goals of <u>presenting truthful and complete history without bending to political correctness pressures.</u>

Howard Ray White is the host of a weekly television show presented in Charlotte, North Carolina by the local Public Access television channel. You can watch past episodes on smart televisions by going to vimeo.com.

White is also the author of an alternate historical fiction novel, *The CSA Trilogy,* which presents an alternate history, in three volumes, of our Confederate States winning their independence and growing into the greatest nation on earth. A happy story about, "what if Confederates had succeeded in defending their land?"

His historical novel, ***Wartime Struggles of a Virginia Farm Slave Family***, allows the reader to experience the struggles slave families dealt with during four years of war in Virginia, near Richmond. Who were their true friends, White people of the North or White people of the South?

White has written and published three books about the War Between the States that can be read in a few hours and impart so much vital understanding about the war that Lincoln fought to conquer the legally-seceded states. 1: *Why and How the North Conquered the South.* 2: *Understanding Abe Lincoln's First Shot Strategy.* 3: "Understanding 'Uncle Tom's Cabin' and 'The Battle Hymn of the Republic'."

White is also the author of ***God's Humans, from Adam to Today***. This is a must-read for people who want to believe in Jesus, but struggle to understand the Holy Bible and Genesis, having acquired the basics of today's scientific knowledge.

His recent book, *How to Study History when Seeking Truthfulness and Understanding*, will be of interest to all who are frustrated with bias among most present-day authors of published history books. Read this well illustrated book and learn how, when reading other books, you can then sort out the important truths and discard the misleading distortions.

Howard Ray White, after extensive research, has written a very important book that everyone striving to make sense of the Civil War should read. It is a biography of Abraham Lincoln, focused on his life from birth to starting the war to conquer the seceded states. It is titled "***Rebirthing Lincoln***." A truthful biography, Lincoln is not a man deserving any praise. Yes, find time to read this one. So, revealing! Unique.

Most widely read is White's triple comparative biographies book, titled "***Musk, Ford, Wrights, Amazing Americans who Fundamentally Advanced Human Travel***." Yes, in this one book you can read comparative biographies of Elon Musk (Tesla and SpaceX), Henry Ford (his company built over 15 million Model T automobiles and created the world's first moving, mass production assembly line) and the Wright Brothers (Orville and Wilbur Wright of Dayton, Ohio, invented the flying machine and taught the world to fly in airplanes). Published in 2023, the Musk biography, a rapidly advancing story, is up to date as of 2023.

Howard hopes you will enjoy reading this epic book, ***Southern Families Made America***. The history begins in Jamestown, Virginia Colony, long before the *Mayflower* landed in what would become New England. It continues through the Republic of Texas, created by Southern families in 1836, an area much larger than today's State of Texas. Ten years later, this Texas Republic merged into the United States ten years later. Shortly afterward, President James K. Polk, of Tennessee, oversees the making of America with our War against Mexico. Clearly, Southern Families made America.

Dedication

Howard Ray White and his wife of sixty-four years, Judith Willis White, are both descended, almost without exception, from people who were in America as colonists and patriots before and during the American Revolution. This couple's early ancestors were among those who settled the coastal South, then pioneered westward across Virginia and the Carolinas and into Middle Tennessee.

Although few people today can trace their entire family tree back 300 to 400 years, many Southern people share the heritage of descent from American colonists. **So, this book is dedicated to Southern people living today, both white and black, who are descended from the Southerners who struggled, fought and pioneered to build our country, from Jamestown to the Republic of Texas and fought on to get the rest out to California.**

And most of these Southerners are still living in our Southland today and are "Trying to Save America," fighting those wild-irrational-liberal political activists who are, sadly, making progress in destroying the America that our Southern ancestors had made. Therefore, I dedicate this book to them as well.

We hear so much today about how people all over America are the same. We hear politicians arguing that "We are all immigrants." Well, many Southerners are descended from families who Made America. They may have no family tree record going back 300 years. They probably have no memories or family stories about immigrant arrivals or struggles to learn English, if not from England, as many were. Yes, the Southerners of whom I speak are, by and large, descended from those Nation Builders. That is why **I am dedicating this book to them whether their ancestries go back to Southerners who came to America from England, Africa, Scotland, Ireland, or from elsewhere.**

Foreword

It seems today that Americans have great difficulty in grasping the notion that America's expansion westward as far as the Republic of Texas was the hard work and sacrifice of Southern families, often large families. This is truthful. But it is not so recognized in today's culture, where achievements of the Southern people are minimized, and the so-called achievements of the Northern people are overly-exaggerated. I am talking about a span of 239 years from the founding of Jamestown in 1607 to the first year of the Republic of Texas, 1846. I am talking about the hard work and sacrifice of both Southern Whites and Southern Blacks. Two hundred and thirty-nine years! Folks, that is a long time – ten generations of pioneering moms and dads and sons and daughters.

Let us look at 1607. That is the year the first settlers arrived at Jamestown, Virginia Colony. Thirteen years later, in 1620, Puritan Separatists, claiming to be heading for Virginia Colony, instead deviated northward to settle what would become New England, where they would establish controlling, church-state colonial governments. More about those Puritan Separatists later.

In 1803, **President Thomas Jefferson**, a Virginian, arranged the Louisiana Purchase, paying France only $15 million for that vast land, which stretched from the west bank of the Mississippi River out to Oregon Territory on the northwest Pacific coast. Thomas Jefferson's government paid France $18 per square mile or 3 cents per acre.

In two treaties with Spain, 1819 and 1821, West Florida and East Florida had been acquired by the United States. The land of West Florida was soon added to Alabama, Mississippi and Louisiana. East Florida would be a United States territory until becoming a state in 1845.

In 1835, **Mexican Texas** was a vast, sparsely settled land occupied by a few native Mexicans and a large number of immigrants from the Southern United States. The following year, 1936, the people of Mexican Texans won their independence from Mexico and established a democratic nation they named the **Republic of Texas**.

After ten years as a successful independent Republic, Texans would vote to merge into the United States and give the U. S. much of the Republic's territory that lay west and northwest of the decided Texas State boundary. Yes, Texans voted to dissolve their nation and become a state based on the United States' merger contractual promise that the **State of Texas** would be allowed to divide itself into five separate states (think 10 senators) when population growth permitted. But, and this is important, Republican Political Reconstruction following the War Between the States would obstruct that promise. Vast Texas still has only two votes in the United States Senate. There is still only one state. There is no East Texas, no North Texas, no West Texas, no South Texas and no Central Texas.

Now let us step back in time. New England had been settled by **Puritan Separatists** from England. Their religion was based on Christianity, but with a strong controlling political feature. Like Muhammad's Islam, Puritan Separatists wanted a church-state government organization and wanted to exclude non-believers in their governments of Massachusetts colony and surrounding New England colonies, all afterward becoming states. This faith was far different from the protestant Christian faiths prevalent in the South, which had no political component. It led to crazy events up there like the execution by hanging of 14 women and 5 men in Salem, Massachusetts colony in 1692 and 1693.

Massachusetts, New York and Pennsylvania were the battleground regions in the first years of the American Revolution, but, up there, the fight became deadlocked. That was when the British decided to attack the Southern Colonies and complete the destruction of the revolutionary movement. After that Southern invasion, **the Southern people fought back** and were primarily responsible for winning the War for Independence against Great Britain at **Yorktown**, Virginia Colony in 1781 and securing a very advantageous treaty in Paris in 1783. That treaty granted Georgia, South Carolina, North Carolina and Virginia control over western land out to the Mississippi River. The Revolution had been over control of western land, not the price of tea, or taxes on imports, or marine shipping restrictions. And that revolutionary fight was won in South Carolina, North Carolina and Southside Virginia.

Following independence for the thirteen colonies, now states, we observe that **Virginia, which held title to the land north and west of the Ohio River, gave their claim on that vast land to the Federal Government for oversight of future territorial settlement and organization of future states**. Virginia's vast land gift would become the future states of Ohio, Indiana, Illinois, Michigan, Wisconsin and Minnesota. And it is important to observe that, in the early years, Southern families were the primary settlers of the southern part that land, the land of southern Ohio, southern Indiana, and southern Illinois, states today considered to be "northern states". Southern families also settled Missouri and Arkansas, west of the Mississippi River.

Native Americans from our Southland, partly volunteering and partly forced to do so, migrated to west of Arkansas to settle in Indian Territory, land that was promised to them by the Federal Government and the Administration of President Andrew Jackson of Tennessee. Sadly, after the War Between the States, Republican Political Reconstruction politicians violated that promise, the promise Andrew Jackson had made, and allowed Whites to move into Indian Territory, beginning in a covered wagon stampede, and eventually resulting in the present-day state of Oklahoma, where Cherokee, Creek, Chickasaw, and Seminole are, today, only a small powerless minority.

During the span of time between Jamestown and the beginning of the Republic of Texas, Southern people were far more prominent in leading the Federal Government than were Northern people. Presidents George Washington of Virginia (8 years: 1789-1797), Thomas Jefferson of Virginia (8 years: 1801-1809), James Madison of Virginia (8 years: 1809-1817), James Monroe of Virginia (8 years: 1817-1825), Andrew Jackson of Tennessee (8 years: 1829-1837), John Tyler of Virginia (4 years: 1841-1845) and James K. Polk of Tennessee (4 years: 1845-1849) led our Federal Government for all but 12 of our first 60 years of existence. **In so many ways, "Southern Families Made America."**

And, within subsequent chapters of this book, you will come to understand how it was that Southern people accomplished such a remarkable event, remarkable even compared to overall world history. Herein, you will experience factual history. You will witness stark contrasts between the Southern Culture and the Northern Culture, in military skills and bravery, and both in terms of attitudes about personal liberty and attitudes about what constitutes good government. You will witness Southern migration, at times **through the lives of Andrew**

Jackson and Sam Houston, because as a writer of history, I am a firm believer in using biographies of important leaders to help you live the history as others of those times lived it.

Well, the **Republic of Texas** was created in March 1836. Ten years later, in February 1846, that vast land became part of the United States. And 3 months after that, on May 12, 1846, the United States declared war on Mexico. The temptation was just too great! It was obvious to the United States Senate and to **President James K. Polk**, of Tennessee, that America could get all of the remaining land west of the former Republic of Texas, out to Mexican Californio, by waging a brief war against Mexico. This was the Southern States' of America's only war of aggression. Men of the Southern Culture were in the majority among the soldiers invading Mexico. Men of New England participated little in the fight to gain Mexican land. Mexico signed the Treaty of Guadalupe Hidalgo on February 2, 1848, granting the United States the coveted western land out to Mexican Californio.

Well, the people of the Northern Culture had been mostly on the sidelines while the people of the Southern Culture had "Made America." Going forward, though, those people of the Northern Culture would resurrect their Puritan Separatist backgrounds, begin a long and persistent campaign to vilify the South, to ignore it's accomplishments, to vilify the past history of slave ownership, to promote abolitionist political arguments, to condemn the Democratic Party, and to win to themselves control over all western territory and the future states that would be created from those national territories, including territories won in the war against Mexico. This Northern campaign would give rise to the creation of the Northern States Republican Party in 1854 and the election of Abraham Lincoln in 1860. Immediately thereafter, Southern States would begin seceding from the United States, an act not in violation of the constitution of our federation of states. To reclaim the seceded states, President Lincoln would launch a war to conquer them. After four years of war and one million unnecessary American deaths, White and Black, all seceded states would be conquered and the Northern States Republican Party's Political Reconstruction would thereafter destroy States Rights and make all people subservient to a much more powerful Federal Government.

<u>Howard Ray White is passionate about his writings of American history.</u> He strives to be truthful in all aspects and to properly honor the hundreds of his and his wife's ancestors and ancestral relatives who lived those years, beginning in Jamestown, Virginia Colony, expanding across Virginia, down into South Carolina Colony and into western North Carolina Colony, fighting with the **Over the Mountain Men** in the Revolutionary War at King's Mountain, arriving as early settlers in the Cumberland River Valley, and helping to found Fort Nashborough, now Nashville, Tennessee. Among Howard Ray White's many important ancestors is Lawrence Washington, great, great, great grandfather of President George Washington. Lawrence Washington, of Sulgrave Manor, England, died in 1616. <u>Howard is also descended from King John of England who granted the Magna Carta in 1215, bringing to Englishmen their first step toward democracy.</u>

The author has underlined especially important sentences throughout this book as an aid to fast readers.

Table of Contents

About Howard Ray White, the Author 2

Dedication 4

Foreword 5

Table of Contents 8

Chapter 1: Europeans Discover the American Continents 10

Chapter 2: The Settlement of North and Central America 12

Chapter 3 — A Review of Life in the 13 English Colonies 36

Chapter 4 — Wars between Britain and France Over Colonies 42

Chapter 5 — 1763 to 1769: People of the Thirteen Colonies Ponder Seizing Control of Their Destiny 50

Chapter 6 — 1775 to 1783: Thirteen Colonies Revolt Against British Rule 65

Chapter 7 — 1784 to 1789: Transition to the Federal Government 111

Chapter 8 — April 1789 to February 1793: The States during the First George Washington Administration 135

Chapter 9 – March 1793 to February 1797: The States during the Second George Washington Administration 151

Chapter 10 — March 1797 to February 1801: The States during the John Adams Administration 164

Chapter 11 — March 1801 to February 1805: The States during the First Thomas Jefferson Administration 172

Chapter 12 — March 1805 to February 1809: The States during the Second Thomas Jefferson Administration 185

Chapter 13 — March 1809 to February 1813: The States During the First James Madison Administration 194

Chapter 14 — March 1813 to February 1817: The States during the Second James Madison Administration 204

Chapter 15 — March 1817 to February 1821: The States during the First James Monroe Administration 229

Chapter 16 — March 1821 to February 1825: The States during the Second James Monroe Administration 239

Chapter 17 — March 1825 to February 1829: The States during the John Quincy Adams Administration 246

Chapter 18 — March 1829 to February 1833: The States during the First Andrew Jackson Administration 255

Chapter 19 — March 1833 to February 1837: The States during the Second Andrew Jackson Administration 277

Chapter 20 — Sam Houston and the Nation Builders Gain Mexican Texas....................280

Chapter 21 — 1836 to 1846: The Republic of Texas under President Sam Houston 290

Chapter 22 — 1836 to 1846: The Republic of Texas under President Mirabeau Lamar – 1838-1841 291

Chapter 23: The Republic of Texas under Sam Houston's Second Term as President, 1841 – 1844...294

Chapter 24: The Republic of Texas under Dr. Anson Jones's Term as President, 1844 – 1846   298

Chapter 25 — President James K. Polk and Southern Nation Builder's Manifest Destiny   301

Chapter 26 – In 13 Short Years, Northern Politicians Would Seize Control of the America that Southern Families had Made 303

Chapter 27: We now fast-forward to Our South as viewed today................................308

Chapter 28 — Today, Their Descendants are Trying, yes, Trying to Save America 309

References Relevant to Southern Families Made America...313

A listing of Published Books Authored by Howard Ray White, all available on Amazon as print books, most as e-books, some as audio-books. 326

My Close 329

Chapter 1: Europeans Discover the American Continents

Christopher Columbus

On October 12, 1492, **Christopher Columbus** set foot on an island in the Bahamas, which he christened San Salvador. Born in Genoa in 1451, Columbus was the commander of 3 ocean-going sailing vessels that had been commissioned by the King and Queen of Spain, Ferdinand and Isabella. The commission agreement stated that Spain would rule over all discovered lands and would own 90% of the gold and silver found there. Columbus was promised that he would receive the title of "Admiral" of the discovered regions and would own the remaining 10% of all gold and silver discovered. Before proposing the voyage, Columbus had convinced himself that he could sail before the wind westward across the Atlantic Ocean for many weeks if he set out from the coast of West Africa, for he had observed that winds in that region seemed to steadily blow toward the west. Even more important, he had convinced himself that he could return to Europe after reaching the other side of the ocean by sailing north on a reaching tack until he picked up the eastward winds, which he had observed most always blowing off the ocean at Portugal and Spain. Columbus had little idea how far east he would have to sail, but he figured he would eventually reach the east coast of Asia, which had been made known to Europeans through the overland explorations of Venetian merchant Marco Polo around 1298. Sailing in 3 little ships, Columbus eventually reached land in the Bahamas. After exploring some islands, he and his men returned to Spain with 6 Native Americans and fabulous tales of discovery.

Actually, tiny Portugal, under the leadership of Prince Henry, had become the primary naval exploration nation prior to the time of Columbus' voyage across the Atlantic Ocean. Nicknamed "the Navigator," Prince Henry, son of King John I, had established a navigation institute at Sagres on Cape St. Vincent and had promoted the application of scientific methods to the problems of navigation and naval exploration. Portuguese naval explorers had explored the west coast of Africa in 1441 and had begun the business of importing into Europe bonded African workers (slaves) from West Africa. In 1455, Portuguese had discovered the Cape Verde Islands, located off the west coast of Africa. In 1486 sailors under the command of Bartholomew Diaz had rounded the Cape of Good Hope at the southern tip of Africa. Six years after Columbus's first Atlantic crossing, Portuguese sailors under the command of Vasco da Gama would pioneer the sea route to India via the Cape of Good Hope, and would soon thereafter launch the profitable importation of Indian spices.

The Pope Sets Boundaries for Spanish and Portuguese for Control of the Americas

In 1493, soon after Columbus' return, Pope Alexander VI facilitated an agreement between Portugal and Spain regarding who owned what. The Pope, a Spaniard, decreed that Portugal, based on its discoveries off the coast of Africa, would rule over, and possess exclusive trading rights over, all newly discovered lands east of a "Line of Demarcation" that was drawn at the longitude equal to 100 leagues (about 300 miles) west of the Cape Verde Islands. That point is in the Atlantic Ocean, well east of even the coast of Brazil. But a year later, a treaty between Portugal and Spain shifted the line west to 370 leagues (about 1,100 miles) west of the Cape Verde Islands. Apparently Columbus had not yet realized that so much of South America and the Caribbean islands lay to the east of his landfall in the Bahamas islands.

Henry II, the King of England, financed a naval exploration across the North Atlantic under the leadership of John Cabot, a Venetian who had moved to England and become a naturalized citizen. In 1497, Cabot's men made landfall somewhere in Newfoundland and then hurried home. Cabot's son, Sebastian, was most impressed with the incredible schools of huge codfish encountered off Newfoundland, reporting that it was hard sailing work just to force the ship through the schools of cod. But it was a long time before English leaders would decide to exploit the fabulous codfish banks, for at that time England was far inferior to Spain and Portugal in naval power.

In 1519, Spain commissioned **Ferdinand Magellan**, a Portuguese, to lead a 5-ship expedition around the southern tip of South America, across the South Pacific, across the Indian Ocean, around Africa and up the South Atlantic back to home. Magellan was killed in the Philippines, and only one ship made it all the way back to Spain. But his voyage, an amazing event in human history, proved the validity of circumnavigation. It is interesting to realize that that one ship, the survivor, had picked up enough spice cargo in India to pay for the whole 5-ship, 3-year voyage.

By 1522, Europeans knew the overall scope of earth's oceans and continents. From this point forward, Europeans would range over the world's oceans seeking colonies for European settlers and profitable trade for European merchants.

Chapter 2: The Settlement of North and Central America

English Settlers Establish Virginia Colony

Humphrey Gilbert, with Queen Elizabeth's financing, led an English voyage to the codfish banks in 1578, but the Spanish navy ran them off. Gilbert reached the codfish banks on a second voyage in 1583, but went down with his ship when it sank while returning to England. His little ship, the *Squirrel*, weighed only 20,000 pounds. The next year, 1584, Walter Raleigh, Gilbert's half-brother, led a 2-ship expedition to the mid-section of North America. Instead of codfish, Raleigh's men, obviously inspired by the huge success of the Spanish, hoped to find gold. The men landed at Roanoke Island in present-day North Carolina, explored the surroundings and sailed back to England to recruit colonists. The following year, Raleigh sent a group of 106 men, led by Richard Grenville and Ralph Lane, to start an English colony at Roanoke Island. Spending most of their time looking for gold, the colonists were ill prepared for the fight that broke out with Native Americans in 1586. A second group of 117 colonists, led by John White, sailed to the Chesapeake Bay region in 1587. But it was not until 1591 that John White managed to sail over to Roanoke Island to check on the settlers stationed there. He found none. The place was deserted. The only clue to their fate was a carving in a tree: "Croatoan." Apparently, these settlers had either been killed or they were far away in the backcountry being assimilated into Croatoan Native American society.

When England made peace with Spain in 1604, Englishmen of wealth, previously convinced by Walter Raleigh of immense investment opportunities in North America, realized that an English colony would probably not be destroyed by a Spanish attack. But, by then, Walter Raleigh had fallen upon difficult times. So, the two colonization businesses that attracted investors and obtained charters from James I were not Walter Raleigh outfits.

Two companies, the **London Company** and the **Plymouth Company**, were incorporated and, in 1606, were assigned land rights by King James I in a compact called the Virginia Charter. This charter granted the London Company a monopoly over trade and colonization activity between the latitudes of 34 and 38 degrees, where the farmland was so attractive. Referring to present-day maps, the lower latitude corresponds to the southern coast of North Carolina, and the upper latitude corresponds to the southern boundary of Maryland's eastern shore and passes near Charlottesville, Virginia.

At the same time, the compact by King James I granted the Plymouth Company a monopoly over trade and colonization activity between the latitudes of 41 and 45 degrees, where the fishing was so fabulous. Referring to present-day maps, these latitudes correspond to the southern shore of Massachusetts (excluding offshore islands) and the northern coast of Maine.

The charter by King James I granted the intervening land between latitudes of 38 and 41 degrees to both companies, with the provision that, in that region, neither company could establish a settlement within 100 miles of the other company.

With the Virginia Company charter enacted, 144 men set sail in December 1606 in 3 ships under the command of Christopher Newport: the *Sarah Constant*, the *Goodspeed* and the *Discovery*. These ships reached the Chesapeake Bay on April 26, 1607. **The 105 men who survived the voyage founded the first successful English settlement in North America.** They named their settlement Jamestown in honor of King James I. These men and those who followed in the next few years were in for dreadful times, but they would persevere. <u>These</u> **Jamestown pioneers** <u>were the beginning of the pioneering families that we can call the first of the Nation Builders.</u>

The first settlers were governed by a council of seven men, including John Smith who would eventually emerge as the top leader of Jamestown settlement. Being surrounded by an immense forest of huge trees and, within about 60 miles of the settlement, about 5,000 Native Americans whose moods switched back and forth between friendly and hostile, the settlers were reluctant to venture far from home to clear farmland, or to hunt and fish. Game procured had to be shared with everyone in the settlement, a policy that discouraged individual initiative and risk-taking. Furthermore, the trees were so huge that clearing a few acres of land with axes must have seemed an impossible task to the inexperienced men. The death rate among the settlers was staggering. Many died during subsequent ocean voyages, one ship losing 70% of the 185 colonists that set out from England. Many died at Jamestown as well. During the first 9 months of settlement effort 65% of the first 105 settlers died. Much of the deaths were caused by the London plague, malaria, and poor nutrition. Furthermore, there was occasional loss of life during attacks by Native American warriors. For example, John Smith was seized by warriors of the Powhatan Nation in December 1607, but escaped execution when Pocahontas, a daughter of the Powhatan Chief, persuaded her father to release the captive.

Far to the North, the French Begin Quebec Colony

<u>A year after the founding of Jamestown, in 1608, men led by Samuel de Champlain founded a French settlement on the Saint Lawrence River, which they</u> **named Quebec.** <u>This was the first permanent French settlement in North America.</u> As Governor of this New France, Champlain oversaw administration and expansion of French interests in North America. Quebec was ideally situated for trading with Native American nations westward to the distant upper Mississippi Valley. Through subsequent explorations and erection of forts, Frenchmen would come to dominate trade with interior Native American nations. Over the course of many decades, Frenchmen would treat Native Americans with more consideration than did Englishmen, but Champlain would make a mistake when, shortly after establishing Quebec, he would lead a raid against Native Americans – members of the powerful Iroquois Federation of Nations – at the southern tip of Lake Champlain. The French raiders would kill some chiefs, prompting the **Iroquois Federation** to prefer trading with the Dutch instead of the French. And the Native Americans would find the Dutch trade especially good. For example, in 1689, records would show that 2 beaver pelts would buy a musket from the Dutch (Albany), but it would take 5 pelts to buy a musket from the French (Montreal). But the growth of New France would be slow. After not quite 50 years, the population of European people in the region controlled by New France would be fewer than 2,500.

Virginia Colony Grows

Jamestown was reinforced in 1608 by the arrival of more colonists in January and more in the fall. By early 1609, **John Smith** became the sole commander of the settlement, and through his military-style leadership, the colonists were effectively organized into productive teams. As a result, survival rates dramatically improved. But, having been wounded by an explosion, Smith returned to England in October 1609, leaving behind about 500 colonists to cope on their own, without benefit of his experienced leadership.

Based on Smith's reports, the shareholders in the London Company reorganized their business, renaming it the "Virginia Company" and securing, in 1609, a new charter from **King James I**. The new charter totally disengaged the Jamestown group from the Plymouth Company, which had not yet established a colony. **The territorial limits of the Virginia Company's monopoly were redefined as being 400 miles along the Atlantic coast and extending "west and northwest" to the Pacific Ocean.** This revision of the northern border meant that Virginia Colony extended northwestward to include much of the future States of Ohio, Indiana, Illinois, Michigan, Minnesota and Wisconsin. One class of stockholders, called "adventurers," invested in hopes of future dividends, but remained in England. A second class of stockholders, called "planters," were indentured to the Company for 7 years, after which they were to receive title to 100 acres of Virginia land and be economically independent of Company responsibilities.

The loss of life at Jamestown during the following winter, following John Smith's departure, called the "starving time," was horrendous. During the short span of only 7 months, 88% of the 500 colonists died. Yet, in spite of the horrific odds of dying within months of a leaving England, stubborn and brave English men and women continued to come to Jamestown. The Colony was saved again by the arrival in May 1610 of another ship from England. At about that time the *Swan* brought over my 10-Greats Grandfather, John Flood (spelled Fludd at that time). He was about 15 years old. At about age 29 he would marry the widow of William Finch, Margaret Finch, who would arrive on the *Supply* in 1620. During the second half of 1610 the Virginia Company reorganized colonial leadership under a stringent military-style Governor whose word was law. The most stringent and most successful of these military-style governors was Thomas Dale, who held the job from 1611 to 1616.

The year after Thomas Dale assumed leadership, **John Rolfe began raising tobacco,** a North American plant that the Native Americans occasionally enjoyed smoking in ceremonial pipes. The first shipment of Virginia tobacco was a big hit in England. Only a few acres of woodland had to be cleared to raise a profitable tobacco crop. And it was easy to dry and ship across the Atlantic. A barrel filled with tobacco would be sold to many more men than a barrel filled with rice or salted fish. Seeing the potential, the Virginia Company financed a tobacco marketing campaign across England, for it recognized tobacco as the cash crop capable of making the Virginia colony economically viable. The stay-at-home class of stockholders must have been overjoyed over the immediate success of tobacco. By 1617 John Rolfe would perfect a curing process for a very successful "sweet tobacco," and in that year Jamestown tobacco exports would total 20,000 pounds. It had taken 10 years at Jamestown, much of it filled with death and suffering, but by 1617 the shareholders of the Virginia Company were seeing their investment paying off. Now, John Rolfe did not accomplish this all by himself. He had important help from the Native American, Pocahontas, also admired by the colonists for her beauty and athletic ability. In fact, with the blessings of her father, the chief of the Powhatan Nation, Rolfe had married Pocahontas in 1612. This marriage launched an 8-year period of peace between the colonists and the Powhatan Nation. John, Pocahontas and their child traveled to England in 1615, where they were welcomed as celebrities. But Pocahontas died in England, and John Rolfe sadly returned with the child to Virginia. The child would survive to raise a family. From that family would descend several prominent Virginians, including John Randolph of Roanoke. But John and Pocahontas Rolfe were the exception.

Unlike Spanish and French colonists, who were customarily almost all men, and who therefore chose wives from among the Native Americans for lack of any alternative, the English colonists would soon number among themselves many women. The vast majority of colonial Englishmen would marry colonial Englishwomen or remain bachelors. The student of history should firmly note that it was the bravery and determination of English women that made the English colonies so different from the Spanish colonies to the south and the emerging French colonies to the north and to the west – yes, **the bravery and determination of English women.** And this historical reality is the driving force that motivated and propelled subsequent large Virginia families toward their destiny to become the ancestors of the Nation Builders.

Now, the Virginians had not been the first to introduce tobacco into England, for Spanish tobacco had been widely enjoyed in England prior to 1615. Furthermore, Dutch marine merchants operating in and out of New Amsterdam were garnering much of the Virginia tobacco shipping business. So, to ensure the success of Virginia tobacco and English marine shippers, the English Government, in 1621, established laws that prohibited the importation of Spanish tobacco and required that tobacco grown in Virginia be exported only to England and carried there only by English ships.

In 1619 a Dutch ship arrived at Jamestown with **20 indentured African workers**. These workers were bought by Jamestown settlers on 7-year indenture contracts and lived and worked on the tobacco farms. After 7 years these Africans would become independent. This was the first importation of settlers of African descent and their indenture contract was the same as indenture contracts for English workers. But, in a few years the English setters would modify the 7-year indenture arrangement for imported African workers, thereafter requiring that they be bonded for life, unless the owner made them independent.

That same year, 1619, the Virginia Company transported more than 90 young, unmarried English women to Jamestown. Each woman was free to marry or to reject any and all offers of marriage. Each lucky suitor had to pay the Virginia Company 120 pounds of tobacco to defray the cost of his bride's ocean voyage. [1]

The Nation Builder were now well grounded.

Puritan Separatists Seek a Church-State Colony in Massachusetts

While men were colonizing Jamestown for the London Company, **Puritan Separatists** migrated from their homes at Scrooby, England, to a site in Holland. There, they hoped to live religious lives, as they collectively wished, totally independent of the Church of England. Over a 2-year period about 100 Puritan Separatists moved from Scrooby to the site in Holland under a shroud of secrecy. Ten years later, concluding that Holland was an inhospitable place for them to practice their religion, these Puritan Separatists would make arrangements to migrate to Virginia.

In June of 1619 Puritan Separatists secured a contract from the Virginia Company for land for a proposed new religious settlement in Virginia. They organized a colonization company that was patterned after the one used for colonizing Jamestown. A share of stock was issued to investors who contributed 10 pounds sterling, but remained behind, and to each man who

---

[1] Within this section you see part of the author's family history.

volunteered to be a settler. After 7 years, land would be divided among the stockholders. That was the plan!

Although most of the Puritan Separatists in Holland, remained behind, many Puritan Separatists boarded the *Speedwell* and departed from Holland in mid-summer of 1620 on the first leg of what was advertised to be a planned voyage to Virginia Colony. The Puritan Separatists board the *Speedwell* docked in England to allow the boarding of more Puritan Separatists and to add a second ship, the *Mayflower*. However, extensive efforts to make the leaky *Speedwell* sufficiently seaworthy for the dangerous Atlantic crossing ended in failure.

Therefore, **110 Puritan Separatists**, 35 of them from the Holland group, crowded into the *Mayflower* for their voyage to Virginia Colony, or so they claimed in their voyage contract. But these Puritan Separatists did not really want to associate with established settlers in Virginia Colony. They wanted to be Separatists, in other words, **to live away from those Virginians.**

The Puritan Separatists left Plymouth, England, on September 6, 1620. After 9 weeks of sailing in stormy weather, they sighted land. On November 11, they sailed into a protected bay, far, far north of Virginia Colony. They were landing at a place they would name Provincetown. We must suspect that, they, or at least their leaders, had planned to settle far north of Virginia Colony long before they departed England.

Those aboard the *Mayflower* arrived and settled in land that would become New England (Massachusetts, Connecticut, Rhode Island, etc.) and those Puritan Separatists would be the beginning of the founding of the **Northern Culture** in the American Colonies.

Immediately after arriving at Provincetown, everyone signed a "compact" whereby all agreed to live as a democratic religious commune where all production was pooled and shared according to need. They elected John Carver as their leader, but he was to receive no pay for his leadership effort. After exploring the surrounding area a bit, they decided to build their religious commune at a site they named Plymouth. The Puritan Separatists had decided to abandon their contract with the Virginia Company and squat on unauthorized land far north of the Virginia Company's jurisdiction. Apparently, the Puritan Separatists aboard the *Mayflower* did not want to associate with Virginia colonists. Puritan Separatists were following an exclusionist, politically-focused religion that had no Biblical basis.

The Puritan Separatists paid dearly for their decision to remain isolated, far from the then-experienced settlers in Virginia Colony. Although the weather was unusually mild, and even though the waters teamed with fish and the forest teamed with game, many died during the winter months. Native Americans were not the problem, for the London Plague, having reached the area some years earlier, had killed off many of the Native Americans in the vicinity of Plymouth.

In March 1621, a Native American named Samoset brought Squanto into the settlement, and **Squanto** offered to help. He had been captured by Europeans in 1615 and sold into bondage in Spain. Successfully running away in Spain, he had made his way to England. He had worked as a sailor out of England, sailing to Newfoundland, then returning to England, and then back to the region that would become Massachusetts. In short, Squanto was experienced in survival and in dealing with Europeans. The Puritan Separatists, who so desired to live in religious isolation, welcomed Squanto's help, for they were dying off rapidly. By April half were dead. Only 4 of the 18 married women remained alive.

Squanto arranged a treaty with Massasoit, Chief of the Wampanoag Nation, on whose land Plymouth was situated. And Squanto was helpful in arranging another treaty with the Narragansett Nation, which controlled land beyond the Massasoit people. Squanto would remain with the Puritan Separatists until his death in 1622, "giving them invaluable instruction in problems of agriculture and hunting."

In 1621 they would obtain a contract from the Council of New England for the land in and around Plymouth because, since their landing, they had been squatting on land that King Charles I had chartered to that organization. In 1623 they would abandon the commune life-style and revert to individual enterprise. By 1642 they would pay off the stockholders who had financed their ocean crossing.

The above is the history of the founding of the **Northern Culture** in America.

Virginia Colony Suffers Growing Pains

The years following the arrival of the women, **Jamestown** was still a very dangerous place in which to live and raise a family. Three years after the women arrived, in 1622, warriors of the Powhatan Nation launched a coordinated surprise night-time attack, beginning with the farms on the outskirts of Jamestown, killing many of the men, women and babies. The massacre would have been more dreadful if a friendly Powhatan, Chanco, had not warned those living in the central village of Jamestown. In all, about one-fourth of the settlers were killed. Opechancanough had succeeded Chief Powhatan, Pocahontas's father, and the new Chief was apparently determined to drive off the English.

The settlers retaliated with "terrible vengeance" and would have no further trouble with Native American warriors in the vicinity of Jamestown until 1644, when Opechancanough would instigate another fight in which 500 settlers would be killed. This time the settlers would shoot Opechancanough and drive the Powhatan people from the land between the James River and the York River.

At that time **my 10-Greats Grandfather, John Flood,** farmed 2,100 acres along the south bank of the James River, across from Jamestown. He was both a military commander and skilled at communicating with local Native Americans. In 1646 he would be named the official interpreter for Virginia Colony. He would train his son Thomas in the Native American tongue. Soon after John Flood's death in 1658, the Grand Assembly held at Jamestown would pass the following resolution: "Whereas Colonel John Flood had long and faithfully served this country in the office of an interpreter and being now deceased, it is enacted that Thomas Flood, son of said Colonel John Flood, being recommended to the Assembly for his ability in the [Native American] tongue, shall be received in the place of his father and have the same salary."

In 1624 **James I, the King of England**, with help from the English courts, reneged on the charter he had granted Virginia Company stockholders in 1609. The Court declared the charter null and void and decreed that Virginia's North American land thereby reverted to Royal ownership. James I thereby owned the land of Virginia himself. Apparently, James I realized the value of potential Government revenues that could be obtained from Virginia tobacco and taxation of settlers. James I had no intention of letting a land mass, as huge as Virginia, continue to be owned by a stockholder-held company. So, the stockholder's investments became worthless. Parliament apparently felt powerless to counter the move, since it had been James I who had granted the original charter, not Parliament. The Virginia Company had spent about 200,000 pounds sterling developing Virginia "with only negligible returns." [2]

The Dutch Establish Hudson Valley Colony

The **Dutch** were also interested in establishing colonies in, and trade with, North America. It had been in 1609 that Henry Hudson, an Englishman in the service of the **Dutch East India Company,** while exploring for a Northwest Passage to the Pacific Ocean, had led a crew of sailors up what he named the Hudson River. He and his men had sailed all the way to the present site of Albany. And the Holland Government of the Dutch had afterward cited Hudson's exploration trip as justification for its claim to the land of the Hudson Valley and the Delaware Valley. Dutch traders had set up fur trading camps soon after Hudson's discoveries. But it was not until 1624 that the first group of settlers would arrive – 30 families.

By 1626, Dutch people had 3 functioning trading posts: Fort Orange (would be renamed Albany), Fort Nassau (across from present-day Philadelphia) and New Amsterdam (would be renamed New York City). The Five Nations of the Iroquois League had already found working with the French traders on the St. Lawrence to be profitable. So, Native leaders offered to trade on friendly terms with the Dutch as well. In fact, Native Americans living in the Mohawk River area to the west was purchasing furs from Native Americans farther west, transporting them to the Dutch posts and making handsome profits reselling them there. This opportunity to profit as both trappers and traders would continue to encourage excellent relations between the Dutch and Native Americans. Fur exports out of Albany would grow. For example, in 1656 about 35,000 beaver and otter furs would be exported from Albany.

Puritan Separatists Divide into Massachusetts and New Hampshire

In 1629 the Council for New England granted the region between the Merrimac and the Kennebec rivers to Ferdinando Gorges and John Mason. This land is now within eastern New Hampshire and western Maine. After a few years without significant settlement, Gorges and Mason split the land into two parcels, Gorges taking the eastern part, which he named Maine, and Mason taking the western part, which he named **New Hampshire**. Neither Gorges nor Mason succeeded in organizing significant colonization from England. So, it was people who moved up from the Boston region and other parts of neighboring **Massachusetts Colony** that settled those regions. And, these settlers from Massachusetts made sure to install a Puritan Separatist, Massachusetts-style, Church-State Government within the land belonging to Gorges and Mason. In 1678, the government of Massachusetts Colony would pay Gorges 1,250 pounds sterling for the right to govern Maine. On the other hand, the next year, the British Government would issue a charter to form a separate royal colony of New Hampshire, thereby allowing its settlers to escape domination by politicians in and around Boston.

In 1629, the Massachusetts Bay Company obtained a charter from **King Charles I** and contracted for a large land grant from the New England Company.

Puritans in England Seek to Dominate Parliament

In 1629, King Charles I dissolved Parliament and began to purge Puritan political control from the English Government. For 11 years, King Charles I would rule England

---

[2] The author's family history

as a pure monarchy, with particular support for Archbishop William Laud, who would constantly hound the Puritan faction of the Church of England clergy. The Puritan faction, whose initial political activism had been directed at imposing their ideas upon the rituals and government within the Anglican Church, had expanded into civil government political activism and had actually gained control of the House of Commons. So, King Charles I had countered by dissolving Parliament and purging the Puritan faction from the Church of England.

This action by King Charles I would persuade many in the Puritan faction to embrace Separatism and flee England. Instead of turning toward Holland, as the earlier Puritan Separatists had briefly done, the new Separatists headed directly toward the American Colonies.

Although the Massachusetts Bay Company had been chartered as a purely commercial enterprise, Puritan Separatists, before departing to America, seized control of that chartered company so they would be in command after retreating from England to the American Puritan Separatist Colony. Puritan Separatist leaders purged the stay-at-home investors from leadership positions and forced the Massachusetts Bay Company to change the site of stockholder meetings to colonial land. By this maneuver, Puritan Separatists could conveniently control the Company that administered their new Colony.

John Winthrop led the first wave of Puritan Separatist colonists in 1630. By the end of the summer, 1,000 Puritan Separatists had arrived. Their main settlement town was Boston. Many more thousands would follow during the subsequent 10-year period, for King Charles I and Archbishop William Laud would continually hound hose that remained in England.

For 19 years, until his death in 1649, **John Winthrop** would rule over Massachusetts Colony as a dictator. Winthrop was a "modest, self-sacrificing man," who was motivated by "high principles," but he "had not faith in democracy." It is important to note that Winthrop and the Boston-area Puritan Separatists did not exercise control over the Puritan Separatists who had come over on the *Mayflower* and founded Plymouth Colony.

It is also interesting to note that the Puritan Separatist who would flee to Massachusetts Colony between 1630 and 1640 would not foresee that their Puritan brethren would repudiate Separatism and remain in England to fight King Charles I. Puritans would, under the leadership of **Oliver Cromwell**, launch an English civil war, execute King Charles I and William Laud, and establish a Puritan Commonwealth that would be ruled by Oliver Cromwell and an all-powerful Parliament.

This history of Puritans, Puritan Separatists, Oliver Cromwell, King Charles I and the English Civil War will be helpful to my readers when, later in this book, they experience the difference in America's Northern Culture and Southern Culture, as well as the rise of the Northern States Republican Party, Southern State Secession, Abraham Lincoln's war to conquer the Seceded Southern States and the Northern States Republican Party's Political Reconstruction, which followed.

Virginia Colony Matures

After the royal take-over of the Virginia Company (Virginia became a royal colony in 1624), the Government of Virginia Colony consisted of a Governor appointed by the King of England and a House of Burgesses elected by the settlers. The House would actually wield significant power at times. For example, in 1635 the House would vote to "depose" John

Harvey when, as Governor, he levied taxes on the people of Virginia Colony without House consent. King Charles I would stick by Harvey for a while, but eventually would replace him with William Berkeley, who would honor most House legislation during his term, which began in 1642. (By the way, my 10-Greats Grandfather, **John Flood**, was a member of the House of Burgess from 1630 to 1652, and would be elected Speaker of the House of Burgesses in 1652.)
[3] As reported earlier, while under Puritan control, the English Government would execute King Charles I in 1649. Three years later the British Parliament would abolish the job of Royal Governor, and Virginia Colony would become an "independent republic" with strong ties to England. It would retain that status until after the death of Oliver Cromwell and the reestablishment of the monarchy with Charles II as King.

Maryland Colony is Carved out of Virginia Colony

In 1632 a new Colony, named **Maryland**, was carved out of Virginia Colony and put under the stewardship of **George Calvert**. Calvert named the Colony after his French-born wife, Henrietta Maria. Calvert, who held the title "Lord Baltimore," named the principal town after himself. Maryland was bound by the Potomac River on the south and the 40th parallel on the north. In March 1634 Leonard Calvert, George's brother, landed with the first colonists and began a settlement on the site of an abandoned Native American village, a few miles from the mouth of St. George's River. The first settlers were led by Catholics and included 2 priests, for George Calvert intended for his new colony to become a haven for Catholics. However, most of the first settlers were Protestants. So, it is not surprising that from 1642 to 1660 Maryland would become embroiled in fighting between Catholics and Puritan Separatists to get control of the Maryland Government.

Conflicts among Puritan Separatists Result in Establishing little Rhode Island Colony

In June 1636 Roger Williams founded the first town in what would become **Rhode Island Colony**. The Government of Massachusetts Colony, under Puritan Church-State control, had banished Williams from its territory 9 months earlier on charges that amounted to religious non-conformity. Not having a charter from England for a new settlement, Williams purchased some land on the western side of Narragansett Bay from the Narragansett Nation and founded a town he called Providence. Unlike the Church-State organization of Massachusetts, Williams patterned the Providence Government after that of Plymouth Colony, which, although formed by Puritan Separatists, granted religious freedom to all settlers. Two years later William Coddington and some friends from Massachusetts purchased, from the Narragansett Nation, Aquidneck Island in Narragansett Bay and formed a town they named Portsmouth. They renamed their island "Rhode Island." Dissention in Portsmouth would persuade some residents to leave town in 1639 to form a new seaport town they would call "New Port." So Narragansett Bay would be shared with Plymouth Colony, which controlled the east side, and Rhode Island Colony, which controlled the mid-bay island and the west side. Both colonies were extremely small by American standards. But both colonies would be a haven for settlers wishing to flee the persecution being inflicted upon those who did not conform to the dictates of the Puritan Church-State organization of Massachusetts Colony. Prominent among those who fled were Governor Henry Vane, Governor John Winthrop's son, and Anne Hutchinson. Like many

---

[3] The author's family history.

Puritans, the Reverend John Wilson, contrary to the teaching of Jesus Christ, had been preaching that salvation was dependent on good works – without good works, one's soul went to Hell. Anne Hutchinson, believing Jesus Christ, who so often emphasized that salvation was a gift to true believers through God's grace alone, publicly challenged Wilson on this paramount and crucial Christian theological issue. Perhaps agreeing with Anne Hutchinson, Governor Henry Vance was inclined to keep his government out of the religious dispute. But when John Winthrop replaced Henry Vance as Governor, Winthrop saw to it that Anne Hutchinson was banished and excommunicated on a charge of "traducing the ministers." So, you are learning more about the evolution of the Northern Culture.

Puritan Separatists Expand into Connecticut Colony

With the blessings of the Massachusetts Colony Government, about 800 settlers "drove their cattle and hogs before them through the forests" into the **Connecticut Valley**. These settlers were attracted to the valley of the Connecticut River because its land was far superior to that around Boston. But they arrived as squatters, for they did not bother to purchase the land from the local Native Americans of the Pequot Nation. And they sought not the permission of the Dutch colonists or the Plymouth colonists, both groups having already established fur-trading posts where the new settlers were preparing to establish farms. These settlers established 3 farm-oriented towns, which they named Hartford, Windsor and Wethersfield. Between 1633 and 1637 warriors of the Pequot Nation occasionally attacked the European Americans in vain attempts to drive them away. Then, in 1637, the men of the region, with help from a militia from Massachusetts, descended upon the villages of the Pequot and "virtually exterminated" the Pequot people. "Many were killed or burned alive." Many captured men were shipped far away where they were sold as bonded workers. For the most part, Pequots who fled to land controlled by rival Native American nations were killed by the warriors of those nations. Having brutally rid the region of Native Americans, the settlers organized the towns of Hartford, Windsor and Wethersfield into a self-governing entity known as Connecticut Colony. During the following 2 years, the settlers drew up a written Constitution for **Connecticut Colony**, which was called the "Fundamental Orders." It established a government much like the one operating in Massachusetts Colony, **so the Government of the Puritan Church and** the civil Government of the Colony were fused into one Church-State organization. Writing this section was difficult for me, but, being a truthful historian, I had to reveal it to you.

Cod Fishing and Building an Ocean Shipping Industry

Fishing was a major enterprise in Massachusetts and surrounding colonies. By 1633, these settlers of the Northern Culture began exporting salted codfish to Spain, France and Portugal. Since the finest fishing grounds in North America extended from Long Island to Newfoundland, the Massachusetts region was at the heart of the cod fishing industry. And the lucrative fishing business would spawn a lucrative shipbuilding industry as well. Soon, the shipbuilding industry would spawn a lucrative bonded African marine transport industry. Later, because live oak was the best wood for building ships, a significant but much less extensive shipbuilding industry would develop in Maryland Colony and Virginia Colony. By 1775 one-third of the ships trading with the American colonies would be American-built, the construction cost of American ships being 25% to 50% of the cost in England.

Swedes Come to Delaware Bay Region

In 1638 a "small band of Swedes" made a settlement on the Delaware River at present-day Wilmington, Delaware. They called the settlement Fort Christina, and they called the colony **New Sweden**. The Swedes purchased the land they needed from the controlling Native American Nation. The Swedes drove out the English and Dutch fur traders they encountered, and, by their presence on the Delaware River, made unprofitable the Dutch fur-trading post farther upstream. Like the Dutch, the Swedes maintained good relations with the area Native Americans by making the fur trade profitable for both seller and buyer and by purchasing all the land that they intended to occupy.

Puritan Church Confirmed as the Massachusetts State Church

In 1646, the Massachusetts General Court called for a conference of Puritan clergymen to be held at Cambridge. The Massachusetts Church-State Government was concerned that the Puritan Church was losing control over the life of the people in Massachusetts, Connecticut and New Hampshire. Church-State leaders were worried about "the double threat of a rising Presbyterian tide at home and the birth of religious toleration in England." The conference resulted in the **Cambridge Platform of 1648**, "which defined Church Government and the relation between Church and State according to Puritan orthodoxy." This confirmed that the Puritan Church was the Massachusetts State Church. Neighboring colonies did likewise. This firm bonding of Church and State in Massachusetts would maintain effective control for over 40 years, until a few years after the Salem Witch Trials of 1692. Although the Puritans of Massachusetts called their church the "Congregational Church," I am calling it the Puritan Church to make the reading of this work less confusing.

English Shipping Monopoly Serves to Benefit Northeast Colonies while Hurting Virginia Colony

In 1650, **Oliver Cromwell's Puritan-dominated English Parliament** passed a stern protectionist act, which forbade foreign marine ships from trading with English colonies. A more rigid protectionist act, passed in the following year, required that all marine imports coming into England must be carried on English ships, English colonial ships or ships from the country which produced the goods. And, all exports from Britain had to be carried on English ships or English colonial ships. This protectionist act greatly stimulated the shipbuilding and merchant marine industries of the American colonies. This act would be preserved after the restoration of the English monarchy, and would be amended, in 1660, by the inclusion of a list of colonial commodities that could be sold only to sister colonies or to England.

The Staple Act

In 1663, **Parliament passed the Staple Act**, which required that all naval shipments bound for the American colonies had to first land in England and be inspected prior to shipment across the Atlantic. The Act also required that from the American colonies to Europe first land in England before being shipped on to other nations. Most notable on the list of colonial export commodities were sugar, tobacco, cotton, indigo, ginger and dyewoods. Important later additions would include rice and molasses (1704), naval stores (1705), beaver skins and furs (1721) and coffee, cacao, iron, and lumber (1764). As the American Independence movement would gain strength, the list would, in 1767, be expanded to include all other commodities. By 1775, colonial ships would be carrying 75% of colonial marine commerce. But, a lot of that growth would result from smuggling by colonial marine shippers, most notably those based in Boston. While the Massachusetts Colony Government refused to recognize the authority of the English Parliament, Boston marine shippers were becoming wealthy transporting goods directly to and from Europe in violation of the English Navigation Acts of 1660 and 1663. But, **while Bostonians prospered, Virginians suffered**, for the price of tobacco declined greatly because Virginia farmers were denied access to cheaper Dutch shippers and to the higher tobacco prices being paid on the European continent.

Colonial Puritans Create the United Colonies of New England

In 1643, the year after English Puritan activists launched the English Civil War, Commissioners from the Puritan-dominated colonies of Connecticut, New Haven, Plymouth and Massachusetts met in Boston and drew up 12 articles, which bound them together as the **United Colonies of New England** (New Haven Colony, located within Connecticut Colony, existed from 1638 to 1665). Consistent with the Separatist Puritan political mood and the English Puritan war to overthrow the monarchy, this regional independent government was established without the sanction of either the English King or Parliament. In fact, the Puritan revolutionaries back in England probably cheered on their religious brethren in and around Massachusetts. This Massachusetts-led action actually approximated a declaration of independence. The Massachusetts Government claimed it already owned Maine, so Maine Delegates had not been invited. Delegates from Rhode Island Colony had not been invited because the Massachusetts Puritans thought themselves too godly to associate with Rhode Islanders, who they considered the "sewer" of heresy. The regional government charter called for 2 Commissioners from each Colony, both being members in good standing at a Puritan church, to meet annually and exercise granted powers, which were rather broad, but lacked a means of enforcement. Anyway, Massachusetts insisted on being able to veto any resolution it did not like. From the beginning of England's Puritan Civil War (1643) to the demise of the English Puritan Commonwealth (1662), leaders in Massachusetts Colony thought themselves above English law. They violated English trade laws, denied religious freedom to the non-Puritans of Massachusetts, refused to allow legal appeals to English courts, and harbored English Puritans who had fled England to escape prosecution on charges of murdering supporters of the English monarchy. In 1662, the demise of the English Puritan Commonwealth having occurred in England, **Connecticut and New Haven would successfully secede from the Massachusetts-dominated United Colonies of New England**. It would be 1686 before the English Government would bring English law enforcement and religious freedom to Massachusetts Colony. This segment reveals a stretch of truthful history that reveals the early days of the Northern Culture. As you read on, the cultural differences between people in the North and people in the South who dominate political control will become strikingly different.

Swedes are Driven out of New Sweden

Swedes lost control of their Colony forever upon its seizure by a Dutch force that came from New York in 1655. Led by **Peter Stuyvesant**, the Governor of New York Colony, 7 Dutch vessels and 300 fighting men took Fort Christina, the leading settlement of New Sweden, in a bloodless siege.

23

King Charles II Grants Charters for Connecticut, Rhode Island and Carolina Colonies

In 1662, **King Charles II** granted a charter to the people of the lower Connecticut Valley, whose region included the land west of Rhode Island, south of Massachusetts and westward to include the "Bible Commonwealth" of New Haven. This charter would be the basis of the **Connecticut** State Government up to 1818.

In 1663, King Charles II granted to the western Narragansett Bay region a charter establishing **Rhode Island Colony**. This charter endorsed the founder's principle of a strict separation of Church and State governments. This charter would be the basis of the Rhode Island State Government up to 1842.

In 1663, King Charles II awarded a charter that granted the **province of Carolina** to 8 "highly influential" men who had been greatly helpful in restoring the British monarchy. Most notable of these men were Edward Hyde (Earl of Clarendon), Anthony Ashley Cooper, William Berkeley (then the Governor of Virginia Colony), and George Carteret. These 8 men were granted "feudal principality" over the land of Carolina, which meant they could retain title to the land while collecting an annual land usage fee from all settlers. As expanded in 1665, the province of Carolina stretched from latitude 36 degrees and 30 minutes (the present Virginia border) to latitude 29 degrees (30 miles north of present-day Orlando, Florida). It stretched westward to the Pacific Ocean. In fact, the grant of Carolina represented, in land area, about 40% of the land of our country's present-day 48 adjoining States. It was huge, and it was in the best farming climate in North America, with a long growing season and good rainfall. The first settlers in Carolina had already arrived from the Jamestown region 10 years before Charles II chartered Carolina Colony. These people had settled around Albemarle Sound in present-day northeast North Carolina. But, the proprietors of Carolina had no success in collecting an annual land usage fee from the squatters around Albemarle Sound.

King Charles II Grants Charters for New York and New Jersey Colonies

In March 1664, Charles II awarded to his brother, James Stuart, a charter for the North American land between the Delaware River and Connecticut Colony. But James Stuart only retained the northeastern half, for he ceded the southwestern half, the portion between the Delaware River and the Hudson River, to 2 of the 8 Carolina Colony proprietors: John Berkeley, brother to the Governor of Virginia Colony, and George Carteret, considered "the richest man in England." James Stuart, who held the title of "Duke of York," called his colony "**New York**." Berkeley and Carteret agreed to call their colony "**New Jersey**," after an Island in the English Channel, which Carteret had previously administered. We next begin discuss the history of the previous settlement of this land.

The two above awarded lands had been settled by the Dutch in 1624 and named New Netherlands, although many English-speaking settlers lived there at the time that Charles II instructed his brother to seize the colony by military force. New Netherland Colony was coveted mostly for its lucrative fur trade, because it held 2 of the 3 rivers that led to the prime fur-trading region of the time. The three rivers were the Hudson, the Mohawk and the St. Lawrence. King Charles II based his claim to New Netherland Colony upon the brief exploration by John Cabot and his men in 1497, but it was obvious that English seizure of New Netherland Colony would be an act of aggression. In August 1664, "four English ships with several hundred men" arrived before New Amsterdam and demanded the surrender of the colonial Dutch government. The Dutch Governor, Peter Stuyvesant, who had 9 years previously led a similar conquest of New Sweden, was unable to rally his men to defend his Government. So, without a fight, Stuyvesant was forced to surrender New Amsterdam and his Colony to the men aboard the British ships, who had, for the most part, been recruited in Massachusetts and surrounding colonies.

James Stuart appointed Richard Nicolls as Governor of New York Colony, who took immediate charge of its government affairs. On the other hand, James Stuart would never come personally to New York Colony. New York Colony was administered by an "autocratic but somewhat benevolent Government." A code of laws provided for "equal taxation and trial by jury."

A few months later, in 1665, Philip Carteret, a relative of proprietor George Carteret, arrived at New Jersey Colony, found Elizabethtown, and establish a government. He found a few settlers were already living in New Jersey Colony: Swedes, Dutch, and Puritans from the Massachusetts area. The New Jersey Colony Government featured "religious freedom, liberal land provisions, representative government, no taxes without legislative consent and rights of local government for the towns."

So, 57 years, equal to two generations, after the first English settlers arrived in Jamestown, Virginia Colony, English were organizing New York Colony and New Jersey Colony.

The Important Carolinas Seaport Town of Charles Towne Is Founded

In 1669, with substantial financial backing from the Carolina proprietors, a successful settlement was established across the river from the downtown section of present-day Charleston, South Carolina. It was called Charles Towne after King Charles II. It was located on the Ashley River, not far from the Cooper River, both rivers being named for proprietor Anthony Ashley Cooper. The fertile soil and mild climate encouraged a fairly rapid growth in the settlement and the nearby sea-islands. Settlers came from Ireland, Scotland, Barbados and New England Colony. In 1680, French Huguenots began to arrive. Attempts were made to develop an export trade based on almonds, raisins, wine, silk and naval stores, but results were "disappointingly meager." However, the introduction of rice farming in 1690 was successful and ensured a thriving export trade. Rice soon became to southern Carolina Colony what tobacco had previously become to Virginia Colony. Bonded African workers were essential to the profitability of southern Carolina rice farming. So bonded Africans were imported in large numbers and made possible the economic success of southern Carolina Colony.

French Quebec Expands Westward along the Great Lakes and Down into the Ohio River Region

Since the founding of New France at Quebec in 1608, the French had been expanding New France across the Great Lakes and Ohio Valley regions and across the upper Mississippi Valley. French forts were established as French trading expanded westward: Montreal at the Ottawa-St. Lawrence junction in 1642, Sault Ste. Marie at the convergence of Lakes Superior, Michigan and Huron in 1668, and St. Fr. Xavier on Lake Michigan in 1669.

In 1673, French exploration of North America received a big boost from the **explorations by Louis Joliet, Father Jacques Marquette** and their support team. Setting out from Sault Ste. Marie, they paddled along the western edge of Lake Michigan and entered Green Bay; then they paddled up the Fox River to near its headwaters. In that region they walked one and one half miles across a low rise and discovered the Wisconsin River. Because it was so easy, this had long been a major Native American canoe portage site for travel between the Upper Mississippi Valley and the Great Lakes. Joliet, Marquette and their men then paddled their canoes down the Wisconsin River to the Mississippi River and proceeded down the Mississippi until reaching a position not far north of the Arkansas River. At that point they became fearful of being captured by Spanish frontiersmen and decided to turn back north. They paddled back up the Mississippi River, then up the Illinois River, where, near its headwaters, they found a portage to the Chicago River, which took them to the southern tip of Lake Michigan. This new French understanding of how to portage and navigate the river systems of the Great Lakes and the upper Mississippi Valley prompted a rapid expansion of French trading posts and French forts: Ft. des Miamis at the southern tip of Lake Michigan in 1679; Ft. Crevecoeur (1680) and Ft. St. Louis (1682) on the Illinois River; Ft. St. Antoine (1685) on the upper Mississippi River, and many more over the following 70 years. **The Hudson's Bay Company,** founded in 1670, would become the most powerful of the French fur-trading companies.

Dutch Effort to Recover Their Lost Colony of New Netherland is Briefly Successful

In 1673 (or 1674) a large Dutch fighting force returned to New York and New Jersey to recover their seized New Netherland Colony. The Dutch fleet of 23 ships appeared before New York City and retook the lost Dutch colony, whose name was immediately reverted to New Netherland. However, Dutch ownership was brief. In a few months, the war between Britain and Holland was settled by the Peace of Westminster (1674) and that settlement ceded New Netherland Colony back to the British.

Northeastern Colonies and Quebec are at War with Natives

Metacom succeeded his father Massacoit as Chief of the Wampanoag Nation, a small Native American nation situated between Plymouth Colony and Rhode Island Colony. Metacom's people had suffered much under the domination of the Puritan Separatists who lived in Massachusetts and neighboring colonies. Much land had been lost, disease was a problem and the Wampanoag culture was being destroyed by zealous Puritan evangelists. Metacom rallied his people to war against the Puritans and was soon allied with the Nipmuc and Narraganset nations. Other nations sent warriors to help the Wampanoag. The resulting war lasted from June 1675 to August 1676. "Small bands of [warriors] attacked settlements . . . from the Atlantic Ocean to the Connecticut River." In this region it was "the bloodiest of all colonial [Native American] wars. . . Sixteen towns in Massachusetts and 4 in Rhode Island were destroyed." The colonists, who surprisingly received military help from Native American nations to the west, were eventually victorious. Metacom was killed and his wife and son, along with many other captives, were shipped to the Caribbean and sold as bonded workers. "It was the final solution of the [Native American] problem in [the region]."

Under the leadership of Governor Thomas Dongan of New York Colony, traders held on to the past Dutch fur-trading alliances with the Iroquois Federation of Nations. Then traders sought to take over the Iroquois trade that was going to the French at Montreal. But,

Massachusetts Colony traders refused to cooperate with the New York traders and the French responded by launching a military raid on the Iroquois, killing some and capturing others and selling them into bondage. The Iroquois retaliated against the French by destroying Lachine and its inhabitants "in the bloodiest massacre in the history of Canada."

You are observing the escalating contrast between our perceptions of the **Northern Culture** and of the **Southern Culture**, the culture that will be evolving into **America's Nation Builders**.

Virginia Colony Suffers under Governor William Berkeley, Sowing the Seeds of Bacon's Rebellion

Meanwhile, **Virginians were suffering** under the tyrannical rule of their royal Governor, **William Berkeley**, who had regained power in 1660. Berkeley prevented elections to the Virginia House of Burgesses, raised taxes, and reduced services. And, he refused to authorize a military response to 1675's bloody Native American attacks upon Virginia settlers. This was the situation when a newcomer to Virginia, **Nathaniel Bacon**, rose to lead a popular counterattack against the Native American warriors. And, his success in that military endeavor, seemed to challenge Berkeley's leadership. But, Bacon overplayed his hand in 1676 as he led a rebellion against Berkeley's rule, which included the burning of Jamestown. Bacon became sick shortly thereafter and died, leaving the resistance movement leaderless. Governor Berkeley quickly regained a firm hand as he executed 20 followers, including William Drummond, whom Berkeley informed upon his being brought before him:

"Mr. Drummond, you are very welcome, I am more glad to see you than any man in Virginia. Mr. Drummond, you shall be hanged in half an hour."

To that, the Virginian, who was a Scotsman, replied:

"What your honor pleases."

Bacon's Rebellion failed, but the actions of Bacon and his followers became seeds that would grow into a successful independence movement that would be led by Virginians such as Thomas Jefferson and George Washington.

William Penn, the Quaker Influence and New Jersey Colony

The brief Dutch retaking of New York Colony must have prompted considerable selling and reselling of New Jersey Colony Stock. In 1674, proprietor John Berkeley sold his share of New Jersey Colony to Edward Byllynge, who sold the share a year later to 40-year-old **William Penn, a wealthy and idealistic heir** to considerable wealth and political influence. William Penn's father, also named William and a wealthy friend of the Stuarts, had died 4 years previously. The deceased father's immense estate included title to 16,000 pounds sterling debt owed the estate by the English King, Charles Stuart II.

In spite of his affluence and connections to the rich and powerful, the young William Penn's religious feelings had been **deeply influenced by Quakers** while he was a student at Oxford. His attraction to the Quakers' socially-leveling, separatist life-style is particularly surprising, considering that the Quakers "renounced all forms, ceremonies, and sacraments; refused to pay tithes, take an oath or bear arms, and found in the 'inner light' a guide to their conduct."

So, it was a wealthy, religiously awakened, Quaker-influenced **William Penn** who had personally purchased half of New Jersey. Penn carved out half of the Colony for himself, calling it "West New Jersey" Colony. Because of Penn's support, West New Jersey Colony soon became a haven for Quakers, since Quakers generally desired to live in segregated religious communities.

In this religiously-fractional colony, conflict afterward developed between the New Jersey Colony Government and the Puritan settlers. And, Puritan leaders managed to involve James Stuart's New York Colony Government and its Governor, who, in 1679, kidnapped and jailed for a time the Governor of New Jersey, Philip Carteret. But, the next year, James Stuart declared he had no further interest in New Jersey Colony. By 1682, proprietor George Carteret's heirs must have wanted no part of New Jersey, for they sold East New Jersey at auction to the highest bidder. William Penn and 23 associates offered the highest bid. At this point, men of the Quaker faith controlled all of New Jersey. And they would keep that control for 20 more years – until they would surrender their proprietor rights in 1702 and permit New Jersey to become a royal colony.

William Penn takes Ownership of Pennsylvania Colony

In March 1681, **William Penn** canceled his deceased father's 16,000-pound debt to King Charles Stuart II for the right to **own Pennsylvania Colony.** This deal made Penn "both landlord and ruler of the most valuable territory ever granted by [an English King] to a single individual." The charter specified that Penn's colony was bounded by the Delaware River on the east, and from there extended westward for 5 degrees longitude. It specified that the colony was bound on the south by the 40 degrees latitude (equal to what was then Maryland Colony's north border) and on the north by the 42 degrees latitude (equal to New York Colony's southern boundary).

Maryland Colony Would Later Lose Much of their Land to Pennsylvania

But Pennsylvania politicians would not be satisfied with a southern boundary on the fortieth parallel, especially Philadelphians who would covet more land to the south of their city. So, about 80 years after William Penn's purchase of the colony, **scheming Pennsylvania lawyers** would allege that the Pennsylvania charter wording that stated "the beginning of the fortieth" really meant the boundary went down to 39.501degrees. They would allege that, since numbers above 39.501 degrees round up to 40 degrees, all land above 39.501 degrees belongs to Pennsylvania Colony. The argument was foolishness, but apparently **Pennsylvania politicians** would have the greater political influence in London, for they would succeed in **stealing a huge amount of land from Maryland Colony**. From 1763 to 1767, surveyors Mason and Dixon would push this false 39.501 Pennsylvania-Maryland boundary so far south toward 39.5 degrees that Maryland Colony would be squeezed to only 2 miles wide at one point in the mountains.

King Charles II Firmly Controls William Penn's Colony

Although William Penn was landlord and ruler of Pennsylvania Colony, King Charles II made sure that the English Government retained significant control – in fact more control than over any previous colony. He required that all proposed future laws governing Pennsylvania Colony, including local tax bills, be sent to him for his approval or veto prior to enactment. He also required that Pennsylvania Colony station an agent in London to be answerable for any violation of English trade laws. Furthermore, Charles II made sure that tax legislation could be initiated by "Act of Parliament in England" at any time, thereby bypassing the Pennsylvania Colony Legislature altogether.

Pennsylvania Colony Grows Greatly from 1682 through 1689.

When William Penn arrived at his newly purchased Pennsylvania Colony in October 1682, he found about 1,000 settlers had preceded him – many of them being English, Dutch and Swedish settlers who had moved in prior to his acquisition. "The colony prospered from the beginning. Indeed, it had no legitimate excuse for failure. Seventy-five years of English colonizing experience lay back of it; the region was healthful and rich in natural resources; provisions could be secured from the Dutch and Swedish settlers already there; many of the Quakers were wealthy, and the [Native Americans] were friendly." Why were they friendly? They were likely friendly because Penn had purchased large tracts of eastern land for his settlers and because the more western Native Americans, who belonged to the Iroquois League, were subduing the most eastern Native Americans. Furthermore, Penn was a thorough and energetic promoter, advertising widely in Europe for new settlers. Penn granted religious freedom to all Christian and Jewish denominations, but, in practice, Catholics and Jews suffered severe discrimination. From the outset, Jews were prohibited from holding office, and Catholics would be similarly barred after 1706. **By 1689,** the population of Pennsylvania Colony would total about 12,000 people – a mixture of English, Welsh, Scots, Irish, Dutch, Swedes, Germans and others. By that date, the colony's capital of **Philadelphia** would be vying to become the **leading town in the American colonies**.

The Origins of Little Delaware Colony

Well, folks, New Jersey Colony had three counties that lay to the **west of Delaware Bay and the final 30 miles of the Delaware River.** Seeing the prosperous beginnings of Philadelphia and Pennsylvania Colony, some influential people living in these three counties sought to be transferred from New Jersey Colony to Pennsylvania Colony. William Penn agreed and James Stewart agreed as well. So, in 1682, these three counties, which included the town of Wilmington, were moved to Pennsylvania Colony. In 1703 they would be permitted to have a separate Delaware legislature, but the 3 counties comprising Delaware would remain subservient to Pennsylvania Colony. The 3 counties comprising **Delaware** would not become an independent State until its leaders, in concert with the Declarations of Independence in other colonies, would declare independence from both Pennsylvania and England.

Strong-Willed Governor Andros and The Dominion of New England

During 1685, King Charles II moved to take control of Puritan-dominated Massachusetts Colony by combining it with neighboring colonies and creating an administrative body to be called the Dominion of New England. His first step was to convert New York Colony into a royal colony. But King Charles II died before his plan was dutifully implemented the following year with the approval of his successor, King James II. **Edmund Andros** arrived in 1686 to be a strongman Governor over the Dominion of New England, which included Massachusetts, Connecticut, Plymouth, Rhode Island and New Hampshire colonies as well as Massachusetts-claimed Maine. Two years later, Governor Andros would add New York Colony and New Jersey Colony to his stewardship, thereby expanding his oversight to 8 colonies. With no Dominion of New England Legislature seeking to share power, and having fully subjugated the old colonial governments to his control, <u>Governor Andros was in full command.</u>

Undoubtedly, <u>Governor Andros understood that his most important objective was to break the Puritan domination over government and life in Massachusetts Colony.</u> He succeeded at that by demanding freedom of religious expression and separation of Church and State. He even forced the Puritans in Boston to share their Old South Church building with a congregation of Anglican believers. To hamper Puritan attempts to rally the people of Massachusetts against his rule, <u>Andros instituted censorship of the press and suspension of the writ of habeas corpus, and he restricted town meetings to only once per year.</u> Cracking down on smugglers and squatters, Andros enforced English laws including those regulating marine commerce and land rent payments. He also levied some new taxes.

So, in the northeastern colonies we observe considerable and controversial political control over settlers and their leaders. This history is much different from Virginia, the Carolinas and Georgia. In the South we are witnessing the growth of the Nation Builders.

The 8-Year War between the English-Dutch Coalition and the French Disrupts the Northeastern Colonies and French Quebec

In early 1689 King James II was forced to flee for his life in the face of a popular uprising against his Catholic advocacy. <u>Parliament then elected, as co-rulers,</u> **William Stadtholder III** <u>of Holland as King and</u> **Mary Stuart Stadtholder**, <u>James's daughter and William's wife, as Queen.</u> William accepted co-occupation of the English throne so he could align England militarily with The Netherlands to defend The Netherlands against an invasion by France, which the **French King, Louis XIV**, was launching. William's action brought to a close the 50-year period of peaceful relations that Englishmen and Frenchmen had enjoyed.

And, in North America, the war between the English-Netherlands coalition and the French would be fought by colonists, especially those living in Massachusetts, New York and Quebec, with help on both sides from Native American mercenaries. Religious hatred was fanned to facilitate a fighting spirit: Quebec Catholics damned Massachusetts Puritans as "infidels" and Massachusetts Puritans damned Quebec Catholics as "minions of Satan." The Native Americans simply fought on both sides to acquire weapons and other prizes of war. But, the big prize for the eventual European victor would be control over many, if not all, of the loser's American colonies.

<u>War strategy demanded that the new administration in London gain firm control of the northern English colonies, so</u> **William and Mary** <u>chose to dismantle Andros's Commonwealth of New England, and before long, Andros and his ruling team were forced to flee.</u> At that point, the 8 colonies reverted to individual administration under newly appointed governors. Six of the 8 were already royal colonies.

<u>The Puritan Church would not have such a firm grip on the Massachusetts Government after 1691, when Massachusetts, Plymouth and Maine were combined into a re-chartered</u> **royal Massachusetts Colony**. <u>The transformation would be complete upon the conversion of New Jersey into a royal colony in 1702.</u>

The war between the English-Netherlands coalition and the French (1689-1697) produced no clear victor, although the English did succeed in severely damaging the French economy and French naval power. Fighting near the English-French border in America, although intense, resulted in a stalemate as well. The people of Schenectady, New York Colony, suffered "the stark brutality of [Native American] warfare in all its savage fury." Furthermore, 2,000 fighting men from the Massachusetts region failed to succeed with their siege of Quebec City.

A European **treaty signed at Ryswick in 1697 was basically a cease-fire,** for it restored the territorial boundaries in North America that had existed before the fighting had begun. But, this 8-year war would leave lasting feelings of hatred between the peoples of Quebec and the northern English colonies.

And, we observe that settlers in Virginia, the Carolinas and Georgia were not involved in the above war. **They would become the Nation Builders.**

Charles Town and Rice Cultivation

Cultivation of rice in southern **Carolina Colony** was first proven economical shortly before 1690 at a farm near Charleston. With that success, rice farming surged along the South Carolina coast. By 1725, South Carolina farmers would export 100,000 barrels of rice. The rice farms would be located upstream of the saltwater incursion along 11 tidal rivers from the Waccamaw to the Savannah. The best land lay at an elevation between low tide and high tide. Bringing a rice field into production required clearing the field of marsh grass, trees, and brush, digging a ditch network, building a levee along the riverbank, and installing irrigation-control gates. This permitted flooding the field at high tide and draining the field at low tide, all without the use of waterwheels. Because bonded Africans had a superior ability to fight off malaria and to endure swampland work, and since they were economical to own, they were imported in great numbers to live and work on these rice farms. Yields ranged from 30 to 50 barrels per acre.

The Northern Colonies Profit from Expanded Slave Trade from Africa

Prior to 1697 the English Government permitted only the **Royal African Company** to transport bonded Africans (slaves) to the American colonies. Prior to that date, no other marine shipping companies had been permitted to transport bonded Africans. And the supply-price structure of the Royal African Company monopoly had served to limit African importation to a small percentage of what would become the total influx of African slaves into the American colonies. But the Royal African Company charter was rescinded in 1697. So, after that date, ships based in the American colonies were permitted to sail to Africa and bring back bonded Africans.

In response to the expanding market for bonded Africans, **gangs of African warriors** expanded their efforts to capture inland Africans and bring them to west-coast ports where they **traded their captives to shipping company buyers for rum and other items.** The African gangs left to die those captives too infirm to bring a price.

Merchant marine companies in Massachusetts, New York and surrounding colonies rushed into the newly opened business of transporting bonded Africans. **Merchant marine companies in Boston, New York City and Newport would soon dominate the bonded African marine shipping business.** The shipping of bonded Africans would eventually make many shipping company owners in Boston, New York and Newport **immensely wealthy**. And, based on this accumulation of wealth, certain prominent families, through future generations, would become leading political and economic powers in New York City and Boston. One example of a man who would be made wealthy by shipping bonded Africans is none other than Peter Faneuil, for whom Boston's famous Faneuil Hall would be named. By 1770, Rhode Island Colony would be the home base for 150 bonded African trans-Atlantic transport ships. Soon after colonial shippers entered the bonded African shipping business, the few colonies that did not permit African American bonding (ownership of slaves) rescinded those restrictions. **Soon, all colonies** had laws in place that **permitted** and regulated the importation and selling of bondage contracts on people of African descent, both importees and those born in the colonies.

Although most bonded African shipping companies were based in the New York-Massachusetts region, and most shipping company employees lived in that region, only a small percentage of the bondage contracts that were sold were sold to people in that part of North America. Fishing was a major business in the northern colonies, but owners of fishing boats apparently found that bonded Africans made poorer fishermen helpers than indentured or wage-earning European Americans. But, farmers in Virginia Colony and South Carolina Colony would find bonded Africans productive and economically attractive farm workers. Yet, politicians in those and neighboring colonies would often strive to reduce the rate of bonded African importation, for they foresaw societal problems arising from an excessive population of bonded Africans. However, the wealthy bonded African shippers in the New York-Massachusetts region would wield sufficient political influence to prevent the imposition of restrictions on the rate of importation.

French Found Biloxi in Present-day Mississippi

Meanwhile, in 1699, 200 Frenchmen, led by brothers Iberville and Bienville, founded **Biloxi** on the Gulf coast in the present-day state of Mississippi. Seventeen years previous to the founding of Biloxi, in 1682, the noted French explorer, Sieur de La Salle, had traveled down to the mouth of the Mississippi River from French forts in the upper Mississippi Valley, "claiming the entire valley for his King and naming it Louisiana in his honor." **The French would control the Mississippi Valley** from her headwaters to her Gulf discharge without interference from the English or the Spanish during the first 50 years of the founding of French settlements in the lower Mississippi Valley. Nineteen years after the founding of Biloxi, in 1718, people from Biloxi **would establish New Orleans** at a site 100 miles upstream from the mouth of the Mississippi River.

The Eleven-Years War between England and the Spanish-French Coalition

From 1702 through 1713 both the northern and the southern English colonies were touched by the European war between England and a coalition of France and Spain. This war derived from the French King's agreement that gave his grandson the kingship of Spain – an alignment the French and Spanish leaders figured was sufficiently powerful to defeat the English. As in the 1689-1697 war, only 5 years previously, this new war produced attacks between settlers in the Massachusetts region and coalitions of French and Native American nations. However, settlers in New York Colony were spared significant fighting because the fur traders at Albany and the Iroquois Federation agreed to keep the peace.

The worst attack in this 11-year war was the massacre at Deerfield on the Massachusetts frontier. The Puritan-dominated Massachusetts Colony Government retaliated by offering to pay Massachusetts settlers (and any cooperating Native American warriors) a bounty for scalps cut from the heads of Native Americans. I suppose a Frenchman's scalp probably earned a Puritan a bounty payment as well. From Massachusetts Colony, English troops and colonial militia launched attacks on French territory to the north and northeast, capturing Port Royal in 1710 and renaming it Annapolis Royal.

The most ambitious attack upon the French was launched in 1711. If it had been successful, it would probably have resulted in the total conquest of France's North American territories and perhaps even her fishing rights off Newfoundland. A large force of New York colonial militia, regular English soldiers and cooperating warriors of the Iroquois Federation gathered at Lake Champlain for an attack on the western Saint Lawrence region. And, in coordination, 70 ships with 18,000 Massachusetts men sailed from Boston with the intent of capturing Quebec and the eastern Saint Lawrence region. But the Massachusetts ships ran aground near the mouth of the Saint Lawrence River. Nearly 1,000 men drowned and the survivors returned to Boston without fighting. Upon hearing that the Massachusetts force had abandoned the fight, the New York force decided to disband as well. So, the attack that had the potential of completely driving the French from North America in 1711 never saw its first battle.

The Pennsylvania-Virginia region was spared any involvement in the 1702-1713 war. But, because the Spanish were allied with the French, this war resulted in some Spanish attacks in Carolina Colony.

A treaty among British, French and Spanish governments was signed at Utrecht in 1713, thus ending the Eleven Year War. **France lost most of its North American power base**. It ceded to Britain the Hudson Bay region and the rights to oversee and trade for furs with the seven Native American Nations of the Iroquois Federation. This cession would make possible the profitable Hudson Bay Company and British expansion westward through the Great Lakes. France also agreed to give to Britain both Newfoundland and Acadia (except for Cape Breton Island and certain fishing rights), thereby giving the British a formidable presence at the mouth of the Saint Lawrence River. Twenty-five years of peace would follow the 1702-1713 war.

Fearing the eventual loss of the remainder of the Saint Lawrence region, France would strengthen its settlement of the Gulf coast near the mouth of the Mississippi River. And, France would invest in holding on to the Saint Lawrence region by building Louisburg on Cape Breton Island, the strongest fortress in eastern North America. They would also attempt to strengthen their presence in North America by encouraging Nova Scotia's French settlers to pursue acts of hostility toward the British, and by encouraging Native Americans to make war by paying them for the scalps of English people they killed.

England and Scotland Merge, Creating Great Britain

The Scottish Government agreed to merge with the English Government in 1707, thereby creating the powerful British Government. From this point forward, I will be referring to the British Government and will drop reference to the English Government and the Scottish Government, although reference will be made to Englishmen and Scots.

Carolina Colony Divides into North Carolina and South Carolina Colonies

In 1719, having been owned by the 8 proprietors for the previous 50 years, the people of southern Carolina Colony, through a "revolutionary movement," secured the right to be re-chartered as a royal colony, thereafter called "**South Carolina Colony**," an arrangement similar the one controlling Virginia Colony.   The northern half of Carolina Colony would, thereby, become **North Carolina Colony**.

In 1729, **King Charles II** would have purchased back the land and governmental rights of seven of the eight Carolina proprietors and, in that year, establish a boundary between **South Carolina Colony** and **North Carolina Colony** and proclaim North Carolina a Royal Colony.

One proprietor, **John Carteret** (Earl Granville), refused to sell his land rights. Carteret surrendered his rights over the government of his land, but he insisted on retaining the rights to lease and grant his land. And Carteret's land was a huge parcel, representing the upper half of North Carolina Colony. Carteret probably had trouble collecting land-usage fees from many of the North Carolinians in the sandy coastal plain, for these rugged men moved about extracting tar and pitch from the vast eastern North Carolina pine forests. They would prepare a cooking pad, fell pine trees, stack pine logs over the cooking pad, set them on fire, maintain a hot cooking environment by partially covering the logs with wet branches, and collect the pine tar and pitch as it drained out of the hot logs. They packed the tar and pitch in barrels and shipped it to shipbuilders in Britain and along the eastern coast of the American colonies. It seems that it was impossible to keep pine tar off of one's feet while working the cooking fires and that is why, to this day, North Carolinians are called "tar heels."

But, by the 1720's, Carteret was benefiting from an inrush of farmers who wanted to settle farther inland along the fall line. By the 1740's, farm families would settle the central Piedmont region in great numbers. Many deeds to North Carolina land can be traced back to the original grant from "Lord Granville."

Georgia Colony is carved out of South Carolina Colony

By the early 1730's, South Carolinians were gravely concerned about potential Spanish expansion into their Colony from **Spain's adjacent Florida Colony**. Concern over Spanish expansion into southern South Carolina Colony had grown in intensity since 1715, the year that Spanish settlers in Spain's Florida Colony had incited the Native Americans of the Yamasee Nation to fight a "bloody war."   But, since few South Carolinians lived in southern South Carolina Colony, defense of the region was precarious. Consequently, both political leaders in South Carolina and London agreed that the best way to encourage families to settle in the southern part of South Carolina Colony was to carve that land away from South Carolina Colony and make it a new Colony with its own Colony Government and its own promoters. At the same time, **James Oglethorpe**, a Member of Parliament, and Chairman of the Committee charged with investigating the "appalling conditions" in English debtor's prisons, put forward a plan to deport people to the southern part of South Carolina Colony when convicted of failing to pay debts. Deportation, Oglethorpe argued, was more humane than debtor' prison and would help Britain defend against Spanish expansion northward from Spain's Florida Colony.

Accordingly, in 1732, **British King George II amended the boundaries of the South Carolina Charter** and granted a new charter for a colony situated between Spain's Florida Colony and the remainder of South Carolina Colony. **The new colony was named "Georgia,"** in honor of the King, of course. Unlike Pennsylvania Colony, Georgia Colony had no proprietor. For its first 21 years of existence, Georgia Colony was to be governed by a non-profit group of "Trustees" – there would be no colonial legislature. King George retained the right to sign or veto all proposed laws. After 21 years (that would be 1753) the trustees were to resign and the Colony was to revert back to King George II or his successor. Initial laws promised religious freedom to all protestant denominations, but banned Catholics, presumably for fear they would be too friendly toward fellow Catholics in Spain's adjacent Florida Colony. No person of African descent was permitted to live in Georgia Colony, so Africans living there in 1732 were presumably moved up to South Carolina Colony. To limit the accumulation of wealth, land ownership was restricted to 500 acres.

Parliamentarian James Oglethorpe arrived with 130 immigrants in 1733 and founded the town of **Savannah, Georgia Colony**. Oglethorpe was initially enthusiastic about his governmental "social engineering program" aimed at helping bankrupt debtors become successful producers in British society. And, Parliament voted 26,000 pounds sterling largely to finance the effort from London. But, "Oglethorpe quickly lost enthusiasm in his plans" for populating the colony with bankrupt debtors, "whom he discovered to be lazy 'wretches.' . . . As an asylum for ex-prisoners the colony was decidedly unsuccessful."

Prospective new settlers generally chose South Carolina over Georgia, for in South Carolina they had a political voice through the Colony Legislature, they could acquire more than 500 acres of land, and they could expand a farming business by using independent or bonded African American workers. Furthermore, many settlers, after a few years of experience in Georgia Colony, moved north to resettle in South Carolina Colony. Perhaps the most common occupation of early settlers in Georgia Colony was acquiring furs and exporting them through the Charleston seaport. Soon after Georgia Colony was established, the total annual revenue from fur exports from Charleston was estimated to be 25,000 pounds sterling. During one year, deerskin exports totaled about 160,000 hides.

But Georgia Colony would not prosper until after the Trustees relinquished control of the Colony in 1751, 2 years before that event was scheduled to occur. Then, with a Colony Legislature in place, removal of land ownership restrictions, and revocation of the ban on Africans, the population of Georgia Colony would begin to grow and settlers would witness success.

Chapter 3 — A Review of Life in the 13 English Colonies

A 1732 Look at 13 Colonies and 685,000 Colonists

It is useful to examine colonial conditions around the time of 1732, the year that Georgia Colony was split from South Carolina Colony, thereby providing the 13-colony structure that would eventually declare its independence from Great Britain. The population, White and Black, of the colonies had grown from about 250,000 in 1700 to about 685,000 in 1732 and would become almost 2,500,000 in 1775. Prior to 1680, at least 90 percent of the European colonists were English, with Dutch and Swedes along the Hudson being the balance. But, from that time forward, many new immigrants came from France, Germany, Ireland, and Scotland.

Scots from Northern Ireland Settle from Pennsylvania to Georgia

During colonial times Scots lived in Scotland and also in the northern region of the island of Ireland. **Scots** had started coming to America around 1650, primarily from the northern region of Ireland. By 1740 great numbers of Scots from Northern Ireland – both emigrants and children of immigrants – would begin settling the Piedmont region of North Carolina Colony, including the land around the future city of Charlotte. After 1750, many Scots would emigrate from Scotland itself. In early colonial days, Scots had primarily settled in Pennsylvania and the southern colonies, apparently shunning the Dutch of New York and the Puritans of the Massachusetts region. They were highly individualistic and self-reliant. They were Presbyterians. They avoided government control wherever possible, figuring the less government the better. They loved big families and maintained strong family ties. They were eager to move to the western frontier region where land was cheap, and there they bravely faced pressure from Native American warriors.

Scots would start coming from Scotland to the American colonies in large numbers after Highland Scots were beaten in the Battle of Culloden Moor in 1746 -- in what would be a failed attempt to place Bonnie Prince Charley on the British throne. Afterward, being "subjected to intolerable servitudes," Scots would leave Scotland in large numbers to settle in the American colonies, especially the southern American colonies. As would be expected, they would arrive with a burning desire to be free of oversight by the British Government.

Germans also begin Settling Pennsylvania, New York and Southern Colonies

German immigration into the American colonies would grow to sizable strength after 1730, but somewhat less in number than Scottish immigration. Germans, especially from the Palatinate District, were fleeing from religious and economic persecution brought about by a succession of wars: the Thirty Years War, the War of the Palatinate, and the War of the Spanish Succession. About half of the German immigrants were settling in Pennsylvania, the remainder settling in New York Colony and the southern colonies. Like the Scots, the Germans steered clear of Massachusetts and the other Puritan-dominated colonies. Many, particularly those choosing Pennsylvania Colony, preferred to cling "tenaciously to their religion, language and customs."

Irish began Settling New York Colony and Southward

Irish from southern and western Ireland were among early colonial immigrants. These native Irish were Roman Catholic and hated British authority with an intense passion. The

Irish, like the Germans and the Scots, avoided settling in Massachusetts and the neighboring Puritan-dominated colonies.

Swiss come to the Colonies

Immigrants from **Switzerland** were a significant contribution to the population in the early years of the American colonies. Swiss came to get away from the subjugation imposed by their nobility-dominated society.

Jews Come as Well

During the early years, **Jews** were also a significant percentage of the immigration into the American colonies. Most were fleeing persecution in Spain and Portugal. Rather than undertake farming, they generally sought to form businesses in towns. Favorite centers for Jewish settlement were New York City and Newport Rhode Island, but some went to other towns, such as Charleston, South Carolina.

The Puritan–Settled Colonies Remain of Pure English Descent

It is instructive to note that, of European Americans, Massachusetts Colony and her neighboring Puritan-dominated colonies were 95 percent populated by people of English descent. No other American colony was made up of a population of such ethnic and cultural purity.

History of Indenture Contracts: Many Colonists Arrive as Indentured Servants

Many of the immigrants coming to the American colonies had been arriving as **indentured servants**. Indentured servants were classified three ways: voluntary, non-voluntary and court ordered. **Voluntary indentured servants** willingly agreed to be indentured for between 2 and 7 years so that the ship's captain could receive payment from an American purchaser for that person's ocean voyage. Normally, a captain charged 5 pounds sterling for ocean passage to the American colonies. The more thoughtful voluntary indenture servants contracted with an American prior to boarding ship. The less thoughtful permitted the ship's captain to sell his indentured contract at auction upon arrival at the American port.

Non-voluntary indentured servants had, at some point, suffered being kidnapped, tricked, robbed of their passage money, or otherwise forced into an indenture contract by profiteers who took advantage of the victim's language difficulty or ignorance. The indentured contracts of these people, false but enforceable, were sold at auction upon arrival at the American port. Voluntary indenture contracts required 4 years of servitude according to the respective colonial laws from Pennsylvania to Georgia. But, Massachusetts Colony law, and the laws of surrounding northeastern colonies, required a much longer 7-year servitude term for voluntary indentured servants arriving on their shores. Often, businessmen would buy large numbers of indenture contracts at port from a ship's captain and take his charges through the countryside, selling their contracts to inland farmers for a profit.

Servants who were indentured by court order, because of debt or crime, were forced to accept indenture to an American, usually for 7 to 14 years, as punishment, particularly by English courts. By 1775, about 40,000 people would thusly be convicted and shipped off to Pennsylvania, Maryland, Virginia and the West Indies as punishment.

As reported previously, indentured servants of African descent had first arrived in Virginia Colony in 1619, the first people having come from the West Indies. Their indenture contracts were similar to the indenture contracts of European immigrants. These early immigrants of African descent had been made independent at the conclusion of their indenture servitude and given land in the same manner as their fellow servants of European descent. But, sometime before 1650, the indenture contracts for incoming Africans had been, by Virginia Colony law, replaced by life-time bondage contracts, which bound the person of African descent to his or her owner for life, and gave the owner responsibility for, and ownership of, each bonded woman's children. But, few people of African descent had been brought to Virginia during the early years of the Colony, the count of indentured and bound servants of African descent being only about 300 of the 405 African Americans living there in 1650.

At the end of the indenture period, **the newly independent person was entitled to specific compensation** to help him or her begin life as an independent person. In Massachusetts and surrounding colonies, the former indenture contract owner was required to pay $5.00 or give tools of equal value, but none received a gift of land from the applicable Colony Government. In Pennsylvania and the colonies to the south, the colony governments awarded a gift of 50 acres of land to each newly independent man or woman. Many prospered thereafter, even gaining powerful political influence. At one time during the first 50 years of its existence, about half of the members of the Virginia Colony Legislature were men who had arrived in America as indentured servants.

History of Land Distribution Rules Differed Among the Colonies

Land distribution differed between the region in and around Massachusetts and the region from Maryland to Georgia. Townships of about 40 square miles were granted to groups of men by legislatures in Massachusetts and surrounding colonies. These men would divide the land, selling tracts to individuals while reserving much of it as common pasturage for everyone in the 40-square-mile township. This practice, which represented a blend of communal and individual enterprise, gave government officials power over an important part of the economic life of each person in the township.

The governments of the **Southern colonies**, from Maryland to South Carolina, handled land distribution differently. In those Southern colonies, land was granted to individuals by the King or by the proprietor of huge tracts, subject to small annual payments. So, since individual enterprise dominated the economic landscape in the Southern colonies, government officials there were normally of minor importance in the economic life of each person. Furthermore, in these Southern colonies, a settler was given 50 acres of land if he brought a new settler over from Europe, such as a wife or brother. As mentioned elsewhere, in these Southern colonies, upon completion of a term of indenture, a settler was granted 50 acres of land as well. **This practice encouraged large families and the spirit of the Nation Builders.**

Hardships of the Atlantic Crossing

The Atlantic Ocean voyage was most difficult and dangerous during the early years of travel to the American colonies. In the early years, the condition of immigrant transport from Europe was only marginally better than the worse voyages from Africa. "Horrible quarters, rotten and often insufficient food, and epidemics of smallpox and other diseases accounted for a heavy mortality. One extreme example of hardships and tragedy is found in the death of two-

38

thirds of the immigrants on a vessel that wandered on the ocean over 5 months; another is the death of 250 passengers out of 312 who began the voyage. Little children seldom reached the land of hope."

The African American Population as of 1775

By 1775, there would be about 520,000 people of African descent living in the American colonies. This was about one-fifth of the colonial population of 2,500,000 people. In Virginia Colony the population of people of pure European descent represented about 58% of the population. In South Carolina Colony, where people of African descent were most numerous, residents of pure European descent represented only 44% of the total population. This enormous growth of the bonded African American population sparked numerous political movements aimed at curbing the African importation business. Political movements to limit the importation of Africans were most persistent in Virginia Colony where 33 distinct campaigns were undertaken to limit African importation. South Carolina Colony sought to limit bonded African importation by enacting a "heavy head tax" on the buyer of each importee. Politicians in Maryland and Massachusetts also periodically undertook efforts to limit importation. However, in Massachusetts, New York and Rhode Island, **owners of bonded African across-the-Atlantic shipping companies successfully blocked meaningful curbs on their lucrative ocean transport businesses**. And, historians note that African Americans lived long lives and produced children – evidence of a local expanding populations and reasonably fair treatment by their owners.

Who Were the Biggest Land Owners in Colonial America?

The **biggest landowners** in the colonies were holders of **New York Colony** land. In that colony, The **Van Renssalaers family** owned 700,000 acres; the **Beekman family** owned 240,000 acres, and Robert Livingston, Sr. owned 160,000 acres. The major landowners in Virginia Colony held far fewer acres. There, Robert Beverley held 37,000 acres, John Carter held 18,500 acres, and William Byrd I held 15,000 acres.

Great Britain and France are Again at War – 1740 to 1748

The British colonies in America became involved again in a war between Britain and France, which lasted from 1740 through 1748. Again, **Massachusetts Colony** was primarily involved in this war and raids on settlers resulted in the death of many women and children. The most important battle was the capture of the fortified French naval harbor on Cape Breton Island, called Louisburg, which the French used to protect the mouth to the St. Lawrence River and Quebec. Louisburg was captured in 1745 by a force of 4,000 Massachusetts militiamen under the leadership of William Pepperrell of Maine. A French fleet, representing half the French navy, was dispatched from France to recover Louisburg, but after pestilence killed 2,000 Frenchmen and the commander, the crippled fleet returned to France without making an attack. Only a remnant made it back. A second French fleet was dispatched to recover Louisburg, but was destroyed by the British Navy.

In 1748, the French and British ended the war by signing the **Treaty of Aix-la-Chapelle**. The terms of the treaty greatly upset the settlers in Massachusetts, particularly those who lost relatives in the fighting. But, reluctant to further empower Puritan Separatist political leaders in Massachusetts Colony, Britain agreed to trade victories won by Massachusetts militiamen for losses suffered by British forces in India and in the Netherlands. Basically, the treaty restored the boundaries in place at the beginning of the war. The 1740-1748 war had little effect in the middle Atlantic and southern British colonies. However, the French were determined to control the Ohio valley west of Virginia Colony and Pennsylvania Colony, so that region promised to be a future battleground.

Schools are started in Massachusetts, Connecticut and Virginia Colonies

The Massachusetts Colony Government passed a law in 1647 that required towns to establish schools for boys. All towns of 50 families were required to pay a £5 fine or provide a schoolteacher to teach all boys to read and write. Towns with 100 or more families were required to pay the fine or establish a school capable of preparing boys for Harvard College. Harvard College was a Puritan school organized in 1636 to train ministers for the Puritan Church. The College of William and Mary, an Anglican institution, was established in Virginia Colony in 1693. Yale College, another Puritan school, was established in Connecticut in 1701.

Puritan Religious-Inspired Murders Climax with the Salem Witch Trials

The **Puritan Church in Massachusetts** reached the height of its religious-inspired murders in America when, in Salem, Massachusetts, it pressed to death an alleged "witch" and then hanged 19 others. As previously reported, Puritan Church authority was centered in Massachusetts Colony, particularly in Boston. Increase Mather and **Cotton Mather** were the top leaders in the Church when they became excited that witches abounded in nearby Salem. The sad story follows:

Between February 1692 and May 1693, more than 200 people in Massachusetts and neighboring colonies were accused of practicing witchcraft. Thirty were found guilty and 19 of those were executed by hanging: 14 women and 5 men. Another man, Giles Corey, was pressed to death. Many of the accused were locked in jails and at least 5 died during confinement. For example, in the spring of 1692, several adolescent girls, after listening to the strange wild tales of a bonded African American servant woman, accused some old women in Salem of bewitching them. Cotton Mather investigated and concluded that many should die. For the total story see the Smithsonian Magazine, October 2007 issue.

Jonathan Edwards and George Whitefield Spark Religious Revivals

Up to this point, you have read numerous historical accounts of people in the Northern Colonies, especially in Massachusetts Colony, using twisted concepts of religion to control political and cultural activities. Thank God, more than 40 years after the Salem Witch trials, in 1734, good news, or perhaps I should say God's news, arrived in the Northern States, finally influencing the Northern Culture as Jesus Christ had intended. In that year, 1734, **Jonathan Edwards**, an evangelist who embraced what was then called "the outworn dogmas of seventeenth-century Calvinism," launched an important religious revival movement in Massachusetts and surrounding colonies.

A few years later, **George Whitefield** arrived from England and assumed leadership of the revival movement begun by Edwards. "Both Edwards and Whitefield pictured the torments of the lost and glories of the saved so eloquently as to drive thousands of the lower classes into the ecstasy of salvation." This movement made more extensive the common man's involvement in church affairs. People involved with the movement founded 4 new religiously oriented colleges in the region: Princeton, in New Jersey (1746), Brown, in Rhode Island

(1764), Rutgers, also in New Jersey (1766) and Dartmouth, in New Hampshire (1769). This evangelical movement primarily won common people for Christ. And, the movement had a powerful influence on many people who lived in the Northern Colonies. **Thank God!**

Carolina Colony Prospers with Indigo

Between 1740 and 1744, Eliza Lucas, a young **South Carolina** farmer, demonstrated that **indigo** could be a profitable upland export crop. Indigo farming required careful soil preparation and cultivation. An indigo processing mill had to be constructed. When the leaves matured, they had to be picked and "soaked and beaten in vats until fermentation produced a yellow liquid, which gradually changed color as it was drawn into successive vats at just the right stages until the final product was dried cubes of blue." Observing Eliza Lucas' success, many other upland farmers turned to indigo as an export crop. Because they were economical to own, many upland farmers bought bonded African American workers to live and work on their indigo farms.

Pennsylvania Colony Succeeds with Iron Furnaces

Although some small **iron furnaces** had been built during the early years of the American colonies, little iron had existed for export prior to 1700. Hardwood trees were cut and converted into charcoal, and that charcoal was used in the furnaces to reduce the iron ore to metallic iron. Because of local availability of hardwood trees and iron ore, the colonial iron industry was centered in **Pennsylvania Colony**. Because a shortage of hardwood trees restricted the growth of iron production in Great Britain, by 1750, more pig and bar iron were being produced in the American colonies than in Great Britain.

Chapter 4 — Wars between Britain and France Over Colonies

Furs and Skins Remain Valuable Exports

By 1750, the value of furs and skin exports from the American colonies totaled about 100,000 English pounds per year. Although many Americans of European descent killed native animals and preserved furs and skins, the vast majority of the exported furs and skins were from animals killed by **Native Americans**.

Virginia Families Migrate Westward Across Mountains to the Ohio River

In 1747, Virginians began a movement to settle western land that would become western Virginia and **Kentucky**. In that year, 1747, a group of Virginians, including George Fairfax, Lawrence Washington, Augustine Washington and Thomas Lee formed a company, which they called the **Ohio Company**, to facilitate settlement of land south and east of the Ohio River. Two years later, the British Government granted the Company rights to 200,000 acres bordering on the Ohio River and promised to grant an additional 300,000 acres if 200 families were settled in the region within 7 years. This was a feat all considered easily accomplished if the settlers could be protected from the French. Furthermore, the British Government gave this organization an exclusive monopoly over fur trade with Native American nations located on western land where rivers drained into the Ohio River.

In 1752, five years after the company was formed, the Ohio Company purchased rights to some western land from a Native American nation and built Fort Cumberland on the Potomac River, deep in the heart of the Appalachian Mountains, where Cumberland exists today. That year they opened a road, called the Cumberland Road, to facilitate migration westward to and beyond Fort Cumberland. It also sponsored a major western exploration expedition under the leadership of Christopher Gist. But, a competitive thrust westward by the **French** presented a much greater problem to the Virginians than did the Native Americans living in the region.

French Armed Forces build Forts in Western Pennsylvania Colony.

The French believed that possession of the Ohio River Valley, including upstream into western Pennsylvania Colony, was essential to **connect widely separated New France and Louisiana**. And the fur trade throughout French America was lucrative, for an "industrious hunter would return with packages of peltry enough to bring him $1,600 or $1,700, an immense sum in those days, and sufficient to procure a great portion of the best land." The French already had a string of forts across that vast land, including several forts along the Great Lakes and river-valley forts on the Ohio, Wabash, Red, Arkansas, Coosa, Tombigbee, Tennessee, Kanawha and Illinois rivers, and several along the Mississippi River. There was another fort in present-day Kentucky, but since there were no Native Americans settled along its Cumberland River at that time, there seems to have been no French fort in that region. And the French, who depended much more on income from American furs than did the British settlers, were determined to block fur trading between Native Americans and agents of the Ohio Company.

So, in 1749, the Government of **New France Colony sent a French army** under the command of Celoron de Blainville into the **eastern Ohio River Valley** with instructions to show French military force and to bury at strategic locations some lead plates claiming French ownership of the region. Four years later, in 1753, the Government of New France Colony sponsored the building of French forts Presque Isle, Le Boeuf and Venango in land within the western region of Pennsylvania Colony.

Since the French wanted to use the Ohio River region for transporting and trading furs, instead of for settlement, and since the French show of force in western Pennsylvania Colony seemed so impressive, the Native American nations of the Iroquois League were choosing to align with the French. But the Pennsylvania Colony Government was **not trying to defend its western land. So, the responsibility for driving the French from western Pennsylvania fell upon the Virginians.**

Virginia Military Fights to Defend Western Pennsylvania.

As a first step, in 1753, Virginia Colony Governor, Robert Dinwiddie, with the blessings of the British Government in London, prepared a formal letter demanding that the French withdraw from the three forts they built in western Pennsylvania Colony, and he arranged for a group of 6 men to make their way northwestward to the French forts and deliver that demand. Among the 6 were explorer Christopher Gist and a Virginian who would become the Father of the future American nation, young **George Washington, age 21**. The six men delivered the letter as planned, but the French commander insisted that his force would remain where they were building forts. Young George Washington, after twice escaping death, managed to return home to Williamsburg, Virginia, in January 1754.

In February, the **Ohio Company** began the construction of its second fort in western Pennsylvania Colony, this one being where the Allegheny and Monongahela rivers join to form the Ohio River, at present-day **Pittsburgh.** But before its completion, a French army of 800 men drove off the Ohio Company workmen and destroyed their structure. Soon afterward, the French constructed a substantial fort at the same river junction and named it Fort Duquesne.

Having been driven from the confluence of the Allegheny and Monongahela rivers, the Ohio Company had George Washington and a modest militia force construct **Fort Necessity**, at the present site of Farmington, Pennsylvania, about 60 miles southeast of Pittsburg. It was midway between the French's **Fort Duquesne** and the Company's **Fort Cumberland**. But, early in July 1754, Washington was forced to surrender Fort Necessity to a much larger attacking French force from Fort Duquesne. These battles between Virginian militia and French soldiers in western Pennsylvania Colony might be considered the beginning of a new war between Britain and France, which would not be formally declared until 2 years later, in 1756.

Albany Congress Tries, but Fails, to Negotiate Peace

In June 1754, the month prior to George Washington's forced surrender of Fort Necessity, delegates from 7 British colonies had convened the **Albany Congress** at Albany, New York Colony, to plan for a coordinated defense against French attack. Virginia Colony had apparently chosen not to attend. Delegates had come from the following colonies: Massachusetts, Connecticut, Plymouth, New Hampshire, New York, Pennsylvania and Maryland. The first order of business had been to negotiate peace with representatives of the Iroquois League, for it was imperative that Delegates dissuade the Native American nations in the Iroquois League from cooperating with French colonists and the French army. During negotiations, the Native American representatives had complained about British settlers squatting on land belonging to Native American nations and about dissatisfaction with fur trading arrangements. However, after accepting many gifts from the Albany Congress negotiators, the Native American representatives had agreed to refrain from siding with the French in any future conflicts between French and British settlers. Actually, they had pledged that the Native American nations would be neutral, offering help to neither side. After gaining the promise of Iroquois League neutrality, the Albany Congress Commissioners, using drafts prepared by **Ben Franklin** of Pennsylvania, drew up a plan for mutual defense against feared French attacks. This plan, called the Albany Plan, proposed a President General to be appointed by the British King and a Pan-Colonial Council composed of Delegates from all of the British American colonies. So, the Albany Plan envisioned joint rule with one branch anchored in the London Government and the other branch anchored in the votes of colonists. The plan proposed that the President General and the Pan-Colonial Council, acting together, would oversee affairs with the Native American Nations, provide for joint defense of the member colonies, and establish laws governing trade and levy taxes, as required, to fund these responsibilities.

However, upon its submission to the individual colonies, the **Albany Plan was uniformly rejected**, yes, rejected. There would be no uniform taxation to fund a coordinated defense against French attack. Primary responsibility for defending against French attack would fall on the British Government.

A new French army sailed for Quebec and under **Edward Braddock's** leadership 2 regiments of British troops arrived in Virginia Colony in March 1755. Virginia militiamen augmented this force, and **George Washington** joined Braddock's staff.

Braddock's Defeat Gives the French a Victory that Impresses the Native Nations

The Pennsylvania Colony Government **did nothing** to help Braddock's combination of British and militia soldiers as they advanced to confront the French at Fort Duquesne. It even failed to fulfill its promise to cut a road from Fort Cumberland to Fort Necessity. So, Braddock's men spent much time and effort cutting a road through the forest as they advanced westward toward today's Pittsburg.

On July 9, 1755, the advance portion of Braddock's combined army-militia force was only 8 miles from Fort Duquesne when it was attacked by the French army that was stationed there. Braddock's men were quickly defeated in their inept effort to fight off the French soldiers. Many Virginia militiamen were killed by British army fire from the rear and the French found the bright red British uniforms easily recognized targets. Braddock was killed as well. But **George Washington** managed to survive and avert surrender, making it back to Fort Cumberland with a remnant of the forward force.

More distressing to the American colonists than the deaths near Fort Duquesne was the effect on the allegiance of the Native American nations of the Iroquois League. Seeing how easily the French defeated the British, League leaders quickly forgot promises of neutrality and allied with the French in the expectation that French military might was powerful enough to protect Native American land from organized westward migration, such as envisioned by the Ohio Company.

Emboldened by French support – accompanied on occasion by French soldiers disguised in war paint – **Native American warriors** moved eastward and attacked frontier settlements in Virginia, Maryland and Pennsylvania, killing and scalping men, women and children.

Frontier settlements within the Alleghenies were consequently abandoned, as George Washington's militia found defense of the region a hopeless task.

However, far to the south, **the Catawba Nation and the Cherokee Nation** would align with the English colonists, for in 1756, the Governor of North Carolina Colony would arrange treaties with the **Cherokee Chief, Atta-culla-culla**, and with the Catawba Nation as well.

London Takes Control of the War against the French-Native Alliance

It was during 1755 that the British Government took direct control of foreign relations between the American colonies and the Native American nations. Prior to this year, foreign relations with Native American leaders had been handled by the government of each colony, resulting in little uniformity in policy. But, the threat from a powerful Native American alliance with the French had compelled London to take over this important function. Two Native American relations departments were set up in London: the **Northern Department, under William Johnson**, and the **Southern Department, under Edmund Atkin**.

In an attempt to win cooperation with the nations in the Iroquois League, Northern Department Manager **William Johnson** rather quickly began advocating that the British Government establish a boundary line west of which European settlement would be prohibited. Johnson recognized that the British Army could not defend settlements in the mountainous frontier in Pennsylvania and Maryland colonies. He also realized that no peace with the Native American nations would be possible as long as frontier settlers kept taking Native American lands. On the other hand, many frontier settlers, eager to gain for their sons' and grandsons' future access to new farmlands to the west, opposed the policies of the Northern Department leader, William Johnson.

William Johnson's advocacy of a western settlement boundary especially angered the Scots who were settling western Virginia, western North Carolina and upper South Carolina. Perhaps it was such frontier opposition in the South that persuaded Edmund Atkin, of the Southern Department, to refrain from joining Johnson in advocating a boundary line. In fact, Atkin made no effort to rescind the charter to the Ohio Company. By 1757, grants of western land to soldiers and companies, north and south, would total about 2,000,000 acres. Eventually it would become clear that the Native American nations, even including the Cherokees, had chosen to side with the French, and could not be won over by restraints on western settlement.

Then, for a while, British Government frontier policy would actually encourage western settlement with the hope that frontier settlers would help them defeat the French-Native American military alliance.

Note the contrast between the Northern Culture's reluctance to press westward and the Southern Culture's eagerness to press westward, those being the future Nation Builders.

It's Now Official: Great Britain and France are At War

Both Britain and France declared war in 1756, thereby formally recognizing that they were fighting for control of North American land west of British colonial settlement, as well as land in the Caribbean, India and Europe. With formal war declared, **Louis-Joseph de Montcalm (Marquis de Montcalm)** came to Quebec and took command of French forces in North America. During 1757 and 1758, Montcalm's French forces held their positions in the western regions of the British American colonies. The British Government was not only fighting the French, it was also striving to overcome the **treasonable actions** of many owners of marine shipping companies, most of them based in **Massachusetts, Plymouth, Rhode Island and New York**, and even a few based in Maryland and Virginia. At times, more than 100 ships from these ports were at anchor at Monte Cristi in Santo Domingo delivering food and supplies to French ships to sustain France's North American military forces. Historian Fred Wellborn would conclude, "Much of the beef and flour consumed by the French North American army was secured in this way."

William Pitt Organizes British Military Campaign against French

At this point, **William Pitt**, a leader in the British Parliament, assumed leadership over British forces in all theaters of war. He immediately arranged for new British Legislation to forbid exports of foodstuffs, except for rice and fish, from the American Colonies to any non-British ports. This measure was aimed at stopping disloyal owners of marine shipping companies based in the colonies from sending cargo to intermediate ports such as Monte Cristi, Santo Domingo. Pitt reorganized and expanded British forces so effectively that the French began losing ground to a reinvigorated British advance. During 1758 the British took Louisburg, Fort Oswego, Fort Frontenac, and, with the help of Cherokee warriors, forced the French to abandon Fort Duquesne at the present sit of Philadelphia.

Sadly, for Cherokees, the French persuaded them to Take Sides against Colonists

On the other hand, through contemptuous settler behavior, the **Southern Colonies lost the support of the Cherokee Nation**. An example:

Cherokee warriors had lost their horses while supporting the British force during the capture of Fort Duquesne and, finding horses running in the woods in Virginia, had taken them. This had enraged the settlers who owned those horses, and they "fell upon the warriors, who were unconscious of any offense, murdering some and making prisoners of others."

French agents from Louisiana soon thereafter won over the Cherokee Nation to support their side in the war. In early 1760, Cherokee warriors raided all the western farms within their reach in southwest Virginia, western North Carolina and upper South Carolina. This prompted British regular troops to join with South Carolina militia and destroy all of the lower Cherokee towns in upper South Carolina. But, in the fall of 1760, Cherokees in the upper towns retaliated by forcing the surrender of Fort Loudon on the Little Tennessee River, which stood in the center of the Cherokee Nation. The men, women and children in the fort, numbering between 200 and 300, were told that they would be allowed to surrender and travel out of Cherokee country. However, they would be set upon and all but 3 would be killed as they traveled off. Those 3 men were spared at the insistence of Chief Atta-culla-culla.

A Huge British Army Captures French Strongholds of Quebec and Montreal

More troops arrived from Britain in 1759 to expand the British army for a final assault on Louis-Joseph de Montcalm's strongholds in **Quebec and Montreal**. A 5,000-man British force, under **James Wolfe**, launched a brave and risky surprise attack on September 13, 1759 and succeeded in capturing Quebec, with both Wolfe and Montcalm among those killed in battle. The following year, a British army under Jeffery Amherst forced Montreal to surrender. **At that point, the war in North America was over**.

By having chosen the losing side, the Native American nations of the Iroquois League and the Cherokee Nation had forfeited their opportunities to strengthen ties of friendship with the settlers that had been and remained intent on moving westward. Perhaps, if the Native Americans, with a population of about 60,000 people, had fought for the British instead of for the French, settlers in future years would have respected their right to maintain their nations on tracts of land sandwiched between the developing states. But the Native Americans had chosen to side with the French and that placed them on the colonists' list of enemies.

Spain Joins France, but British Secure Victory and Win the Land that will become Canada

During 1760, the British continued to fight with success in Europe and in the Caribbean. In 1761, the Spanish made the mistake of joining in the war in support of the French. Just when it appeared that France would be crushed by British military success, the newly crowned British King, George III, forced a quick end to hostilities, partially to prevent Parliament leader, William Pitt, from becoming popular enough to challenge British royal authority. Preliminary peace terms were agreed to in 1762 and a final agreement was signed in Paris on February 10, 1763. It stipulated that **France give England her claims to all of present-day Canada** except for 2 small islands in the Gulf of St. Lawrence, and her claims to all land east of the Mississippi River, except for the land around New Orleans. French claims in the Caribbean were reduced to Guadeloupe, Martinique, Santa Lucia and the western half of Santo Domingo (which would become Haiti).

France Gives Louisiana to Spain and Spain Gives Florida to the British

As part of the peace agreement, France gave to Spain her claim to the land around New Orleans and her claims to land west of the Mississippi River. **Finally, Spain gave Britain her claim to Florida** and Spain recovered its claim to Cuba. By this agreement, France lost all of her vast land claims on the North American continent.

At this point it was clear that North America's destiny was to be controlled by English-speaking settlers. The Dutch had lost their colony in 1674, and the French had lost theirs in 1763. The Spanish still had vast claims in Mexico and western North America from the Rocky Mountains to the Pacific. But Spanish military strength had long been incapable of challenging the British. So, political observers at Paris knew that, with France so severely defeated in North America, no insurmountable obstacle stood in the way of eventual British seizure as well of those Spanish claims west of the Rocky Mountains.

French in Upper Mississippi Valley Persuade Native Americans to Attack Colonial Settlers

While the British, French and Spanish were dealing out titles to North American and Caribbean land, leaders of the various Native American nations – whose people were most affected – were rather ignored. This information vacuum permitted Frenchmen in the upper Mississippi region to trick many Native American leaders into believing that they could still defeat the westward-migrating colonial settlers, if only they coordinated their attacks. And Frenchmen convinced them that a huge French army would come to join them if only they led the way and showed how easily the colonial settlers could be driven back across the eastern mountains. **The Native Americans** took the bait and launched, in May 1763, a ferocious and coordinated attack on British fortifications and settlements throughout the northern Mississippi region. The coordinated, preemptive strike "resulted in the capture of nearly all the forts, the annihilation of their garrisons and the plundering of the settlements they had been established to protect." British soldiers and settlers retained control of only Fort Pitt, Fort Niagara and Fort Detroit. The most famous fight was the resistance mounted by the soldiers and settlers in Fort Detroit who successfully withstood the Native American siege led by Chief Pontiac. Many settlers and British soldiers lost their lives and their scalps to Native American warriors during this coordinated attack.

During this Nine Years War, British Colonists had Suffered far More than British Troops

Overall, during this just related Nine Years War, colonial settlers had suffered more than British soldiers and sailors. From the inception of war with the French in 1755 to the peace achieved with Native Americans in 1764, the death toll of colonial settlers, many being women and children, had far exceeded the death toll among British soldiers and sailors fighting in North America. That is true in spite of the fact that regular uniformed British soldiers and sailors were the predominant fighting forces in most of the major battles of the war. Settlers could say they suffered the most loss of life, but the British Government could say, funded by taxes in the British Isles, their soldiers and sailors had won the war and given peace to the colonial settlers. So, both British Government leaders and colonial settlers were arguing that they deserved the majority of the fruits of victory. Leaders in London claimed the **British Government deserved taxes** from colonial settlers to help fund its ongoing defensive operations. Settlers claimed they deserved the right to purchase land from Native Americans and form settlements through and beyond the Appalachian Mountains, with the organizational support of large land companies such as the Ohio Company, which was operated by investors in Virginia.

London Decides it cannot afford to Protect Colonists from Attacks by Native Americans

It seems that the British had defeated the French in Europe, but they could not economically defeat Native Americans on the frontier. The British Government simply did not want to spend huge sums of money paying full-time British soldiers to patrol a land that was as big as the European continent – especially when colonial settlers were so resistant to paying taxes to help offset the huge Government expense of such a thing. So, that was the reason that the British Government considered proclaiming that **the land of westward-flowing waters belonged to the Native American Nations** for the foreseeable future.

Since France had been severely defeated and Spain was incapable of challenging British might, the British Government was confident that it could control the colonization of all of North America from the Atlantic to the far reaches of the Mississippi River, and after that it could probably take the far west away from Spain.

But, could the British Government in London retain the loyalty of the American colonial settlers when British military might would be no longer needed to defend against French attack? Up until 1763, colonial settlers needed British military support. After 1763, they did not – and Government officials in London and political activists in the colonies knew it!

The history through September 1763 is now at a close. The history progresses to October, the month that witnessed the launch of the **Independence Movement in the American Colonies**.

Chapter 5 — 1763 to 1769: People of the Thirteen Colonies Ponder Seizing Control of Their Destiny

Late 1763

An Independence Political Movement is Born

The political movement to win limited sovereignty for the legislatures in the 13 Colonies began in late 1763. At this time, the effort was not an Independence Movement, for most politicians preferred a compromise whereby the Colonies became states that left foreign affairs issues to the British Government, but where each state was individually sovereign with regard to internal matters and with regard to administration of the Native American lands that stretched westward to the Mississippi River.

The King's Proclamation Line Sparks a Revolutionary Movement in the Back Country

On October 7, 1763, the British Government issued a proclamation through the King's executive office that would seed a powerful revolutionary movement in the American Colonies. This new British law established the **King's Proclamation Line**, which followed the eastern continental divide across North America. All land west of the Proclamation Line belonged exclusively to the Native American nations.

The intent of the Proclamation Line was to make peace with the Native American nations, for, perhaps, one generation and hopefully even longer, while keeping settlers within governing distance of British-controlled seaports, and away from Spanish influence along the Mississippi River – the natural highway to the sea for the people who were beginning to settle along the Ohio River and the Tennessee River. However, the British Government was careful to keep secret when it might open Native American land to settlers. As far as settlers knew, the Proclamation Line would be a permanent barrier for generations yet unborn.

The line ran from the upper Saint Lawrence watershed (at the boundary of the new British colony of Quebec) down to the new British colony of East Florida. The destination of creeks and rivers defined Native-versus-Settler access to the land, for the Proclamation Line was not surveyed. If a creek sent its water to the Saint Lawrence, the Ohio, the Tennessee or the Gulf of Mexico, the land around it was to be reserved for Native Americans – Colonial settlers and African Americans were to be excluded. If a creek sent its water to the Atlantic Ocean, the land around it was to be reserved for colonial settlers and African Americans – Native Americans were to be excluded. **So, the Proclamation Line was designed to separate the Natives from the Settlers.** Native Americans could only live west of the line and colonial settlers and African Americans could only live east of the line. Land of westward flowing waters was decreed to belong to the Native American nations, subject to the oversight of the British Government. Colonial settlers were firmly prohibited from buying a parcel within the land of westward flowing waters, even if Native Americans in the area seemed eager to sell some of their land.

The new law meant that British troops would probably be sent inland to expel settlers from settlements that had previously been legally located within the lands of westward-flowing waters. Such military action would reverse the role of the British soldier. He would be fighting to preserve Native American land instead of fighting to take Native American land. Situations could be expected whereby the British soldier would be a friend of the Native American and a foe of the colonial settler. Furthermore, the Proclamation stipulated that any colonial seeking to travel west of the Proclamation Line to conduct trade with Native Americans had to first obtain a trading license from British authorities.

Colonial settlers living inland in the foothills and inland valleys – from Massachusetts to Georgia – saw the Proclamation Line as a new reason to hate the British Government. Many were of Scottish ancestry, and that alone had imbued within their hearts a rather natural inclination to hate the British Government – in fact a natural hatred of any government that was at all imposing.

So, the Proclamation Line simply further fueled a natural tendency among inland settlers to an **intensified hatred of the British Government**. But, in eastern towns, such as Boston, New York and Philadelphia, where manufacturing and trade were important, the Proclamation Line was generally accepted as reasonable.

This apparent acceptance by seaport, trading and manufacturing towns would deceive British authorities into believing that the Proclamation boundary would be generally accepted as a proper barrier to western migration.

London was well aware that many European settlers were already living in the land of westward-flowing waters. But surveying and marking a boundary that curved about to include almost all existing European American frontier settlements seemed an impossible task in 1763. So, the British had seized upon the geographic watershed as the only practical boundary concept. This trapped European settlers who were living along the New River, which flowed north out of North Carolina into Virginia before turning west to cut through the Appalachians on its way to the Ohio River. It would also trap settlers in the French Broad River Valley of western North Carolina. **Settlement on the Watauga River** in present-day northeast Tennessee would begin in 1768 in defiance of the King's ban and rapidly grow thereafter.

And European American settlers, including my ancestor **William Wiseman**, would, before 1778, cross over the Blue Ridge Mountains and establish new farms along North Carolina's South Toe River, which flowed westward through the Appalachian Mountains to the upper Tennessee. Wiseman and his family were living on the eastern slope of the Blue Ridge Mountains when the Proclamation Line was decreed, and were hunting on the western side of the ridge. He liked the land on which he hunted and would eventually move there and establish a farm. William Wiseman and his family would be fighting mad over the possibility of British soldiers coming in over the mountains to force them off what they considered to be *their land*. [4] Additional examples abounded in the backcountry. Every year that the British Government failed to enforce the Proclamation Line resulted in more frontiersmen living in defiance of the ban and vowing to fight to retain their maturing farms.

Daniel Boone Explores Western Regions of Virginia and North Carolina Colonies

At the time of the King's Proclamation, a party of frontiersmen, which included **Daniel Boone** of the Yadkin River in the North Carolina Piedmont, was exploring and hunting in what would become southeast Kentucky. Boone was exploring for the Henderson Company, which

---

[4] Author's family history.

planned eventually to purchase large tracts of land from the Cherokee Nation and resell the land to frontier settlers. Upon his return home, he would hear that settlement on the land he had explored had recently been prohibited. But Boone and likeminded men were to defy the King's Proclamation.

Back Country Settlers Included Scots, Scots-Irish and Germans

Scots from Scotland and the northern section of Ireland were the dominant group living in the backcountry. And there were German-speaking people living in the backcountry as well. Both groups were easy to anger when confronted with oppressive British Government laws enforced by British soldiers. The Scots had always been distrustful of a London-based government, and had often behaved defiantly. Furthermore, the German-speaking settlers in the backcountry simply felt no loyalty toward the British, so they would be easily persuaded to follow the example set by their Scottish neighbors.

It would not be until 1780, long after the Declaration of Independence, that the British military, during the latter years of the Revolutionary War, would seriously threaten to force these frontier settlers from their homes. Then the settlers would rise up en masse and, at **King's Mountain**, inflict upon British authority the first of the string of Carolinas-region military defeats that would lead, 12 months later, to the British surrender at Yorktown in southeast Virginia. **These frontier settlers were America's Nation Builders!**

The King's Proclamation Also Created East Florida, West Florida and Quebec Colonies

The King's Proclamation also created 3 new colonies. It established **West Florida Colony** along the western Gulf Coast, in what are now the coastal regions of the States of Alabama, Mississippi, and eastern Louisiana, less the land around New Orleans. In 1863, West Florida Colony extended about 50 miles inland from the Gulf Coast, but the following year it would be expanded farther north to about 150 miles inland. The Proclamation also created **East Florida Colony**, which approximated today's State of Florida.

In the far north, the Proclamation created **Quebec Colony**, which centered on the St. Lawrence River. Quebec Colony included Quebec City and Montreal and ran westward to within 150 miles of Lake Huron.

1764

British Agents Negotiate with Natives for Peace along the Proclamation Line

Negotiations between the British and the Native American Nations began in 1764. The centerpiece of the British offering was British patrols along the new Proclamation Line. I suppose that Native American negotiators scoffed, "but settlers have not yet moved off our land." And it is probable that the confident-sounding British negotiators replied, "Oh, but we will make them move as soon as our treaties are signed." The Native American Nations recognized the British offer was a better deal than they had expected, given how they had so recently fought alongside the French.

British Attempt Modest Taxation in Coastal Towns

In 1764, the war with France being concluded, the British Government thought a **modest tax on certain imports and business transactions** would be accepted in the Colonies without sparking a resistance movement. The British Government certainly needed the money because, under the best of circumstances, it would take many years to pay off the debt incurred during the last war with France. And, patrolling the Proclamation Line would be expensive. It is true that the Colonies were indirectly earning money for the British Government through the trade restrictions imposed on commerce in and out of the Colonies. But the Government believed direct taxation was also needed. Surely, the colonists would understand that it took money to maintain British soldiers in the Colonies and British naval vessels in the West Atlantic and the Caribbean Sea.

King George III had appointed **George Grenville to the job of Prime Minister** in 1763. Among many other issues, Grenville had looked at the financial situation in the Colonies. Paraphrasing Grenville's thinking, historian Christopher Hibbert would write:

> "Now the time had come to pay not only for these [past] victories [over the French in North America] which, in Grenville's opinion, the American colonists had done very little to achieve, but also for the cost of defending and administering the territories, which they had secured. In helping to meet these expenses, Grenville considered that it was only proper that at least part of the **high cost of maintaining a force of 10,000 men in America**, as a safeguard against French revenge and [Native American armed resistance], should be met by the American colonists themselves. After all, it was their homelands which were to be protected, and their taxes were so relatively slight that it was calculated that an American paid no more than sixpence [½ shilling] a year against the average English taxpayer's 25 shillings. In 1764 Grenville accordingly announced that a direct tax would be imposed upon the Colonies within a year if no other suggestions were forthcoming as to how the required sums might be raised. He also announced that there must be [policing] in the ways in which customs duties were collected and evaded in [the Colonies]. Smuggling must be stopped and an end put to the present disgraceful mismanagement, whereby it [had been costing] £8,000 to collect £2,000-worth of customs duties in [colonial] ports."

No better ideas surfaced, so, in 1764, the British Government announced that the tax on imported molasses would be cut down to 3 pence per gallon from the higher tax rate decreed by the tax law that had been issued 31 years earlier. The old law was still on the books, but smugglers had largely evaded payment of that tax. Now, the British Government warned smugglers that the new, lower 3 pence per gallon molasses import tax would be strongly enforced and collected with renewed determination. Much of the molasses being imported into the Colonies was used by liquor distilleries in Massachusetts Colony to make rum. So, this import tax could be expected to cut into that sector's profit margin more than elsewhere.

1765

Prime Minister George Grenville Recommends a Little More Colonial Taxation

The following year, 1765, George Grenville recommended a second revenue-generating tax. This was a move to extend to the Colonies the **Stamp Tax** program that had long been in place in Great Britain. By that program, "all manner of legal and other documents were declared to be null and void in [the Colonies] unless bearing stamps of varying denominations, which had to be purchased from official distributors. Passports had to bear stamps, as did liquor licenses, playing cards, ships' papers, insurance policies, almanacs, newspapers and pamphlets. The stamps had to be paid for in sterling." And, it was obvious that evasion would be difficult because "cases involving breaches of the law were to be tried in the courts in which offenses against maritime law were considered and in which judges, appointed by the government, decided the issue without reference to juries." The Stamp Tax would increase the business costs of lawyers, distillers, newspapermen and printers.

It is Now Time to Introduce the Andrew Jackson Family

It is now time to introduce the Jackson family. **During 1765 Andrew Jackson, father to the future President of the same name**, arrived in the **Waxhaws**, a region that straddled the North Carolina-South Carolina line just south of **Charlotte**. He arrived with his wife Elizabeth, who had several relatives who were already established in the Waxhaws. Her sister, Jane, who had arrived 5 years earlier with her husband, James Crawford, was already prosperous by frontier standards. Three other sisters had established themselves in the region as well: Margaret and her husband, George McKemey, Mary and her husband, John Lessley, and Sarah and her husband, Samuel Lessley. The best land was already taken, so future father Andrew bought 200 acres of marginal Waxhaw land where "the red soil was washed and thin" and "the stand of pine and hickory and oak was drubbed and scrubby-looking." But it was close enough to Elizabeth's sisters.

Boston Suffers Riot in Opposition to the New British Stamp Act Taxation Law

On a hot August day in 1765 the first riot against British authority took place at **Boston, Massachusetts**. Boston was a likely place for a riot. Historian Christopher Hibbert would describe Boston as it looked in 1765:

> "[Boston was] a town of some 16,000 inhabitants many of whom worked in its [liquor] distilleries, fisheries, ropewalks and shipyards. It had once been the most prosperous port on the American coast, but was now a less flourishing and less orderly place in which a third of the adult population had no regular employment and the carriages of rich merchants were likely to be insulted and even pelted by crowds in the poorer parts of the town down by the wharves."

Protesters hanged the Stamp Tax Collector, in effigy, from an elm tree in Hanover Square. Attached to the effigy was a sign: "What greater joy did New England see, than a stamp man hanging on a tree." That stamp man was the well-known and wealthy merchant, Andrew Oliver, who had just accepted the job of "Distributor of Stamps for Massachusetts Bay." So, Oliver would be the man selling for the British Government those tax stamps that had to be affixed to passports, liquor licenses, playing cards, ships' papers, insurance policies, almanacs, newspapers and pamphlets. In fact, he already had a stamp office under construction on Oliver's Wharf.

The protest turned violent when an organized gang of rioters came into Hanover Square, pulled down the effigy, set it on fire as they hurled insults, proceeded down to Oliver's Wharf, pulled down the partially-constructed stamp office, proceeded to Oliver's fine home elsewhere in the city, broke out the windows, forced their way inside, smashed the furniture and "briefly contemplated" violence against Oliver and his family. During that "brief contemplation"

Oliver's brother-in-law, **Thomas Hutchinson**, arrived with the Sheriff. Hutchinson was a politically powerful man, wealthy, well connected by family ties, and firmly committed to continued British protection and governmental rule. Officially, Hutchinson was both the Colony's Chief Justice and the Colony's Lieutenant Governor. After shouting insults and throwing bricks at Hutchinson and the Sheriff, the rioters dispersed.

The next day men connected with the rioters warned Oliver that his house would be burned down and he might be killed if he sold those British tax stamps. The men issued a similar threat to brother-in-law Thomas Hutchinson. Hutchinson defied the threat. But Oliver submitted, and men connected with the rioting posted signs about town announcing Oliver's upcoming public resignation:

> "The True-born Sons of Liberty are desired to meet under [the] Liberty Tree at [noon today] to hear the public Resignation, under Oath, of Andrew Oliver, Distributor of Stamps for [Massachusetts Colony]."

Resistance organizers then unleashed their riot mob upon Hutchinson's house. "The mob completely wrecked it, threw out smashed furniture and family manuscripts, including a history of Massachusetts which Hutchinson had written, and broke into a strongbox to steal all the money it contained. **Hutchinson himself was considered lucky to have escaped with his life**."

Nine Colonies Establish an Anti-Stamp Act Congress

In October, 1675, Representatives from 9 of the 13 Colonies met in New York City to plan a coordinated effort to oppose the Stamp Tax. No representative came from Virginia Colony, North Carolina Colony or Georgia Colony. They would have sent representatives if the respective Colony Governors had permitted it. This body, calling itself the **Stamp Act Congress**, issued a Declaration of Rights and Grievances. Perhaps the most important language in this rather long declaration was the assertion that the "only representatives of the people of these colonies are persons chosen by themselves, and no taxes ever have been, or can be, constitutionally imposed upon them but by their respective Legislatures."

Tax collections for items requiring Stamps began on November 1. That day, organized rioters in New York City stole Lieutenant Governor Cadwallader Colden's carriage, chopped it up into firewood, and used the wood to burn his effigy. Then, the rioters rushed to the home of a prominent British officer and burned it down. There was violence in other commercial centers as well.

1766

Natives Agree to Abandon Land East of the King's Proclamation Line, but Western Settlers Balk

Treaties based on the King's Proclamation Line were concluded with the Native American nations in 1766. Those nations gave up any residual claims to land east of the Proclamation Line, and recognized that the British, not the French, were in control of European settlement of North America. **Yet, frontiersmen in western North Carolina and southwest Virginia were ignoring the Proclamation Line**.

James Smith set out to explore the land previously given up by the Cherokees and Shawnees, which was situated between the Ohio River and the Cherokee River (the Cherokees called it the Watauga River). A major river in present-day eastern Tennessee, the Watauga would be renamed the Holston River. Accompanied by Joshua Horton, his bonded African American servant, Uriah Stone, and William Baker, the James Smith party explored present-day Tennessee, including the **Cumberland River from Stone's River to the Ohio River**. Named for Uriah Stone, the name Stone's River would be transformed into Stones River, as if it had been named for the many stones in the riverbed instead of for Uriah Stone. During the Federal invasion of the Confederacy, a major battle would take place at Murfreesboro on both sides of Stones River. My grandfather would later buy a farm on that battlefield, and beginning in childhood, I would ponder upon the bloodstains in Grandfather's farmhouse floors. As a retired adult, I would write many published books about the Civil War in attempts to educate today's Americans about a needless war that resulted in one million unnecessary deaths, white and back. Those bloodstains had inspired me to become a writer.

Parliament Repeals the Stamp Act because it is too Expensive to Enforce

Meanwhile, the violence in coastal towns greatly disturbed British Government officials, since they realized that the Colonies were so vast that they could easily spend more money enforcing the collection of a protested modest tax than the tax was worth to the Government treasury. During this time, **Charles Rockingham** replaced George Grenville as **Prime Minister**. In February, after only 4 months of Stamp Tax collections, **Parliament repealed the Stamp Tax by a vote of 274 to 134**. The colonial resisters in the North had won.

But Parliament warned protestors that it reserved the right to levy future taxes on people living in the Colonies without consulting Colony legislatures. Parliament was insisting upon its sovereign power "to make laws and statutes" and "to bind the Colonies and people . . . in all cases whatsoever."

1767

Parliament Enacts Taxes on Colonial Imports of Glass, Lead, Paint, Paper and Tea

In early 1767, the British Government moved again to enact revenue-generating taxation on the American Colonies. Hoping to thwart protestors, Parliament skirted direct taxation of individuals as it voted to impose **import taxes on glass, red and white lead, painters' colors, paper and tea**. Since tea was the most widely consumed commodity on the tax list, protest organizers chose to focus upon the tea tax. They announced a **boycott on tea**. In fact, a man caught drinking tea might be the victim of a mob attack, particularly in the colonial seaport towns where protestors were focusing their activities. "There were riots in which customs officers were abused and attacked, tarred and feathered. In New York City, there were clashes between demonstrators and [British] soldiers who, by a recent Quartering Act, were entitled to occupy rooms in taverns and empty houses if barracks were inadequate or unavailable." In one incident, a Boston mob surrounded a customs officer's house and the besieged man fired his gun into the crowd, killing a young protestor.

Around the same time, British authorities caught a wealthy Boston merchant and smuggler, **John Hancock**, evading import taxes and **seized his sloop**, *Liberty*, for unpaid taxes. In apparent retaliation, an organized mob stole a tax collector's boat and burned it to ashes in front of Hancock's large and grand house on Beacon Hill. It seems that Hancock's father had become wealthy through many years of plying the illegal smuggling trade and the son was aiming to preserve the profitability of the smuggling business.

Andrew Jackson's Father dies in Dreadful Accident

Andrew Jackson (the future President's father) died tragically in March 1767. He had injured himself handling a heavy log on his Waxhaw, North Carolina, farm, and died shortly afterward. His wife Elizabeth, who was near full-term in her third pregnancy, shortly after the burial, gave birth at the house of her sister Jane Crawford. A son was born that day, March 15. Elizabeth named him **Andrew for his father**. Andrew had 2 older brothers, Hugh, 4, and Robert, 2. Elizabeth remained with her boys at the Crawford house, since the Crawford family had ample room. Andrew would show promise as a young lad, learning to read by the age of 5, and receiving an elementary education at a school at Waxhaw Church, a prominent Presbyterian church in the region.

1768

Colonists from Virginia and North Carolina settle the Watauga River Region of Present-day Tennessee

In defiance of the King's Proclamation Line, settlers started, in 1768, to settle on the **Watauga River in present-day northeastern Tennessee.** Settlement was begun by 10 families from near Raleigh, North Carolina Colony. Many other families would be coming from western North Carolina Colony and southwestern Virginia Colony.

1770

British Soldiers Have Difficulty Dealing with a Protest along a Ropewalk in Boston

On March 2, 1770, **several British soldiers went to Boston's ropewalk** to apply for any available laborer jobs by which they might earn some money to supplement their meager military pay. Since widespread unemployment had elevated feelings of hatred toward anyone competing for the limited number of available jobs, these applicants were immediately targeted for abuse. It must have been rather easy to rally Boston workers to beat off any British soldier seeking an available job. A man who had a job at the ropewalk taunted one of the applicants, Patrick Walker, and told him, if he wanted work, he "could go and clean his shit house." Offended, Patrick knocked the taunting man down and 8 or 9 of Patrick's fellow soldiers gathered around him with clubs in an attempt to stand firm. A larger group of ropewalk workers "rushed at the soldiers with [the] thick slats they used in their work and beat them off." But the soldiers returned with 20 or 30 more comrades. In fact, they arrived with ceremony, behind an African American man beating a drum. One of the ropewalk workers taunted: "You [African American] rascal, what have you to do with [European American] people's quarrels? . . . I suppose I may look on," the man replied. There was another fight with improvised clubs beating upon flesh and bone and again the **ropewalk workers drove away the soldiers.**

"Fire, Damn You, Fire" – Five Killed in Boston

In the evening, 3 days later, **gangs of Boston men taunted and fought with soldiers** in the streets. Fire bells were rung and crowds gathered. Young apprentice workers were taunting a soldier standing sentry duty outside Boston's Custom House when the soldier lost his temper and struck one of the young men with the butt of his musket. A large crowd swarmed about the lone sentry and hurled snow and ice at the man as they shouted insults. As the snow and ice pelted him about the body and face, the besieged sentry fixed his bayonet and loaded his musket. From behind or within the crowd the sentry heard a man taunt: "Fire, damn you, fire! Fire and be damned! You coward, you dare not fire!" One would assume that the heckler was safely behind those at the front who would be killed by the gun-blast he was so passionately encouraging. And one would assume the sentry realized that, if he obeyed the heckler and fired his single-shot musket, the crowd would rush at him from all sides and club him to death. So, the sentry did not fire and no one rushed at his bayonet.

But, a group of soldiers patrolling the streets soon arrived to rescue the besieged sentry. Their officer, Thomas Preston, firmly commanded his men to stand firm but hold their fire. The crowd turned their taunts toward these soldiers in an attempt to break their discipline. "Damn you, you sons of bitches, fire! You can't kill us all!" Perhaps the heckler, positioned safely at the back of the crowd, was again doing his thing. An unidentified man somewhere behind the soldiers called out, "Fire! By God! I'll stand by you, whilst I have a drop of blood. Fire!" At that moment someone in the crowd knocked down one of the soldiers with a block of wood.

That exasperated soldier got up, bruised from the blow he had just suffered, and defied his commander's firm order. Shot from his musket ripped through the crowd and tore into flesh. A few other soldiers fired into the crowd in support before the officer who commanded the group could shout, "Damn ye rascals, what did you fire for?" and then badger them back under his control. The officer and the protest leaders inspected the dead, dying and wounded. Casualties in the crowd came to 3 dead, 2 dying and 5 wounded but destined to survive. Now the protest leaders had their cherished martyrs. The 2 or more Bostonians who had been heckling the soldiers to "Fire, damned you! Fire!" must have been pleased. One of those hecklers may well have been none other than **Samuel Adams** himself.

Massachusetts Colony authorities brought Thomas Preston and his men before the court on charges of murder. Lawyers Josiah Quincy and **John Adams** handled the soldiers' defense. John Adams and Samuel Adams were cousins. Despite pressure from the judge, both lawyers encouraged an attitude of martyrdom toward the dead and wounded, for they called them nothing more than "a motley rabble of saucy boys." Samuel Adams watched the proceeding intently, hoping by his very presence to ensure no one was allowed to suggest that those "saucy boys" had been manipulated by "political puppeteers" such as himself. But, despite the cover-up, enough truth surfaced about the crowd's behavior to persuade the Jury to find the commander and all but 2 soldiers not guilty. Those 2 soldiers were convicted of manslaughter, branded on the thumbs and permitted to return to their military units.

Headlining the incident, the "**Boston Massacre**," propagandists railed against British authority, and solemn ministers delivered sermons titled "Slaughter of the Innocents."

Parliament Rescinds Tax on Glass, Lead, Paint, and Paper, but Retains Tax on Tea

In April 1770, the British Government decided to rescind the American import tax on glass, red and white lead, painters' colors and paper. **But it left intact its import tax on tea**. British leaders reasoned: one token import tax must remain in place to remind colonists that they are British citizens with some minimal obligation to financially support the Government. But despite the amazing leniency of British authorities, agitators in New York, Massachusetts and neighboring colonies would continue to harass British soldiers and applauded tea smugglers. **We see here an image of puzzling, nonsense behavior by politically active men of the Northern Culture**.

Far West of the Proclamation Line, at Watauga, James Robertson gets reports on the Cumberland River Valley, located much further west.

Meanwhile, during 1770, **the Watauga settlement** in northeastern Tennessee continued to grow. **James Robertson** arrived in time to make a corn crop. Robertson was probably excited over the reports from the Casper Mansco hunting party that had returned from the Cumberland River Valley, which would become middle Tennessee. Leaving the New River Valley of southwest Virginia, these hunters had been out west for a full year. They reported that no one lived in the vast Cumberland River Valley at the time in spite of the presence of fertile and potentially very productive soil. They found evidence of past Shawnee occupation and the remains of a French fort on the bluff where Nashville now stands and they observed much evidence of long-ago Native American occupation, but, at the time that they were there, the country held no human occupants. However, Robert Crocket was killed by a Native American hunting party as it traveled north on the War Trace Path that connected the Cherokee and Shawnee Nations. "All the country through which these hunters [had] passed was covered with high grass, which seemed inexhaustible; no traces of any human settlement could be seen, and the primeval state of things reigned in unrivaled glory; though under dry caves, on the sides of creeks, they [had] found many places where stones were set up, that covered large quantities of human bones. They [had] also found human bones in the caves, with which the country abounds." And, at the French [Salt] Lick, "they saw an immense number of buffaloes and wild game, more than they had ever seen at any one place. The lick and all the adjoining lands were crowded with them. Their bellowing resounded from the hills and forests; some of these animals they killed, and got their hides to cover the boats."

Within a few years, James Robertson would be leading settlers to the region. He would later establish Fort Nashborough (now Nashville) and play a major leadership role in the founding of the State of Tennessee.

1772

Rhode Island Agitators Seize British Ship, the *Gaspee* and Wound the Captain

In June 1772, agitators from Providence, Rhode Island Colony, swarmed aboard a British navy ship, the *Gaspee*, which had become accidentally grounded. They seized the grounded ship, put the wounded commander and his crew into small boats, and then destroyed it. I suppose they were boycotting tea and drinking something else. But destroying the *Gaspee* makes no sense.

Watauga Establishes a Government West of the Mountains

By 1772, there were sufficient settlers in Watauga to justify a local government. So, settlers "formed a written association and articles for their conduct." They appointed 5 Commissioners to govern the association, one being **James Robertson**. Earlier in the year, Virginia Colony had agreed to a 36-degrees-30-minutes boundary between Virginia and

Cherokee land and this clearly placed the Watauga settlement south of Virginia as well as west of the King's Proclamation Line. Watauga was west of North Carolina, too. However, "some of the Cherokees expressed a wish that [settlers of Watauga] might be permitted to stay if they would make no further encroachments." To seal the agreement, **James Robertson** and an associate negotiated an 8-year lease with the Cherokees "for all the country on the waters of the Watauga."

1773

British Government Allows Cheap Tea to Arrive in the American Colonies

During 1773, once again, the British Government decided to **appease the defiant protesters**, this time by authorizing the East India Company to ship tea directly from its storehouses in India to the American Colonies, thereby substantially cutting transportation costs. This move was computed to reduce tea prices at American ports so much that one-pound sterling could buy two pounds of tea instead of just one pound of tea, import tax included. Government authorities expected the big price cut would make it impossible for political activists to continue to use a tea boycott to rally resistance to British authority, because tea would be uncommonly cheap. And, the East India Company welcomed the change, for it had been complaining that, with its Indian warehouses stuffed full with 15 to 20 million pounds of tea, it faced bankruptcy if it did not receive Government help. So, the British Government had agreed to exempt the East India Company from the normal requirement that it bring its America-bound tea shipments into English ports prior to shipping them on to the American Colonies. **Cheap tea was on the way to the American Colonies!** But, would protestors succeed at turning away the tea-bearing ships as they had previously done in New York City, Philadelphia and Charleston – even cheap tea? Perhaps so. In those port cities, protestors had forced tea agents to resign their jobs, so, smugglers and their agents had gained control of those tea markets.

But perhaps the **East India Company** could successfully off-load a shipment of cheap tea at Boston harbor and thereby make the smuggling business unprofitable. **Thomas Hutchinson** was Governor of Massachusetts Colony and his 2 sons had been set up as legitimate tea distribution agents.

Not to be Denied a Tea Protest, Agitators Dress Up like Natives and Riot in Boston Harbor

Well, Boston protest leaders were not about to let cheap tea defuse their political movement. In seaport cities and towns, far from the western frontier, where the crucial issue of land access actually anchored the true passion for independence, tea had been a useful symbol about which seaport protestors could propagandize – the tea boycott had to be sustained. **So, when a boatload of cheap East India Company tea arrived in Boston Harbor aboard the *Dartmouth* in November, protestors and their leaders sprang to action to prevent unloading the cargo.** The ship's captain entered the cargo in the log at the Boston Custom House, but protest leaders, the most prominent being Samuel Adams, apparently succeeded in blocking payment of the import tax and completion of related import paperwork. So, the *Dartmouth* remained tied up at the dock, still full of chests of tea subject to British tax. As the days became weeks, Samuel Adams, and other protest leaders, sustained passions through frequent rallies staged at Boston's Old South Meeting House. At one point, the ship's captain grew so tired of the fuss that he announced that he was going to sail away with his tea. But Governor Hutchinson warned him that he would order the fort's artillerymen to sink the *Dartmouth* if he attempted to sail her out of the harbor. It seems that Hutchinson was determined to break the tea boycott in Massachusetts Colony and thereafter defuse the protest movement. Meekly, the captain of the *Dartmouth* remained in the harbor for additional weeks. During this time, two more ships bearing loads of tea subject to British tax, the *Eleanor* and the *Beaver*, sailed in and tied up at the docks, apparently unaware until too late that they would also be trapped in a boycott war being waged between the Governor and the protestors. The climax arrived on December 16 when, urged on by **Samuel Adams** and **John Hancock**, an organized band of **protestors, disguised as Native American warriors** of the Mohawk Nation, descended upon all three tea ships, broke into the cargo holds, hauled up the 342 tea chests, broke them open and **dumped the 35,000-pound cargos into the water**. **Paul Revere** was among the men masquerading as Mohawk Native Americans. Afterward, as the disguised protestors filed past the home of John Montagu, British Commander-in-Chief of the North American Station, Montagu called down to them: "Well, boys, you've had a fine, pleasant evening for your [Native American] caper, haven't you? But mind, you have got to pay the fiddler yet." And one of the disguised men returned a threatening reply: "Just come down here, if you please, and we'll settle the bill in two minutes."

Not long thereafter, an organized band of New York City protestors broke into the cargo hole of the *Nancy* and destroyed its cargo of tea subject to British tax.

Well, **these tea tax protesters were not the Nation Builders**. The Nation Builders were the families of the Southern Colonies, moving westward settling in the mountain valleys and beyond, along the westward flowing waters, defying the King's Proclamation Line.

Officials in the British Government were getting angry.

1774

Now, British Government Officials are Getting Mad

The Governor of Massachusetts Colony, **Thomas Hutchinson**, resigned and set out for the safety of London, and to consult with Government officials. During February, he advised them to set aside ideas of further appeasing the protestors and turn, instead, to forcing them to submit to British rule. Firm force in Massachusetts Colony would result in "speedy submission," he predicted. Others advised likewise. For example, shortly before Thomas Gage left London for the Colonies to assume the job of Commander-in-Chief of the North American British Army, he discussed the political situation with King George III. Gage told him that "So long as the British [Government] behaved like lambs, the colonists would play the part of lions, but that, if the Government were resolute, the [colonists] would 'undoubtedly prove very meek'." **The Prime Minister, Frederick North**, was similarly inclined to assume a tough stance. And North was determined to try the tactic first on the people of Massachusetts Colony, for they had been the most violent protestors, and the British Government had previously taken control of the Massachusetts Colony Government.

With the support of **King George III** and under the leadership of Prime Minister Frederick North, Parliament authorized punitive measures designed to bring Massachusetts protestors into submission. Parliament voted to enforce the following new laws beginning on June 1, 1774.

Boston Harbor was to be closed until citizens paid for the 35,000 pounds of tea they had destroyed – they had to **either pay up or see their seaport-based economy destroyed.** Members of the Massachusetts Colony upper legislative body were to be appointed by the British Government, instead of being elected by the lower legislative body as in the past. So, the Massachusetts Colony Legislature, still technically a subservient body, would be further removed from contact with the people. British troops were ordered back to patrol duty in Boston, and officers were empowered to demand quarters in private taverns, even homes if no other housing could be obtained. So, British presence would be all over town. **Thomas Gage's job responsibilities were expanded beyond his main assignment of Commander-in-Chief over all British soldiers in the colonies, for he was also instructed to take on Thomas Hutchinson's old job of Governor of Massachusetts Colony.** **That meant that Massachusetts would be under military rule.** And Parliament further empowered Gage, in his capacity as Governor, to direct Massachusetts courts to send accused colonists to England for trial in any situation where, in his opinion, the case could not be fairly tried in Massachusetts. King George III was confident that the Prime Minister and Parliament were taking the proper action. George wrote: "The die is cast, the colonies must either submit or triumph. I do not wish to come to severe measures, but we must not retreat. By coolness and an un-remitted pursuit of the measures that have been adopted, I trust that they will come to submit." And William Dartmouth, Secretary of State for the American Colonies, instructed Thomas Gage to first seek "by mild and gentle persuasion to induce submission," resorting to overwhelming force only as a last resort.

Misunderstanding the Root of the Rebellion, Parliament Makes a Big Mistake and Further Limits Western Land Access

It is instructive to note that the most fundamental objection to British rule was not addressed by Parliament as it clamped down on Massachusetts protestors – apparently because the 1763 British restriction on westward expansion was not being protested in Massachusetts Colony. But, shortly thereafter, **Parliament defined as Canadian Territory the land in present-day Michigan and much of the land in present-day Illinois.** This was viewed with alarm in New York Colony, Pennsylvania Colony and Virginia Colony, for people living there had hoped to eventually expand westward through the Great Lakes regions. This act of Parliament had nothing to do with the seaport fuss about the price of tea; this land transfer act was a deliberate and fundamental restriction on colonial aspirations.

Reasonable Colonial Leaders become Engaged – Convene the First Continental Congress

In August, the Virginia Colony Legislature threatened to meet illegally as a revolutionary First Virginia Convention. But, soon afterward, many other colonies had that idea. So, **delegates from the 13 Colonies** gathered in Carpenters' Hall at **Philadelphia** for the **First Continental Congress**, which opened on September 5. Emphasizing a strengthened resolve to sustain a boycott on imported goods, the First Continental Congress appealed to all colonists to shun every kind of nonessential import. Then, **Paul Revere** arrived with resolutions from Suffolk County, Massachusetts, which asked the First Continental Congress for its support of an armed resistance to any British Army attempt, by force of arms, to imposed British law on the colonists of Massachusetts. And, it was about this time that Massachusetts political activists set up a provisional revolutionary state government. The Continental Congress voted to support an armed resistance campaign, if necessary, but did not vote to declare independence from

British rule. Too many Delegates still hoped for a settlement whereby the British Government would provide some protection and oversight, but leave the colonies as almost-independent states.

West of the Proclamation Line, Natives and Colonials are Fighting

During October, there was significant fighting on the western frontier of Virginia and North Carolina colonies. Settlers of Watauga, in present-day Tennessee, and settlers of western Virginia Colony were defending against attacks by warriors from the Shawnee Nation and other Native American nations located north of the Ohio River. Of course, this conflict was taking place far west of the King's Proclamation Line.

About 300 militiamen were camped where the Kanawha River flows into the Ohio River in present-day West Virginia. James Robertson and Valentine Sevier, both of Watauga settlement to the south, were among the militiamen. Shortly before dawn, both were hunting about a half-mile from the camp when they spotted Native American warriors advancing toward the camp. In the predawn darkness, they fired their guns to startle the warriors and then succeeded in running back to camp to warn the others. The warriors were led by Cornstalk, a Shawnee Chief, who directed his 800 men with skill. A horrendous fight ensued all day between 800 warriors and 300 militiamen. Eventually the warriors retreated. The militia lost 160 men killed or wounded, and it was believed the natives lost a comparable number.

1775

Big Mistake – A leader in Parliament, Samuel Johnson, Advocates Arming Natives and Negroes to Put Down the Emerging Rebellion

On March 8, 1775, **Samuel Johnson**, a literary "titan" and influential member of the British Parliament, issued a pamphlet titled, *"Taxation, no Tyranny, An Answer to the Resolution and Address of the American Congress."* There, Johnson submitted: "**he who accepts protection, stipulates obedience**." He reminded colonists that the British Government had "always protected" the American colonists. For those reasons, he continued, the British Government may subject them to its rule. Wherever colonists were "governed by [British] laws, entitled to [British] dignities, regulated by [British] counsels, and protected by [British] arms," the British Parliament reigned supreme. The American colonies were part of the widespread British community. Parliament had the authority to collect taxes "from part of the community for the benefit of the whole." But, application of force had become necessary. With "the least injury possible to their persons and possessions," rebellious colonists must be forced to accept the rule of Parliament. Samuel Johnson's argument had been logical and convincing up to this point, but he overstepped the bounds of prudence when he unwisely threatened to ignite racial warfare if British troops proved unequal to the task. As a last resort, Johnson suggested "let us give the [Native Americans] arms, and teach them [military] discipline, and encourage them now and again to plunder a [colonial farm]." That was a practical military move, because Europeans had often persuaded various Native American nations to take up arms and fight for or against the French or the British. Furthermore, the root cause of colonial rebellion was over the land of westward-flowing waters, not the price of tea, and only well-armed Native Americans could hope to defend those lands from colonial invaders, for the British army would always be far too small. We recall that the British Government had never previously encouraged any Native American Nation to go to war against American colonists.

Yet, it was a practical concept. But Johnson did not stop there. He mused that it might also be necessary to send British soldiers into the countryside with instructions to take African American men off the farms, organize them into armed bands and send them forth to crush the rebellion. John Wesley and Robert Orne were complimentary of Parliament member Samuel Johnson's pamphlet, as were many others, although most British men surely thought it a bit premature to threaten racial warfare.

Recognizing that the British might attempt to incite racial warfare, the Continental Congress had already adopted a resolution forbidding the importation of bonded Africans after December 1, 1774. And the individual sovereign states would cooperate, as Delaware would outlaw bonded African importation in 1776 and Virginia would do the same in 1778.

Chapter 6 — 1775 to 1783: Thirteen Colonies Revolt Against British Rule

April 1775

Boston Rebels Seize British Arms and Launch a Revolution in Massachusetts Colony

Thomas Gage, Commander-in-Chief of the North American British Army, made his first move to gain control over the stashes of armaments in the countryside around Boston – including the armaments **stored at an armory at Concord**. At the same time he planned to arrest prominent protest leaders, such as **Samuel Adams** and John Hancock. The mission had been previously mapped and planned. However, spies in Boston knew that a raid was being planned, so when spotters noticed troops gathering after nightfall, **Paul Revere** set out on a good horse to warn protestors at Lexington, and farther down the road at Concord. A group of sixty protestors, armed and organized into a military unit, gathered at Lexington to offer resistance, but seemed reluctant to do so when the British soldiers arrived. However, without official sanction from the leader of the protestors, one man fired at the British soldiers from behind a rock wall and drew return fire. The British return fire toward the unsuspecting protestors was deadly, for it killed eight and wounded nine others, plus the group's leader. Apparently, the protestors ran off without firing again. But, one protestor managed to wound a British soldier in the back as the unit marched on toward Concord. Another organized group of armed protestors was present at Concord when the British unit arrived. Initially, the Concord protestors made no move to bar British access. But again, one sniper fired at the British soldiers, and that prompted the soldiers to fire toward the protestors. This time the protestors fired back and the skirmish commenced. The first protestor volley killed three British soldiers and wounded four British officers. Outgunned, and in unfamiliar territory, the British began their retreat to Boston. This advance force would soon be glad to receive help in their retreat, because British Lieutenant General Hugh Percy was already heading up the road toward them with cannon and a large force of soldiers. And they needed all the protection they could get, because "From farm walls, hedgerows and wayside boulders, from the windows of houses and the roofs of barns, hundreds of [protestors], including women, kept up a steady fire on the retreating [soldiers], shooting many in the back." A head count back in Boston would show that the British effort to gain control over outlying stashes of armaments **claimed the lives of 250 officers and soldiers**.

This time the protestors did not disperse and return to their farms and businesses. They gathered more supporters and moved on toward Boston to put the city under siege. Growing stronger every day, the protestors had evolved into revolutionaries. Massachusetts Colony had evolved from a colony undergoing a sometimes-violent political protest movement to a colony in revolution. Those revolutionists will henceforth be called "Rebels." By the end of April, there were **10,000 armed Rebels dug in along the siege lines enveloping Boston**.

Meanwhile, far to the Southwest, Watauga Settlers Conclude a Treaty with the Cherokee Nation

And, **on the North Carolina frontier**, well west of the King's Proclamation Line, settlers were acting totally independent of British law. During the month of April, the Watauga settlers in what would become the tip of northeastern Tennessee concluded their land acquisition treaty with the Cherokee Nation. This treaty provided for ownership of the land in and around the

Watauga settlements near present-day Johnson City, Kingsport and Bristol. The major Cherokee leader, Atta-culla-culla, favored the sale, but a lesser chief, said to have been Oconostota, appealed to fellow Cherokees to refuse the deal. In a desperate speech Oconostota reviewed the history of the European American settlements, first only along the coast, and then growing farther and farther inland. He warned that, because of the European American's insatiable thirst for more land for new farms, the Cherokees would be driven far to the west and eventually, when there was no place else to which they could flee, the remnant would be slain until the Cherokee was extinct. "But he did not prevail, and the [sale] was made."

In Charlotte, Mecklenburg County, North Carolina Colony, a Large Region in the Piedmont, Independence from British Rule is Declared.

After word arrived of the fight at Lexington, Massachusetts Colony, but shortly before word arrived of a Rebel siege of Boston, 27 leaders in **Mecklenburg County, North Carolina Colony**, were duly elected by the people and agreed to take a firm stand against British rule by proclaiming that their vast County was thereby independent of the British Government. Gathering in Charlotte on May 20, 1775, in a small log courthouse at the intersection of Trade and Tryon Streets, these leaders **issued a Declaration of Independence**. The Mecklenburg leaders approved 6 "Resolves" which collectively declared Mecklenburg County to be independent of British rule and directed that the Declaration was to be "laid before the Continental Congress" at Philadelphia. Consisting at that time of 2,647 square miles, Mecklenburg County was more than twice as big as Rhode Island Colony and one-third larger than Delaware Colony. Settlement by Scots and Germans had begun around 1740. The Mecklenburg action was the first official Declaration of Independence in the Thirteen Colonies. The Declaration's second and third "Resolves" are presented below:

Resolved, That we, the citizens of Mecklenburg County, do hereby dissolve the political bonds which have connected us with the mother country; and absolve ourselves from all allegiance to the British crown, adjuring all political connection with a nation that has wantonly trampled on our rights and liberties, and inhumanly shed the innocent blood of Americans at Lexington.

Resolved, That we do declare ourselves a free and independent people; that we are and of right ought to be a sovereign and self-governing people, under the power of God and the general congress; to the maintenance of which independence we solemnly pledge to each other our mutual cooperation, our lives, our fortunes and our most sacred honor.

This Declaration of Independence was signed by **Abraham Alexander, Chairman**, and 26 leading men of the County. By signing, these men were putting their lives on the line, for documented rebels of that high order would be hung by the British if captured.

By the way, after they would suffer defeat at Yorktown, Virginia on October 19, 1781, leaders in the British Government would recall that **Mecklenburg County had been the first to officially declare its independence**. They would remember that western North Carolinians would crush British attempts to conquer their region, that North Carolinians and South Carolinians would chase the British Army to the southeast Virginia coast and thereby make possible a decisive siege at Yorktown, which would be manned by themselves, by George Washington's army just arrived from the Northern States, by a French Army, and by a section of the French Navy.

Yes, there, in western North Carolina Colony were the homes and farms of the Nation Builders!

And, the British would eventually learn more than they wanted to know about an 8-year-old lad who, in May, was reading the Mecklenburg Declaration of Independence to a gathering of neighbors in the Waxhaw region, which straddled the Mecklenburg County border. Why? Because that lad would play a major leadership role in defeating British attempts to conquer the United States in 1812. The lad's name was **Andrew Jackson**. No wonder that, 5 years after the **Mecklenburg Declaration of Independence**, the British Commander, at that time attempting to conquer the Carolinas Piedmont, would declare, while passing through Charlotte, that the region was a "**Hornets' Nest**." He would be discovering that both Mecklenburg County and the surrounding regions were teeming with fervent Nation Builders.

A footnote about the Mecklenburg Declaration of Independence is warranted. On April 6, 1800 the written records of the Mecklenburg Convention of May 1775 and the written copies of the Mecklenburg Declaration of Independence were destroyed in a fire that consumed the home of John McKnitt Alexander, who had been the Secretary of the Mecklenburg Convention in May 1775. The copy that was expressed to Philadelphia by James Jack was considered, at that time, premature by the President of the Continental Congress and was not preserved either. Remember, if confiscated by British officials, the Mecklenburg Declaration would be considered treason, and the men who had signed it would be apprehended and executed. So, the wording I have presented above is based on the recollections of Alexander and others, who recreated the document after the fire. Without a doubt, the Mecklenburg Convention took place in May 1775 and there was no British rule in Mecklenburg County afterward.

In Boston, the Rebel Siege Line Expands to 15,000 Men

At the same time, in May, the Rebel force in the siege line around Boston grew to 15,000 men. But, Rebel leaders were not content simply to keep British forces bottled up in Boston. Some set off for Fort Ticonderoga, which lay 150 miles to the north. The French had originally built the fort, then calling it Fort Carillon, to protect the strategic route between French Quebec and the upper Hudson Valley region of British New York Colony. **Fort Ticonderoga contained heavy cannon, which the Rebels wanted to deploy in their siege of Boston**. The Rebels caught the British soldiers at Ticonderoga by surprise at 3:30 in the morning and captured men and cannon without firing a shot. The fort contained more than 100 iron cannon and several mortars, along with gunpowder and projectiles, which would obviously be of immense value to the rebel army. Thomas Gage, Massachusetts Colony Military Governor, would soon learn that he had committed a huge blunder by not beating the Rebels to this strategic resource. Under the leadership of Henry Knox, Rebels began building sleighs and carts and acquiring pack animals to haul the mortars and many of the cannon, including the gunpowder and projectiles, to the Boston siege lines. The task would take many months.

British Expand Top Military Command in America, adding William Howe, Henry Clinton and John Burgoyne to give aid to Commander Thomas Gage

About the time that Rebels seized the cannon at **Fort Ticonderoga**, the British leaders in London dispatched 3 additional top commanders to help Thomas Gage direct efforts to suppress the rebellion. The American Colonies covered a huge area, and, even before the loss of the cannon at Fort Ticonderoga, London leaders knew they needed more high-ranking field leadership. The 3 commanders, **William Howe**, **Henry Clinton** and **John Burgoyne**, arrived at Boston aboard the *Cerberus* toward the end of May.

British Find Northern Colonies Difficult and Southern Colonies Hopeless

Although the British found the situation in Boston, New York and Canada difficult, the situation in Virginia and points south was rather hopeless. On June 5, Rebels in Williamsburg forced the **Governor of Virginia Colony, John Murray**, to abandon his house and take refuge in the British frigate, *Fowey*. Declaring that Murray had abdicated, the Virginia Colony Legislature transferred his power to a Rebel Committee. Without success, Murray gathered up a few British ships and raided farms along the James River, luring a few bonded African Americans to join his campaign along the way. Murray issued a proclamation declaring any bonded African American to be independent if he ran away and joined the British Army. And Murray unsuccessfully sought help from Native Americans living in the Ohio Valley. Murray's improvised army, under the command of Charles Fordyce, made an attack at Long Bridge, about 20 miles south of Norfolk. Fordyce and his men were slaughtered by a Virginia militia of "expert marksmen, mostly entrenched behind a loop-holed stockade, 7 feet high and well supplied with ammunition." A survivor would later write: "We are now retired on board ship, cut off from all communications from the shore."

British Make Foolish Effort to Break the Boston Siege Line at Bunker Hill

Prodded by the newly arrived trio of top British commanders, Thomas Gage directed his first major Boston siege breakout attempt on the afternoon of June 17. It was an ill-conceived frontal attack on Rebels who had recently advanced to **Bunker Hill** and dug in. The base of Bunker Hill was situated between Boston and nearby Charlestown, within range of British Navy cannon. Thomas Gage planned to use cannon aboard his warships to protect the landing site, for his men had to row over to that spot and rush to shore to find available cover prior to staging their attack. Henry Clinton advised an alternate route that would have permitted the British soldiers to cut off retreat and thereby capture a few hundred of the Rebels, but Gates insisted on his frontal attack plan. So, British troops landed from rowboats near the foot of the hill and organized for their advance against the dug-in Rebels. Those poor British soldiers were killed in great numbers before the Rebels safely retreated back to more remote siege-line trenches. A frontal attack to simply take a hilltop, with no prospect for taking prisoners, was a foolish military strategy. This engagement was the first major military battle of the American Revolution and the Rebels clearly won a major victory. The British soldiers had managed to kill or wound over 400 Rebels. But they had suffered 27 killed officers and 226 killed soldiers, plus 63 wounded officers and 828 wounded soldiers, for a total of 1,144 casualties. The high casualty toll was devastating, for it represented about 40 percent of the British force that had been occupying Boston. The dreadful news would reach London in about 2 weeks.

British Command Ponders Options

British authorities knew that their problems with rebellious activity were not limited to Boston. Boston had simply been the site of the most violent protest actions. In Boston, British soldiers had been present in large numbers, unemployment had been crushing, disparities between rich and poor had been dramatic, and the historic Puritan compulsion to intertwine religious and political fervor had been at work. Authorities knew that maintaining control over the northern colonies included overseeing Newport and Plymouth, 2 other prominent coastal towns within 60 miles of Boston. It included overseeing New York City. Strategically, New York City was the most important seaport of all, for the Hudson-Lake Champlain corridor, which stretched northward through vast New York Colony from New York City to Canada, was the passageway to Quebec Colony. There, the British were lucky. Yes, populated by French-speaking people, the newly acquired citizens of Quebec showed no inclination to join the protestors in English-speaking colonies to the south. So, British officials figured that they could best crush the protest movement by sweeping down through the northern colonies from bases in Quebec. British officials also wanted to occupy the Hudson-Lake Champlain corridor so they could have access to the **160,000 Native Americans living to the west**, hopefully persuading them to help defeat the Rebels. The Iroquois League of Six Nations comprised the Mohawk, Oneida, Onondaga, Cayuga, Seneca and Tuscarora nations. Other Native American nations were combined in the Western Confederation.

South of New York Colony laid **the largest town of all, Philadelphia.** With a population of 30,000, this was "the most important commercial center in the British Empire after London and Liverpool." British officials were also concerned about the vast backcountry in Pennsylvania Colony. They were also concerned about controlling Baltimore, Norfolk, Wilmington, Charleston, and Savannah for these were the major seaports for Maryland, vast Virginia, vast North Carolina, South Carolina and Georgia. They knew that controlling the seaports would be easy, relative to controlling the vast back-country farmland in those 5 southern colonies, much of it populated by independent-minded Scots and their German neighbors.

George Washington of Virginia Colony Takes Command of the Continental Army

About 2 weeks after Massachusetts Rebels had decimated the British force in the battle at Bunker Hill, George Washington arrived to take command of the Rebel siege lines surrounding Boston. **The Continental Congress had recently appointed Washington as Commander-in-Chief of all Rebel armed forces.** Many Delegates had argued that, since the fighting was taking place in Massachusetts Colony, a Massachusetts man should be named Commander-in-Chief. And these Delegates had pointed out that Bostonian **John Hancock** was eagerly seeking the job. But most Delegates were more impressed with Washington's leadership ability, his past military experience, and his willingness to accept the job without pay. Bostonian **John Adams** strongly urged Washington's appointment in hopes that it would attract urgently needed support from the other 12 colonies. Adams knew that, alone, Massachusetts had no hope of defeating the British Empire, and that the leadership of a skilled Virginian would prove most valuable. Before departing for Boston, Washington had explained his appointment in a letter to his wife, Martha:

> "I assure you in the most solemn manner that, far from seeking this appointment, I have used every endeavor in my power to avoid it, not only from my unwillingness to part with you and the family, but from a consciousness of its being a trust too great for my capacity."

George Washington arrived at the Boston siege lines in early July. He would consume 8 months transforming the undisciplined and disorganized Boston siege force into a Continental Army capable of defeating the British. The 3,000 soldiers who had just arrived from Pennsylvania, Maryland and Virginia needed training. Powder and shot were needed, for there was not enough to launch even one sizable offensive. Henry Knox and his men were still building sleighs and carts and acquiring horses and mules to bring over the captured Fort Ticonderoga artillery. That vital siege artillery was still months away from arrival. Washington would have to cope with the fact that enlistments would expire at the end of the year, which was about the time he hoped to complete his training and equipping program. Furthermore, many of the officers were simply incompetent. But, during those 8 months, Washington would rebuild the command team, as he fired many officers for cowardice, dishonesty and for being uncooperative. At one point he would court-martial 8 officers and have one flogged before his men. Washington would demand much from the soldiers as well, including clean and orderly camps, and he would punish soldiers for breaches of discipline. He would even seek authority to hang anyone who deserted in violation of his enlistment contract. Among the top officers helping Washington at the siege lines were **2 Virginians, Horatio Gates and Charles Lee.** But Washington knew that **Henry Knox**, out at **Fort Ticonderoga**, was the most important commander on his team.

Washington Orders Attacks Against British in Montreal and Quebec

While George Washington and Henry Knox were transforming the Boston siege force into a disciplined and well-armed Continental Army, Rebels under **Benedict Arnold** and Richard Montgomery were struggling to drive the British Army out of Canada. Among these Continentals was **Alexander McMillan**, who had emigrated from Ireland earlier in 1775, having landed in Boston. Soon after arriving, he had signed up to fight with the Continentals in Quebec.

By the way, **Alexander McMillan** would later fight alongside **my ancestor, and his uncle, William McMillan**, at King's Mountain. And, as an old man he would fight the British again with **Andrew Jackson** at New Orleans.

Washington had figured the best way to defeat the British Government was to drive the British Army from its safe haven in Canada. So, Washington had directed Richard Montgomery to lead a 2,400-man attack force to capture Montreal, and then proceed east to reinforce Benedict Arnold's force of 1,100 men, which would be laying a siege on Quebec City. Montgomery had set out from Fort Ticonderoga with his men in late August, and Arnold had set out from Maine with his men the following month. Montgomery was very successful. In November, defeated British forces **fled Montreal** for Quebec City. But Arnold found that conquering Quebec City was a tougher assignment. Inadequate clothing and supplies had diminished Arnold's force to 600 men by the time he arrived at the outskirts of Quebec. When Montgomery arrived, he came with only 300 more men, for he had dispersed most of his force at forts along the way. British defenders numbered 1,200, but only about 70 were British Army regulars, so the commander, Guy Carleton, was especially concerned about the fighting spirit of his men. Yet, the fortifications at **Quebec City** were withstanding occasional bombardment by the light field artillery the Rebels had managed to bring along. The Rebels attacked on December 31, but without success. Richard Montgomery was killed in that action, leaving Benedict Arnold in full command.

Efforts to create an Independent New Hampshire State

Meanwhile, political activists in New Hampshire Colony, being close to this fighting and with the blessing of the Continental Congress, were moving toward the adoption of a constitution for a sovereign State of New Hampshire.

1776

Washington's Tactics are Successful – British Evacuate Boston

Henry Knox and his men arrived at the Boston siege line from Fort Ticonderoga on January 24, 1776. The men arrived with **43 cannon**, **16 mortars**, and shot and gunpowder for all. By this time, George Washington had completed equipping, training and organizing his siege army. **So, by February, with a competent Continental Army of 17,000 men and ample siege artillery, George Washington was ready to drive the British out of Boston.**

On March 2nd, Washington's men took, without a fight, Dorchester Heights, and placed artillery there to bring much of Boston and some of the harbor within range of the newly arrived cannon and mortars. Even without a fight, the British force in Boston knew it was beaten. The top commander, William Howe, sought and obtained Washington's pledge not to fire upon his men if he evacuated the British force without destroying the city. The British desperately needed more ships to carry out the evacuation, but they had to make do with what they had. On March 17, the British started loading the ships for a planned 16-day voyage to the safe Canadian port of Halifax. All military supplies that could not be loaded onto the ships were destroyed. Crammed into and upon the ships were 12,000 soldiers (regular British soldiers, mercenaries, and local recruits) and more than 1,000 Bostonians who had supported the British and feared reprisals from Rebels if they remained behind. Most of the evacuating Bostonians had boarded with their children on the first day, and sadly, many of the children died of suffocation before, 10 days later, the ships caught the wind and sailed out of Boston harbor "packed with their human cargoes and with as many horses and stores as could be crammed aboard them." **George Washington** and his "triumphant men of the Continental Army marched down into Boston as the British ships disappeared beyond the horizon." Virginian George Washington had forged the Boston siege force into a fearsome Continental Army and had driven off a 12,000-man British force without engaging in a significant battle. **It was a major triumph!**

The flight to Canada by more than 1,000 Bostonians should not be construed as indicative that citizens who wanted to be loyal to the British Government lived only in Boston. It is instructive to realize that many settlers in the Colonies wanted to be loyal to the British Government. In Virginia, the "honorable and widely respected Lawrence Washington," a brother to George Washington (or half-brother) was actively loyal. In New Jersey, William Franklin, son of Benjamin Franklin and the Governor of New Jersey Colony was the head of the Board of American Loyalists, which attempted to supply organization to a Loyalist movement. During the course of the British effort to re-conquer the 13 newly independent States, **about 19,000 colonial settlers would fight in British military units**. Looking at the situation another way, at any one time during the defense of the thirteen States' declaration of Independence, no more than 6% of the population of fighting-age men would be fighting for the Continental Army. The other 94% would be uninvolved or supporting the British Government.

Parliament is Outraged Over the British Retreat from Boston

When news of the forced evacuation of Boston reached Parliament, the **Opposition Party** lashed out vehemently against the officials who were responsible for directing British efforts in the Colonies. In the House of Commons **Charles Fox** called **Frederick North** a "blundering pilot who had brought the [British] Nation into its present difficulties. William Chatham, the King of Prussia, nay, Alexander the Great, never gained more in one campaign than [Frederick North] has lost – he has lost a whole continent." But, perhaps more responsible for American Colony affairs than North was George Germain, Secretary of State for the American Department. Germain was "largely responsible for the conduct of the war in America and for defending it in the House [of Commons]."

Sadly, for the British, their Army and Navy, were Far Too Small to Retain Control of the Vast British Empire

And Germain knew that the British Government had insufficient men under arms in 1776 to defeat the Continental Army and militia that were spread out across a land as big as Europe. Navy strength had dwindled from a 1774 high of 21,000 men down to 16,000 men. Army strength was widely dispersed. There were 16,000 in England and Scotland, 12,000 in Ireland, and 9,000 men spread out across India, Africa, Minorca, Gibraltar and the West Indies. And there were 8,000 in Canada and protected enclaves within the rebellious Colonies. But the British Army in North America was greatly augmented by local American recruits. British soldiers received very little pay, because most of their meager compensation was in the food, shelter and uniforms provided. Actually, much was made of the "smartness" of the British uniform, as that was perhaps the most powerful recruitment lure.

The "Brown Bess" shoulder-gun issued to a British soldier did not represent the highest technology of the day. For example, **Patrick Ferguson had invented a breech-loading rifle** and would stage a most impressive demonstration during the same year that Washington's siege army forced the British to evacuate Boston. The Brown Bess was a 44-inch muzzle-loading musket, which an average soldier managed to fire 2 or 3 times a minute, with a range of 100 yards. But Ferguson's rifle was capable of 6 shots per minute with improved accuracy and range. During the war a small number of British soldiers would receive a form of Ferguson's breech-loading rifle, but **the British would not convert to the rifle fast enough** for it to be a significant factor in its attempt to re-colonize the American States. In addition to recruitment of loyal colonists, a suitable manpower build-up would require recruiting Native American warriors from the Iroquois League of Nations and the Western Confederation of Nations, and recruiting thousands of mercenaries in Europe, particularly in German-speaking regions. And some British leaders held the futile hope that a large force of African Americans could be persuaded to join the cause of the British Government.

Heroically, British Forces Break the Siege of Quebec

Hoping to prevent the fall of Canada, the British Government had dispatched a rescue fleet to the besieged city of Quebec. The 50-gun *Isis* had set out in early March, and other ships had followed in early April. Using sail power, the commander of the *Isis* forged a path through the ice with heroic determination as other ships followed. The rescue fleet reached Quebec City at dawn on May 6. The frigate *Surprise* bombarded the Rebel entrenchments as British troops disembarked from the transports. Seeing that he had no chance of taking a reinforced Quebec

City, **Benedict Arnold** immediately ordered a withdrawal from Canada. The Rebels left behind "several pieces of their artillery and much of their baggage." British soldiers found the Rebel "tents still standing and their breakfasts laid out on tables."

British Succeed in Tricking Cherokees into an Alliance

Meanwhile the British Government was encouraging the **Cherokee Nation** to ally with the British cause and help defeat supporters of the new American states. Through its Superintendent, John Stuart, who had fled South Carolina to a refuge in Florida, the British War Department had directed Alexander Cammeron, its agent for the Cherokee Nation, to win the Cherokees to the British cause. Cammeron argued for the British cause before the Cherokee chiefs, promising "large presents in clothing, the plunder of the conquered country, and that part of it which was on the western waters to be reserved for their hunting-grounds." Although the Cherokee people had difficulty understanding why British people would go to war against British people, and although many considered the Watauga settlers to be friends, the leaders of the Cherokee Nation decided to align with the British and to go to war against the frontier settlers in Watauga, western North Carolina, and upper South Carolina. But a Cherokee woman, Nancy Ward, alerted the Watauga settlers of the Cherokee realignment and warned them that attacks were imminent. These settlers would build more forts and prepare to defend their farms and their women and children.

Major British Naval Effort to Retake Charleston, South Carolina Colony Fails Dramatically

This report is a dramatic win for the newly-organized State of South Carolina. It demonstrates that the **Southern Colonies were the homes and farms of the Nation Builders**.

On June 28 a British Naval fleet under the command of **Peter Parker** attempted to take back **Charleston, South Carolina**. But the South Carolina militia was ready for the British attack. And Samuel Davis may have joined the militia by this time. The future father of Jefferson Davis, Samuel had left or was about to leave his widowed mother to take food and clothing to his two half-brothers, Daniel and Isaac Williams, who were at the coast fighting the British. Samuel, then about 19 years old, would remain to fight alongside his half-brothers. Guarding the harbor entrance from the fort on Sullivan's Island were Continentals under **William Moultrie** (a more substantial fortress at the site would later be named Fort Moultrie). And among the men guarding the land invasion routes was the Waxhaw militia, which was commanded by young Andrew Jackson's uncle, **Robert Crawford**. Jackson would have been there had he not been so young. It was a hard fight, and the fort's walls held. The damage inflicted upon the British fleet was devastating. Parker's flagship, the *Bristol*, lost her mizzen, her main mast and her captain. All 5 frigates were damaged, and the *Actaeon*, having run aground, was destroyed. The British suffered nearly 200 killed and wounded compared to light Continental losses of 12 killed and 24 wounded. The British fleet limped away toward New York City, having no intention of attacking again. In fact, **the British Government would soon decide to forego any further attempts to conquer the lost colonies of Maryland, Virginia, North Carolina, South Carolina and Georgia**, and concentrate available forces on retaking the northern colonies from Pennsylvania through Massachusetts, because there the people were congregated around larger seaport towns, and a British base in Canada was nearby.

Therefore, it appeared that a greater part of the people in the northern colonies could be persuaded to be loyal to the British Government.

Earlier, on May 10, the Continental Congress had advised political activists in the Colonies to establish separate sovereign State Governments, each best suited to "the happiness and safety of their constituents." By this time, political activists in New Hampshire and South Carolina had Constitutions in place and Virginia activists were in the process of establishing a Virginia State Constitution.

Bravely, Delegates in the Continental Congress Issue the Declaration of Independence

On July 4, Continental Congress Delegates in Philadelphia, representing what had been the 13 colonies and what was becoming 13 sovereign States, issued a **Declaration of Independence**. Like the **Mecklenburg County Declaration** issued from Charlotte, North Carolina, 13 months earlier, the Second Continental Congress' Declaration of Independence proclaimed that the region covered was independent from British rule. Most importantly, the designated region covered by the Continental Congress Declaration consisted of all the land within the Colonies that lay between Spanish-speaking Florida and French-speaking Canada. It was understood that the land of westward-flowing waters was also included, for it was clear that the Declaration had been written by a team of Nation Builders who fully intended to overrule the British law that prohibited settlers from moving west into the land of westward flowing waters. That vast land, which the British Government had been unsuccessfully attempting to preserve for Native American nations, was to be controlled by the 13 sovereign States, either jointly or separately.

Andrew Jackson, then 9 years old, read a copy of the Declaration of Independence to interested Waxhaw settlers who were gathered at Robert Crawford's house. Like inland settlers throughout the thirteen States, Waxhaw settlers understood that the Declaration of Independence had a lot more to do with access to western land than with the price of tea or papers bearing British government stamps. Nation Builders, not micro-economists, wrote the Declaration of Independence. And, there were hints in the wording of Thomas Jefferson's draft that these Nation Builders were eager to discontinue the British-sanctioned importation of bonded African workers. But, the details of when and how would remain undecided and await another debate. Hereafter, what I have been calling the "thirteen Colonies" will be called the "thirteen States." And, "States" will be capitalized to remind us of the sovereignty of each. Unlike after the American Civil War, these "thirteen States" were not States within a nation, they were sovereign States acting together for their common defense under the leadership of a Continental Congress. In some ways, Congress resembled today's North Atlantic Treaty Organization – NATO. Bringing these thirteen sovereign States together, under a constitutionally-limited Federal Government, would take place many years later.

The Thirteen Colonies Organize as Thirteen Independent State Governments

At this time, political activists were busy creating constitutions for their respective sovereign States. Prior to July 4, State Constitutions were in place in New Hampshire, South Carolina, Virginia and New Jersey. By the end of the year, 1776, new State Constitutions would be established for 4 other sovereign States: Pennsylvania, Delaware, Maryland and North Carolina. By July 1780, State Constitutions would be established for 3 more States: New York,

Georgia and Maryland. In the remaining 2 States, Connecticut and Rhode Island, political activists would choose to "slightly revamp" their Colony Charters, thereby avoiding establishing new State Constitutions. The State Constitutions were, and would be, "brief and strikingly similar." Power resided in the two-house legislatures, or, in the case of Pennsylvania and Georgia, in the one-house legislature. Frequent elections were required, most often once per year. The governor had very little power, except in Massachusetts, which allowed a governor's veto that could be overridden by two-thirds of the votes in both legislative houses. But no governor was authorized in the Pennsylvania State Constitution.

George Mason had written the Declaration of Rights section of the **Virginia State Constitution**, and that was serving as the pattern for comparable sections in the other State Constitutions. The Virginia Declaration of Rights stipulated, "That all men are by nature equally free and independent, and have certain inherent rights," and that included "life and liberty." Other political principles included "popular sovereignty, separation of legislative and executive powers, freedom of elections, speedy jury trial, no general search warrants, freedom of the press, a militia instead of a standing army, and religious freedom." Each State established a judicial system, and these were similar to the respective earlier colonial systems. Voters selected judges in Georgia, but legislatures or governors appointed judges in the other States.

Applying the principle of "no taxation without representation," only men who paid taxes were allowed to vote. But, the value of taxable land required to qualify to vote varied considerably from State to State. North Carolina permitted all men to vote for lesser offices, but required ownership of 50 acres to vote for higher offices. Virginia required ownership of 50 acres to vote for all offices. Pennsylvania allowed all taxpayers to vote, without regard to the size of their landholdings. In a similar manner, Georgia allowed all or most taxpayers to vote. A man in Massachusetts needed landholdings worth 60 pounds sterling to qualify to vote. Religious freedom was granted to all, but some States denied Catholics access to the polls and most denied access to Jews as well. The Pennsylvania State Constitution and the South Carolina State Constitution required a voter to testify that he believed in God, and the Delaware State Constitution required a voter to testify that he believed in God, Jesus Christ and the Holy Ghost. But Virginia and New York applied no religious test to prospective voters.

Continental Agents Seek Arms Purchases in Europe

Arriving in France in 1775, **Silas Deane**, a Connecticut merchant, had been the first representative of the Continental Congress to be stationed at Paris. His job had been to "buy arms for which he would receive a 5% commission." Congress had wanted **Thomas Jefferson** to go to Paris as its primary representative, but Jefferson had declined because, at the time, his wife was having difficulty with her pregnancy. So, Congress had then asked 2 other men, **Arthur Lee** of Virginia and **Benjamin Franklin** of Pennsylvania, to join Deane in Paris. Congress had named Lee the principal representative. Even before Lee and Franklin had arrived, Dean had won the clandestine support of the French Foreign Minister, Comte de Vergennes, "who was eager to recover for France all that she had lost during [the fighting that had spanned from 1756 to 1763."

In fact, the French had been supporting the Continentals since 1775, for, since that year, help was being received from "two French officers" and "at least 200 Frenchmen" acting as "artillerists and engineers." And, during 1776, a 19-year-old Frenchman of unusual ability joined the Continental Army as a high-ranking officer – a young fellow named **Marie-Joseph du Motier Lafayette**. In the early days of the conflict, De Vergennes had dispatched observers to the American States and learned from their reports that the citizens were overwhelmingly behind the Continental Congress and that they controlled the vast majority of the countryside. The arrival of Lee and Franklin served to expand Vergennes' confidence in Congress' eventual success. With de Vergennes' approval, Pierre-Augustin Caron de Beaumarchais, through a fictitious company, had been supplying arms, for which the French Government officially expected to be paid, but which Arthur Lee "assured Congress were a gift." And those arms – valued at over 6,000,000 livres – would be very important in the capture of British General Burgoyne's 4,000 men at Saratoga, New York State.

Cherokees and Watauga Settlers are At War

Meanwhile, during July, **Cherokee warriors descended on frontier settlements in the Watauga region.** But, a militia of 170 men met the warriors in open field at the Island Flats and, through superior organization and marksmanship, forced them to flee after the loss of about 40 warriors, including several chiefs. Amazingly, none of the militiamen were killed and the 5 wounded would recover. On the same day, **James Robertson**, **John Sevier** and 38 other settlers began holding off a band of Cherokee warriors until relief would arrive 3 weeks later. A third band of Cherokee warriors, commanded by The Raven, invaded Carter's Valley, but would leave after finding all the settlers well defended behind fortifications. But settlers along the Clinch River would be unable to repulse the band of Cherokee warriors that invaded their territory, and most of the farms would be burned and many settlers would be killed. Similar Cherokee attacks were launched against frontier settlers in southern North Carolina, northwest South Carolina and northeast Georgia. The Cherokee Nation seemed determined to clear settlers from the land of western flowing waters.

Frontier settlers quickly gathered **sizable militia forces to punish the Cherokees** for going to war against frontier settlements in alliance with the British Government. Virginians under William Christian arrived in the Watauga region and drove the remaining warriors from the region. A North Carolina force of 400 militiamen joined the Virginians toward the end of the month, as did militiamen from the Watauga settlements. By early September, this militia force of 1,800 frontiersmen confronted a Cherokee force of 3,000 warriors at a crossing of the French Broad River. But the warriors did not contest this militia force as it crossed the river and headed south to destroy upper Cherokee towns. The militiamen burned 4 towns – Neowee, Tellico, Chilhowee and Tuskega – before the upper Cherokee agreed to peace.

At about the same time an army of 2,400 men from the Piedmont region of North Carolina, under the command of **Griffin Rutherford**, invaded the middle towns and valley towns of the Cherokee Nation, which were located west of present-day Asheville, in southwestern North Carolina, and in upper South Carolina. Rutherford's men "destroyed 36 towns and villages, cut up and wasted the standing and gathered Cherokee's corn, and drove off and destroyed all the flocks of domestic animals that could be found."

A third army of South Carolina militiamen, under **Andrew Williamson**, "consisting of a powerful force," penetrated the [Cherokee region] in the far northwestern part of present-day South Carolina and destroyed numerous Cherokee towns.

A fourth army of **Georgia militiamen, commanded by Leonard McBury**, destroyed all the Cherokee towns on the Tugulo River in present-day extreme northeast Georgia.

So, within a few months the once proud Cherokee Nation suffered grave devastation for its decision to ally with the British Government. Almost all of the Cherokee people had survived the attacks by fleeing into the mountains, but their power, self-sufficiency and strength was severely weakened.

British Land Huge Army in New Jersey

Meanwhile, during July, the British had landed a huge army on New Jersey's Staten Island, just below New York City. "With naval support of 10 ships of the line and 20 frigates, and in command of the **largest British army which had ever been landed on an alien shore**, [British commander] **William Howe** was ready at last to make his long-planned **assault on New York State**, to take command of the Hudson River, the most convenient overland route to Canada, and thus to drive a wedge between the Rebels, who could then be defeated separately, first [to the east] of New York [State], and [then to the south of it]." George Washington, by this time in control of New York City and Long Island, was in command of Rebel forces. But Washington was outnumbered, having only 10,000 men compared to the British force of 20,000 men. The Continentals were **forced to abandon New York City** on September 13. The presence of 20,000 British soldiers must have destroyed the fighting spirit of Rebel forces, for, by early December, **Washington's Continentals** had been reduced to about **3,000 men**, and many of these would desert upon crossing the Delaware River with him at Trenton, New Jersey. Only a remnant of Washington's Continental Army would winter over with him in Pennsylvania State. During this time, the British force that had failed at Charleston, South Carolina, landed without opposition at the tiny State of Rhode Island. The next major British target would be Philadelphia, the key to controlling the major State of Pennsylvania.

British Succeed in Driving Rebel Forces from the Quebec-Montreal Region

After liberating besieged Quebec City, the British Army had **cleared Rebel forces from all land between Quebec City and Montreal**. Finding 2,000 Native Americans gathered at a pow-wow near Montreal, John Burgoyne had talked 1,500 into joining his men in a sweep down the Champlain-Hudson corridor, but most had returned home after a while. Surprisingly, the British pursuit had come to rest at the northern end of Lake Champlain. Instead of hauling supplies and artillery around the shoreline, the British had decided to cut trees and build boats. The British had even dismantled the ocean-going warship, *Inflexible*, and dragged it piece by piece to a reassembly site at the north end of the lake. At the south end of the lake, around Crown Point and Fort Ticonderoga, Rebel the commander, **Benedict Arnold**, who would later be proved a British spy, had decided to also occupy his men with cutting down trees and building boats. Well, the British had built better boats and armed them with better cannon. On October 11, the winds being favorable, the British boats set off toward the south end of Lake Champlain. In addition to the *Inflexible*, the *Marie*, the *Carleton* and a huge raft named the *Thunderer*, there were 500 small transport boats containing soldiers. In a fierce lake battle the British boats defeated the Rebel boats, but the survivors managed to beat their boats back to Crown Point at the south end of the lake. The Rebels then burned the Crown Point fort and retreated south to Fort Ticonderoga. Thinking that winter was too near at hand, John Burgoyne then retreated with his men to winter quarters in the British region that would become Canada.

It was probably a mistake, for a determined winter campaign aimed at securing the Hudson-Champlain corridor might well have overcome the Continentals. Burgoyne's men had not accomplished much more than drive the Continentals out of their forward base in Canada.

Continental Congress Authorizes a Large Troop Buildup

After the loss of lower New York State and eastern New Jersey State, it was obvious to the Continental Congress that the British Government was determined to force the States to submit to British rule by escalating its force to whatever size it took to ensure success. A much larger Continental Army would be needed to permanently drive them out. Accordingly, the **Continental Congress voted to authorize an army of 60,000 men**, each enlisted for **3 years**, or longer if necessary. The Congress also authorized **George Washington** to enlist an additional 15,000 men whenever he thought it prudent. The problems were 1) persuading men to enlist, 2) obtaining arms and supplies, and 3) financing such a large undertaking. Furthermore, at the time, Washington had only 3,000 men under his immediate command. To reach the authorized level of 60,000 men, Washington needed to create an army that was **20 times bigger** than the one he then commanded. But, the small size of his army did not drive Washington to despair, for he was determined to make the best of his difficult situation. **George was a Nation Builder!**

Washington and Continentals Surprise British Forces at Trenton, New Jersey

On the morning after Christmas, George Washington's army launched a surprise attack on the German mercenary force that occupied **Trenton, New Jersey**. The attack was well planned. **Washington** had gathered enough men from Philadelphia and from other commands to double his force to 6,000 men. He had chosen the morning after Christmas to attack Johann Rall's German mercenaries, because all of them would have celebrated Christmas with excessive drinking the night before. The plan worked perfectly. Washington's men caught the German mercenaries by complete surprise, capturing 1,000 and a fine storehouse of military supplies. General Charles Cornwallis responded by dispatching 7,000 British soldiers from bases on the Hudson, but Washington's men managed to stay one step ahead of them.

1777

Washington Leaves Trenton in the Night

Leaving Trenton during the night, Washington's men **moved quickly to Princeton** and, on January 3, 1777, successfully attacked the British force that occupied that town. Washington's men inflicted more than 300 casualties and captured most of the guns at Princeton. Then they speedily moved away. The weather being extremely cold, **British General Cornwallis** decided to call off further pursuit. The Continental Army's winter-time success at Trenton and Princeton boosted sagging spirits at a most critical time, for Washington knew he would need a large, spirited army to repulse the British attack on Philadelphia that was expected during the coming summer.

Confident of Independence, Settlers Stream Westward

During this time, the States were dealing with the **steady stream of settlers who were moving westward across the mountains to settle in the lands of westward-flowing waters.** With the independence of the thirteen States declared and being defended militarily under the leadership of the Continental Congress, these courageous settlers were simply ignoring the British Proclamation line that forbade settlement in the land of westward-flowing waters. Parts of frontier Virginia that was within westward-flowing waters had been settled for many years, but vastly more attractive land stretched westward from the State's frontier line to the Ohio River and, beyond that, to the Mississippi River. And for several years settlers had been moving into the fertile bluegrass region of that frontier. Since the States were sovereign, each to its own, and the Continental Congress was only a military-defense organization, the legislatures of States with large western frontiers were moving to annex western land to their respective governments. In 1776, the **Virginia State Legislature** had annexed the land to its west and organized it as **Kentucky County**. In May 1777, agents representing Virginia and North Carolina negotiated a treaty between their States and the Cherokee Nation, which established a boundary line between the Watauga settlements and the Cherokee Nation. In November, the **North Carolina State Legislature annexed the Watauga settlements and organized the region as Washington County**. A land sales office was established immediately for selling Watauga land: up to 640 acres per head of household, and 100 additional acres for his wife and for each child. "Great numbers of persons [would come] to [Watauga] from the eastern parts of North Carolina to enter land [purchases]." Payment was not due until January 1779.

Far to the north, in June 1777, the **three Allen brothers, Ethan, Ira and Levi**, who claimed 300,000 acres of land between the southward-flowing Connecticut River and the prohibited northward-flowing Lake Champlain, and who had defended that land against British attack with an army known as the Green Mountain Boys, organized their land holdings and adjacent land into the **Republic of Vermont**. And, recognizing that bonded Africans had no future in far-north Vermont the Allen's stipulated in their Constitution that bonded Africans were prohibited. It was to ensure their 300,000-acre claim was legally validated that the Allen's were defying the claims to that land by New York State and New Hampshire State, for precedent and colonial charters placed the Allen land within those two States. As would be expected, the Thirteen States refused to admit Delegates from the Allen's' Republic of Vermont into their Continental Congress.

British Army Moves Southward, below the Great Lakes, and Heads for Albany

On June 20, **John Burgoyne's British army**, which was based in Canada, set sail from the north end of Lake Champlain. The invasion force was led by Native American warriors in a fleet of canoes, followed by Americans and Canadians. Next came the British soldiers and the German mercenaries. Next came "boats laden with provisions, ammunition [and] cattle." In the rear followed servants, sutlers, tradesmen and the women. Ten days later, the invasion force reached the southern shore, a few miles from the twin forts of Ticonderoga and Mount Independence, which were defended by 3,000 Continentals under **Arthur St. Clair** and **Anthony Wayne**. The British, shrewdly, and with much sweat and muscular effort, hauled heavy cannon up to the top of nearby Sugarloaf Hill. By July 4, British artillerymen were sighting directly down into **Fort Ticonderoga**. Realizing that they were about to be overwhelmed, the Continentals evacuated the fort and retreated southward. Slowly, the British plodded southward as well, tediously clearing the trees that had been felled by Continentals to clear a path for the heavy cannon Burgoyne insisted on bringing along. The British consumed 20 days in covering the first 20 miles. And there were fights as Burgoyne's men continued toward their goal of Albany. For example, Native American warriors and German mercenaries attempted a raid on militia stores at Bennington. In that effort, the invasion force lost "4 cannon, numerous muskets, tons of stores," nearly all the Native American warriors, many of whom simply ran off, and "perhaps as many as 900 soldiers."

Another example of British failure was taking place to the west, where a Continental force of 600 men was defending Fort Stanwix. This fort, located at the headwaters of the Mohawk River, was about 60 miles east of British-held Fort Oswego, located on the south shore of Lake Ontario. A British-led force of Canadians, American recruits, Native American warriors and British soldiers, about 1,600 men in all, advanced from Fort Oswego toward Fort Stanwix and arrived there shortly before the arrival of 800 Continental reinforcements lead by Nicholas Herkimer. The British attempt to ambush the reinforcements fared badly, the fort held, and many warriors and several of their chiefs were killed. After the surviving warriors ran off, the outnumbered British decided to abandon their attack and return to Fort Oswego. Meanwhile, Burgoyne's British force plodded slowly toward Albany.

British Win a Great Victory – Seize Philadelphia

Earlier, on July 9, more than 14,000 men had boarded 260 ships in the vicinity of New York City to begin a mission to capture **Philadelphia, Pennsylvania**. Instead of marching overland directly through New Jersey, the British commander, **William Howe**, had decided on a much longer sea route down the Atlantic coast and up through Chesapeake Bay. After a difficult voyage of 47 days, in which most of the horses had died, the invasion force disembarked, on August 25, near Head of Elk, Maryland. **George Washington's** defensive force of about 16,000 Continentals and State militia was waiting in entrenched positions outside Philadelphia. On September 11, the British attacked the section of entrenchments above Brandywine Creek. Two weeks later, on September 25, after hard fighting, Howe's victorious British Army entered Philadelphia "behind a parade of heavy guns with bands playing triumphant airs." **Delegates to the Continental Congress had evacuated with their papers sometime earlier**. On October 4, Washington's Continentals, reinforced to 11,000 men, launched a counterattack on British positions at Germantown, located just north of Philadelphia. This fight resulted in 537 British casualties, 652 Continental casualties, and 438 Continentals captured. But the British secured their occupation of Philadelphia, but not much else, for Washington's men set up a camp 14 miles from the city. During the months ahead Howe's men would not be able to expand their control over much more Pennsylvania territory than a supply-line corridor up the Delaware River valley toward New York City. Washington's men would winter not far from Philadelphia in **Valley Forge**.

Continentals and British are Advancing toward a Major Battle at Saratoga, New York

About this time, having received 3,000 fresh reinforcements at New York City, **Henry Clinton** felt that he had sufficient manpower to, during the first week of October, move up the Hudson River and take some of the Continental-held forts. And he was worried about Burgoyne's men. Still far from their objective of Albany, Burgoyne's 5,000-man British force remained pinned down near Saratoga. So, Burgoyne certainly needed a diversionary attack along the Hudson Valley to draw off some of General Horatio Gates's 12,000-man Continental Army, which was threatening to capture all of Burgoyne's British army. And, George Washington was also dispatching, under the command of **Benjamin Lincoln**, some of his

Philadelphia-area Continentals to the Saratoga area to further strengthen Horatio Gate's forces. Continentals had already captured the 3 British companies standing guard over the British flotilla at the head of Lake George. And Continentals under Benjamin Lincoln would soon be taking Fort Ticonderoga, further cutting off Burgoyne's favored line of retreat through Lake George and Lake Champlain.

So, **General Henry Clinton** was aiming at both diversion and expanded control of the Hudson valley as he led his 3,000-man British force up the Hudson River during the first week of October. They took Fort Montgomery on October 8, and then Fort Clinton, where they captured 66 cannons, a 10-gun sloop and 300 Continentals. But Clinton's victories along the Hudson River failed to draw Continentals from the 12,000-man force that was steadily closing in on Burgoyne's men. Furthermore, Horatio Gates had 4,000 more Continentals at the ready to come quickly when called.

By October 8, **Burgoyne's British force had retreated back to Saratoga** after a failed attempt to break through the Continental lines. The plight of Burgoyne's men quickly became hopeless. **Gates and Burgoyne engaged in surrender negotiations.** On October 17, "with their drums beating, the British and German troops marched out of their lines to pile their arms in front" of the [Continental] camp. . . In all, there were scarcely half the number that had left Quebec in such confidence that summer – **fewer than 4,000 British, some 2,400 Germans.**" The British and German prisoners were marched about 200 miles to Boston and confined in prisoner-of-war camps on Winter and Prospect Hills. Eventually many would take oaths of allegiance to the Continental Congress and settle in America, including half of the 2,400 Germans. **The defeat at Saratoga, New York, was by far the worst defeat suffered by the British up to this point in their campaign to re-colonize the American States.** The impact upon the political situation in London and Paris would be immense.

Continental Congress Approves the Articles of Confederation

Enthused by the major military victory at Saratoga, Delegates at the Continental Congress voted to approve the "**Articles of Confederation**," which, if ratified by all 13 sovereign States, would bind those States under a strictly limited **Confederation Government** over a new country to be known as the **United States of America**. The wording of the Articles of Confederation had been crafted shortly after the issuance of the Declaration of Independence, but had failed to garner much support until the victory at Saratoga. State sovereignty was firmly retained by the wording of the second article:

"Each State retains its sovereignty, freedom, and independence, and every power, jurisdiction, and right, which is not by this Confederation expressly delegated to the United States, in Congress assembled."

And the third article added:

"The said States hereby severally enter into a firm league of friendship with each other, for their common defense, the security of their liberties, and their mutual and general welfare, binding themselves to assist each other, against all force offered to, or attacks made upon them, or any of them, on account of religion, sovereignty, trade, or any other pretense whatever."

Agreed to by the Continental Congress on November 15, the Articles of Confederation were thereby submitted to the Legislatures of the 13 sovereign States for their individual ratifications.

But it would be many years before all 13 States would ratify the Articles of Confederation and thereby establish the United States of America.

Parliament Reels over Loss of Saratoga and Failure to Advance beyond Philadelphia

When news reached London that Burgoyne's 4,000 men had surrendered at Saratoga, **William Chatham**, a member of Parliament's Upper House who belonged to the **Opposition Party**, rose up to denounce the British war effort in the strongest possible language:

> "No man thinks more highly than I of the virtue and valor of British troops; I know they can achieve anything except impossibilities; and the [re-colonization] of [the American States] is an impossibility. You cannot, I venture to say it, you cannot conquer [the American States] . . . What is your present situation there? We do not know the worst, but we know that in 3 campaigns we have done nothing, and suffered much . . . Conquest is impossible: you may swell every expense and every effort still more extravagantly; pile and accumulate every assistance you can buy or borrow; traffic and barter with every pitiful German prince that sells his subjects to the shambles of a foreign power; your efforts are forever vain and impotent; double so from this mercenary aid on which you rely; for it irritates to an incurable resentment the minds of [the citizens of the American States] . . . If I were [a citizen of those States], as I am an Englishman, while a foreign troop was landed in my country, I never would lay down my arms, never – never – never!"

1778

On February 2, 1778, the British House of Commons engaged in a serious debate over efforts to re-colonize the American States. **Opposition Party leader, Charles Fox,** denounced the Government's attempt to re-colonize the American States in a speech that the *London Chronicle* called "masterly, forcible, and expressive." Fox presented the "most striking proofs of judgment, sound reasoning and astonishing memory." Historian Christopher Hibbert would describe the speech as follows:

> "Fox went on to survey the course of [the British Government's] dispute with [its American ex-colonists] and to show how the [effort to re-colonize the American States] had been mismanaged. He suggested that to recognize [the] independence [of the American States] was not necessarily to harm Britain's interests: an independent [group of American States] could be a powerful [political] friend. To continue to seek blood in [those States] would endanger the hope of that [potential] friendship. Now that there were so many reasons to fear that [the French Government] would enter the war [in support of the American States], it would be unwise to send reinforcements across the Atlantic. [Fox] proposed a motion that no more regiments of the Old Corps, that was to say the existing [British] Army, should be allowed to leave [the British Isles]."

Charles Fox's motion not to escalate the re-colonization campaign was defeated by a vote tally of 259 against to 165 for. But the Opposition was making itself felt. **British Prime Minister Frederick North** was clearly worried as he sought support from political leaders throughout Europe: "If [North America] should grow into a separate empire, it must cause a revolution in the political system of the world, and if Europe did not support Britain now, it would one day find itself ruled by [North America] imbued with democratic fanaticism." But, perhaps Prime Minister Frederick North secretly agreed with Opposition leader William Chatham that "the conquest of [the American States] is an impossibility," for he wrote King George of his desire to resign: "Your Majesty's service requires a man of great abilities, and who is confident of his abilities, who can choose decisively, and carry his determination authoritatively into execution. . . . I am certainly not such a man." With full knowledge that it would mean the end of British efforts to re-colonize the American States, North suggested that King George put **William Chatham**, leader of the Opposition, in the Prime Minister job. But King George was horrified by such a thought:

> "Nothing, the King protested, could ever induce him to approach [William] Chatham 'or any other branch of the Opposition.' 'Honestly,' he continued, 'I would rather lose the crown I now wear than bear the ignominy of possessing it under their shackles . . . No consideration in life will make me stoop to Opposition . . . It is impossible that the nation will not stand by me . . . If they will not, they shall have another King'."

Surprisingly, King George understood the British people rather well. In spite of the surrender of thousands of troops at Saratoga, New York, and the failure to make meaningful progress in re-colonizing the American States, the announcement by the French Government that it was entering a military alliance with the American States would produce a groundswell of British patriotism. And, that patriotic outpouring would provide thousands of additional British soldiers bent on fighting the combined military might of France and the American States.

A Huge Development – France Enters into a Joint Military Alliance with Continentals

A military alliance between France and the American States was signed in Paris on February 6. Without question the capture of Burgoyne's men at Saratoga had convinced the French that the Continentals were powerful enough, with French help, to completely drive the British out of the American States. And, the French figured they might win back Quebec in the deal. Most importantly, this military alliance would prove to be the margin of victory for the American States. And, at this point in our history, victory was still far from sight. Using State militia and the Continental Army, the American States had been trying for 3 years to defeat the British Government's re-colonization campaign. But the war had long ago degenerated into raids and counter-raids. The British had not been able to hold any State of significant size on a year-round basis, and the Continentals had not been able to drive the British completely out of any seaport region that they wished to use as a base of operations. The independence of the 4 large States of Virginia, North Carolina, South Carolina and Georgia **had not been seriously threatened**. But, for 3 years, the independence of the 2 large States of Pennsylvania and New York and the 7 small States of Maryland, Delaware, New Jersey, Connecticut, Rhode Island, Massachusetts and New Hampshire had been repeatedly threatened by British raids from bases in New York City, Quebec and the Hudson River Valley. It would be fear of the French that would move the British Government to escalate its military effort and – foolishly, events would prove – **attempt to re-colonize the 4 large southern States** of Georgia, South Carolina, North Carolina and Virginia.

Foolish, indeed!

Virginia, North Carolina, South Carolina and Georgia held the homes, the farms and the large families of the Nation Builders!

British React to the French Decision to Support the American Colonial Rebellion

The British changed tactics in reaction to the French decision to officially enter the conflict in support of the American States. In fact, the British Government viewed the French threat more seriously than the threat from the American States. Perhaps British leaders even worried about more European nations joining the French action. For example, **Benjamin Franklin** observed from Paris: "Every nation in Europe wishes to see Britain humbled, having all in their time been offended by her insolence." Jeffrey Amherst, the principal British military adviser, insisted that "the object of the war being now changed, and the contest in [the American States] being a secondary consideration, our principal object must be distressing France." And **Frederick North** made one more effort to negotiate a political arrangement between the American States and the British Government, proposing something between the status of Scotland and the future Commonwealth of Canada. North's agents told Commissioners from the Continental Congress that the British Government was prepared to recognize the Continental Congress, to suspend all objectionable Acts of Parliament, and to give up the right of taxation. Furthermore, the British Government would even consider admitting American Members to the House of Commons. However, in exchange, the American States had to ensure the return of all property seized from Americans accused of being loyal to the British Government, and had to ensure the payment of all debts due to British citizens. Furthermore, the American States had to permit King George III to appoint all military officers and had to let Parliament regulate import and export trade. Finally, the Continental Congress had to withdraw the Declaration of Independence. That was Frederick North's peace offer. Foolishness! The Continental Congress received the offer, considered it and refused its terms. There would be no peace. So, the British Government elevated Henry Clinton to Commander-in-Chief, to replace William Howe, and urged him to take ruthless action to re-colonize the American States.

Henry Clinton Takes Command of British Forces

Henry Clinton arrived in Philadelphia on May 8 to take over William Howe's job as **Commander-in-Chief**. Howe would be returning to England. "[Clinton's] orders, framed in the light of the new [American] alliance with France, were to withdraw the British troops from Philadelphia and other outposts and concentrate them at **New York City**. If necessary, a temporary retreat to Canada might even be considered, leaving garrisons at Rhode Island State and Halifax. At the same time, Clinton was to embark 5,000 men for an attack on St. Lucia, a small island, but one of the most important French harbors in the Caribbean, another 3,000 men for the coast of Florida, and smaller detachments for Bermuda and the Bahamas." But, Clinton's first job would be to minimize losses from attacks from Continental forces that his men would suffer, upon **abandoning Philadelphia**, as they made their way back to British bases in and around New York City.

General Clinton set out from Philadelphia with 10,000 men on June 18. Clinton's force departed encumbered with "hundreds of wagonloads of baggage, private carriages, bakeries on wheels, laundries, blacksmiths' shops, boats, pack-horses, hospital tents and stores, and a 12-

mile-long trail of camp followers and Americans who were supporting the British cause, as well as numerous women who had disobeyed his orders to go to New York City by sea."

Continentals attacked the British caravan near Freehold, New Jersey, on June 28. The fighting was fierce, but the British managed to drive off the attacking Continentals. The British soon thereafter made their way to Staten Island and New York City. The British force had lost 300 men from the fighting near Freehold, 60 men from sunstroke, and 600 men, mostly German mercenaries, from desertion. Continental losses had been slightly higher.

French Fleet under Comte d'Estaing Arrives

A few days after completion of the British crossing to Staten Island and New York City, a large French fleet consisting of 12 ships of the line and 5 frigates, under Comte d'Estaing, arrived on the hunt. But the large French ships, having too much draft, could not cross over the sand bar that stretched from Sandy Hook to Staten Island, thereby permitting the British ships to lay safely at anchor behind the bar. So, **George Washington** and **Comte d'Estaing** agreed on a joint attack to dislodge the British hold on tiny Rhode Island State. On August 8, the French fleet weighed anchor and set sail for Rhode Island State. However, by chance, a large British Navy fleet, including 13 ships of the line and fresh British troops, was approaching New York from England at that very moment. And British spotters stationed high up in the sailboat's crow's nests spotted the French fleet moving out. The combined Continental-French attack on Rhode Island began on August 9 with the landing of Continental soldiers under protective fire from cannon aboard the French warships, while other Continentals advanced via land routes. The attack force numbered perhaps 10,000 men in all. Commanders of the various Continental units included de Lafayette, John Hancock, Nathanael Greene and John Sullivan. Sullivan's men had been stationed in the vicinity for many months. The attack lost momentum shortly after it had begun. The just-arrived British fleet, plus the ships that had been hiding behind the sand bar at Staten Island, had given chase and were just arriving off Rhode Island – 35 ships in all. The British fleet, under Richard Howe, sought to delay a fight until the winds strengthened to improve maneuverability, because many of the French ships were larger and held more powerful guns. But, when the wind did stiffen on the evening of August 11, it became a "violent gale," which "blew the fleets apart, dispersing and dismasting the larger French men of war." The French flagship, "the 90-gun *Languedoc*, with her tiller broken, her bowsprit as well as her lower masts lost, was badly mauled by the 50-gun *Renown*." Beaten, and in danger of capture, the **French fleet fled to Boston Harbor** for repairs under the protection of the Continental forces stationed there. Shortly afterward, the Continental land forces gave up their attack and returned to posts elsewhere.

After repairs were completed in Boston, d'Estaing's French fleet boarded 4,000 French soldiers and **sailed off toward the West Indies**. There, he would take the small island of St. Vincent and the larger island of Grenada, but he would fail to recover the small island of St. Lucia. That island, which had harbored one of the most important French ports in the West Indies, had been conquered a few weeks earlier by British forces out of New York City. During the battle for St. Lucia, the French would lose 500 men compared to a British loss of only 200 men. After this battle, d'Estaing would decide to sail his French fleet back to the American coast.

1779

Three Years, Seven Months after the Mecklenburg Declaration of Independence, British Decide to Challenge the Independence of the Southern States – British Attack Georgia

The year 1779 began with key action in Georgia State. A British force of 3,500 men, under **Archibald Campbell,** having sailed from New York City, had landed on Tynbee Island in the **State of Georgia** on December 29, 1778. And Campbell was expecting reinforcements, under Augustin Prevost, from the British Colony of East Florida. The British force out of New York was about 25% Scottish, 25% German mercenaries, and 50% American settlers who supported the British cause, many of them of Irish descent.

This Georgia landing was the beginning of the British Government's new southern States invasion effort. After three and a half years of intense fighting in the northern States, the British had accomplished nothing more than to hold the region around New York City and tiny Rhode Island. And the French alliance made prospects for victory in those States less likely. So, the desperate British Government had decided to resort to an attack on the 4 large southern States of Georgia, South Carolina, North Carolina and Virginia. From the beginning British leaders had considered victory in these States their most difficult challenge, and for that reason, the southern line of attack had never been previously attempted, except for one unsuccessful attack on Charleston, South Carolina. Perhaps, some British leaders dreamed that many citizens from those 4 States would come forth and join the British Army. Perhaps, others dreamed that many African American men would turn on the European American citizenry and thereby make easier a British conquest. It was not that British officials had immense faith in such things happening. They simply hoped for that response from an untested region, one that they had not previously dared to invade. They were first trying to **conquer the weakest State, Georgia.** The port city of **Savannah** "[laid] a little way upstream beyond a bend in the river."

The independence of Georgia had not been seriously threatened since it had become an independent State. And the Continental force at the capital, Savannah, about 1,500 men under **Robert Howe, a North Carolinian,** would prove inadequate to fight off a powerful surprise British attack. Archibald Campbell ordered an attack before the East Florida force arrived. And, under Campbell's skillful leadership, the British conquered Savannah. Campbell proudly reported back to George Germain in London that his men had taken 38 officers, 415 soldiers, 48 cannon, 23 mortars, 94 barrels of gunpowder, the Savannah Fort and all its stores. He claimed full control over Savannah and Savannah harbor. He reported that the British Army faction of the invasion force had only suffered one officer and 3 soldiers killed and 9 soldiers wounded. Campbell threw the prisoners into the holds of some of the ships and proceeded upriver to gain control over more territory. Eventually many of those prisoners would die from intense heat within the holds of the ships. By January 10, Campbell's men gained control over Savannah River farmland in the vicinity of the capital. About the same time Prevost's men, marching up from the colony of East Florida, conquered a Continental fort at Sunbury, taking 40 cannon and 200 Continentals. Before long Campbell and Prevost's men would have control over a string of forts from Savannah to Augusta. But and this is important, they had not yet conquered the State and its people. **Georgians were among the Nation Builders!**

Confident of Independence, Watauga Settlers Move West, to the Cumberland River Valley of Western North Carolina (Now Tennessee) to Establish Fort Nashborough

James Robertson of the Watauga settlements and **Casper Mansco** of southwest Virginia were not going to let a British invasion threat in the east prevent them from leading settlers to the Cumberland River Valley in what would become **Middle Tennessee**. Early, in 1779, Robertson led 8 men from the Watauga settlements to the vicinity of the French Lick and the bluff where Nashville now stands. There, the men would plant corn and construct cabins while Robertson would make his way to the Illinois country to "purchase the cabin rights of George Clark." During the fall, Mansco would lead "a number of families to the country, who [would settle] at Bledsoe's Lick, Mansco's Lick, and at other places." Mansco realized that game was plentiful at the salt licks, and good farmland was nearby. Three of Robertson's men would remain on the Cumberland while the remainder would return to Watauga to guide family members and additional settlers to the region.

However, settlement of the Cumberland region would prove to be more difficult than Robertson and his men were figuring, for the **Cherokee Nation** and the **Creek Nation**, having recently aligned with the British, were looking for easy prey. Encouraged by British military success in the southern States, about 1,000 Native American warriors divided into small fighting units and launched supportive raids along the frontier. These warriors, drawn from various nations from the Ohio to the Cherokee region, were under the overall leadership of Dragging Canoe, who was based at Chickamauga, a lower Cherokee town. "[**Dragging Canoe's warriors**] committed more depredations on the frontiers from Georgia to Pennsylvania than all other [nations] together." In response, the governments of Virginia and North Carolina authorized a joint militia of 1,000 men under the command of **Evan Shelby** of the Watauga region and arranged for him to be reinforced by a supplemental group of army soldiers under **John Montgomery**. Since both States were unable to advance money for supplies or boats, "these were procured by the indefatigable exertions and on the individual responsibility of Isaac Shelby." The force embarked down the Holston River in small boats and canoes in April 1779. "The troops descended so rapidly as completely to surprise the [Cherokees], who fled in all directions to the hills and mountains without giving battle. The [troops] pursued, and hunted them in the woods and killed upward to 40 of them, burned their towns, and destroyed their corn and every article of provision, and drove away their great stocks of cattle." A few months later, in September, about 550 men would gather for another invasion of the Cherokee Nation. This force would be composed of Virginia soldiers under **Arthur Campbell**, Watauga militia under Isaac Shelby and another group of Watauga militia under John Sevier. These men would march southward through the Cherokee Nation into Chickamauga and down the Coosa River to Vann's Town. The American force would kill all the cattle and hogs they found, burn many towns and villages, and would "spread over the face of the country a general devastation, from which [the Cherokee people] could not recover for several years." And, during 1779, "such a current of population [was pouring] into Kentucky and into the settlements on the Holston [that it would give] a permanency to the establishments in the 2 [future States of Tennessee and Kentucky that] no efforts of the [Native Americans] and British could ever break up."

Fighting Continues in Savannah, Georgia

Meanwhile, Continental leaders had dispatched a fast ship to the Caribbean to appeal for help from Comte d'Estaing's French fleet, and George Washington sent Benjamin Lincoln to relieve Robert Howe as commander over the army's defensive effort in the State of Georgia. Under **Benjamin Lincoln**, Continental forces consolidated to drive the British forces from the line of forts from **Augusta to Savannah**. A Continental force of 1,500 men dislodged the British from the fort at Augusta without a fight, and then commenced to harass other outposts. Augustin Prevost sought to lure Lincoln's Continentals away from the Georgia backcountry by **marching a 2,000-man British force to Charleston, South Carolina**, but he found the defensive force at Charleston too well prepared to risk an attack. So, the British force made camp out on James' Island and John's Island. Eventually Lincoln's Continentals arrived at Charleston and **forced the British force to withdraw from the islands**.

British Face Mounting Trouble – Spain Declares War, too

Matters became worse for the British Government when, on June 16, the **Spanish Government declared war on Great Britain**. By July, a combined French and Spanish fleet of 66 ships would be cruising the English Channel. This combined attack force would have taken Plymouth harbor had the weather cooperated, and had many sailors in the attack force not become sick. After a few weeks, the immediate threat would subside. In defending its coast, the British would be fortunate to lose only one major ship of the line.

Also, the British were constantly wary of adventurous Continental warships such as the converted merchant vessel, **_Bonhomme Richard_**, which was commanded by **John Jones**. Concerns heightened after the sailors on Jones' ship overcame the crew of the _Serapis_ off the English coast, thereby capturing this far more powerful warship for Continental use. And Jones bested the _Countess of Scarborough_ as well. Born in Scotland, Jones had immigrated to Virginia in the early 1770's and joined the Continental Navy in 1775. Operating off the coast of France and the British Isles, Jones' sailors would take numerous prizes before peace would be consummated in Paris. The Continental's effort to defend their independence was escalating into a large-scale war between far-off European nations. In European fighting, the British would retain Gibraltar, but lose Minorca. Thoughts of a British invasion of New Orleans were totally abandoned.

British Forces in New York City Region are too Weak to Advance into the Countryside

Meanwhile, having sent so many men to the Caribbean and to Georgia, General Henry Clinton believed his remaining force too small to attempt anything more than occasional raids out of the main British network of bases in and around New York City. Henry Clinton had even ordered the **abandonment of the British base at tiny Rhode Island State**, fearing he had insufficient manpower to defend 2 military bases. The British advances were nothing more than hit-and-run raids, but the people living in targeted areas were often treated brutally. Of the raids, the New London _Gazette_ reported that British and German troops "entered the houses, attacked the persons [of both loyalties] indiscriminately, breaking open desks, trunks, chests, closets, and taking away everything of value." But the British soldiers operating out of the New York City military base were also occasionally suffering at the hands of the Continental Army. On July 16, Continentals under Anthony Wayne, by executing "a dashing bayonet charge," captured Stony Point Fort on the Hudson River, taking more than 500 prisoners. A month later, on August 18, Continentals under Henry Lee, then known as **"Light Horse Harry Lee,"** and later as the father of the Confederacy's General Robert Lee, took 150 prisoners in an assault on Paulus Hook Fort. But, a large group of militia recruits would fail in an elaborate effort to take a new British coastal fort being built at Penobscot, then part of Massachusetts State, but now in the State of Maine.

A militia force of 3,000 recruits and 19 ships, mostly transports, assembled at Boston and set out to drive the British from **Penobscot Bay**. They arrived in late July with ample resources to take the place. But, the Continentals, being without aggressive leadership, wasted about 2 weeks shelling a pesky 50-man British force of Scots, which held the partially-constructed fort. That stubborn resistance purchased the time needed for the arrival of a powerful British warship, the 64-gun *Raisonnable* and 4 accompanying frigates. A combined land-sea action then quickly destroyed most of the Continental ships and dispersed the poorly-led militiamen into the wild and unpopulated forest, through which most would eventually make their way back home.

British Troops are dispatched to Ensure Quebec Remains Loyal

A few days later, on August 26, Henry Clinton received the year's first contingent of new British troops – about 3,400 men – but most of them were sick with fever. Within a few weeks there would be 6,000 sick British soldiers at the New York City base. Clinton could order no further raids until his men recovered from the fever. But, after their recovery, George Germain would direct Clinton to send 2,000 of his men to Quebec. Apparently, France's alliance with the Continentals was producing enthusiasm for a revolution among a significant number of **French-speaking Canadians**. British leaders in London apparently would conclude they needed reinforcements in Canada to prevent a potential rebellion among settlers of French descent. And, perhaps leaders in London were seeing a decline in support for the new independent governments of the 8 northern States, which stretched from Massachusetts to Pennsylvania, for monetary criminal activity in the region had become immense.

British encourage Criminal Activity in the Northern States

Because of vast criminal counterfeiting activity, the **paper money** issued by the Continental Congress was being so diluted that it was worth a little as two cents in coin to a dollar in paper. British authorities hoped that, perhaps, the loss of economic stability and the rise of economic crime would compel the citizens of the commercially oriented northern States to return to the security they had known in British currency and British law. And British leaders planned to increase financial distress by shutting down more lucrative agricultural exporting ports, which were so necessary to supporting the Continental dollar. Savannah was shut down. Charleston would be next.

French and Continentals Fail to Drive British Out of Savannah, Georgia

On September 2, **Comte d'Estaing arrived at Savannah** with an immense French fleet of 22 ships of the line and 11 frigates, plus many transports filled with troops. The French immediately captured a British frigate, a 50-gun warship, and 2 stores ships. A week later, the Fleet moved up the Savannah River and landed troops in preparation for an assault. Unable to safely position their big warships within cannon range, the French, with help from **Lincoln's Continentals**, struggled with a sparsity of horses to move cannon overland into assault position.

On October 4, the combined **French-Continental force** began shelling the British entrenchments around Savannah. But, after 4 days, it was apparent that the French guns were not dislodging the British. Anxious to get the job over with and get back to sea before the winter storms began, d'Estaing urged Benjamin Lincoln to agree to an immediate but premature attack. "Lincoln was aghast; it seemed to him a suicidal venture." Yet he reluctantly agreed. The attempt to drive the British from Savannah failed. **The French and Continentals withdrew.** The French had lost 637 men. The Continentals had lost 264 men. And the well-protected British force had lost only 54 men. Lincoln's Continentals departed for Charleston to strengthen its defenses. And, Comte d'Estaing and the French fleet sailed away, some heading for France and the remainder returning to the West Indies.

More Watauga Settlers Arrive at Fort Nashborough on the Cumberland River

On the other hand, far from the war, **James Robertson**, **Casper Mansco** and their followers had their sights set on settling the Cumberland River Valley. **John Donaldson**, his family (including 13-year-old daughter Rachel) and others departed the Watauga settlements on December 22 aboard a boat they had named *Adventure.* Other boatloads of settlers departed at the same time and, as soon as weather permitted, a convoy of boats was proceeding down the Watauga River toward the Tennessee River. They all planned to float down the Tennessee to the Ohio, then, work their way a short distance up the Ohio River to the mouth of the Cumberland River, which they would ascend until they reached the French Lick and the bluff where Nashville now stands. Meanwhile, James Robertson, John Rains and other men were already traveling overland to that same destination, herding before them Rains' stock of 21 cattle and 17 horses. Unfortunately, the winter would be the coldest on record and the Cumberland River would freeze over to a great depth.

1780

With Savannah, Georgia Secure, British Launch a Massive Attack on Charleston, South Carolina

As winter made Henry Clinton's hit-and-run raids more difficult in the northern States, he decided to gather up his available force in a massive attempt to conquer Charleston, South Carolina. On December 26, Clinton set out from his New York City base with **7,600 men** aboard 90 transport ships. The difficult voyage took one month. By the time the convoy reached Johns Island, from which they intended to attack Charleston, Clinton's convoy had lost 9 troop transports from gale-force winds. With little opposition, the British troops disembarked at Johns Island and advanced to James Island. Looking across the two-mile span of the Ashley River, the British viewed the seaport city of Charleston and her defenses. Entrance to the harbor was guarded by Fort Johnston on the north shore of James Island and Fort Moultrie on the south shore of Sullivan's Island. There was no Fort Sumter in the middle of the harbor at that time. **Charleston** was the most important city, and the most important seaport in the 4 southern States. Although many Charlestonians, particularly women and children, quickly evacuated upon sighting the British ships, the city normally had a population of 12,000. Charlestonians were mostly of English descent, but people of Scottish, French, Spanish and German descent lived there as well. Many African Americans, mostly bonded, lived there. Charleston was the cultural center to which well-to-do South Carolina farmers and their families retreated, when the situation at home permitted.

The commanding British Navy officer, **Marriot Arbuthnot**, waited off shore for the most favorable weather – a stiff offshore wind in combination with a strongly flowing incoming tide and poor visibility – for he hoped to gain entrance by racing between the 2 forts while absorbing minimal damage.

Believing the wind, tidal flow and foggy weather optimum in the middle of the afternoon on April 9, Arbuthnot ordered the warships to run the course. An observer among the German mercenaries would write:

"This afternoon our men-of-war passed Fort Moultrie. At 4 o'clock they came out of Five Fathom Hole with a splendid wind and a strong tide, and aided by fog. Marriot Arbuthnot went ahead in a jolly boat and piloted. Snape Hammond led the vanguard with the *Roebuck*. At half past four he passed the fort, which belched fire out of 40 pieces, most of them 24-pounders. [The *Roebuck*] replied with a broadside and then sailed by without loss and without delay. . . Then came the *Richmond*. . . The *Renown* formed the rear guard."

That same day, Henry Clinton led the British land force up the south bank of the Ashley River. About 12 miles upstream of Charleston, the force crossed over to the north bank where they spread out to block a Continental retreat. Then they began advancing toward Charleston to prepare a siege. About this time, 2 detachments of British, one under **Patrick Ferguson** and the other under **Banastre Tarleton**, overran a Continental supply depot at Monck's Corner, which was about 30 miles upriver from Charleston. Apparently the men in the Continental cavalry units at **Monck's Corner** and Biggins Bridge, who were under the command of Isaac Huger, were caught off-guard and most of them fled on foot, leaving 400 horses and their arms and equipment for the British to use to advantage. The men in Tarleton's unit butchered about 100 trapped Continentals so mercilessly that Ferguson threatened to shoot the most bloodthirsty offenders, but Tarleton would not permit it.

More Settlers Arrive at Fort Nashborough on the Cumberland River After a Remarkable River Journey

Meanwhile, while the Continental Army was attempting to defend Charleston, the boat-weary settlers from **Watauga** were finally arriving at the vicinity of what would become Nashville. On April 24, the *Adventure* with **John Donaldson** and his family arrived at Big Salt Lick where they were greeted by **James Robertson**, who must have been greatly relieved to see the travelers. The exceptionally cold winter had forced the river travelers to delay descending the Tennessee River until February 27. It had been a most difficult journey and Native American attacks had been more prevalent than expected. At this time, the population of settlers in the Cumberland region was about 200 single men and families. Ephraim Peyton, who had traveled overland with Robertson was pleased to find that one of the boats contained his baby daughter, who had been born en-route to his wife on March 7. But tragedy had struck while passing Cherokee towns in March. A boat with 28 settlers aboard had been asked to follow at the rear at a considerable distance, for some were sick with smallpox. Cherokee warriors had attacked this trailing boat, killing or taking prisoner all aboard and receiving a dose of smallpox virus at the same time. Several more settlers had been killed while passing through the Muscle Shoals region of the Tennessee River. The boats had reached the Ohio River on March 20. Some settlers had set out for Natchez and some for Illinois, but most had struggled upstream on the Ohio to the mouth of the Cumberland River, which they had reached

4 days later. Then, it had taken over 4 more weeks to struggle up the river to the Cumberland settlements at **present-day Nashville**. For ten dollars, each settler would be able to buy 1,000 acres from Richard Henderson, based on his 1775 purchase from the Cherokee Nation. And, as the new settlers explored and cleared their lands, they would report evidence of a long-ago rather dense population of Native Americans: "At many springs is the appearance of walls enclosing ancient habitations, the foundations of which were visible wherever the earth was cleared and cultivated, to which walled entrenchments were sometimes added. These walls sometimes enclosed six, eight, or ten acres of land; and sometimes they are more extensive." The utter vacancy of the vast Cumberland River Valley must have persuaded settlers to firmly believe that their movement to settle the land and build a prosperous State was consistent with God's will. Why should such highly productive land be left to only the animals, they must have asked? There was no evidence that the Cherokees or the Shawnees needed the land. Except to facilitate rare treks by infrequent hunting parties, neither Native American nation showed any interest in living in the land. Yet, the settlers must have puzzled at why the land was once settled, but now vacant. I do not know the answer, but suspect that, in the aftermath of the great depopulation brought on by contact with European diseases, the natives retreated toward their central homelands to sustain viable and protected towns: the Cherokees eastward toward the mountains, the Creeks southward to below the Tennessee River, and the Shawnees northward to above the Ohio River.

Continentals Withdraw from Charleston, South Carolina as British Move In

Meanwhile, far to the east, Charleston, South Carolina, was on the verge of **surrender**. Charleston was under siege from all directions; all land and sea supply routes and escape routes were cut off. On May 4, British troops landed on Sullivan's Island and began preparations to lay a siege upon Fort Moultrie. The fort on James Island was overrun. British warships were roaming the Cooper and Ashley rivers. On May 8, **General Henry Clinton** demanded the surrender of the city and its forts.

The commanding officer over Continentals in Charleston, Benjamin Lincoln, realized the situation was hopeless, but Charlestonians prevailed upon him to keep fighting. The shelling became more intense. Finally, four days later, on May 12, **the hopeless Charleston defenders surrendered**. The British took **2,571 Continentals and 800 militiamen as prisoners**. In spite of the intense shelling the British had only suffered 76 killed and 189 wounded, and the Continentals and militia had only suffered 89 killed and 138 wounded. However, an accidental explosion in a storage building would kill 200 soldiers and citizens within 3 days. The Continentals also lost 343 artillery guns of various sizes, 6,000 muskets, 376 barrels of gunpowder, 30,000 rounds of ammunition and large stores of rum, rice and indigo. The 800 militiamen were immediately paroled, and the Continentals were sorted for parole or imprisonment based on rank and a loyalty evaluation.

French Establish a Base in Rhode Island, but Have to Remain There

Locating and surveying land in present-day Kentucky when Charleston fell, Isaac Shelby of the Watauga region would learn of the fall of Charleston on June 16, and quickly return home to organize his militia to meet the expected British advance into upper South Carolina and western North Carolina.

Henry Clinton pulled out of Charleston on June 8 and headed back to his base at New York City. He returned with "4,000 troops, most of the army's horses and wagons, and a good deal of equipment." To hold Charleston and to expand British control inland, Clinton left behind **Charles Cornwallis** with 4,000 men, including officers **Patrick Ferguson** and **Banastre Tarleton**, and some navy ships under **Marriot Arbuthnot**. Clinton was probably concerned that the French might shift the balance of power toward the Continentals in the northern States because a French fleet of 7 ships of the line, 3 frigates and transports carrying 6,000 French troops had arrived at tiny Rhode Island State. But Clinton was surely pleased that a British Fleet had arrived to reinforce military actions at the northern States shortly afterward and, with those reinforcements, he felt capable of holding the French fleet in check. The 6,000 French troops, under **Jean Compte de Rochambeau**, would remain **pinned down in Rhode Island State** for the remainder of 1780. **George Washington's Continentals**, having suffered through a record cold winter, would prove incapable of shrinking the British strongholds during his remaining military campaigns of the year. The effort to defend the independence of the northern States was stalemated. And morale in the Continental ranks was low and deteriorating. It appeared that the British might succeed at re-colonizing the American States if they could only defeat the Continentals and the militia in the Carolinas.

Under Charles Cornwallis, British Advance into South Carolina Countryside

Soon after Henry Clinton's departure, Charles Cornwallis dispatched 3 large military units into the interior of South Carolina, one to the far upstate region around Ninety-Six, one up the Savannah River to Augusta, and one, which Cornwallis himself led, up the Santee River to Pine Tree Hill, later renamed Camden. I will call Pine Tree Hill "Camden" hereafter. Before reaching Camden, Cornwallis learned that about 400 Virginia militiamen under Abraham Buford were far ahead, retreating on foot toward North Carolina. So, Cornwallis ordered Tarleton to take 270 cavalrymen and ride ahead in pursuit. After 54 hours of hard riding, and after switching to many stolen horses along the way, **Tarleton's cavalrymen** came upon **Buford's Virginia militiamen** near **Waxhaw**, near the border between South Carolina and North Carolina, about 25 miles south of Charlotte, North Carolina. The Virginians misjudged the speed of the cavalry attack and got caught firing too late. Many were hacked to death with sabers while they attempted to reload. Then, the survivors tried to surrender, but Tarleton's men ignored the attempt. Eventually the last of the Virginians went down hopelessly fighting back. A much less bloodthirsty surgeon, Robert Brownfield, was with Tarleton's men. He would later write:

> "Tarleton with his cruel myrmidons was in the midst of [his men] when commenced a scene of indiscriminate carnage never surpassed by the ruthless atrocities of the most barbarous savages. The demand for quarters, [which means to be allowed to surrender] . seldom refused to a vanquished foe, was at once found to be in vain. Not a man was spared. . . [Tarleton's dragoons] went over the ground plunging their bayonets into everyone that exhibited any signs of life, and in some instances, where several had fallen over the others, these monsters were seen to throw off on the point of the bayonet the uppermost, to come at those underneath."

We now learn more about young Andrew Jackson. As they drove their livestock before them, young Andrew Jackson, who was 13 years old, his mother and brothers, his uncles, aunts and cousins were all fleeing north, further into North Carolina, to escape from Tarleton's men and to enable the men among them to join the guerilla-style militia commanded by Thomas Sumter.

The slaughter of Buford's Virginia militiamen would become the future rallying cry of Continentals and militiamen when they would seek their revenge against overpowered British soldiers. Then the Continentals would cry out, "Remember Tarleton's quarters."

But, unusually cruel violence in South Carolina was not limited to fights between British soldiers and Continental or militia soldiers. Alarmed by the British invasion, South Carolinians who supported their new independent State turned on fellow South Carolinians thought to be supportive of the British re-colonization effort. The result: thousands killed, robbed and burned out. Charles Cornwallis would lament: "Every friend of [the British re-colonization effort] has been carried off and his [farm] destroyed." Cornwallis was witnessing how his presence had incited a civil war between two political factions of South Carolinians.

Charles Cornwallis surely realized that expanding his military reach into North Carolina would be tough. He had all that he could handle in Georgia and South Carolina with his forces widely dispersed at 4 coastal bases (Savannah, Georgetown, Beaufort and Charleston) and 7 inland sites (Augusta, Ninety-Six, Cheraw Hill, Cross Creek, Rocky Mount, Camden, and Hanging Rock). The British were **suffering from guerilla raids** by militiamen under **Thomas Sumter, Andrew Pickens** and **Francis Marion**, who was called "the Swamp Fox."

The most capable men in Sumter's 600-man unit were in the squadron of dragoons commanded by William Davie of Waxhaw. Andrew Jackson's uncle, **James Crawford**, rode with the dragoons, along with 2 sons and 3 nephews. Thirteen-year-old Andrew Jackson and his older brother, 16-year-old Robert, rode with the dragoons as messengers, a job "for which I was well fitted, being a good rider and knowing all the roads," Jackson would later tell. It was under these conditions that, in mid-June, Cornwallis pondered how to deal with 3,050 Continental troops marching southward through North Carolina under **Horatio Gates**, the acclaimed hero who had led the Continentals to their greatest victory, which was at Saratoga, New York. Gates' men were headed straight for Cornwallis' British force at Camden. But Horatio Gates was about to plunge from hero to cursed.

Militia from Watauga and other Western Regions Challenge the British Advance toward the Mountains

Cornwallis did not appreciate it at the time, but he would be facing a greater threat from the rugged, skillful and well organized militiamen from the western frontier of Georgia, South Carolina, North Carolina and southwest Virginia; under commanders such as North Carolina's **Isaac Shelby, John Sevier** and **Charles McDowell**. All of their men were skilled marksmen and battle-tested in fighting Cherokee warriors. It was in mid-July, from the Watauga settlements, that Isaac Shelby led out 200 mounted riflemen and John Sevier led out a similar force. Upon arriving in upper South Carolina, they joined McDowell's men, who had been reinforced by 600 Georgia militiamen under George Clarke. McDowell detached the forces of Shelby, Sevier and Clarke with orders to take a British-held Fort on the Paccolet River, which had been constructed about 7 years previously by frontiersmen as protection against Cherokee warriors. The British in the Paccolet fort surrendered without a fight. But the greater threat was the large 2,000-man British army led by Patrick Ferguson, which was foraging nearby.

Shelby's men fought an advance party of 600 of Ferguson's army on August 1. Both sides retreated after an hour of battle, but Shelby's men inflicted the greater damage.

Continentals, under Horatio Gates, Suffer a Horrible Defeat at Camden, South Carolina

On August 15 Cornwallis' force of just over 2,000 men encountered the Horatio Gates Continental army of 3,050 men near **Camden, South Carolina**. The next morning, relying heavily on an attack upon the Continental rear by Banastre Tarleton's cavalry, the British scattered the Continentals and butchered many, despite the American's 3-to-2 numerical advantage. The British force killed almost 1,000 Continentals, and took almost 1,000 prisoners. This tremendous defeat suffered by the Continental army would dishearten many men who were otherwise inclined to fight to defend independence. On the other hand, the huge Continental loss embolden other men who, figuring the British were destined to re-conquer the States, wanted to be on the winning side. Many Americans, to their future sorrow, would at this time align with the British cause.

South Carolinians under Thomas Sumter Suffer Defeat by Tarleton's British Cavalry

Cornwallis led his soldiers back to Camden while Tarleton's cavalry went off looking for Thomas Sumter's 800-man guerrilla force. Sumter's men had recently captured a British supply train and was falling back to defend the Waxhaws. **Tarleton's men** located the guerrilla force at Fishing Creek on August 18 and managed to sneak up to their camp that night. In a sudden surprise raid, **Sumter's guerrilla force suffered the loss of 150 killed and wounded and 200 taken prisoner.** The proficient Tarleton cavalrymen suffered only one killed and 15 wounded. But Thomas Sumter and the rest escaped to fight again. "Sumter escaped to Charlotte on an unsaddled horse and without a hat, accompanied by a naked drummer boy who was taking a bath in the creek when the British cavalry struck." Andrew Jackson's uncle, James Crawford escaped on foot, but his 2 sons, William and Joseph, were captured. **Andrew Jackson** was at Waxhaw Church attending to wounded at the time.

Western Militia Fight British in Upper South Carolina

At about this time, Isaac Shelby, while fighting with his men in upper South Carolina, learned that **Patrick Ferguson** had just received reinforcements of 600 crack British troops. This knowledge persuaded Shelby to order his men to abandon their attack plans and instead prepare a defensive breastwork of logs in anticipation of a determined British attack. Shelby put about 25 skirmishers out front to initially engage the British and deceive them into chasing those 25 men directly into his well-protected main force of crack riflemen. The plan worked. All the British officers were killed and about 200 British soldiers were captured.

But, the toll in British killed and wounded was not determined because Shelby just then received an urgent message from Charles McDowell advising him of the August 18 defeat near Camden of the large Continental army under Horatio Gates. Realizing that his men were weary and not capable of fighting a much larger British force, **Shelby** ordered his men to retreat toward the mountains with their 200 prisoners. They were pursued by the British, but by exerting the greater effort, they managed to escape into the mountains with the prisoners. The news of Gates' defeat sent waves of panic among many of McDowell's other militiamen, who broke into smaller units and retreated west into the mountains.

Too slow to catch the retreating militiamen, and unwilling to cross over into the Watauga settlements, British commander Patrick Ferguson directed his men to make camp at Gilbert Town. There, on September 12, Ferguson grabbed a prisoner who was related to Isaac Shelby, a fellow named Samuel Phillips, paroled him and told him to take a message over the mountains to his kinsman, which stated: "If [the men over there] did not desist from their opposition to [the British re-colonization campaign], he would march his army over the mountains, hang their leaders, and lay their country waste with fire and sword."

A threat such as this would prove to be the big mistake that would cost Ferguson his life and reverse the military fortunes of the British Government. Upon receiving Ferguson's threat from Phillips, Isaac Shelby rode to the other side of the Watauga settlements to confer with John Sevier. They agreed that, instead of waiting to defend Watauga on their soil, they should raise the largest possible army and **take the fight to Ferguson's camp**. **Shelby and Sevier were of the Nation Builders!**

Over The Mountain Men Begin the Continental's Unstoppable Drive to Force the British to Grant Independence

It is most important to realize why the men "over the mountains" were especially dedicated to defeating the British re-colonization effort. Their dedication derived from King George's Proclamation of 1763 whereby all the land of westward flowing waters was reserved for the Native American nations. **Men who lived "over the mountains" had settled the westward-flowing, upper Tennessee Valley** – land that, according to British law, belonged to the Cherokee Nation. Families who lived "over the mountains" realized that, if the British Army succeeded in re-colonizing North Carolina and Virginia, Cherokee warriors, with British help, would drive them from their homes and farms, thereby taking back their land within the westward-flowing waters. So, it was with uncommon dedication and resoluteness that **840 Over the Mountain Men gathered at Sycamore Shoals** in the upper Tennessee Valley, and, on September 26, set out to **destroy Patrick Ferguson's British Army before it reached Charlotte**. They were led by **Charles McDowell, William Campbell, John Sevier** and **Isaac Shelby**.

Along the way the **Over the Mountain Men gathered more fighters** including relatives of **my Wiseman and Burleson ancestors**, who had wrested new farms from the wilderness and the Native American cornfields in the **South Toe River Valley**. Also present among these determined men were my ancestor **William McMillan and his nephew, Alexander McMillan**. Alexander McMillan was a veteran of Continental campaigns in Quebec. Later he would get another shot at fighting the British when, at 63 years of age, he would be with Andrew Jackson at New Orleans to finish the American victory in the War of 1812.

After emerging from the mountains, the Over the Mountain Men were reinforced by about 350 western North Carolina men under Benjamin Cleveland, and shortly thereafter by about the same number of South Carolinians under John Williams. It was early October.

Cornwallis Leads British from Camden, South Carolina to Charlotte, North Carolina, where the Mecklenburg Declaration of Independence had been Signed Over Four Years Earlier

Back on September 8, **Charles Cornwallis** had led his 2,000-man British force out of Camden, South Carolina, though almost 3 weeks of sniper fire to just south of Charlotte, North

Carolina. He had stayed in James Crawford's temporarily abandoned house in the Waxhaw region for one or more nights as he oversaw the advance. While guerillas slowed the British advance, Waxhaw settlers were fleeing north toward Charlotte. **Andrew Jackson**, his mother and his brother Robert passed through Charlotte's guerilla defensive line on September 26 and made their way to homes farther north.

North Carolina was to be a fateful undertaking, for Cornwallis would find Charlotte a "**Hornet's Nest**." And he would find North Carolina to be the region where the British re-colonization effort would be proven a lost cause. Cornwallis and his men would struggle along a zigzag path through North Carolina, and finally into southeast Virginia, where, at Yorktown on the Chesapeake Bay, he would hope for rescue by the British navy. But the French Navy would beat the British Navy to Yorktown, and Continental and French troops would descend upon his men from the south, from the west and from the north. There, Cornwallis would surrender everything. So, the history of the defense of independence in North Carolina is critically important. **North Carolina is where the Nation Builders began their heroic and determined effort aimed at Making America.**

On or about the night of September 25, Charles Cornwallis' army had camped at the spring beside Providence Presbyterian Church near where I live today. Arriving at Charlotte the next day, Cornwallis had figured he would stay a while. Many of his men were sick at that point, and he could write to London that he had, in fact, entered North Carolina, though by just a few miles. One of his officers thought Charlotte "an agreeable village, but in a damned rebellious country."

Over The Mountain Men Defeat Ferguson's Troops at Kings Mountain, West of Charlotte

Meanwhile, British commander **Patrick Ferguson** had been leading a force of about 1,000 men eastward toward Charlotte, where he and Cornwallis would join their forces. Ferguson had found slim pickings along the way as he scoured the South Carolina upstate foothills for recruits with which he might increase the size of his British army. An officer had written that the region was "composed of the most violent young Rebels, particularly the young ladies." Ferguson did not know it at the time, but every rider he dispatched to Charlotte to plead for help from Charles Cornwallis had been or would be cut down by either local militia or militia from "over the mountains."

Realizing that the **Over the Mountain Men** were hard on his heels, British commander Patrick Ferguson, on October 6, pushed his army toward Charlotte on a hard, 16-mile morning march. When he came to **King's Mountain** around mid-day, he directed his men to make camp on top of the mountain, thinking it the best available defensive position. King's Mountain was a low ridge that sat upon a rolling countryside. It was rather far from the Blue Ridge Mountains over which the Over the Mountain Men had crossed a few days earlier, for South Carolina lay a short distance to the south. It was 30 miles farther to Ferguson's destination of Charlotte. It, and nearby Crowder's Mountain, were the remnant of an ancient mountain chain that had almost completely weathered away. And its moderately steep slopes were heavily forested with large pines. The ridge of the mountain was only about 600 yards long. Atop waited British Commander Patrick Ferguson's 1,100 men, all recruits gathered in the States, mostly within South Carolina and Georgia. They were armed with short-range, bayonet-fitted muskets, so they were equipped for close-in fighting. By 3 o'clock in the afternoon the **Over-the-Mountain men were spreading out around the base of King's Mountain to prevent escape.** They were led by Isaac Shelby, John Sevier, Joseph McDowell (Charles' brother), John Williams, and William Campbell of southwest Virginia, who was elected commanding officer of the day. The Over the Mountain Men were equipped with **long rifles** without bayonets. So, they were prepared for long-distance fighting.

The Over the Mountain Men began their advance up the mountain slope, from tree to tree, firing their long-range rifles with deadly accuracy. Many being experienced in fighting Native American warriors, the Over the Mountain Men steadily picked off Ferguson's men, one by one, but rapidly. Whenever, the British force gathered up and charged down the slope with their bayonets, the Over the Mountain Men in the front rushed downhill a short distance while their backups shot away at the bayonet charge, forcing Ferguson's men back to the top lest they all be killed. **Within an hour, the Over-the-Mountain Men were closing in on the top of the ridge from all sides.** There were so many large trees that Ferguson's British field cannon were of little use. In desperation, Patrick Ferguson rode about attempting to rally his force. But it was not to be his day.

A few years earlier Ferguson had invented a long-range, accurate, breach-loading rifle that would have made his men victorious. Victorious if 1,100 such weapons had been atop King's Mountain that day. But there were none up there. "In a desperate bid to rally them, Ferguson charged forward on his horse, shouting, 'Hurrah, brave boys, the day is ours!', brandishing his sword, knocking aside 2 white flags raised in surrender, riding on through the shot, his hat and hunting shirt shot to pieces, wounded in both arms and in the chest, until he fell dead from the saddle and his horse tumbled over and down the slope.

James Collins, who had advanced up King's Mountain with Shelby's men, would write:

"On examining [Ferguson's body] it appeared that almost 50 rifles must have been leveled at him at the same time. Seven rifle balls had passed through his body, both his arms were broken, and his hat and clothing were literally shot to pieces."

The British force suffered 225 killed and 879 taken prisoner, of which 163 were wounded. "This battle dispirited [supporters of the British campaign], and almost demolished their hopes."

In fact, the overwhelming British defeat at King's Mountain signaled the beginning of the end of the British re-colonization effort. And, in itself, the battle represented a condensation of the whole American independence movement:

1. The battle illustrated how the movement for thirteen independent American States was primarily driven by a passion to collectively control, without interference from London, access to the western frontier.

2. It illustrated how the British, though capable of establishing seaport military bases, had no realistic hope of controlling the vast backcountry.

3. It illustrated how the Scots, traditionally a fiercely independent people, when operating in their backcountry environment, were quite capable of defeating a British army recruited from the coastal regions of the American States.

4. <u>And finally</u>, **it reminded all future historians that the American independence movement was about land, land, land** – <u>not about the price of tea, not a fuss about tax stamps, not a conflict over import-export trade policy. The American independence movement was</u> **a fight to control the western frontier.** <u>It was</u> **a fight by the Nation Builders** <u>aimed at securing victory.</u>

Cornwallis Retreats to South Carolina and Sets Up Winter Quarters

<u>Soon after</u> **General Charles Cornwallis** <u>learned that Patrick Ferguson had been killed and all his men either killed or captured, he decided to begin</u> **a retreat into South Carolina,** <u>toward Winnsboro.</u> Reaching Winnsboro on October 29, Cornwallis instructed his men to establish their winter camp. Another British force under Francis Rawdon would establish winter quarters in Camden, South Carolina. Continental Militia under Francis Marion and Thomas Sumter would often intercept British wagon trains seeking to reach those winter quarters with supplies from Charleston. Sumter's men would repulse a British force at Fishdam Ford on November 9. Two weeks later, Banastre Tarleton, the notorious British cavalry commander, would lose almost one quarter of his men in an impetuous charge at Blackstock's Farm. In December, Continental cavalry, under William Washington, a kinsman of George Washington, would force the surrender of Henry Rugeley's men.

Meanwhile, Cumberland Valley Settlers Deal with Raids by Natives

Meanwhile, settlers far west in the Cumberland Valley in what would become **Middle Tennessee**, were beginning to experience raids by Native American warriors, although to a much lesser degree than they would soon suffer. During 1780, two settlers were killed, one was wounded and many feared much larger attacks were forthcoming. Furthermore, they were distressed by the summer's crop failures. "A considerable part of them went this year to [what would become] Kentucky and Illinois." And the remainder stayed close to the 2 major forts that had been constructed for defense. On the other hand, the hunting was exceptionally good. A hunting party of 20 men "returned in canoes with meat and hides from 105 bears, 75 buffaloes and more than 80 deer."

1781

George Washington replaces Horatio Gates with Nathanael Greene – a Brilliant Decision that Yields a Major Continental Victory at Cowpens, South Carolina

While Charles Cornwallis had been wintering in Winnsboro, South Carolina, many of the Waxhaw settlers had returned home, including Robert Crawford, Andrew Jackson and his brother Robert. During the first week of January 1781, Charles Cornwallis began moving his men out of Winnsboro, South Carolina, and back towards Charlotte, North Carolina. He would again pass through the **Waxhaw** region. At this point, a small party of his men would attack **James Crawford, Andrew Jackson** and 4 other men at a farmhouse that they were defending. After 2 defenders were killed and James Crawford was wounded, the situation looked bleak. But just then a bugle sounded and that seemed to scare the British away. "The defenders were mystified until a solitary neighbor, Mr. Isbel, appeared with a bugle." Andrew Jackson was lucky to escape.

<u>In the aftermath of the humiliating defeat of Horatio Gates' Continental army at Camden, South Carolina,</u> **George Washington** <u>had sent</u> **Nathanael Greene** <u>to North Carolina to take</u>

command of Continental defenses in the southern States, and, at this time in our history, Greene was headquartered at Charlotte. Soon after Cornwallis' men left Winnsboro, Greene divided his force, sending half, under Daniel Morgan, westward to attack the British outpost at Ninety-Six, South Carolina. Cornwallis likewise divided his force, sending half, under Banastre Tarleton, to intercept Morgan's Continentals. Tarleton's men caught up with Morgan's men along a branch of the Broad River, about 15 miles northeast of Spartanburg, South Carolina, and about 5 miles south of the State line. The place was a new clearing called **Hannah's Cowpens**, a group of fenced feeding lots where cattle were fattened for market. It was January 17. **Tarleton** launched an immediate attack, but Morgan's Continentals fought back with excellent discipline and won a major victory. The British suffered about 100 dead soldiers, 10 dead officers, and 800 captured. The Continental losses totaled only 72. Cornwallis was surely shaken by this loss; for, unlike Ferguson's locally-recruited men, who were defeated at King's Mountain, Tarleton's men were all seasoned troops and cavalrymen brought from Great Britain. An aide to Cornwallis called the defeat at Hannah's Cowpens "the most serious calamity since Saratoga."

It's All about Control Over Western Land – Deals are Struck – All Thirteen States Agree – The United States of America is Created

While the British army was struggling to avoid defeat in North Carolina, Delegates to the Continental Congress from the smaller States, sensing victory was close, gained confidence that control of the western frontier would eventually be passed from State control to Continental Congress control. Delegates from the smaller States, which had no frontier lands, were encouraged by New York's offer to give up its claim to western land, even though it was based only on old treaties with the Iroquois League of Nations, and thought to be of little legal validity. More importantly, they were satisfied by Virginia's offer to give up her vast claims north of Kentucky County, which were real and important claims. Virginia's claim was based on exploration and settlement, and on its 1609 Virginia Colony Charter, which extended its boundary "up into the land throughout, from sea to sea, west and northwest." The offers by New York and Virginia satisfied the Delegates from Maryland, the State that had been severely squeezed many years earlier by Pennsylvania Colony's aggressive land grab. So, on March 1, 1781, the Maryland Delegates in the Continental Congress signed the **Articles of Confederation** on behalf of their State and **thereby created the United States of America**, since Delegates representing the other 12 States had previously signed it. But, the claims of various States to western land would continue to dominate the frontier political landscape. Since the Continental Congress would not accept the vast Virginia northwestern land cession until 1784, prior to that time, Virginia would continue to claim all land between the Kentucky southern boundary, the Great Lakes and the Mississippi River. But, citing its colonial charter that extended its western boundary to the Pacific, Massachusetts acknowledged the validity of New York and then claimed a strip of the Virginia land that ran from Lake Huron to the Mississippi River. Likewise, citing its similar charter, Connecticut claimed a strip of Virginia land that ran from Lake Erie to the Mississippi River. North Carolina claimed that its western boundary extended to the Mississippi River. South Carolina claimed a narrow strip below what would become Tennessee, and Georgia claimed western land between the South Carolina claim and West Florida, which the British were destined to give to Spain during the negotiations in Paris. This would be the situation when the British would sign the Treaty of Paris in 1783.

Despite these State frontier land claims, the United States of America was born in March 1781. I will call the government of the United States, as constituted by the Articles of Confederation, the "Confederation Government." I will call the subsequent government the "Federal Government."

British under Cornwallis and Continentals under Greene Fight Hard at Gilford Court House, North Carolina

Immediately after the British defeat at Hannah's Cowpens, North Carolina, British General Charles Cornwallis recombined his force and **pursued Nathanael Greene's Continentals.** But Greene kept his men tantalizingly beyond reach as he led the British on an exhausting chase toward Virginia. However, on March 15, when his men were just south of the **Guilford County Court House,** Greene decided to stop and give Cornwallis' men a stiff fight. Greene had about 4,500 men, twice the number in the British force. The fighting was bloody with heavy losses on both sides. And the Continentals eventually retreated, leaving valuable ammunition and guns behind. But they had inflicted heavy losses on the British force, since between one third and one quarter of its men had been killed or wounded. On March 18, **Cornwallis, having decided to give up on defeating Greene's Continentals, began a retreat across North Carolina toward the coast at Wilmington.** He would arrive in Wilmington 3 weeks later.

Andrew Jackson Learns to Hate the British

Andrew Jackson, his brother Robert and about 40 others were at the **Waxhaw Presbyterian Church on April 9 when the group noticed some men on horseback approaching by the road.** Dressed as farmers, the approaching men seemed harmless; perhaps they were reinforcements. But, suddenly, the "farmers" turned off the road revealing "a company of British dragoons with sabers drawn" charging toward the church. Eleven of the Waxhaw men were captured and the church was set afire. Andrew Jackson and his cousin Thomas Crawford fled across a marshy stretch of Cane Creek, with a dragoon in hot pursuit. Andrew managed to get across, but, when Crawford's horse mired, the dragoon wounded him and took him captive. The next morning **Andrew and his brother Robert** were **captured by British dragoons** when they visited the Crawford house to report that Thomas had been wounded and captured. Later, as punishment for not cleaning his boots as directed, the officer over the dragoons "lifted his sword and aimed a violent blow" at Andrew. Andrew "threw up his left hand" to ward off the blow, receiving a cut to the bone as well as "a gash on his head" that would leave a scar for the remainder of his life – and the scars would forever remind him how much he hated British authority. The dragoons forced Andrew and his brother Robert to march 40 miles to the British prisoner-of-war camp at Camden. Robert arrived with a raging infection from the wound he had received in the mud of Cane Creek. And "a few days after the boys' arrival" a **smallpox epidemic** struck the crowded prison. Andrew was stricken shortly before his mother Elizabeth arrived at the prison gate to bargain for the release of her 2 boys. She "had ridden all the way from the Waxhaw region to second the request of an American militia captain for an exchange of prisoners, and to ask that her 2 wounded boys be among the number." She successfully won the release of Andrew, Robert and 3 Waxhaw neighbors. But Robert was seriously ill. "Robert was so weak from smallpox and an infection of his wound that he had to be held on a horse. [Elizabeth] rode another pony. Andrew walked, barefooted, bareheaded and without a coat." And they were chilled by rain. **Robert died 2 days later, but Elizabeth managed to nurse Andrew back to health.**

Abandoning North Carolina, Cornwallis Leads his British Troops toward Virginia's Chesapeake Bay

On April 25 Cornwallis led his discouraged troops out of Wilmington toward Virginia's Chesapeake Bay. He was abandoning for the time efforts to re-colonize North Carolina. In Virginia he would oversee 2,000 men under the notorious traitor **Benedict Arnold** and 2,500 more men under William Phillips. So, arriving with 1,435 weary men at **Petersburg**, **Virginia**, on May 20, **Cornwallis would expand his oversight to a respectable force of about 6,000 men**. Six days later, he would write Henry Clinton at the British base in New York: "I shall now proceed to dislodge [the Continentals under Marie-Joseph Marquis de] Lafayette from Richmond."

British Abandon Camden for their Military Base at Charleston, South Carolina

On April 25, the same day that Charles Cornwallis had departed Wilmington, British troops under **Francis Rawdon** had left their base at Camden, South Carolina, to attack Nathanael Greene's Continentals before they could join up with Francis Marion's guerrillas. Marion's guerrillas had already forced a British surrender at Fort Watson. The fight between Rawdon's men and Greene's Continentals resulted in heavy casualties. Rawdon, having suffered 270 killed and wounded, decided to **abandon Camden and retreat toward Charleston**. And, **British presence in South Carolina was being reduced back** to the original Charleston seaport military base. The British had surrendered at Fort Granby, then at Fort Motte and then at Orangeburg. Fort Galpin and Georgetown also reverted back to the Continentals. Augusta, Georgia, would be liberated on June 5.

Watauga Settlers and Cherokees move toward Peaceful Coexistence

Meanwhile, in the mountains of western North Carolina, **John Sevier** and his men were keeping the **Cherokee warriors** in check by rather severe measures. Sevier and 130 of his men had raided the middle Cherokee towns in March. At Tuckasejah they had killed 50 Cherokee men and captured 50 women and children. Before leaving that region, Sevier's men had burned 15 or 20 more Cherokee towns and had destroyed all the corn granaries they found. The Cherokees had been so defenseless that Sevier's men had suffered only one man killed, and the one wounded man was recovering. Then, during the summer, Sevier set out again with about 100 men to confront a band of about 50 Cherokee warriors who were advancing toward the Watauga settlements to plunder and raid. Sevier's men located the warriors, killed 17 and drove off the remainder. At this point, with their British allies facing defeat and the frontiersmen bent on punishment, the **Cherokee Nation seemed eager for peace**. And peace would be achieved in the summer of 1781.

Cornwallis Commands 7,000-Man British Army at Lower Chesapeake Bay Base in Virginia

By summer, **Cornwallis** had a force of 7,000 men at the lower Chesapeake Bay. His men had **run Lafayette's Continentals out of Richmond**, but had not hurt them much in the process. From his headquarters in Williamsburg, he was considering Portsmouth and Old Point Comfort as sites for a new fortified British naval base, but was leaning toward constructing the facility at Yorktown. He was convinced the British needed a fortified naval base in the region. Virginia, which controlled the entrance of the Chesapeake Bay, was the key to a significant British presence in the American States. And the past year had taught him that the British had no hope of controlling the back-country until it had secured the major seaports. Virginia was best. New York was too far north and Charleston was too far south. Furthermore, Charleston was isolated and subject to being retaken by Continental forces.

But George Washington and French allies were making plans to put Cornwallis' British force under siege before he could complete fortifications and to thereby force his surrender.

Lafayette's Continentals and French Fleet Prepare to Trap Cornwallis' Army

At Tyree's Farm, 20 miles from Cornwallis' base at Williamsburg, Virginia, Lafayette's Continentals celebrated the fifth anniversary of the American States' joint Declaration of Independence. "Bands played; flags were waved; passages from the Declaration were declaimed; guns were fired; soldiers marched and trotted by Continentals from New England and New Jersey, from Pennsylvania and Virginia, militiamen and artillerymen, dragoons in new uniforms, riflemen in buckskin breeches and coonskin caps." On August 2, Cornwallis began landing men at Yorktown to begin building a naval base there. On August 14, **George Washington** received a message that **Francois Marquis de Grasse**, with 29 ships and more than 3,000 troops had left the Caribbean for the Chesapeake Bay. The next day he and **Jean Rochambeau** agreed to march their armies south by an overland route to join Lafayette's Continentals and de Grasse's fleet in a **massive siege of Cornwallis' British force at Yorktown**. Washington and Rochambeau chose to march instead of sail to avoid the British fleet, which was very powerful in the Atlantic between Massachusetts and Virginia. And Washington and Rochambeau could better deceive Henry Clinton of their plans by **marching overland**. The French fleet, under de Grasse, was at anchor off Yorktown by August 31. But Henry Clinton did not realize until September 2 that Washington and Rochambeau were headed for Yorktown with their armies. **A British fleet of 19 ships out from New York** under **Thomas Graves** and fought de Grasse's fleet in the Atlantic outside the Chesapeake Bay on September 5. **The French fleet under Jacques-Melchior Comte de Barras, which had been based at Newport, Rhode Island, managed to arrive during the battle and slip into the Chesapeake uncontested.** So, when Graves' attempt to defeat de Grasse failed, he knew he had no hope of defeating the combined fleets of de Grasse and de Barras. Leaving Cornwallis' army to its fate, **Graves took his fleet back to New York**.

Meanwhile, British Suffer Losses in Upper South Carolina

The British situation in the Carolinas was just as bleak. By June, except for the main British base in Charleston, the fort at Ninety-Six had been the only fort in the Carolinas held by British forces. The British at Ninety-Six had withstood an attack by Greene's Continentals on June 17. Then on, September 8, a bloody fight took place at **Eutaw Springs** in which each army lost about 600 killed and wounded, but the **Continentals managed to capture 500 British soldiers and 1,000 guns.** So, with every fight, the British forces in the Carolinas were growing weaker, despite the absence of any overwhelming Continental victories. **Nathanael Greene was persistent**. He knew that fighting to a draw, then retreating, was a formula that would eventually repulse the British effort to re-colonize the American States. He wrote the **French Minister, Chevalier La Luzerne**, "We fight, get beat, rise, and fight again." And he wrote to John Sevier asking him and Isaac Shelby to raise militia from the Watauga settlements and travel to the Santee River of eastern South Carolina and reinforce the guerrilla forces under

Francis Marion to help prevent a potential retreat from Yorktown to Charleston by Cornwallis' men.

Continentals and French begin Siege of Yorktown, Virginia

Having combined the Continental armies at Williamsburg, Virginia, George Washington, Marquis de Lafayette and Jean Rochambeau set out on September 28 for Yorktown with their 16,000-man force to lay a siege line. Completing the first major 4,000-foot trench in front of the British defenses on October 6, they began bringing up siege cannon. With the French fleet at his back and the combined French and Continental armies at his front, **Cornwallis' 7,000-man British Army appeared to be doomed.** Although a powerful French fleet was in Chesapeake Bay, de Grasse and de Barras were unable to move their warships up the York River to within range of the British Yorktown fortifications without exposing their ships to damaging British fire. So, they situated the **French Fleet** in the Chesapeake Bay and near the Atlantic entrance to be **sure the New York-based British Fleet could not get in and rescue Cornwallis' men.** On October 9, the Continentals and French began an intense bombardment of the British gun placements. George Washington fired the first cannon shot himself, the projectile pushing through several houses before "it went through the one where many [British] officers were at dinner, and over the tables, discomposing the dishes," and striking the fellow at the head of the table. About 3,600 more cannon balls were dispatched that day. The Continental and French artillerymen could see their targets, and the Frenchmen were so skillful that they bragged of being able to put 6 consecutive projectiles in the embrasures of the British batteries. On October 14, the Continentals and Frenchmen had completed a forward trench and moved even closer to the heart of the British compound. About 1,000 British soldiers managed to cross the York River to Gloucester in boats during the night of October 16, but a gale force wind delayed any further crossings. By the time the winds subsided, **Cornwallis realized that he must surrender.** So, he called the men back from Gloucester. Figuring that the French and Continentals were firing about 100 guns, a witness wrote, "The whole peninsula trembles under the incessant thunderings of our infernal machines."

Later in the day "a drummer boy in a shabby bearskin hat followed by an officer waving a white handkerchief" emerged from behind the British earthworks and, in the "drifting gun smoke," walked down the slope toward the Continental-French lines. Washington refused Cornwallis' request to let his surrendered soldiers return to Europe, and his request to pardon people in Yorktown who had supported the British re-colonization effort. Washington demanded unconditional surrender. **At two o'clock on the afternoon of October 19, in new uniforms, the British paraded out into a field, encircled with mounted French troops, to give up their weapons and surrender.** Charles Cornwallis was not among them. Too embarrassed over his defeat, he pretended to be sick. The surrendering British passed between two lines of allied troops: the French lined up on one side in their white uniforms with black gaiters, and the Continentals lined up on the other side in a variety of rather drab clothes. Cornwallis' designated officer, Charles O'Hara, attempted to symbolically surrender to the French as he presented his sword to **Jean Comte de Rochambeau**, but the French commander refused: "We are subordinates to the Americans," he explained. "General Washington will give you your orders." O'Hara then offered his sword to George Washington. Washington, believing it proper that his subordinate deal with Cornwallis' subordinate, motioned to

Benjamin Lincoln. So, O'Hara then turned to Lincoln. **Benjamin Lincoln** tapped O'Hara's sword. **The British Army at Yorktown had surrendered to the Continental forces under the command of George Washington**.

Marie-Joseph Marquis de Lafayette turned to a friend and remarked: "The play, sir, is over."

But, on that same day of October 19, Henry Clinton did not realize "the play" was "over." It was that day that he and Thomas Graves, the British naval commander, set sail from the New York British military base with 7,000 men, bound for Chesapeake Bay. Five days later, upon reaching the mouth of the Chesapeake, Clinton's men asked for the local news from 3 men in a little boat they spotted. The news was bad. The men in the little boat told Clinton that all of Cornwallis' men had surrendered at Yorktown to the combined Continental-French force. At that point Clinton realized that his 7,000 men had arrived too late. He then ordered his fleet to turn around and sail back to the relative safety of their New York military base.

News in London of Cornwallis' defeat would first reach **George Germain**. Germain would then immediately inform Frederick North. Immensely distraught over the defeat and fearing that it signified the end of British efforts to re-colonize the American States, **North would exclaim to Germain: "O God! It is all over!"**

Continentals Turn Full Effort toward Liberating Charleston, South Carolina

Cornwallis had surrendered shortly before **John Sevier** and **Isaac Shelby** arrived at **Francis Marion's** guerrilla base on the Santee River with **500 militiamen from the Watauga settlements.** So, the Continentals turned their full effort toward the liberation of Charleston. On one occasion about 550 men were sent to take a British fort on the Cooper River that was manned primarily by German mercenaries. The British officer in charge of the fort refused to surrender to the first officer who approached with that demand. But, wishing to avoid an unnecessary battle, Isaac Shelby proposed to personally appeal to the British commander for his surrender. "Shelby approached the garrison and assured the commander-in-chief that should he be so mad as to suffer a storm, every soul within would be put to death, for there were several hundred mountaineers at hand who would soon be in with their tomahawks upon the garrison. The officer inquired of Shelby if they had any artillery, to which he replied that they had guns which would blow him to atoms in a moment, upon which the officer said, 'I suppose I must surrender,' and immediately threw open the gate." Shelby's men had no artillery, but he had not felt obligated to be truthful about it.

British soldiers from a nearby fort contemplated attacking the Continentals while they were organizing their hoard of 150 prisoners, but decided instead to retreat to Charleston upon learning that Marion's men had been reinforced by "a large body of riflemen from the west." The expertise of the riflemen from over the mountains, whose reputation had been validated at **King's Mountain**, seemed to strike fear in the hearts of British and German mercenaries alike.

Jackson Family Suffers Greatly, but Andrew Survives to Lead the New Country Militarily and Politically

Shortly after young **Andrew Jackson** had regained his health, **his mother, Elizabeth**, had joined with two other women from the Waxhaws and **set out for Charleston to help nurse the sick men who remained imprisoned in British ships in the harbor.** Many of the captives had been dying from the plague, so the situation was dire, and only the brave dared attempt to help. Among the captives were 2 of James Crawford's sons, Joseph and William. The women had been able to nurse William to health, but Joseph had succumbed to the plague. **And Elizabeth tragically caught the plague as well. She died sometime in November, leaving Andrew Jackson without a mother**. He had suffered much family grief. His father had died of an accident a few days before he had been born. Then his brother Robert had died from smallpox and a wound received at the hands of the British dragoons. Finally, his mother had died bravely attempting to save the lives of prisoners in the hellish British prison ships anchored in Charleston harbor. But Andrew Jackson was tough. He was a survivor. He would persevere. **He would lead America's Nation Builders**.

A Year-end Recap of Events in the Cumberland Valley of Future Middle Tennessee

Before leaving the year 1781, I should recap the situation in the **Cumberland Valley**. During 1781, settlers in the Cumberland Valley had suffered major attacks by Cherokee raiding parties. About 45 Cherokee warriors had attacked Freeland's Station at midnight, January 15. And raids by large groups of warriors had persisted throughout the year. The warriors had "burned up everything before them: immense quantities of corn and other produce, as well as houses, fences, and even the stations. . . All who could get to [Fort Nashborough] or Eaton's Station did so, but many never saw their comrades in those stations. Some were killed sleeping; some were awakened only to be apprised that their last moment had come; some were killed at noonday, when not suspicious of danger; death seemed ready to embrace the whole of the adventurers. . . [They] could never learn the exact loss they sustained" during 1781, but contemporary historian John Haywood would list the names of 13 killed, 2 scalped but surviving, and 4 wounded.

1782

The British Government Faces Reality – the Thirteen American Colonies are Lost Forever

As 1782 opened, the **British Government still had about 30,000 fighting men** under its command in the American States, including British soldiers and sailors, Americans disloyal to their State governments and European mercenaries, most of whom spoke German. And, many of these were stationed at the British military bases in and around New York City. But, despite the presence of such a huge fighting force, the capture of Cornwallis' force at Yorktown persuaded many more influential British political leaders to advocate abandonment of the military campaign to re-colonize the American States. Yet, George Germain and Frederick North remained dutifully loyal to King George III.

Charles Fox, leader of the Members of Parliament who advocated abandoning the re-colonization effort, warned that the American terrain presented "a unique diversity of difficulties," because it possessed "obstacles of rivers, of a deep intersected country, of impassable marshes, of a disaffected people," and, worst of all, was populated with "timid friends" and "inveterate enemies." A newspaperman for the London *Courant* wrote that Fox's "arguments against the nefarious war were unanswered and unanswerable." William Pitt deplored "the accursed, cruel, unnatural, wicked American war, a war of injustice and moral depravity, marked by blood, slaughter, persecution and devastation." Edward Gibbon declared: "I shall never give my consent to exhaust still further the finest country in the world in this prosecution of a war from whence no reasonable man entertains any hope of success. It is better to be humbled than ruined."

Yet, **Frederick North** managed to win defeat of a House of Commons resolution declaring, "all further attempts to reduce the [American States] to obedience [to Britain] are contrary to the true interests of this [nation]." And, North won defeat, by slim margins, of further moves to force withdrawal of British troops. But North was compelled to discharge the 2 chief leaders of the conquest effort: George Germain and Henry Clinton. Then, on February 22, the **House of Commons**, after a memorable speech by **Henry Conway**, came within one vote of passing a resolution to abandon the re-colonization effort. Conway's motion was brought forth again 5 days later. It passed by 19 votes.

The next day, Frederick North wrote King George III proposing that the North Administration be replaced by a group of new men. Refusing to accept the resignation of North and his ministers, George III declined to become, "in the smallest degree, an instrument in a measure that would annihilate the rank in which the British Empire stood among the European States." A month later, North submitted another resignation. George III replied: "If you resign before I have decided what I will do, you will certainly forever forfeit my regard."

Four hundred members of the House of Commons took their seats on March 20 to debate a motion to discharge Frederick North and the ministers who comprised his administration. Just before debate began, to everyone's surprise, North appeared. Shortly afterward, Charles Surrey rose to present a motion to discharge. But, before Surrey could begin, North rose and declared, "I rise to speak to that motion." After a brief hassle over his right to interrupt the designated speaker of the moment, North, being permitted his speak, told the members that he opposed the motion because he had handed in his resignation and his administration was in effect already dissolved. North encouraged the House to find a man of greater abilities, but warned them that it would be exceptionally difficult to find "a successor more zealous for the interests of his country, more anxious to promote those interests, more loyal to [King George III], and more desirous of preserving the Constitution whole and entire." With that, **Frederick North left his position of leadership in the British Government**. A week afterward, a new administration was in place under the leadership of **Charles Rockingham**.

Western Settlers in Future Tennessee Struggle, but They are Tough

During September some Cherokee warriors around Chickamauga and the lower towns sought revenge against frontiersmen by attacking and killing some settlers and stealing their horses. John Sevier responded by raising a militia of 100 men and by marching south into the upper Cherokee towns, which were at peace. There, he persuaded a Cherokee man to join him as guide and spokesman. The man was John Watts, who would later become a "celebrated chief of the Cherokee Nation." Accompanied by Watts, Sevier's men destroyed Vann's Town, Bull Town and Estanaula.

Further west in the **Cumberland Valley**, **settlers** were hunkered down in Fort Nashborough, for that was the only way the remnant that remained in that region could defend themselves **against persistent Cherokee raids.** These people were tough, as the following example will attest:

"In the spring of 1782 a party of [warriors] fired upon 3 persons at the French Lick and broke the arms of John Tucker and Joseph Hendricks, and shot down David Hood, whom they scalped and stamped, as he said, and followed the others toward [Fort Nashborough]. The people of the fort came out and repulsed them and saved the wounded men. Supposing the [warriors] gone, Hood got up softly, wounded and scalped as he was, and began to walk toward [Fort Nashborough], when, to his mortification, he saw standing upon the bank of the creek a number of [warriors], the same who had wounded him before, making sport of his misfortunes and mistake. They then fell upon him again, and having given him in several places new wounds that were apparently mortal, they left him. He fell into a brush-heap in the snow, and next morning was tracked and found by his blood and was placed, as a dead man, in one of the out-houses and was left alone. After some time, he recovered and lived for many years."

Many of those hunkered down in **Fort Nashborough** advocated abandoning the region and fleeing north toward the Ohio River, because most of the horses had been stolen, hunting was dangerous, and raiding parties of warriors even made it impossible to raise a nearby corn crop. But **James Robertson** "pertinaciously resisted the proposition," while warning how difficult it would be to reach the Ohio to the north or the Watauga settlements toward the east without suffering heavy casualties at the hands of the many Cherokee raiding parties that were roaming the region. Robertson argued that they were isolated and had to make the best of the situation without reliance upon outside help. Information about most settler casualties was apparently lost to history, for current historian John Haywood would only name 5 killed, 5 wounded and 1 captured.

1783

During 1783 land sales were resumed in the Watauga settlements based on an expanded territory, much of which had previously been considered as belonging to the Cherokee Nation. Yet, the Cherokees had ample land west of the Tennessee River and south of the Pigeon River. Tracts of 5,000 acres or less could be purchased at a price of 10 pounds per 100 acres. By late May 1784, "vast quantities of land" would be recorded as having been purchased.

Spanish and British make Secret Deal Aimed at Arresting American Westward Migration

Prior to the culmination of peace negotiations between Great Britain and the allied nations, consisting of France, Spain and the Union of the 13 American States, **Spanish leaders made a secret pact with the French leaders in Louisiana to bar American access to navigation on the Mississippi River** and to carry out other measures designed to thwart western expansion by American pioneers. At this point, "the Spanish cabinet applied to the French minister at Madrid, Monsieur de Montmorin, expressing their apprehensions of the advancing American settlements, and that it was the true policy of Spain not to open to them the navigation of the Mississippi, as it would enable them to acquire the commerce of [New] Orleans and Mexico." And, it was agreed that the **Spanish would encourage the warriors of the Cherokee, Creek, Chickasaw and Choctaw Nations to pursue a protracted guerrilla war** against pioneers from the east to retard settlement of the western lands that would soon be certified as belonging to the American States.

British and Americans Sign the Treaty of Paris – Each of the Thirteen Former Colonies is Now an Independent State

On September 3, King George III's ministers concluded the negotiations with the allies, consisting of the **American Peace Commissioners, Benjamin Franklin, John Adams and John Jay**, who represented the thirteen American States, the French negotiating team, and the Spanish negotiating team. Although Spain had not been nearly as active in support of the American States as had the French, the Spanish Government had declared war on Britain and had fought the British at Gibraltar and Minorca. So, the Spanish Government claimed some prizes of the war. Thomas Jefferson had been named to the Commission, but had asked to be excused because of unexpected personal problems. The resulting agreed upon document was called the "**Treaty of Paris.**" **It recognized the independence of the 13 American States, individually and collectively, and established western, northern and southern boundaries for the group.** Franklin had insisted for months that the British Government cede Canada to the States, but that effort had failed. The northern boundary of the States approximated the present-day eastern Canadian-American boundary. But, fishermen in the American States were granted the right to fish off Newfoundland and the St. Lawrence River, and to "dry and cure fish in the unsettled bays, harbors and creeks of Nova Scotia, the Magdalen Islands and Labrador."

The southern boundary was 31 degrees latitude, which was about 50 miles inland from the Gulf of Mexico, for Britain ceded East Florida and West Florida to Spain.

The treaty set the western boundary as the Mississippi River.

And, most importantly, it imposed no obligation upon the American States to honor the sovereignty of the Native American nations in the **lands of western-flowing waters**. It appealed to creditors "on either side" to pay debts "of the full value in Sterling Money." It obligated the Confederation Government to recommend earnestly to the various State Legislatures, which were regarded as sovereign, that they respectively enforce the return of confiscated property to British citizens who were abroad or who had been accused of supporting the failed British re-colonization effort. The treaty forbade any further confiscation of property by the States or their citizens. It obligated the British to withdraw from its military bases within the American States "with all convenient speed."

A few weeks after the signing of the Treaty of Paris, the last remaining **British forces withdrew from the New York military base**. George Washington's Continentals swept in behind the departing British to take control of the vacated military base and adjacent New York City.

It Really Was About Control Over the Western Land

News of the Treaty of Paris boosted settlement of the Cumberland Valley. Many settlers who had fled the Cumberland Valley for safer places returned during the remaining months of 1783, and many more new settlers arrived from Watauga and North Carolina, giving "strength and animation to the settlements." Commissioners with defensive guards would arrive early in 1874 to begin surveying land. In appreciation of their pioneering courage, the North Carolina Legislature had granted 640 acres to every head-of-household and single man among the settlers of the Cumberland Valley who had arrived before June 1, 1780. Those who had fled during 1781 and 1782, but returned, had to pay for their land, but those who had remained to defend the region received their land free of charge. Seventy of these recipients were named. Also, families who had lost a member to warrior attacks received their land free. Sixty-three such families were named, including the family of James Leiper (also spelled Leeper and a probable relative to my ancestors).

The North Carolina Legislature had given similar tracts to veterans of the Defense of Independence. <u>Veterans were entitled to choose land east of the point where the Cumberland River emerged from present-day Kentucky and west of the Tennessee River, if it lay within 55 miles of the present-day Tennessee-Kentucky boundary.</u> **Fort Nashborough** and nearby **French Lick** was at the center of this vast region. Furthermore, the North Carolina Legislature, in appreciation of brilliant military leadership, gave **Nathanael Greene** a 25,000-acre tract of land.

Although the growing population of Cumberland settlers was adding a measure of improved safety against raids by bands of warriors, current historian John Haywood would name 16 killed, and 1 wounded during 1783. Both Cherokee and Creek warriors were involved. Spanish authorities, such as Don Esteban Miro, Governor of Louisiana and West Florida, who had supplied arms, ammunition and supplies to facilitate attacks, had encouraged the young warrior's innate enthusiasm for war.

The Confederation Congress found meeting in Philadelphia too difficult after about 80 Continental Army veterans marched from Lancaster, Pennsylvania, and threatened to rob the bank that held what little money the Pennsylvania State Government owned. These men wanted their past-due military pay. Feeling powerless to deal with potential lawlessness in Pennsylvania, Representatives voted to relocate the Confederation Congress to a site across the river in New Jersey.

Chapter 7 — 1784 to 1789: Transition to the Federal Government

1784

British Are Slow to Withdraw from South of the Great Lakes

Although the British promised in the Treaty of Paris to surrender, with "all convenient speed," all military posts on land belonging to the American States, **London officials secretly commanded officers to hold the British posts along the southern edge of the Great Lakes.** These military posts were needed to maintain British fur trade with the Native Americans who lived south and southwest of the Great Lakes. And they facilitated the armament of Native Americans and continued favorable relations with their political leaders. Perhaps, British officials hoped that, by arming and encouraging these Native Americans to defend their land against pioneers arriving from the east, they would succeed in maintaining or expanding British control of the Great Lakes region. There were 3 British forts located on the southern edge of the Saint Lawrence River and 5 located on the southern edge of the Great Lakes. They were, from east to west, Dutchman's Point, Pointe au Fer, Oswegatchie, Oswego, Niagara, Erie, Detroit and Michilimackinack. **The British would continue to hold these forts for 12 years**, until 1796, but the forts were too far from the Ohio River Valley to stop western migration to land west of Virginia and north of Kentucky County in the Ohio River valley, which was the land most sought by farmers.

Spanish Sign Treaty with Creek Nation

It should be remembered that Spain was claiming an expanded northern boundary for **West Florida** because that had been the boundary when the territory had been a possession of Great Britain. **On that basis, Spanish West Florida contained the land that represents about half of today's states of Alabama and Mississippi**, the claimed northern boundary falling at 32 degrees and 28 minutes, which was a few miles north of present-day Vicksburg, where the Yazoo River empties into the Mississippi. **The Spanish Government further claimed all the land below the Tennessee River by the right of conquest.** So, this was a very large territory where many Creeks, Chickasaws and Choctaws lived. It included present-day west Tennessee, Mississippi and Alabama. **On June 1, "in the Spanish fort of Pensacola, the capital of West Florida, Governor Don Esteban Miro, Governor Oneille and Don Navarro, on behalf of the Spanish [Government] on the one side, and Alexander McGillivray for the Creek Nation on the other, made and signed a treaty** by which the Creek Nation engaged to maintain inviolable peace with the Spaniards; to expose their lives and fortunes for the King of Spain; to obey the orders which should be received from the Governor of Louisiana or the Governor of Florida, and the laws of the great King of Spain in points compatible with the character and circumstances of the Creeks, who should conform themselves to the municipal usages and customs, established or to be established, in Louisiana and both Floridas." It was furthermore agreed that the Creeks would not admit into their towns any European American who did not have a Spanish passport. So, by this treaty the Spanish were offering to gradually incorporate the Creek people into their Spanish American Colonies, if they obeyed orders from Spanish authorities, such as repulsing the westward advances of settlers from North Carolina, South Carolina or Georgia. The most exposed and most isolated settlers would be those in the Cumberland Valley. And Creek warriors were becoming more aggressive than Cherokee warriors had been. Current historian John Haywood would record the names of 10 settlers of the Cumberland region who were killed by warriors during 1784.

North Carolina Cedes Its Western Territory (Future Tennessee)

The North Carolina Legislature, during their April session at Hillsboro, passed an act that ceded to the Congress of the United States all of the North Carolina land west of the highest ridgeline of the Appalachian Mountains. This land would eventually become the State of **Tennessee**. The act stipulated that the cession would become void if Congress failed to accept, by April 1786, the ceded territory and establish an appropriate Territory Government. But, when it would meet again in October, the Legislature would recognize that Congress had no intention of accepting the cession anytime soon. So, the Assembly would then repeal the cession act and set up the **District of Washington** to govern over Watauga settlements and Cumberland settlements. But, the 6-month span during which the region would be ceded, but not accepted, would spawn political movements in the Watauga and Cumberland settlements. This vacuum in government authority would give rise to a Watauga Secession Movement by Watauga settlers and it would cause some Cumberland settlers to flirt with authorities in Spanish Louisiana.

1785

Confederation Government gets Land Cessions from Natives West of Pennsylvania and Establishes 640 Acre Survey Rules

In January 1785 the Confederation Government, at Fort McIntosh on the upper Ohio River, obtained **land-cession treaties** with the Chippewa, Delaware, Ottawa and Wyandot nations. Three months previously, a similar cession had been obtained from the Iroquois Nation at Fort Stanwix. By these land cessions, the United States considered that most of the land in the present state of Ohio could be offered for sale to interested frontier settlers. At this time, it is estimated that the land west and north of the Ohio River contained a population of about 2,000 French settlers and about 2,000 American settlers, mostly from Pennsylvania and Virginia. There were probably 40,000 Native Americans in the region. Congress intended to sell tracts of this land to facilitate settlement and to raise desperately-needed revenue.

Confederation Congress Approves the Land Ordinance Act

In late May, the Confederation Congress approved the **Land Ordinance Act** that had been drafted by a committee chaired by **Thomas Jefferson**. It provided for an organized method of surveying and selling territorial land. It stipulated townships of 6 miles square, which contained 36 sections of 640 acres each. Five sections were reserved as compensation to soldiers and sailors who fought to defend independence, one section was reserved to pay for a public school and the remaining 30 sections were to be sold for $640 each. Smaller tracts could not be sold, but families, friends or relatives could pool their funds and purchase a tract in the name of one of the groups. The most common method of raising the money was probably to sell a farm east of the Appalachian Mountains and use that money to purchase land in Ohio Territory. But the high price of the land would discourage many and sales would be slow.

Watauga Settlers Establish the State of Franklin

Watauga political leaders, at an organization convention held in December, established a constitution for a <u>new independent</u> **State of Frankland** and called for election of legislators to first meet early in 1785. <u>Apparently, the repeal of North Carolina's cession act, aimed at eventually creating the state of</u> **Tennessee**, <u>had not dissuaded these Watauga leaders from their movement to carve out a state of their own.</u>

The Assembly at Frankland met for the first time in early 1785 and legislated for the new state. <u>The legislature elected for</u> **Governor**, **John Sevier**, for Superior Court Judge, David Campbell, and other men for additional officers as they saw fit. The Assembly notified **Alexander Martin**, the Governor of North Carolina, that it had become the official government for the Watauga settlers, and therein listed their reasons for seceding from his State. Governor Martin was not pleased. In his April "manifesto", he told Frankland officials why they had erred. Martin proceeded to ignore the Frankland Government as if it did not exist. Yet Frankland officials concluded a peace treaty with the Cherokee Nation on June 2 whereby they gained considerable land south of the French Broad River and the Holston River as far as the dividing ridge between the Little River and the Tennessee River. That same month, Governor Martin proclaimed as fully operative the system of North Carolina courts that had been designed to serve Watauga settlers and he named judges to each court. Frankland officials persevered anyway, establishing laws governing taxation, militia, judicial courts, monetary policy, etc. Furthermore, Frankland officials dispatched William Cocke to the Confederation Congress in an unsuccessful attempt to seek admission as the State of Frankland. The proposed boundaries covered much of present-day West Virginia, East Tennessee, including the western foothills of the Cumberland Plateau, and the upland regions of present-day Alabama and Georgia. **But, the Assembly of Georgia countered by organizing all the land below present-day Tennessee as Houston County, Georgia**, including "all the territory that belonged to Georgia on the north side of the Tennessee River." So, two separate and overlapping governments would rule **Watauga** settlements during 1786.

Confederation Congress Signs Treaty with Cherokee Nation

<u>"On [November 28], the [Confederation Congress] on the one hand and the Cherokees on the other, concluded a treaty at Hopewell, in the Keowee, in which it was stated that the [thirteen States]</u> **gave peace to the Cherokees** <u>and received them into favor and protection under certain conditions.</u> The Cherokees acknowledged themselves to be under the protection of the [Confederation Congress], and of no other [nation, including Frankland]." The Cherokees were invited to send a "deputy of their own choice to Congress whenever they thought proper." And the land designated as belonging to the Cherokee Nation was liberally defined as follows:

"Beginning at the mouth of Duck River, on the Tennessee; thence running north-east to the ridge dividing the waters running into the Cumberland from those running into the Tennessee; then eastwardly along said ridge to a north-east line to be run, which shall strike the Cumberland River 40 miles [upstream of] Nashville; thence along the said line to the river; thence up the river to the ford where the Kentucky road crosses the river; thence to Campbell's line, near Cumberland Gap; thence to the mouth of Cloud's Creek to [Watauga]; thence to the Chimney Top Mountain; thence to Camp Creek, near the mouth of Big Limestone, on Nolichucky; thence a southwardly course 7 miles to a mountain;

thence to the North Carolina line." And the sentence continued defining boundaries in South Carolina and Georgia.

Since this treaty designated as Cherokee-owned a considerable amount of land in the Watauga region that had already been settled by European Americans, including land recently ceded to Frankland, Congressman William Blount of North Carolina fought the treaty with all the political power he could muster. He argued that the land involved still belonged to North Carolina and consequently the treaty exercised powers "not given to Congress by the Articles of Confederation." The treaty did give the settlers on the Cumberland a measure of peace during 1785. However, current historian John Haywood would only record the names of 4 settlers killed by Native American warriors.

1786

Serious Rioting in Massachusetts over Abusive Foreclosures on Farmland

Intense rioting was commonplace in Massachusetts in the latter half of 1786. Farmers were having difficulty paying interest on mortgages, especially since creditors were demanding payment in gold and silver coin. The Massachusetts courts and aggressive lawyers were combining to ruin marginal farmers. These farmers felt "squeezed and oppressed" as their plight served to "maintain a few lawyers" who were growing "rich on the ruins of their neighbors." **With lawyers at their side creditors were dragging delinquent farmers into county court and foreclosing of their farms**. The Massachusetts House of Representatives had refused in June to authorize a new issue of paper money to increase the money supply. After that setback, rioters surrounded courthouses in several farming counties, and the court was prevented from sitting in 4 counties. The Governor dispatched the State militia under the command of Benjamin Lincoln. The rioters scattered when confronted by the militia and the Government regained control of the court system. Although this rioting was confined to Massachusetts and lasted only a few months, some politicians feared that it might spread if not addressed.

Movement to Revise the Articles of Confederation Begins

The Virginia Government and the Maryland Government attempted to involve all the sister States in an interstate trade policy meeting in September at Annapolis, Maryland. During 1785, at his Mount Vernon farmhouse, George Washington had sponsored a previous discussion between Virginia Delegates and Maryland Delegates concerning navigation of the Potomac River. The 2 State legislatures had subsequently endorsed the agreed policy, and this progress had prompted the call for a September meeting at Annapolis, to be attended by Delegates from all States, to discuss interstate commerce. This meeting was a disappointment, for only 5 States sent Delegates. But there was a positive result because the attending Delegates agreed to recommend to the Confederation Congress that it call a meeting of Delegates from all the States, "to take into consideration the situation of the United States, to devise such further provisions as shall appear to them necessary to render the Constitution of the [Confederation] Government adequate to the [pressing needs] of the [Confederation of States]." Many thought that improvements in interstate commerce policy required that the Articles of Confederation be expanded to empower Congress to exercise greater power over trade, and possibly over taxation. Congress concurred and, in February, issued a call for a Convention to open on May

14, 1787, at Philadelphia, to be attended by Delegates from all 13 States, "for the sole and express purpose of **revising the Articles of Confederation**."

Wagon Road from Watauga to Fort Nashborough is Begun

Meanwhile settlement of the Cumberland Valley was accelerating. Thanks to the political efforts of **Representative James Robertson,** the Assembly of North Carolina authorized the construction of a **wagon road from the Clinch River to Nashville,** said road to be built by about 300 men who would take half of their pay in land at the rate of 400 acres of Cumberland Valley land per year worked. This valuable road would be opened for traffic in 1787. This was a rather peaceful year in the Cumberland, for current historian John Haywood would list only 4 men wounded by Cherokee warriors.

1787

North Carolina Government Stops the State of Franklin Movement

But, the 2 competing governments overseeing the **Watauga** settlements were feuding. In early February 1787, a local Watauga sheriff moved to execute an order received by officials of the North Carolina Government. The order was directed at John Sevier, the Governor of the competing State of Frankland. Acting on this order, the Sheriff seized many of **John Sevier's** bonded African Americans to sell them for payment of the imposed fine. And the Sheriff temporarily put them at John Tipton's farm on the Nolichucky River. Tipton was a Representative in the North Carolina Legislature. At the time, Sevier was on the frontier conferring with others on how best to defend their region from attacks by Native American warriors. Upon learning that his bonded African Americans had been taken by the Sheriff of the competing government, Sevier gathered a posse of 150 supporters and traveled to Tipton's farm. Tipton and 15 of his supporters meanwhile barricaded his farmhouse and awaited Sevier's posse. Sevier's men surrounded the farmhouse and aimed a small cannon at the place. Then Sevier demanded their surrender. Tipton answer was: "Fire and be damned." Reluctant to fire, Sevier began a waiting game while the house remained surrounded. During the night a Tipton supporter managed to sneak out and call for help. But others attempting to sneak out were less successful, as a supporter named Webb was killed and another, named Vaun, was wounded. But help was on the way in the form of a posse of 180 men led by George Maxwell, commandant of the militia of neighboring Sullivan County and also a Representative in the North Carolina Legislature. John Sevier planned to storm Tipton's farmhouse when dawn broke on the second day of the siege. But Maxwell's militia arrived in time to prevent the launch of Sevier's attack. Rather than fight, Sevier's supporters fled. The Sheriff of Washington County, who supported Sevier, was killed in the conflict, but the toll of dead and wounded was remarkably light. John Sevier got away but his two sons, James and John, were taken prisoner, and "Tipton forthwith determined to hang them." But cooler heads prevailed and the sons were released. "With this battle the **Government of Frankland** came to an end."

Constitutional Convention Proposes a Federal Government

Delegates from 12 States gathered for a Constitutional Convention at Philadelphia and, on May 25, began debating issues concerning a **new Federal Constitution for a new Federal Government**. The State of **Rhode Island** would never participate. The group seemed to give little consideration to merely revising the Articles of Confederation, for the majority seemed to be enamored with wiping the slate clean and constructing a new Federal Government from the ground up. There was some coming and going, but, during the course of the Convention, a total of 55 Delegates would attend. Twenty-one had fought to defend independence and 8 had signed the Declaration of Independence. Seven had been Governors and 39 had been in Congress. Over half of the Delegates were lawyers, but many were farmers, merchants and physicians. About half had graduated from a college. The average age was 42 years.

Virginians played the major role in the Convention, its delegation consisting of **George Washington**, **James Madison**, Edmund Randolph, George Wythe, George Mason and John Blair. James Madison of Virginia was "the best-informed man of any point in debate." He was "so well informed and active" that he would become known as the "**Father of the Constitution**." Madison "brought to Philadelphia a fund of information concerning ancient and modern confederacies, as well as a carefully studied analysis of the peculiar weakness of the [Confederation Government]." South Carolina sent John Rutledge, Charles C. Pinckney and Charles Pinckney, as well as Pierce Butler.

Pennsylvania sent **Benjamin Franklin**, Robert Morris, Gouverneur Morris, and James Wilson. At 81 years of age, Franklin took little part in the proceedings, but James Wilson was second only to James Madison in his level of activity. The noteworthy Delegates from Massachusetts were Elbridge Gerry and Rufus King. The New York Delegation was divided in philosophy, with **Alexander Hamilton** tugging to strengthen Federal powers while his companions fought to weaken them. Connecticut sent Oliver Ellsworth, Roger Sherman and William Johnson. New Hampshire Delegates would not arrive until July 23, and little Rhode Island would boycott the Convention altogether.

So, at first, **11 States were represented**. The 7 large States were Massachusetts, New York, Pennsylvania, Virginia, North Carolina, South Carolina and Georgia. The 4 small States were Connecticut, New Jersey, Delaware and Maryland. Voting was by State, each State having one vote, and the large States would predominate. All deliberations were secret, so we have no details about them.

The Virginia Delegation, empowered by James Madison's superb preplanning, arrived at the Convention with a definite proposed constitution structure. **Edmund Randolph** presented Virginian's plan 2 days after the Convention opened, and it became the basis for further debate. The Virginian's plan stipulated an executive, a judiciary and a two-house legislature. If adopted by a sufficient number of States, the old Confederation Government would terminate its activity in deference to the new Federal Government. After a few days, New Jersey Delegates pushed a movement to scrap the Virginian's plan and simply strengthen the powers of the existing Congress under the Articles of Confederation. Three other small states offered New Jersey their support. Although Alexander Hamilton objected, his fellow New York Delegates also voted to support the New Jersey proposal. However, no other large State joined the movement, so it faltered because 6 large States opposed it.

The big struggle occurred over the voting strength of the respective States in the House and Senate of the new Congress. This struggle was concluded by yielding to the desires of the small States. Both large and small States accepted a compromise in which seats in the House of Representatives were awarded in proportion to population, and seats in the Senate were awarded on the basis of 2 seats for each State. Another major issue was allocation of representation for bonded African Americans. Many in the northern States would argue that they should not be counted at all in figuring allocation of seats in the House of Representatives and in the Electoral College, but a compromise would be accepted whereby **each bonded African American was to be counted as three-fifths of an independent person**.

There was much debate about empowering the Federal Government to enact import taxes and export taxes. Delegates from the northern States favored import taxes to permit local manufacturing companies to raise their prices. And Delegates from the southern States favored no import or export taxes so as to ensure free trade and maximum access for their export goods in foreign markets. A compromise on this issue would grant import taxation power, but prohibit export taxation power.

The majority of Delegates in the States, both the northern States and the southern States, wished to outlaw further importation of bonded Africans. But Massachusetts Delegates wanted to extend importation of bonded Africans to continue to enrich Massachusetts shipping companies, and Georgia Delegates figured a few more bonded Africans were needed in their State before importation was concluded. These interests were satisfied by permitting importation for a few more years, until the end of 1808, at which time it would be prohibited.

Delegates would agree that the President was to be chosen by Electors who were to be sent by each State as it saw fit. Electors could be elected by a state's legislature or by its voters, as each State Government would decree. Each State was empowered to send the number of electors that matched its allotment of Representatives and Senators in Congress. By adding the two Senators in the count, this formula would reduce the Electoral College disadvantage of the small States. A majority was needed to elect a President in the Electoral College and, if the Electoral College failed to arrive at a majority, after many voting attempts, the House of Representatives would choose a President from among the 5 people receiving the most Electoral College votes.

The Constitutional Convention would conclude its work on September 17 and 39 Delegates would sign the proposed document. "The members [would dine] together and [take] cordial leave of one another." The most significant constitution ever drafted by human beings would be ready for submission to the 13 States. The new Government would not to be called a National Government for that would imply that the Government was sovereign. Instead, it would be called a Federal Government to emphasize the fact that the States were sovereign in all but the few segments of government that were delegated to Federal officials. This restriction of Federal Power would be clearly stated in the Tenth Amendment, a part of the Bill of Rights section. It would say: "**The powers not delegated to the [Federal Government of the] United States by the Constitution, nor prohibited by it to the States, are reserved to the States respectively, or to the people**."

But, over the ensuing years, lawyers would steadily defy this firm limitation imposed by the Federal Constitution, as they would take small word groupings out of context and allege that such obtuse logic empowered the Federal Government to assumed new powers never intended by the framers.

While Delegates were debating replacing the existing Congress, which acted under the Articles of Confederations, that body remained legislatively active. In fact, it approved the **Northwest Ordinance Act** in July 1787 – a very important piece of legislation. This act provided a government for the National Territory west and north of the Ohio River and for eventual statehood for 3 to 5 future States. Most importantly, it stipulated that these future States would have political powers equivalent to the existing States. The initial Territory Government would consist of a governor, a secretary and 3 judges. When the population reached 5,000 males, the settlers of the Territory would be permitted to elect a Territory Legislature of 2 houses and to send a non-voting Representative to Congress. This National Territory was to be eventually divided into between 3 and 5 sections, each of which could apply for statehood upon reaching a population of 60,000 inhabitants in its section. At that point, the inhabitants could call a Constitutional Convention, write a State Constitution and apply for statehood "on an equal footing with the original States, in all respects whatever."

No **bonded African Americans** were permitted to live in this "**Northwest Territory**," for it was to be reserved for European Americans and the few independent African Americans who might choose to live there. Congress apparently assumed that ample land was available to bonded African Americans south of the Ohio River. Called the "Northwest Ordinance," this act contained 6 "articles of compact," which guaranteed individual rights such as religious liberty and trial by jury.

The Confederation Congress had procrastinated in passing the Northwest Ordinance until **a group of speculators in Boston**, Massachusetts, had proposed a scheme for purchasing up to 1,500,000 acres in what would become the southeast corner of the State of Ohio. Through their [New] **Ohio Company**, these speculators had demanded a 33% discount and said it would pay with Continental Congress paper money at face value. But, this highly depreciated paper was trading at about 12 cents to the dollar. These speculators had probably bought up a lot of the paper money at a steep discount and figured Ohio land would be the most profitable use of their paper. The [New] Ohio Company would eventually purchase 750,000 acres, for which it would pay the equivalent of about $60,000. And, the Bostonians who owned the Company would manage to sell enough of the land to make the payment to Congress without advancing any capital of their own. It was a slick deal that profited a politically connected group of **wealthy Bostonians**. But it did spur faster settlement of the Northwest Territory. Nine months after the passage of the Northwest Ordinance, 48 men would establish an Ohio River settlement that they would name Marietta.

Arthur St. Clair would be appointed Governor of the Northwest Territory, would arrive in July 1788, and soon thereafter would establish his headquarters at the new settlement of Cincinnati, which was founded in that year on a parcel of the huge tract of land purchased by **John Cleves Symmes of New Jersey** for about 8 cents per acre. Like the Boston speculators previously mentioned, Symmes must have had very profitable political connections.

Cumberland Valley Settlers Are at War with Creeks

Meanwhile Creek, and to a lesser extent Cherokee, warriors were making life in the Cumberland Valley exceedingly dangerous, even though the population was growing and settlements were expanding toward the Red River. Current historian John Haywood would name 35 settlers killed during 1787. During one raid at Station Camp Creek, warriors "broke into a house in which were Price and his wife and family. They killed the old man and woman, and chopped the children, and left them wounded." They also killed a boy by the name of Baird.

118

Bent on retaliation for these and many other killings, **James Robertson gathered a militia of 130 men in June, obtained 2 Chickasaw guides and set out to punish the Creeks in their own towns.** The militia reached the Tennessee River just downstream of Muscle Shoals and located a Creek town near the mouth of Coldwater Creek. There they killed many Creeks. They also killed 3 French traders and a woman of European descent as they were trying to flee with the Creeks. Twenty-six Creeks were killed as they tried to flee across the river, but this was only a fraction of the total carnage. The militia also "wounded and took captive the principal trader and the owner of the goods of 5 or 6 other Frenchmen who lived there as traders and had in the town stores of tafia, sugar, coffee, cloths, blankets, [Native American] wares of all sorts, boxes full of salt, shot, [Native American] paints, knives, powder, tomahawks, tobacco and other articles suitable to [Native American] commerce." They also located the scalps of 2 of the men who had been recently murdered in the Cumberland Valley. Then, as Robertson's militiamen were descending the Tennessee River with the captured goods, they encountered a convoy of French traders with additional goods. They surprised these traders and captured their goods as well. All of these captured goods were brought back to the Cumberland Valley and sold, and the proceeds were divided among the militiamen. It appears that the retaliation inflicted by the Cumberland militiamen was bloodier than the attacks they and their women and children were suffering at the hands of raiding parties of warriors. Their attitude must have been to inflict the greater punishment in hopes that would deter further attacks.

But the Creeks were not so easily dissuaded, because, a month later, a party of 200 Creek warriors headed north toward the Cumberland settlements promising that "they would not do much harm this time," but, if the people of the Cumberland settlements invaded Creek territory "after the blow which they meant to give the people of the Cumberland, they might expect a merciless war." But, the **wagon road from the Watauga settlements to Nashville** would be completed in a few months and "by these improvements emigration into the new [Cumberland] settlements [would be] greatly facilitated and encouraged."

Andrew Jackson is at Salisbury, North Carolina, becoming a Lawyer

Andrew Jackson, now 20 years old, returns to our history. He had arrived in Salisbury, North Carolina by late 1784 and had managed to connect with some influential men in that important Piedmont town. He had become well known, as one acquaintance would later report: "Andrew Jackson was the most roaring, rollicking, game-cocking, horse-racing, card-playing, mischievous fellow that ever lived in Salisbury." In March 1783, he had inherited between 300-and-400 pounds sterling from his deceased grandfather, Hugh Jackson of Carrickfergus, Ireland. But young Andrew had wasted most of that money on gambling and playful activity by the time he had arrived in Salisbury. He had obtained some advanced schooling at Queen's Museum in Charlotte and had taught a school in the Waxhaw region, so he had sufficient education to begin reading law and clerking with a leading Salisbury lawyer. He had worked first with Spruce Macay, then John Stokes.

In September 1787, **Jackson was admitted to practice law in North Carolina**. He would become friends with John McNairy, who, 3 months later, would be appointed by the North Carolina Legislature to be the judge of the newly established Superior Court for the Cumberland settlements, in what would become Middle Tennessee. Jackson would get McNairy to agree that, if he accompanied him to Nashborough, he would receive an appointment to the new public prosecutor job. <u>Andrew Jackson was eager to go west and establish his new lawyer career in the Cumberland settlements.</u>

The Federal Constitution **Should be Required Reading** -- So Here it Is!

<u>As previously reported, the Federal Constitution was approved on September 17, 1787, for submission to the 13 States.</u> Approval of the Conventions of 9 States would be sufficient to bind those under the new Federal Government. <u>This was the most important political document ever written by mankind.</u> Its wording and the intent of its wording would be hotly debated during the political era, 70 years into the future, which preceded southern State secessions and the Federal invasion of the Confederacy. All histories that I have read, and I expect all histories that you have read, relegate the Federal Constitution to an appendix section if it is reproduced at all. <u>However, I think you should read the document, word for word.</u> If you find that task too tedious, then please read the segments that I have highlighted in italics. Much of the politics that would produce southern State secessions and the Federal invasion of the Confederacy would revolve around the wording and intent of the Federal Constitution. <u>And remember, the primary leaders in the creation of this Constitution were Virginians, who were of the **Southern Families that Made America.**</u>

The Constitution of the United States of America

We, the people of the United States, in order to form a more perfect union, establish justice, ensure domestic tranquility, provide for the common defense, promote the general welfare, and secure the blessings of liberty to ourselves and our posterity, do ordain and establish this Constitution for the United States of America.

Article 1

Section 1. *All legislative powers herein granted shall be vested in a Congress of the United States, which shall consist of a Senate and House of Representatives.*

Section 2. *The House of Representatives shall be composed of members chosen every second year by the people of the several States*, and the electors in each State shall have the qualifications requisite for electors of the most numerous branch of the state legislature.

No person shall be a representative who shall not have attained to the age of twenty-five years, and been seven years a citizen of the United States, and who shall not, when elected, be an inhabitant of that State in which he shall be chosen.

Representatives and direct taxes shall be apportioned among the several States which may be included within this Union, according to their respective numbers, which shall be determined by adding to whole number of free persons, including those bound to service for a term of years, and excluding [Native Americans] not taxed, three-fifths of all other persons. The actual enumeration shall be made within three years after the first meeting of the Congress of the United States, and within every subsequent term of ten years, in such manner as they shall by law direct. The number of representatives shall not exceed one for every thirty thousand, but each State shall have at least one representative; and until such enumeration shall be made, the State of New Hampshire shall be entitled to choose three, Massachusetts eight, [Rhode Island] one, Connecticut five, New York six, New Jersey four, Pennsylvania eight, Delaware one, Maryland six, Virginia ten, North Carolina five, South Carolina five, and

Georgia three. [Note that the total for Pennsylvania northward was 35 and for Maryland southward was 30].

When vacancies happen in the representation from any State, the Executive authority thereof shall issue writs of election to fill such vacancies.

The House of Representatives shall choose their Speaker and other officers; and shall have the sole power of impeachment.

Section 3. *The Senate of the United States shall be composed of two senators from each State, chosen by the legislature thereof, for six years*; and each senator shall have one vote. [Note: election of senators would later move from legislatures to popular vote.]

Immediately after they shall be assembled in consequence of the first election, they shall be divided as equally as may be into three classes. The seats of the senators of the first class shall be vacated at the expiration of the second year, of the second class at the expiration of the fourth year, and of the third class at the expiration of the sixth year, so that one-third may be chosen every second year; and if vacancies happen by resignation, or otherwise, during the recess of the Legislature of any State, the Executive thereof may make temporary appointments until the next meeting of the Legislature, which shall then fill such vacancies.

No person shall be a senator who shall not have attained to the age of thirty years, and been nine years a citizen of the United States, and who shall not, when elected, be an inhabitant of that State for which he shall be chosen.

The Vice President of the United States shall be President of the Senate, but shall have no vote, unless they be equally divided.

The Senate shall choose their other officers, and also a President pro tempore, in the absence of the Vice President, or when he shall exercise the office of President of the United States.

The Senate shall have the sole power to try all impeachments. When sitting for that purpose, they shall be on oath or affirmation. When the President of the United States is tried, the Chief Justice shall preside: and no person shall be convicted without the concurrence of two-thirds of the members present.

Judgment in cases of impeachment shall not extend further than to removal from office, and disqualification to hold and enjoy any office of honor, trust or profit under the United States; but the party convicted shall nevertheless be liable and subject to indictment, trial, judgment and punishment, according to law.

Section 4. The times, places and manner of holding elections for senators and representatives, shall be prescribed in each State by the legislature thereof; but the Congress may at any time by law make or alter such regulations, except as to the places of choosing senators.

The Congress shall assemble at least once in every year, and such meeting shall be on the first Monday in December, unless they shall by law appoint a different day.

Section 5. Each house shall be the judge of the elections, returns and qualifications of its own members, and a majority of each shall constitute a quorum to do business; but a smaller number may adjourn from day to day, and may be authorized to compel the attendance of absent members, in such manner, and under such penalties as each house may provide.

Each house may determine the rules of its proceedings, punish its members for disorderly behavior, and, *with the concurrence of two-thirds, expel a member.*

Each house shall keep a journal of its proceedings, and from time to time publish the same, excepting such parts as may in their judgment require secrecy; and the yeas and the nays of the members of either house on any question shall, at the desire of one-fifth of those present, be entered on the journal.

Neither house, during the session of Congress, shall, without the consent of the other, adjourn for more than three days, nor to any other place than that in which the two houses shall be sitting.

Section 6. *The senators and representatives shall receive a compensation for their services, to be ascertained by law, and paid out of the treasury of the United States. They shall in all cases, except treason, felony and breach of the peace, be privileged from arrest during their attendance at the session of their respective houses, and in going to and returning from the same; and for any speech or debate in either house, they shall not be questioned in any other place.*

No senator or representative shall, during the time for which he was elected, be appointed to any civil office under the authority of the United States, which shall have been created, or the emoluments whereof shall have been increased during such time; and no person holding any office under the United States, shall be a member of either house during his continuance in office. [This paragraph outlaws the corruption that had been so prevalent in the British Parliament]

Section 7. *All bills for raising revenue shall originate in the House of Representatives*; but the Senate may propose or concur with amendments as on other bills.

Every bill which shall have passed the House of Representatives and the Senate, shall, before it become a law, be presented to the President of the United States; if he approves, he shall sign it, but, if not, he shall return it, with his objections to that house in which it shall have originated, who shall enter the objections at large on their journal, and proceed to reconsider it. If after such reconsideration two-thirds of that house shall agree to pass the bill, it shall be sent, together with the objections, to the other house, by which it shall likewise be reconsidered, and if approved by two-thirds of that house, it shall become a law. But in all such cases the votes of both houses shall be determined by yeas and nays, and names of the persons voting for and against the bill shall be entered on the journal of each house respectively. *If any bill shall not be returned by the President within ten days (Sundays excepted) after it shall have been presented to him, the same shall be a law, in like manner as if he had signed it, unless the Congress by their adjournment prevent its return, in which case it shall not be a law.*

Every order, resolution, or vote to which the concurrence of the Senate and House of Representatives may be necessary (except on a question of adjournment) shall be presented to the President of the United States; and before the same shall take effect, shall be approved by him, or, being disapproved by him, shall be re-passed by two-thirds of the Senate and House of Representatives, according to the rules and limitations prescribed in the case of a bill.

Section 8. *The Congress shall have power*

to lay and collect taxes, duties, imposts and excises, to pay the debts and provide for the common defense and general welfare of the United States; but all duties, imposts and excises shall be uniform throughout the United States;

to borrow money on the credit of the United States;

to regulate commerce with foreign nations, and among the several States, and with the [Native American Nations];

to establish an uniform rule of naturalization, and uniform laws on the subject of bankruptcies throughout the United States;

to coin money, regulate the value thereof, and of foreign coin, and fix the standard of weights and measures;

to provide for the punishment of counterfeiting the securities and current coin of the United States;

to establish post offices and post roads;

to promote the progress of science and useful arts, by securing for limited times to authors and inventors the exclusive right to their respective writings and discoveries;

to constitute tribunals inferior to the Supreme Court;

to define and punish piracies and felonies committed on the high seas, and offenses against the law of nations;

to declare war, grant letters of marque and reprisal, and make rules concerning captures on land and water;

to raise and support armies, but no appropriation of money to that use shall be for a longer term than two years;

to provide and maintain a navy;

to make rules for the government and regulation of the land and naval forces;

to provide for calling forth the [various State] militia to execute the laws of the union, suppress insurrections and repel invasions;

to provide for organizing, arming, and disciplining, the [various State] militia, and for governing such part of them as may be employed in the service of the United States, reserving to the States respectively, the appointment of the officers, and the authority of training [their respective State] militia according to the discipline prescribed by Congress;

to exercise exclusive legislation in all cases whatsoever, over such district (not exceeding ten miles square) as may, by cession of particular States, and the acceptance of Congress, become the seat of the government of the United States, and to exercise like authority over all places purchased by the consent of the legislature of the State in which the same shall be, for the erection of forts, magazines, arsenals, dockyards, and other needful buildings; and to make all laws [that] shall be necessary and proper for carrying into execution the foregoing powers, and all other powers vested by this constitution in the government of the United States, or in any department or officer thereof.

Section 9. *The migration or importation of such persons [meaning bonded Africans] as any of the States now existing shall think proper to admit, shall not be prohibited by the Congress prior to the year one thousand eight hundred and eight, but a tax or duty may be imposed on such importation, not exceeding ten dollars for each person.* [This paragraph permitted the marine shippers of Massachusetts and neighboring States to continue to profit from the triangular trade route that included hauling bonded Africans to the United States, and it permitted the rapidly expanding southern agricultural regions to gain more laborers to clear land and establish new farms. But importation would be outlawed in just twenty years – 1808 – so any importation past that point would be illegal smuggling.]

The privilege of the writ of habeas corpus [(which prevents the long-term imprisonment of a person without benefit of trial)] shall not be suspended, unless when in cases of rebellion or invasion the public safety may require it. [By falsely alleging that the Confederate Government did not exist and that the people in the seceded States were rebelling against their respective State governments, Abe Lincoln would point to this paragraph as his justification for the imprisonment of many Democrats]

No bill of attainder [(a bill that withdraws civil privileges)] or ex post facto law [(a law that punishes for past offenses)] shall be passed.

No capitation [(a Federal tax levied on each individual)], or other direct tax shall be laid, unless in proportion to the census or enumeration herein before directed to be taken. [The Constitution did not envision or provide for an Internal Revenue Service; all Federal taxes were to be paid by the States, which were expected in turn to gather taxes from their property-holding population.]

No tax or duty shall be laid on articles exported from any State. [The exporting farming States insisted on free trade for exports.] No preference shall be given by any regulation of commerce or revenue to the ports of one State over those of another; nor shall vessels bound to, or from, one State, be obliged to enter, clear, or pay duties in another. [Ensures tax-free interstate commerce.]

No money shall be drawn from the treasury, but in consequence of appropriations made by law; and a regular statement and account of the receipts and expenditures of all public money shall be published from time to time.

No title of nobility shall be granted by the United States: and no person holding any office of profit or trust under them, shall, without the consent of the Congress, accept of any present, emolument, office, or title, of any kind whatever, from any king, prince, or foreign State.

Section 10. *No State shall enter into any treaty, alliance, or confederation; grant letters of marque and reprisal; coin money; emit bills of credit; make any thing but gold and silver coin a tender in payment of debts; pass any bill of attainder, ex post facto law, or law impairing the obligation of contracts, or grant any title of nobility.*

No State shall, without the consent of Congress, lay any imposts or duties on imports or exports, except what may be absolutely necessary for executing its inspection laws; and the net produce of all duties and imports, laid by any State on imports or exports, shall be for the use of the Treasury of the United States; and all such laws shall be subject to the revision and control of the Congress. No State shall, without the consent of Congress, lay any duty of tonnage, keep troops, or ships of war in time of peace, enter into any agreement or compact with another State, or with a foreign power, or engage in war, unless actually invaded, or in such imminent danger as will not admit of delay.

Article II

Section 1. *The executive power shall be vested in a President of the United States of America. He shall hold his office during the term of four years, and, together with the vice-president, chosen for the same term, be elected as follows.*

Each State shall appoint, in such a manner as the legislature thereof may direct, a number of electors, equal to the whole number of senators and representatives to which the State may be entitled in the Congress: but no senator or representative, or person holding an office of trust or profit under the United States, shall be appointed an elector.

The electors shall meet in their respective States, and vote by ballot for two persons, of whom one at least shall not be an inhabitant of the same State with themselves. And they shall make a list of all the persons voted for, and of the number of votes for each; which list they shall sign and certify, and transmit sealed to the seat of the government of the United States, directed to the President of the Senate. The President of the Senate shall, in the presence of the Senate and House of Representatives, open all the certificates, and the votes shall then be counted. The person having the greatest number of votes shall be the President, if such number be a majority of the whole number of electors appointed; and if there be more than one who have such a majority, and have an equal number of votes, then the House of Representatives shall immediately choose by ballot one of them for President; and if no person has a majority, then from the five highest on the list the said House shall in a like manner choose the President. But in choosing the President, the votes shall be taken by States, the representation from each State having one vote; a quorum for this purpose shall consist of a member or members from two-thirds of the States, and a majority of all the States shall be necessary to a choice. In every case, after the choice of the President, the person having the greatest number of votes of the electors shall be the Vice-President. But if there should remain two or more who have equal votes, the senate shall choose from them by ballot the Vice-President. [Amendment XII would be similar to this paragraph, but require electors to vote separately for President and Vice-President]

The Congress may determine the time of choosing the electors, and the day on which they shall give their votes; which day shall be the same throughout the United States.

No person except a natural born citizen, or a citizen of the United States, at the time of the adoption of this constitution, shall be eligible to the office of President; neither shall any person be eligible to that office who shall not have attained to the age of thirty-five years, and been fourteen years a resident within the United States.

125

In case of the removal of the President from office, or of his death, resignation, or inability to discharge the powers and duties of the said office, the same shall devolve on the Vice-President, and the Congress may by law provide for the case of removal, death, resignation or inability, both of the President and Vice-President, declaring what officer shall then act as President, and such officer shall act accordingly, until the disability be removed, or a President shall be elected.

The President shall, at stated times, receive for his services, a compensation, which shall neither be increased nor diminished during the period for which he shall have been elected, and he shall not receive within that period any other emolument from the United States, or any of [the States].

Before he enters on the execution of his office, he shall take the following oath or affirmation:

"I do solemnly swear (or affirm) that I will faithfully execute the office of President of the United States, and will to the best of my ability, preserve, protect and defend the constitution of the United States."

Section 2. *The President shall be commander in chief of the army and navy of the United States, and of the militia of the several States, when called into the actual service of the United States;* he may require the opinion, in writing, of the principal officer in each of the executive departments, upon any subject relating to the duties of their respective offices, and he shall have power to grant reprieves and pardons for offenses against the United States, except in cases of impeachment.

He shall have power, by and with the advice and consent of the Senate, to make treaties, provided two-thirds of the senators present concur; and he shall nominate, and by and with the advice and consent of the Senate, shall appoint ambassadors, other public ministers and consuls, judges of the Supreme Court, and all other officers of the United States, whose appointments are not herein otherwise provided for, and which shall be established by law. But the Congress may by law vest the appointment of such inferior officers, as they think proper, in the President alone, in the courts of law, or in the heads of departments.

The President shall have power to fill up all vacancies that may happen during the recess of the Senate, by granting commissions [that] shall expire at the end of their next session.

Section 3. *He shall from time to time give to the Congress information of the state of the union, and recommend to their consideration such measures as he shall judge necessary and expedient;* he may, on extraordinary occasions, convene both houses, or either of them, and in case of disagreement between them, with respect to the time of adjournment, he may adjourn them to such time as he shall think proper; he shall receive ambassadors and other public ministers; he shall take care that the laws be faithfully executed, and shall commission all the officers of the United States.

Section 4. *The President, Vice-President and all civil officers of the United States, shall be removed from office on impeachment for, and conviction of, treason, bribery, or other high crimes and misdemeanors.*

Article III

126

Section 1. *The judicial power of the United States shall be vested in one Supreme Court, and in such inferior courts as the Congress may from time to time obtain and establish. The judges, both of the supreme and inferior courts, shall hold their offices during good behavior*, and shall, at stated times, receive for their services, a compensation, which shall not be diminished during their continuance in office.

Section 2. The judicial power shall extend to all cases, in law and equity, arising under this Constitution, the laws of the United States, and treaties made, or which shall be made, under their authority; to all cases affecting ambassadors, other public ministers and consuls; to all cases of admiralty and maritime jurisdiction; to controversies to which the United States shall be a party; to controversies between two or more States, between a State and citizens of another State, between citizens of different States, between citizens of the same State claiming lands under grants of different States, and between a State, or the citizens thereof, and foreign [nations], citizens or subjects.

In all cases affecting ambassadors, other public ministers and consuls, and those in which a State shall be party, the Supreme Court shall have original jurisdiction. *In all the other cases before mentioned, the Supreme Court shall have appellate jurisdiction*, both as to law and fact, with such exceptions, and under such regulations as the Congress shall make.

The trial of all crimes, except in cases of impeachment, shall be by jury; and such trial shall be held in the State where the said crimes shall have been committed; but when not committed within any State, the trial shall be at such place or places as the Congress may by law have directed.

Section 3. *Treason against the United States, shall consist only in levying war against them, or in adhering to their enemies, giving them aid and comfort.* [Note that at this point in history the United States are plural, acknowledging that, in most areas of law, each State is sovereign]. No person shall be convicted of treason unless on the testimony of two witnesses to the same overt act, or on confession in open court.

The Congress shall have power to declare the punishment of treason, but no attainder of treason shall work corruption of blood, or forfeiture except during the life of the person attainted. [This prevents seizure of land inherited from a person convicted of treason.]

Article IV

Section 1. Full faith and credit shall be given in each State to the public acts, records, and judicial proceedings of every other State. And the Congress may by general laws prescribe the manner in which such acts, records and proceedings shall be proved, and the effect thereof.

Section 2. *The citizens of each State shall be entitled to all privileges and immunities of citizens in the several States.*

A person charged in any State with treason, felony, or other crime, who shall flee from justice, and be found in another State, shall, on demand of the executive authority of the State from which he fled, be delivered up, to be removed to the State having jurisdiction of the crime.

No person held to service or labor in one State, under the laws thereof, escaping into another [State], shall, in consequence of any law or regulation therein, be discharged from such service or labor, but shall be delivered up on claim of the party to whom such service or labor may be due. [Judges would frequently violate this requirement in support of political activists who sought to prevent run-away bonded African Americans from being returned to their home States for trial.]

Section 3. *New States may be admitted by the Congress into this union; but no new State shall be formed or erected within the jurisdiction of any other State; nor any State be formed by the junction of two or more States, or parts of States, without the consent of the legislatures of the States concerned as well as of the Congress.* [During the Federal invasion of the Confederacy, the Republican-controlled Federal Government would deal with this requirement by setting up a puppet Virginia legislature that would vote to let Federals confiscate Virginia land to make a new State of West Virginia.]

The Congress shall have power to dispose of and make all needful rules and regulations respecting the territory or other property belonging to the United States; and nothing in this Constitution shall be so construed as to prejudice any claims of the United States, or of any particular State.

Section 4. *The United States shall guarantee to every State in this union a republican form of government, and shall protect each of them against invasion; and on application of the legislature, or of the executive (when the legislature cannot be convened) against domestic violence.* [A republican government is defined as a representative government in which voters elect people to represent them in the government. To justify their 1861 invasion, officials in the Republican-controlled Federal Government would falsely allege that each of the seven seceded States in the Confederacy was suffering from a revolt against its "republican form of government" and, that each revolt was so violent that Federal forces had to invade each State and blockade the seaports of each State to restore to each State a "republican form of government."]

Article V

The Congress, whenever two-thirds of both houses shall deem it necessary, shall propose amendments to this constitution, or, on the application of the legislatures of two-thirds of the several States, shall call a convention for proposing amendments, which, in either case, shall be valid to all intents and purposes, as part of this constitution, when ratified by the legislatures of three-fourths of the several States, or by conventions in three-fourths thereof, as the one or the other mode of ratification may be proposed by the Congress; provided, that no amendment which may be made prior to the year 1808 shall in any manner affect the first and fourth clauses in the ninth section of the first article; and that no State, without its consent, shall be deprived of its equal suffrage in the Senate.

Article VI

All debts contracted and engagements entered into, before the adoption of this Constitution, shall be as valid against the United States under this Constitution, as under the Confederation.

This Constitution, and the laws of the United States which shall be made in pursuance thereof; and all treaties made, or which shall be made, under the authority of the United States, shall be the supreme law of the land; and the judges in every State shall be bound thereby, any thing in the Constitution or laws of any State to the contrary notwithstanding.

The senators and representatives before mentioned, and the members of the several State legislatures, and all executive and judicial officers, both of the United States and of the several States, shall be bound by oath or affirmation, to support this Constitution; but *no religious test shall ever be required as a qualification to any office or public trust under the United States.*

Article VII

The ratification of the conventions of nine States, shall be sufficient for the establishment of this Constitution between the States so ratifying the same.

[Closing Testament]

Done in Convention, by the unanimous consent of the [twelve] States present, the seventeenth day of September, in the year of our Lord 1787, and of the independence of the United States of America the twelfth [year]. In witness whereof we have hereunto subscribed our names.

Signatures

*[The President of the Convention, **George Washington** and, 39 Delegates from 12 States signed the document. Some of the Delegates did not sign. And Rhode Island did not even send Delegates to the Convention.]*

State Ratifications Progress

Ratification had to be by a majority of specially elected Delegates to a State Convention called for that purpose alone. **James Madison, of Virginia,** explained that the signers did not want to let a State Legislature provide the ratification because "A compact between independent sovereign [States], founded on ordinary acts of legislative authority, can pretend to no higher validity than a league or treaty between [those States]." Three States speedily ratified the Federal Constitution, completing the task by December 1787. Delaware, Pennsylvania and New Jersey ratified in that order. The votes in the Delaware Convention and the New Jersey Convention were unanimous, but the Pennsylvania Convention split 46 for, versus 26 against. Pennsylvania advocates of ratification had "resorted to every device known to politicians, including even actual force," in garnering the necessary votes for passage. In fact, the opposition was so angry that, the party thrown to celebrate ratification "broke up in a fistfight and the burning of [a copy of] the Constitution."

1788

Two States, Georgia and Connecticut, ratified the Federal Constitution in January, 1788, bringing the total to 5. Four more were needed to create the new Federal Government. The vote in the Georgia Convention was unanimous, but the vote in the Connecticut Convention was split 128 for, versus 40 against. [R118;290]

The Massachusetts Convention, after a heated and protracted debate among almost equal factions, in February, approved the new Federal Constitution by a vote of 187 for, versus 168 against. A swing of 5 votes would have reversed the result. Boston merchants, bankers and marine shippers were the power behind those favoring ratification, because they looked forward to high Federal import taxes to permit raising prices for manufactured goods, and they looked forward to Federal regulations to benefit the marine shipping industry. Three more State ratifications were needed.

Settlers in Cumberland Valley Suffer More Raids by Creeks

Meanwhile, **attacks in the Cumberland Valley were intensifying. James Robertson's family suffered a death at the hands of Creek warriors** when the warriors attacked and killed a son, Peyton, during an early March attack on a sugar camp. During the same attack, the warriors captured John Johnston, and Creeks would hold this youth captive in a Creek town for several years. Current historian John Haywood would record the names of 12 killed and one captured during 1788. Settlers could understand why Cherokees might resent settlement on land that used to be remote Cherokee hunting grounds, but attacks by Creeks could be explained only as incitement by Spanish authorities or banditry or both, for the Creeks had never occupied or claimed as hunting grounds any land north of the Tennessee River.

A few days before his son's murder, James Robertson had written the Chief of the Creek Nation, Alexander McGillivray, asking him to explain why Creek warriors were attacking settlers north of the Tennessee River. McGillivray wrote back in early April:

"I will not deny that my nation has waged war against your country for several years past, and that we had no motives of revenge for it, nor did it proceed from any sense of injuries sustained from your people; but, being warmly attached to the British, under their influence our operations were directed by them against you, in common with other Americans. After the general peace had taken place you sent us a talk, proposing terms of peace, by Samuel Martin, which I then accepted and advised my people to agree to, and which should have been finally concluded in the ensuing summer or fall. Judging that your people were sincere in their professions, I was much surprised to find that, while this affair was pending, they attacked the French traders at the Muscle Shoals, and killed 6 of our nation who were trafficking for silverware. These men belonged to different towns, and had connections of the first consequence in the [Creek Nation]. Such an unprovoked outrage raised a most violent clamor, and gave rise to the expedition against Cumberland, which soon took place. But, as that affair has been since amply retaliated, I now once again will use my best endeavors to bring about a peace between us."

So, **McGillivray**, whose ancestry was partially European, placed considerable blame on the killing of French traders and their Creek counterparts during the past attack by Cumberland militia at Muscle Shoals, which the Cumberland settlers had believed to be an act of retaliation.

Ratification of the Federal Constitution Becomes a Huge Struggle

Back in the States, there was more debate over the Federal Constitution. Delegates to the **Maryland Convention approved** the Federal Constitution in late April by a vote of 63 for, versus 11 against. The next month, the **South Carolina Convention approved** the Constitution by a vote of 149 for, versus 73 against. The approval of only one more State was needed to establish the new Federal Government.

By a close vote of 57 for, versus 47 against, Delegates to the **New Hampshire Convention approved** the Federal Constitution on June 21. It was a close vote similar to the Massachusetts vote, but **it was a ratifying vote**, and this being the ninth State to ratify, it was **sufficient to empower the new Federal Government**.

Delegates at the Virginia Convention approved the Federal Constitution a few days later by another close vote of 89 for, versus 79 against. The people of the Piedmont, the mountain valleys and the Kentucky region, where Scots were very influential, stood opposed to ratification. But, the populous and politically powerful Tidewater region favored ratification. Delegate Patrick Henry, horrified by the proposed government's political strength, had called the Federal Constitution "the most fatal plan that could possibly be conceived to [subjugate] a people." But **George Washington** and **James Madison** had persuaded **Edmund Randolph** to switch from the opposition to the proponent faction, and this became a telling blow to the opposition. By another close vote, **Virginia** had been added to the list of States that would join her sisters under the already-approved Federal Government. The only major States yet to ratify were New York and North Carolina. Little Rhode Island did not much matter.

Advocates of the new Federal Government concentrated their persuasive powers upon the Delegates in New York State because that State, if outside the new government, would isolate Massachusetts and her neighbors from the Pennsylvania-Maryland-Virginia heartland. Three advocates had been publishing editorial essays in New York newspapers since October 27, 1787, beginning their series only 5 weeks after the Federal Constitution had been approved for submission to the States. After a time, these essays were bound together in book form under the title of "*The Federalist: A Commentary on the Constitution of the United States.*" This group of 85 essays – each addressed, "To the people of New York" – were written by **Alexander Hamilton**, the leader of New York advocates of ratification, John Jay, the wealthy and talented political leader who was based in New York City, and Virginia's James Madison, the Constitution's most productive framer.

The essays most significant to my study were numbers 43, 44, 45, and 46, all 4 having been written by **James Madison**. Published in January 1788, these essays discussed the limitations on the power of the Federal Government, and the retained areas of State sovereignty. He commented on the provision in the Federal Constitutional which empowered the Federal Government "to guarantee to every State in the [Federation] a republican form of government [(meaning a government controlled by freely-elected representatives of the people)]; to protect each [State] against invasion; and, [at the request] of [a State] legislature, or [a State governor if the legislature is adjourned], [to protect that State] against domestic violence." Concerning invasion, Madison stated: "A protection against invasion is due from every society to the parts composing it. The latitude of the expression here used seems to secure each State, not only against foreign hostility, but against ambitious or vindictive enterprises of its more powerful neighbors." He recognized the possibility of an insurrection within a State launched by either a minority or a majority of the people, but he believed that in almost all cases of insurrection, the State Government would be capable of subduing the effort, and, for that reason, he believed that "insurrections in a State will rarely induce a Federal [Government] interposition." Madison assured Americans that "the States will retain, under the proposed [Federal] Constitution, a very extensive portion of active sovereignty." And, he thought it more likely that the State governments would gain power and weaken the Federal Government instead of the opposite, which, as we all know, did occur about 70 years later, and is continuing to this day. Madison wrote: "the more I revolve the subject, the more fully I am persuaded that the balance is much more likely to be disturbed by the preponderancy of the [State governments] than of the [Federal Government]." He closed his 4 essays on this issue with an assurance that the proposed Federal Government would not, over time, destroy the planned degree of State Government sovereignty. He had great faith in the judgment and collective wisdom of the voters in each State. He believed evil Federal politicians would be "restrained" from "forming schemes obnoxious to their constituents," by the voters or by the State governments. He rebutted politicians who were opposing ratification: "All those alarms [that] have been sounded of a meditated and consequential annihilation of the State governments, must, on the most favorable interpretation, be ascribed to the [imaginary] fears of the authors of them."

These "authors" who feared the demise of State sovereignty had indeed been advocating changing the Federal Constitution to better guarantee the perpetuation of the planned degree of State sovereignty.

Based on my sampling of historical documents, there was no significant discussion of the right of a State to secede from the Federation at some future date. I find no record of future State Secession being a debate topic during the 4 months in which the Delegates wrote the Federal Constitution. And, I find no record of that being a debate topic in the *Federalist* and *Anti-Federalist* papers that are handed down to us in convenient book form. However, there was much discussion of the extent of State sovereignty and the dangers to the State governments from erosion of State sovereignty. All agreed that Federal powers were strictly limited and that the power to dispatch a Federal army and/or militia from one or more States on an invasion of a State was strictly limited to opposing an insurrection within the targeted State that threatened the existence of the legitimate State Government, empowered by representatives elected by the voters, such as a *coup d'etat* establishing a monarchy or a dictatorship. The Federal Constitution did not in any way provide for a Federal response to the future secession of a State. So, it was clear that, if the voters in a State did at some future date elect Delegates to a State Convention to vote for or against secession, there was no lawful way that the Federal Government or opposed States could legally invade the seceded State and force it to rejoin the Federation.

The right of State secession seemed to be a foregone conclusion. So, discussion of State secession rights was of little concern in 1787 or 1788. The right of a State to secede was assumed to exist. In fact, it would not be challenged when, some years in the future, politicians in Massachusetts would threaten to call a State Convention to vote for the secession of their State.

However, the right of State secession was apparently of concern to the Delegates in the Virginia Convention because they won passage of a proviso to their ratification act that asserted that voters of Virginia had the right to put back within their State Government "the powers [being] granted [to the Federal Government] under the [Federal] Constitution" if and when "[the Federal Government] shall be perverted to their injury or oppression." So, Virginia went of record attesting that State secession would be considered a legal process.

One month after Virginia's ratification, **Delegates to the New York Convention** finally voted for ratification by a vote of **30 yes, versus 27 no**. **John Hancock** had finally persuaded and badgered enough opposing Delegates to switch sides. Advocates of ratification had even threatened to remove New York City from their State if its Delegates did not switch sides. But, the most persuasive force during July of 1788 was the realization in New York that 10 States had already ratified the Constitution and that it would be isolated if it continued to refuse to ratify.

Ratification had proven very difficult. Three large States – Massachusetts, Virginia and New York – had, each, approved ratification by only a 53% majority. And the creation of a viable Federal Government was obviously dependent on acceptance by at least 2 of those States. So, the States came exceedingly close to retaining the old Confederation Government directed by the old Congress. But ratification had been achieved and the old Congress voted to establish the first Wednesday in March as the date that the **new Federal House and Federal Senate would convene in New York City**. It directed the legislatures in the ratifying States to **choose Presidential Electors** on the first Wednesday in January. Electors would cast their votes for President and Vice-President on the first Wednesday in February. So, voters in the ratifying States proceeded to launch the Federal Government by electing Representatives and by their legislatures electing Senators and Presidential Electors. The people of North Carolina and little Rhode Island simply watched.

Andrew Jackson and Others Travel the Wagon Road Westward to the Cumberland Valley

Meanwhile, westward migration continued. **Andrew Jackson**, who would become the first Federal President from Tennessee, joined the first wagon train to use the full length of the new road across the Cumberland Mountains, which had been completed in September. Accompanied by 16 guardsmen employed by the State of North Carolina, Jackson and his newly purchased bonded African American servant girl departed Knoxville, crossed the Cumberland Mountains and arrived at Nashville on October 26. Jackson was a new 21-year-old lawyer looking to beat competing lawyers to an emerging region where he could find plenty of business dealing with land claims. Being a single man, he figured the servant girl could handle all the domestic chores, so he would be free to work long hours at his lawyer business. The following month, the North Carolina Legislature would establish a District Court over the 3 counties that comprised the Cumberland region. And, to everyone's surprise, the sponsor of the bill establishing this new District Court attached the name "Mero District" to the thing. Why would a Tennessean advocate naming his district for Don Esteban Miro, the Governor of Spanish Louisiana and Spanish West Florida? Would such political flattery entice Miro to open up the Mississippi to river traffic from Tennessee? Anyway, the name stuck, including the misspelling.

Andrew Jackson would soon find that he could work in both the County Court and the District Court without leaving Nashville. Jackson would board at the home of John Donelson's widow. There, he would become a friend of the widow's married daughter, **Rachel Donelson Robards** and other members of the Donelson family, and he would become a friend of another newly arrived lawyer, John Overton, who was also boarding with the widow Donelson. Jackson probably sensed that 21-year-old Rachel was having marital problems for she spent considerable time at the house while her husband, Lewis, was at their Cumberland farm or at his family property in Kentucky County, Virginia. Jackson was attracted to Rachel, but respected her marriage obligations.

In a separate wagon train, at about the same time, 22 families also traveled to the Cumberland from the Watauga settlements by way of the new wagon road across the Cumberland Mountains. They were escorted by 100 guards who had come over from the Watauga settlements to ensure a safe journey. So, the **Cumberland settlements** were to see rather rapid growth. And, that growth might well be further encouraged by peace with the Native American nations to the south.

Settlers were encouraged by a December letter from the chief of the Creek Nation, **Alexander McGillivray**, in which he advised James Robertson that he knew that the Cherokees were encouraged toward peace by the recent peace offer from the Confederation Congress, which had restored considerable Cherokee land south of the early Watauga settlements. He furthermore admitted that the Cherokees had earlier asked for Creek [military] assistance, which his Creeks had furnished during the fall months. But, just recently, he had agreed with Cherokee chiefs Little Turkey, Bloodyfellow and Dragging Canoe to thereafter "refrain from all hostilities" against European American settlers.

1789

George Washington of Virginia Elected to become the First United States President

In February, **Presidential Electors from 10 States elected George Washington, of Virginia, as Federal President** and John Adams of Massachusetts as Federal Vice President. Washington's election was unanimous but, Adams's election was a closely contested affair, since 11 men received second-choice votes. Electors from only 10 States had participated in the Electoral College voting, because Electors from the eleventh State had failed to arrive in time.

Chapter 8 — April 1789 to February 1793: The States during the First George Washington Administration

Before relating the history of the Federation's first 4 years, it is appropriate to summarize George Washington's life, the Federation elections and the organization of the first Washington Administration. At the conclusion of this summary, the narrative history will resume. This format will be repeated at the beginning of every 4-year period from this point forward. By presenting each 4-year Federal Administration as a stand-alone summary, I will enhance your understanding of how the Federal Government contributed, and sometimes retarded, the westward expansion of Southern families across North America to, eventually, settle Mexican Texas and win its independence. My primary resource for these segments is *The Complete Book of U. S. Presidents*, by William A. DeGregorio.

George Washington, of Virginia, ex-commander of the Continental Army, was elected the first Federal President by the unanimous vote of all 69 Electors. John Adams, of Massachusetts, was elected Vice President. They were inaugurated into their offices in New York City on April 30, 1789.

George Washington was the son of Augustine Washington of the Potomac region of Virginia. Augustine was a large-scale farmer, an iron manufacturer and a businessman with business in England, which often required his attention. He died when George was 11 years old. Because Augustine was away on business so much of the time, George spent little time with his father. His mother was Mary Ball Washington, whom Augustine had married after his first wife died. George Washington's 3-greats grandfather was the Reverend Lawrence Washington of Essex, England.

By the way, I am also descended from the Reverend Lawrence Washington. Lawrence is my 11-greats grandfather.[5] George Washington's great-grandfather, John Washington, came to Virginia about 1656 to pick up a load of tobacco and chose to make his home in Virginia when his ketch sank as he began his return sail toward England.

At age 16, George Washington worked in a survey party on an expedition across the Blue Ridge Mountains in western Virginia. A year later, he was appointed Surveyor of Culpeper County, Virginia. At 20, George inherited his half-brother's farm, named Mount Vernon, located on the south bank of the Potomac River across from present day Washington, DC. As a major, then as a lieutenant colonel, Washington fought against the combined forces of French militia and Native Americans from 1752 to 1758 in support of the Virginia effort to control western lands in the mountains of present-day West Virginia, Maryland and Pennsylvania.

Washington was elected to the Virginia House of Burgesses in 1759 and served in that capacity until 1774 – a period of 15 years. Afterward, Washington was a member of the Virginia Delegation to the First and Second Continental Congresses (1774-1775). In June 1775, the Second Continental Congress elected Washington to the position of Commander in Chief of the newly authorized Continental Army. On October 19, 1781, under Washington's leadership, the Continental Army and supporting French forces secured the surrender of the British at Yorktown, Virginia. Two years later, in November 1783, a formal peace treaty was signed in Paris. Two

---

[5] I am referencing my family history.

months afterward, Washington resigned his commission and returned to manage the neglected fields of his farm.

Five years afterward, in 1787, Washington was elected a Virginia Delegate to the Constitutional Convention where the other Delegates unanimously elected him President of the Convention. During debate, Washington generally advocated motions that strengthened the power of the Federal Government that the Delegates were striving to create. Under his oversight, the Constitution of the United States of America was drafted and submitted to the 13 independent States for their individual ratification.

Washington was elected the first Federal President without significant opposition. William DeGregorio summarizes Washington's election as follows:

"Washington, a Federalist, was the obvious choice for the first President of the United States. A proven leader, Washington's popularity transcended the conflict between Federalist and those opposed to a strong central government. He was most responsible for winning independence, a modest [farmer/surveyor] with a winsome aversion to the limelight. He so dominated the political landscape that not 1 of the 69 electors voted against him. Thus, he carried all 10 States – Connecticut, Delaware, Georgia, Maryland, Massachusetts, New Hampshire, New Jersey, Pennsylvania, South Carolina and Virginia. (Neither North Carolina nor Rhode Island had ratified the Constitution yet. New York was unable to decide in time which electors to send). Washington [remains] the only President elected by a unanimous electoral vote. John Adams of Massachusetts, having received the second-largest number of votes, 34, was elected Vice President."

Washington's Cabinet was made up of **Secretary of State Thomas Jefferson of Virginia**, Secretary of the Treasury Alexander Hamilton of New York, Secretary of War Henry Knox of Massachusetts, and Attorney General Edmund Jennings Randolph of Virginia.

During the first 2 years of the first Washington Administration, Federalists held a 17 to 9 majority in the Senate and a 38 to 26 majority in the House. The opposition was termed the "Anti-Federalists." During the second 2 years, Federalists held a reduced 16 to 13 majority in the Senate and a reduced 37 to 33 majority in the House. The opposition had coalesced into the Democratic-Republican Party, which I will hereafter call the Democratic Party, for this organization would evolve into the modern Democratic Party we know today.

The State of Vermont was admitted into the Federation in 1791.

The State of Kentucky was admitted in 1792.

The Bill of Rights, composed of 10 Amendments, was ratified by the States and made a part of the Federal Constitution.

The more significant events involving African Americans during the 4 years of the first Washington Administration will now be presented. The 1790 census recorded 753,403 people with some African heritage. This represented 19.3% of the population of the States. Of these people, 92% were bonded. The population in the States from Connecticut to Maine was 16,822, of which 22% were bonded. The population in the States of Pennsylvania, New Jersey and New York was 50,298, of which 72% were bonded. And the population in the States from Georgia to Delaware was 686,283, of which 95% were bonded. The population of independent African Americans was almost evenly split between the southern States and the northern States.

In 1790, the Federal Government outlawed the granting of citizenship to immigrants who were of African descent. Some bonded African Americans were inspired by the bloody and successful revolution by bonded workers of African descent who overran the western third of the Caribbean Island of Hispaniola in 1791 and established the nation of Haiti. Benjamin Banneker, a noteworthy independent African American, worked with the commission that surveyed the District of Columbia and planned the new City of Washington. He also began publishing an almanac for Maryland and neighboring States.

This concludes the overview of the first George Washington Administration. The narrative history resumes with first attention going to the first days of the new Federal Government.

The Narrative History Resumes – March 1789

New Federal House and Senate Convene

In April and May of 1789, **the Federal House and Senate, convened at its temporary quarters in New York City** and settled on import taxes as the chief source of revenue for the Federal Government. The import tax was to go into effect on August 1, 1789. Import taxes were popular with businessmen, such as iron producers, and the few farmers, such as wool producers, who were competing with imported goods, for import taxes permitted them to raise the prices they charged for their goods. But, import taxes were not popular with exporters, such as cotton, tobacco and rice farmers, because import taxes meant they paid more for purchased goods and faced retaliatory import taxes at the European ports to which their products were exported. But, of more importance to American commerce was the tax levied on marine shippers. By this Federal tax, marine shippers entering American ports had to pay an entrance fee of 6 cents per ton of vessel displacement per year if built and owned in America – a modest tax not considered a burden. However, marine shippers entering American ports had to pay 30 cents per ton if the vessel had been built in America, but was owned abroad, and that payment was due each time the vessel entered an American port, not merely once per year. Furthermore, if the vessel was both built and owned abroad, the fee rose to 50 cents per ton. The Federal Government was subjecting foreign owners of marine vessels to such high taxation that it created a boom in American investment in ship construction and ownership. So, the first major industries to benefit from Federal commerce legislation were the manufacturing, shipbuilding and marine shipping industries, which were concentrated in the **New York-Massachusetts** region of the Federation. On the other hand, the first major industries to suffer from Federal commerce legislation were the farmers who raised **export crops, such as cotton, rice and tobacco.**

The State of Georgia Proposes Settlement of its Western Lands

During this year, 1789, the **Georgia State Government offered for sale** all of the land between the western border of the State and the Mississippi River. Georgia political leaders chose to ignore that, although they had preferential rights over other foreign European nations, such as Spain or France, this land needed to be first purchased from owners: the Cherokee, Creek, Chickasaw and Choctaw nations. Georgia politicians merely alleged that the land west of Georgia's western settlements belonged to the people of Georgia, as expressed through their State Government. This concept was in agreement with precedents in North Carolina, which had claimed the land that would become Tennessee, and in Virginia, which had claimed the land that had become Kentucky County. The Georgia claim was a vast amount of land, stretching from the Tennessee border at 35 degrees latitude down to the West Florida border at 32 degrees and 28 minutes (the expanded boundary claimed by Spain). And, a small part of the sale also included land below 32 degrees and 28 minutes. Since the Confederation Government had, in 1786, ensured the region's Native American nations that the land was reserved for them, **George Washington** issued a proclamation directing United States citizens to shun involvement in Georgia's western land sale program. And, he directed the Governor over Federal Territory south of the Ohio River, William Blount, to "keep settlers off the lands that the [Federal] Government had reserved for Native Americans."

Cumberland Valley Settlers Suffer War with Creeks, which is Instigated by the Spanish

Meanwhile, frontiersmen struggled in the Cumberland Valley. During June, Native American warriors, probably Cherokee or Creek, attacked settlers near **James Robertson's farm**. A militia of about 60 men quickly gathered at the farm and set off toward the Duck River in rapid pursuit. Andrew Jackson, a new Nashville lawyer, was among those men. A 20-man portion of the militia, which included Jackson, eventually caught up with the warriors and executed a surprise morning attack, killing 1 and wounding 5 or 6. They did not pursue further, but returned to Nashville with considerable captured goods, including 16 guns. Current historian John Haywood names 23 Cumberland settlers who were killed, plus 4 wounded, during the year 1789. And, he attests that many more were killed, but without a surviving record of their names. Furthermore, Creek warriors killed a Chickasaw chief and his son, both of whom were visiting the Cumberland settlements at the time. The population of the Cumberland region was growing, but so was the death toll from raiding bands of Native American warriors.

Spanish Officials make More Trouble for Southern Settlers moving Southward and Westward

Meanwhile, the Spanish leaders began courting the American settlers west of the Appalachian Mountains. **Don Esteban Miro, the Governor at Spanish Orleans**, issued a proclamation in early September in which he invited citizens of other countries to **emigrate to Spanish Louisiana and Spanish West Florida.** He promised unfettered passage down the Mississippi with all the livestock and possessions emigrants wished to carry. And, he promised a gift of between 240 and 800 acres of **free land**, "in proportion to the numbers," plus exemption from taxation. The only thing required of new settlers was the taking of an oath of allegiance to the Spanish Government. To a young man whose attitude toward American democracy was rather indifferent, the Spanish Government's offer must have been very tempting. And that was the idea, for Spanish officials viewed with alarm the steady westward migration of English-speaking pioneers. Perhaps, they could persuade many of these settlers to switch their allegiance to Spain before the foreseen battle for control of the Mississippi River erupted. Many years later, the Mexican Government would attempt the same ploy when it would invite English-speaking pioneers to settle Mexican land in what is now southwest Texas.

But there was another side to Spanish policy. Spanish authorities in Louisiana and West Florida were arranging to arm the Cherokee, Creek, Chickasaw and Choctaw nations out of the Spanish armory at Pensacola. During late August, two Cherokee chiefs, John Watts and

Talotiskee, returned from Pensacola with Spanish arms to Wills Town in the Cherokee Nation. "The Cherokees assembled from all parts of the Nation at Wills Town" to participate in the Green Corn Dance festival and "to hear Watt's report from Pensacola." Watts read to the assembled crowd a letter from **Governor Oneil, the Spanish ruler of West Florida**. "It stated that his master, the King of Spain, had sent to his care at Pensacola arms and ammunition in abundance, for the use of the 4 southern [Native American] nations, which he had divided into 4 separate warehouses."

And, Watts reported that Governor Oneil had reminded him of a crucial difference between the settlement agenda of Spanish and English people. Oneil had argued: "the Spaniards never wanted a back country. Wherever they landed they sat down; even such a sand bank as [Pensacola] was sufficient. They were not like the Americans – first take your lands, then treat with you, and give you little or nothing for them." And, Governor Oneil recommended that the current year "was the time for them to join quickly in war against the United States, while they were engaged in the war against the northern [Native American nations]." And he promised to keep a warehouse stocked with Spanish arms at Wills Town. Emboldened by fresh arms and promises of Spanish help, John Watts concluded with an appeal to war: "All you young men who like war go with me. Tomorrow we will have a great many more men, and we will settle matters better when we all get together."

Fortunately, Cherokee Leaders are Not Fooled by Spanish Tricks

But, **The Bloody Fellow**, an older and perhaps wiser Cherokee chief, rose to present a contrary argument. **He argued that the Americans "were good people,"** and pointed to the recent "presents I received for myself, and likewise for your warriors." Then he challenged: "When was the day you went to your father and brought from him as much?" The Bloody Fellow closed with this stern advice: "You had better take my talk, and stay at home and mind your women and children."

Then **Cherokee Chief Talotiskee** countered, "I too have been to Pensacola, and saw the [Spanish] Governor as well as [did John] Watts, and heard his talk. I think a great deal of it. I shall try to do as he directed me." But The Bloody Fellow persisted: "Look at that flag. Do you see the stars in it? They are not towns, but nations. There are 13 of them. They are people who are very strong, and we are the same as one man. If you know when you are well, you had better stay at home and mind your women and children."

Yet, **John Watts** was not turned from his objective, for he rose and announced, "The day is come when I must again imbrue my hands in blood. Tomorrow I shall send off a runner to the Creek Nation to bring on my friends. Then I shall have people enough to go with me to Cumberland, or any place that I want to go." That concluded the conference.

The men then stripped to the flap, painted their bodies black and **danced the war dance around the United States flag.** When darkness fell, they removed to the town house and "continued the war dance all night." There was more debate the following day, when The Bloody Fellow admonished: "I would wish none of you to go to war, but to stay at home in peace, as I intend to do myself. I can go over the mountains and live in peace." A Shawnee warrior, who had lived for many years with a small group of Shawnees in Cherokee country rose and asserted: "With these hands I have taken the lives of 300 men; the time is come when they shall take the lives of 300 more. Then I will be satisfied, and sit down in peace." Two days later the Cherokees agreed to plans to attack the Cumberland settlements in 4 divisions, and to clear the country of all living people. But the Cherokees put their trust in a Frenchman named Derogue, and a man named Fendleston, who was partly of European American descent. These 2 were asked to quickly go to the Cumberland settlements and report back on defenses. But, upon reaching Nashville on September 15, Derogue revealed the joint Cherokee-Creek attack plan to James Robertson and this gave the Cumberland settlers time to prepare.

On September 30, a large war party of about 450 Creeks and 200 Cherokees attacked a small fort at Buchanon's Station. It was manned by only 19 Cumberland militiamen, but the fortress walls were sound. John Watts led the charge, but the warriors were unable to penetrate the fortress, and no defender was killed. The warriors lost a Shawnee chief and a Creek chief and John Watts took a miniball in the thigh, and several warriors were killed and several were wounded.

Then a strange thing happened: the huge war party of Cherokees and Creeks retreated back to their homes. Why had John Watts decided to assault a fortified position when it would have been so much wiser to instead bypass the thing and move on to attack unprotected settlements? Wasn't the object to kill as many settlers as possible? Or had John Watts really been secretly influenced by the wiser talk of The Bloody Fellow? Perhaps Watts realized that, since the young warriors had to have a war adventure to fulfilled manhood, he would lead them to Cumberland, but throw them against a small fort, where only a few would be killed, and then lead them home to "mind their women and children," leaving Cumberland rather quickly so as to not incite a retaliation.

"This was the last formidable invasion that the Cherokees ever made upon the Cumberland settlements."

Federal House and Senate Establish a Federal Courts System

Meanwhile, on September 24 in New York City, proponents of a strong Federal Government pushed through Congress a **Judiciary Act** that established the structure of a Federal Court System within the Federal Government and decreed the types of cases to be adjudicated by Federal courts – instead of by State courts as in the past. These new Federal courts – a Supreme Court, 16 District Courts and 3 Circuit Courts – were empowered to accept appeals from the various State courts and to adjudicate cases involving Federal laws, the Federal Constitution, and treaties with foreign governments. By making the Federal court system "the supreme law of the land," the Federal Congress was, at this early time, already threatening the principle of "State Sovereignty" as guaranteed by the Federal Constitution.

The Bill of Rights Become Part of the Constitution

On September 28, the Federal House and Senate finally passed the long-awaited group of Amendments to the Federal Constitution, which is known collectively as the **"Bill of Rights."** Proponents of the Federal Government, during their campaigns to win ratification of the Federal Constitution in the separate legislatures of the independent States, had encountered heavy criticism that the Constitution did not guarantee personal liberties and State sovereignty. So, proponents had promised State legislators that amendments would be submitted to them once the Federal Government was established. Early attention by the House and Senate to revenue and organizational issues, prior to submitting the awaited amendments, had produced apprehension among citizens who cherished State sovereignty and protection from government intrusion into their private lives.

James Madison, after reviewing more than 100 suggested personal liberty amendments, had selected several and submitted them to the Federal House. The House passed 17. And the Federal Senate passed 12. Then the 12 authorized Amendments were submitted to the States for ratification.

The Massachusetts State Legislature would refuse to ratify any of the Amendments, demanding that a pet amendment be added to the list before ratifying the 12 Amendments already submitted. In fact, the Massachusetts State Legislature would not ratify the ten Amendments known as "The Bill of Rights" until December 1939, when I was a 16-month-old toddler. But enough States would ratify 10 of the Amendments by December 15, 1791, thereby enabling those 10 to become part of the Federal Constitution. The other 2 would never be ratified.

The most important of these 10 Amendments was the **Tenth Amendment**, which reinforced the guarantee of State sovereignty. In language easily understood by a grade school boy, the **Tenth Amendment stated**:

"The powers not delegated to the [Federal Government] by the [Federal] Constitution, nor prohibited by it to the States, are reserved to the States respectively, or to the people."

It was as simple as that. By approving the Federal Constitution, the several States had "delegated" certain identified powers to the Federal Government, and "reserved" the balance to themselves, to each of the states.

Alexander Hamilton is Appointed Secretary of the Treasury

George Washington made **Alexander Hamilton**, of Massachusetts, his **Secretary of the Treasury** on September 11, 1789. Washington had chosen Hamilton, in spite of his young age of 32 years, because he was brilliant and passionately in favor of a strong, credit-worthy Federal Government. And, Washington probably agreed that past government debt should be redeemed at, or near, face value. Certainly, Hamilton wanted to pay, at full face value, holders of Confederation debt – and even the State debts that had been incurred during the defense of Independence – even though the going market rate for **those bonds had fallen to about 25 cents on the dollar**. Aware that Hamilton might succeed, wealthy men and bankers with money to invest were sending their agents across the States buying up Government bonds, sometimes for as little as 10 cents on the dollar. Such agents were particularly successful at buying bonds cheaply in the southern States, where rural bondholders were less aware that a powerful political movement was underway to redeem them at face value. **Before long, wealthy individuals and banks in New York City, Philadelphia and Boston owned much of the debt that Hamilton proposed redeeming at face value**. Political leaders in Virginia and States to the south, even if they agreed with Hamilton's redemption proposals in principle, were infuriated that passing legislation to that effect would make wealthy men in those 3 cities vastly more wealthy.

But, attempts to prevent such speculators from making huge profits failed to win passage because **Thomas Jefferson** stepped into the picture, as will be explained shortly.

Spanish Command at Natchez Seeks Settlers from the States

Meanwhile, **Andrew Jackson** was drawn to **Natchez** by Don Esteban Miro's offer encouraging emigration by citizens of the United States. Jackson traveled to Natchez in the winter months of 1789-1790, and made friends of two influential Virginia emigrants, brothers Abner and Thomas Green. Jackson was impressed that the Greens had finer homes than any he had seen in the Cumberland settlements. So, he acquired "a tract of excellent land where Bayou Pierre meets the Mississippi 30 miles above Natchez." And he would build a log house on the property before returning home by the Chickasaw Road "in time for the 1790 term of court at Nashville."

During 1790, Manuel Gayoso de Lemos, the Spanish commandant at Natchez, made a treaty with the Choctaws and Chickasaws to acquire a portion of the Walnut Hills region, which lay just north of present-day Vicksburg, Mississippi. Although the Spanish often appealed for Native American cooperation by claiming that it was the English-speaking people of The States who craved land, the Spanish were behaving the same way in the Walnut Hills region.

Thomas Jefferson is Secretary of State

George Washington had made Thomas Jefferson of Virginia his Secretary of State, and Jefferson began work at his new job upon his return from France on March 22. Immediately upon his return, Alexander Hamilton alleged to Jefferson that, unless past government bonds were redeemed at face value through the issue of new Federal Government bonds, the Federal Government would collapse from lack of credit. But Jefferson failed to investigate this allegation thoroughly before he hosted a dinner to which Hamilton was invited. Over wine and food, Hamilton and Jefferson struck a deal. Jefferson agreed to support Hamilton's proposal to pay Confederation bondholders at face value and Hamilton agreed to relocate the Federation Capital to the northern boundary of Virginia, after a 10-year temporary residence in Philadelphia to allow construction of the new Federal facilities. Jefferson would later complain that Hamilton had tricked him, but the fact remains that locating the Capital adjacent to Virginia was of great importance to Virginia politicians. Furthermore, 29 of the 64 Representatives in the House stood to personally profit from issuing new Federal Government bonds. So, the deadlock in the House and Senate was broken and past government bonds would be redeemed at face value, **greatly enriching wealthy speculators** in New York City, Philadelphia and Boston.

The Ohio River Experiences Settlement on Both Sides

Meanwhile, far off settlements along the Ohio River greatly concerned Federal officials, because warriors of the Native American nations situated north of the Ohio were still attempting to repulse the unlawful European American invasion north of the Ohio River. Furthermore, British authorities in the Great Lakes region were facilitating Native American arms purchases and offering encouragement.

As you know, European Americans were in complete control of land south of the Ohio River, which the State of Virginia had organized in 1776 as **Kentucky County**. But, by 1790, there were substantial settlements on both the South side and the North side of the Ohio River. As you further know, between the Ohio and the Great Lakes, westward to the Mississippi River, was a vast land that would become the States of Ohio, Indiana, Illinois and, eventually, far-north Michigan. Floating downriver in one-way float-boats and paddling upriver in canoes or by walking overland, settlers had first occupied Kentucky County along the banks of the Ohio. Some crossed from Kentucky County to the north bank of the Ohio River and began near-river settlements.

Well, Native American warriors had found it impossible to prevent settlements along the north bank by the application of large-scale military tactics, since settlers had only to escape across the river to Kentucky County. So, warrior defensive efforts were confined to guerrilla raids where a few settlers could be isolated and killed. Even so, by 1790, the population around the Marietta settlement exceeded 1,000 and the population around Cincinnati was more than that. The old French settlement of Vincennes, located on the Illinois River well north of the Ohio River, was growing as well.

At Fort Harmar, during the previous year of 1789, Arthur St. Clair, acting as "governor" of the Cincinnati region, had arranged for a land treaty with local Native Americans that granted permission for European American settlements along the north bank of the Ohio. But, the treaty did not give up title to the land. Aiming to defend and expand European American settlements north of the Ohio, **George Washington**, in 1790, persuaded the Federal Congress to fund a 2,000-man army to build and man a string of **Federal forts on the north side of the Ohio River**.

Federals Organize Territory South of the Ohio River

North Carolina had ratified the Federal Constitution on November 21, 1789, thereby inferring no conflict over governing the land that would become Tennessee. Six months after the ratification, on May 25, 1790, the Federal Government organized all Federal territory south of the Ohio River under one Territory Government called, **"Territory of the United States of America South of the River Ohio."** William Blount of North Carolina Colony, appointed Governor of the vast Territory, would, by October, move to Knoxville to establish his office. **Daniel Smith** was appointed Secretary. Governor Blount would arrange for John Robertson to pick up Smith's old job of military commander of the Cumberland region. And he would arrange for John Sevier to become military commander of the Watauga region. Dr. James White would be elected as the Territory Representative to the Federal House. On December 15, 1790, **Andrew Jackson** would be named **Attorney General of the Cumberland** region, a job that included being public prosecutor.

Creek Nation Appears More Cooperative

Alexander McGillivray, **leader of the Creek Nation**, traveled to the Federal Capitol at New York City and negotiated a **treaty with George Washington**, which was signed on August 7. This treaty called for the Creek Nation to give up its claim to the land previously taken by the State of Georgia in exchange for a $100,000 payment from the Federal Treasury. In addition, Washington agreed to give McGillivray the title of "Brigadier General" and pay him a salary of $1,800 per year. By this move, Washington was hoping to switch the Creek Nation from its past alignment with the Spanish Government to a new alignment with the Federal Government. You will soon learn that bribing McGillivray would not sustain peace.

Current historian John Haywood would name 10 Cumberland settlers killed in 1790 by Native American warriors, plus 3 who were scalped and survived and 3 who were wounded and survived. Of 5 victims of one attack Haywood would write: "They wounded John McRory, and caught and scalped 3 of Everett's children and killed John Everett."

1791

Vermont Granted Statehood

The Federal House and Senate granted statehood to Vermont on February 18. Vermont was the first State that had not existed as a colony prior to the formation of the Federal Government. **The land within Vermont was actually part of New York State**. So, the people of Vermont had sought independence from the New York State Government in Albany. And, the previous year, the New York State Government had agreed to give up their land within Vermont. The reason: political leaders in the States north of Maryland wanted two more Federal senators from their region. **Splitting New York into two States increased the number of senators from north of Maryland to 18, versus only 12 from Maryland south.**

Alexander Hamilton's Federal Whiskey Tax Sparks Rebellion

Eager to raise more tax revenue beyond that expected from the new Federal taxes on imports and on owners of foreign marine shipping companies, **Alexander Hamilton** had advocated, on December 13, 1790, a new tax – **a tax on people who made distilled liquors**, such as whiskey and rum. The Federal House and Senate had obliged and Federal collection of this new tax, which amounted to about 25% of the selling price, was scheduled to begin on March 3, 1791. Efforts by Federal Revenue agents to collect the tax in the western regions of the new nation, particularly in western Virginia, would incite **a rebellion by small farmers** who converted corn to whiskey during the fall and winter months as a way of raising hard cash. These farmers had found that hauling a few kegs of whiskey across the difficult mountain roads to the eastern markets was a lot more profitable than hauling several wagon-loads of dried corn – that is, before the introduction of the Federal tax on whiskey. The legislatures of Virginia, North Carolina and Maryland would soon protest the high tax rate, and Congress would, on May 8, 1872, relent by reducing the tax to 7 cents per gallon, which was about 14% of the selling price.

Alexander Hamilton Proposes a United States National Bank

For some time, **Alexander Hamilton** had been examining the United States' banking industry. There was not much to it. During the latter half of the colonial period, colonial businessmen needing major financing had used the Bank of England, which had been chartered by the British Government in 1694. For minor financing, especially to purchase land, settlers had been able to use local land banks, whose activities were limited to loaning money while receiving land as collateral and issuing limited amounts of paper money backed by the banks' land holdings. Although **land banks** suited the needs of farmers reasonably well, a businessman could not turn to them to finance the construction of industrial enterprises, such as an iron-works facility or a shipbuilding yard. Looking to fill those needs, Robert Morris of Philadelphia, in 1781, had founded the first full-service bank, which he called the Bank of North America. It could finance industrial enterprises and issue larger amounts of paper money backed by various types of collateral, and, I suppose, some gold reserves. Two more full-service banks had been founded in 1784, one in Boston and the other in New York. Although businessmen had begun launching a full-service bank in Baltimore in 1790, none was in

144

operation in the southern farming region from Maryland to Georgia, when, <u>on December 14, 1790, the House had received Alexander Hamilton's report advocating the establishment of a national bank to be called the</u> "**Bank of the United States**."

Historian Fred Wellborn would write:

"[Hamilton] urged that growing business, and the [Federal Government], needed the facilities as well as the stable bank-note currency which a great national bank could provide. Specifically, the principal advantages were: (1) an increase of actual capital – the result in part of an enlargement of the bank notes in circulation, (2) the greater ease with which the [Federal Government] might secure loans, (3) the greater opportunities for the individual to borrow money, and; because of the increased circulation, to pay [Federal] taxes." But Wellborn, who would come to understand economic theory better than had Hamilton, would add this footnote: "In other words, Hamilton believed that a bank could create capital (i.e., that the 'credit' of the [Federal Government] could be called upon to do the work of capital), an idea that is contrary to a law of economics that capital can be produced only through labor and frugality."

<u>Representatives and Senators from the farming States stretching from Maryland to Georgia, for the most part,</u> **were opposed to a national bank**. <u>They feared it would destroy State-chartered banks and overly involve the Federal Government in finance, to a degree they thought dangerous to the welfare of the American people.</u> The primary opposition tactic against those favoring the national bank was to persuade them that a national bank violated the limited powers laid down in the Federal Constitution. <u>But Hamilton's forces steered through the House and Senate a bill that chartered a Philadelphia-based national bank for 20 years and gave it a monopoly on all Federal Government financial activity.</u>

George Washington polled his Cabinet and listened to **Thomas Jefferson's** strong arguments against establishing a national bank, but <u>he was, nevertheless, persuaded to sign the bill and make it the law of the land, which he did on February 25, 1791.</u>

<u>When $10,000,000 worth of stock in the Bank of the United States was offered for sale, it was grabbed up in a mere 4 hours,</u> $2,000,000 of that stock being purchased by the Federal Government itself, exchanging Federal bonds for bank stock, I suppose. Eventually the bank would establish branches in 8 other cities. It would immediately enjoy a monopoly arrangement in dealing with all Federal Government banking, including being the depository for Federal bonds. <u>Only bank notes issued by the national bank, or gold or silver coins, would be valid when paying taxes collected by the Federal Government. The Bank of the United States would be a roaring success in financial terms.</u> By the summer of 1791, bonds issued by the new national bank would be selling at a premium in London. The Federal Government's international credit was enhanced by the bank's success, but, more importantly, there had been a significant economic recovery in The States since 1789. Within 2 years, Europeans would become embroiled in wars that would increase demand for American exports, further stimulating the economy.

Andrew Jackson and Rachel Donelson

<u>Our history now presents the saga of</u> **Andrew Jackson's** <u>efforts to help</u> **Rachel Donelson**, <u>her divorce from</u> **Lewis Robards**, <u>and Rachel's marriage to Jackson.</u>

In Nashville, Andrew Jackson took his new job as Attorney General rather seriously, but availed himself of every opportunity to aid Rachel Donelson Robards in her continuing conflict with her husband, Lewis Robards. For example, Jackson had traveled to Kentucky in July 1790 to bring Rachel from her husband's home to her sister's home near Nashville, because she had wished to get away from her husband.

Well, you will recall that Jackson had purchased a small parcel of land in Spanish Louisiana Colony that overlooked the Mississippi River and had built a small log cabin there. Apparently, Rachel wanted to relocate to Spanish held Louisiana Colony for a time, perhaps until her divorce from Lewis Robards finalized. So, a plan was hatched for her to migrate to Louisiana Colony and spend time with the Abner Green and his family.

Well, Jackson had not been content to let Rachel travel, unescorted, to the Spanish town of **Natchez** with the Spanish trader John Stark and his crew of boatmen, for Jackson knew that such travel was hazardous. Rachel had tried to assure Jackson that, as a child, "from the deck of the *Adventure*, she had heard [Native American] arrows sing and seen the glint of scalping knives," and that "she did not fear them now." But Jackson had not been dissuaded. So, he turned over the legal responsibilities of the Attorney General's office to John Overton and joined the Stark trading party to help ensure a safe float trip to Natchez, on the Mississippi River, in West Florida.

The trading party is reported to have departed Nashville "in the winter or spring" of 1791, for the exact date is unknown. Upon arriving at their destination, Jackson would make sure that Rachel was safely situated in the home of **Abner Green**, whose farm lay 23 miles from Natchez. The Greens had arrived as prosperous immigrants from Virginia and Natchez was "second in importance only to New Orleans and the focal point of most of the American emigration." In his new surroundings, Abner Green wealthy, having purchased the farm and summer home that had belonged to Manuel Gayoso de Lemos, the Spanish commandant. Jackson would return to Nashville by the rather dangerous Chickasaw Road, a trading path that would later be renamed the **Natchez Trace**.

By the way, when a much younger man, I rode my bicycle on the Natchez Trace from Nashville, Tennessee to Natchez, Mississippi along with a first cousin. Great trip. We were going south. Jackson had been going north.

Andrew Jackson married Rachel Donelson Robards at Thomas Greens' "stately brick" **home near Natchez, in Spanish Louisiana Colony**. The marriage took place in August 1791. Both were 24 years old. After the wedding "the couple retired to Jackson's establishment at Bayou Pierre, where a log house in a clearing on the bluff looked down on the incredible Mississippi" (you will recall that Jackson had purchased the property during a previous visit to Natchez in late 1789). **But the marriage was actually illegal!**

The newlyweds had probably believed reports that the Virginia General Assembly had granted a divorce to Rachel's first husband, Lewis Robards. But, the bill, "An Act concerning the Marriage of Lewis Robards," passed on December 20, 1790, just 12 days before Kentucky County ceased to be a part of the State of Virginia, had in fact merely directed Robards to "publish [his divorce intent] for 8 weeks successively in the *Kentucky Gazette*" and then seek to have a jury grant the divorce in a Territory Court. The act had concluded with: "Thereupon the marriage between the said Lewis Roberts and Rachel shall be totally dissolved." Perhaps there had been confusion from the misspelling of Robards' name, for the person recording the act had written: "Lewis Roberts."

Furthermore, Lewis Robards had encouraged the Donaldson family's misconception that the Virginia General Assembly had fully granted his plea for a divorce. For example, he had written Rachel's brother-in-law Robert Hays requesting that Cumberland land held jointly by he and Rachel be divided, so that he would receive half of it. On the other hand, perhaps sensing that Robards intended to punish Rachel further by delaying the divorce for a few years, Jackson may have figured the best legal recourse was to leave the United States and marry Rachel in Spanish Louisiana Colony.

And Robards would in fact wait 2 years, until September 1793, before quietly seeking the divorce in a Kentucky court. Furthermore, he would fail to announce in 8 issues of the *Kentucky Gazette* his intent to seek a divorce, as had been required by the Virginia General Assembly. According to John Overton, one of Jackson's brothers-in-law, Jackson would be stunned by the 1793 news that the divorce had been delayed 2 years. Upon hearing the news, Jackson would insist that "every person in the country" understood that Rachel had become his wife in Natchez. But, after much persuading, **Jackson would agree to a second marriage ceremony in Nashville in January 1794**.

This misunderstanding over Robards' divorce status would haunt Andrew and Rachel in the years to come when political opponents would use the incident to disparage the character of both. Many observers would believe that the political slander during the year Andrew was elected Federal President so distressed Rachel that it contributed to her tragic death shortly after moving into the White House at Washington City.

Hamilton and Jefferson Lead America's First Two-Party Political Movement

Political parties began to form during the latter months of George Washington's first term as President. **Alexander Hamilton** was the political leader and hero of the wealthy merchants, manufacturers, shippers and bankers of the States from Pennsylvania to Massachusetts. Thomas Jefferson was rising to become the political leader and hero of America's farmers – both small-scale farmers and large-scale farmers. Hamilton was an elitist who, distrusting the collective political wisdom of the average man, believed in government by the wealthy class. Jefferson was a democratic idealist who, trusting the collective political wisdom of the average man, advocated government by the people. **Washington** was distrustful of political parties and wished talk of them would go away. He dreamed of a Federation where politicians worked together, without much conflict, with equal desire to do what was good for America and good for its people.

Hamilton was becoming leader of the party in power – **the Federalists. Jefferson was becoming leader of the party out of power – the Democrats**. Actually, Jeffersonians would call their party the Republican Party, and historians would call it the Democratic-Republican Party, but it would become known as the Democratic Party under the leadership of Andrew Jackson. (As mentioned earlier, I am going to call Jefferson's party the "Democratic Party" from the beginning to make this work easier to read and understand.)

The **strength of Hamilton's Federalists was the wealthy people of the northern States** from Pennsylvania to Massachusetts. The strength of Jefferson's Democrats was the farming people, particularly the farming people from Maryland to Georgia extending from the Atlantic coast to the western frontier.

Back in 1789, Alexander Hamilton had encouraged John Fenno to establish a newspaper that would advocate a strong and dominant Federal Government. Fenno's newspaper, the *Gazette of the United States*, was established in New York City and was moving to Philadelphia in conjunction with the relocation of the United States Capital. As the Federalist Party grew in political organization and its political agenda firmed, Fenno's newspaper would be at work dutifully disseminating Party rhetoric and advocating adoption of favored programs.

But the emerging Democratic Party had no comparable newspaper until James Madison, Henry Lee and Aaron Burr succeeded at encouraging fellow Princeton classmate Philip Freneau to go to Philadelphia and helped him establish the *National Gazette* there, which began publication in October 1791. Before long, editors Fenno and Freneau were attacking each other and leaders of the opposition parties in "scathing rhetoric." They even devised poetry to strengthen the impact of their insulting attacks. Historian Fred Wellborn would conclude: "Never did newspapers perform greater service in sharpening political antagonisms."

A New 2,000-man Federal Army is Raised to Defend Settlers North of the Ohio River, but it is decimated by Native Americans Fighters

George Washington persuaded the House and Senate to approve a **Federal force of 2,000 new recruits to provide protection to settlers on the north side of the Ohio River.** This force, under Arthur St. Clair, poorly paid and poorly trained, set out for **Cincinnati** in October, intending to build forts along the way. But, in early November, Native American warriors attacked St. Clair's Federal force about 100 miles north of Cincinnati, killing 600, wounding most of the remainder and gaining renewed confidence that they could defend their land, if they only received enough British support. But, this first major military defeat for the Federal Government **would not deter President George Washington** from organizing a new Federal Army to protect settlers north of the Ohio.

African American Events During 1791

The year 1791 was when bonded African Americans began a revolt on the large Caribbean **Island of Hispaniola**. They were taking advantage of the chaos throughout the French domain that was caused by the **French Revolution**, which was underway in Europe. At this time the island's more prosperous European Americans were, as Royalists, generally supporting the government of the King of France and the less prosperous European Americans were generally supporting the French revolutionaries. The island's independent farmers, of mixed African and European descent, were supporting the French revolutionaries and were opposing a revolt by the island's bonded people of African descent that was taking place.

Hispaniola's bonded people of African descent were taking advantage of this ongoing conflict between the island's Royalists and Revolutionaries and fighting to become independent people themselves. The bonded people of African descent would be intent on winning their independence. And a former bonded man, **Francois Dominique Toussaint L'Ouverture**, would emerge as the leader of the revolt of the bonded people of African descent. This would be a protracted struggle lasting until 1804.

Cumberland Valley Settlers are still suffering from Native Attacks while Spanish at Natchez continue their Settlement Efforts

Settlers in the **Cumberland Valley** were still suffering attacks. Current historian John Haywood would name 15 Cumberland-region settlers killed in 1791 by Native American warriors. Of 3 victims, Haywood would write: "On June 2, 1791, they killed John Thompson in his own cornfield, within 5 miles of Nashville. On June 14, they killed John Gibson and wounded McMoon, in Gibson's field, within 8 miles of Nashville."

1792

Spanish Governor at Natchez Gains More Land

Toward the beginning of 1792, **Manuel Gayoso, the Spanish Governor at Natchez**, acquired for Spanish settlement much more land stretching south from present-day **Vicksburg, Mississippi**. He obtained by treaty with the Choctaw Nation "a large tract of country, beginning at the mouth of the Yazoo; thence 10 miles up it; thence southeast to a river which empties into Lake Pontchartrain, and down that river." Spanish leaders had been lying about only wanting to settle the coastal part of Spanish West Florida.

First Federal Mint Established in Philadelphia, Pennsylvania

The Federal Congress set up a mint in Philadelphia, which began to stamp out gold and silver coins in 1792. This would be the only Federal coin manufacturing facility until 1835, when Federal mints would be added at Dahlonega, Georgia, Charlotte, North Carolina, and New Orleans, Louisiana. The financial prowess of Philadelphia, of Pennsylvania, and of the northeastern States, was and would be enhanced by the presence in Philadelphia of the sole Federal Mint and the sole National Bank.

Kentucky Granted Statehood

The Federal House and Senate granted statehood to Kentucky in June 1792. Several years previously, Virginia had given Kentucky County to the Federal Government and it had been governed thereafter as part of the Federal Territory South of the Ohio River. So, Kentucky was carved from an original State as Vermont had been 16 months previously. Kentucky statehood increased the number of Federal Senators from Maryland southward to 14, versus 18 from north of Maryland.

Native Attacks on Cumberland Settlers Intensifies

During 1792, Native American attacks on settlers in the Cumberland region had become much more commonplace than in previous years. Current historian John Haywood would name 44 people killed, one scalped and surviving, 13 wounded and surviving and 4 captured. Among the dead he would list: "Robert Sevier and William Sevier, sons of Valentine Sevier," who was a brother to the prominent Watauga settlements leader, **John Sevier**.

President George Washington Agrees to Serve a Second Term

As the 1792 elections approached, the Federalist Party and the Democratic Party examined their strengths and weaknesses. The Federalist Party seemed assured of keeping the Presidency if George Washington would agree to run for a second term. Otherwise, they might well lose to the new Democratic Party. But Washington was 60 years old, had devoted about 37 years of his life to Virginia and the United States, and simply wanted to go home. Alexander Hamilton and other Federalists begged Washington to reconsider working the job just 4 more years. Even Thomas Jefferson, leader of the opposition, begged him to run for a second term for the sake of national stability. **Finally, Washington relented and agreed to run for a second term**. He was easily reelected. And the fall election for Federal Representatives and Senators went very well for the **new Democratic Party**, for their candidates won a majority of the seats in the **Federal House**.

Chapter 9 – March 1793 to February 1797: The States during the Second George Washington Administration

Before resuming the narrative history, it is appropriate to present an overview of the national elections and the organization of the second George Washington Administration.

George Washington, a farmer, surveyor and military commander from Virginia, was easily reelected to a second term. Vice-President John Adams, a lawyer and politician from Boston, Massachusetts, was reelected to the office of Vice-President as well. William DeGregorio summarizes Washington's reelection as follows:

> "Despite the growing strength of [the Democratic Party], Washington continued to enjoy virtually universal support. Again, he won the vote of every elector, 132, and thus carried all 15 States - Connecticut, Delaware, Georgia, Kentucky, Maryland, Massachusetts, New Hampshire, New Jersey, New York, North Carolina, Pennsylvania, Rhode Island, South Carolina, Vermont and Virginia. Vice President John Adams of Massachusetts received the second-highest number of votes, 77 and thus was again elected Vice President."

Washington's Cabinet was little changed from the one that had served him during his first term. Edmund Jennings Randolph, of Virginia, moved from Attorney General to Secretary of State for 2 years, after which that position was held by Timothy Pickering, of Massachusetts. Alexander Hamilton, of New York, remained 2 years as Secretary of the Treasury, after which that position was held by Oliver Wolcott, a lawyer from Connecticut. Henry Knox, of Massachusetts, remained as Secretary of War for one year, after which that position was held by Timothy Pickering. After Pickering's move to Secretary of State, the War position was held by James McHenry, a physician from Maryland. William Bradford, of Pennsylvania, was Attorney General for the first year, followed by Charles Lee, of Virginia.

During the first 2 years of the second Washington Administration, Federalists retained a 17 to 13 majority in the Senate, but the opposition Democratic Party organized the House with a 57 to 48 majority. During the second 2-year segment, Federalists enlarged their Senate majority to 19 versus 13 and Federalists regained control of the House with a slim majority of 54 versus 52.

The new **State of Tennessee** was admitted in 1796, thereby advancing the United States to the Mississippi River.

The Eleventh Amendment to the Federal Constitution, which excluded the Federal Government from jurisdiction over litigation between a State and a citizen of a different State or a foreign power, was ratified in 1795.

In his farewell address in 1796, President Washington warned of the future danger of powerful political parties in the hands of unscrupulous and ambitious men. It was as if he foresaw the domination of parties by ambitious lawyers and the rise of the sectional Republican Party 60 years into the future. **George Washington warned:**

> "[Political parties] serve to organize faction, to give it an artificial and extraordinary force to put, in the place of the delegated will of the Nation, the will of a party; often a small but artful and enterprising minority of the community; and according to the alternate triumphs of different parties, to make the public administration the mirror of the ill-concerted and incongruous projects of faction, rather than the organ of consistent

and wholesome plans digested by common counsels, and modified by mutual interests. However, combinations or associations of the above description may now and then answer popular ends, they are likely in the course of time and things, to become potent engines, by which cunning, ambitious, and unprincipled men will be enabled to subvert the Power of the People and to usurp for themselves the reins of Government; destroying afterwards the very engines which have lifted them to unjust dominion."

The more significant events involving African Americans during the 4 years of the second Washington Administration will now be presented. In 1793, **Eli Whitney invented a cotton engine,** a machine that stripped the cotton fibers away from the cotton seeds, which had been tedious and time-consuming hand work prior to this date. This invention would greatly improve the productivity of cotton farms, and free African Americans to spend more time in fieldwork and other more productive tasks. A 1793 Federal law required that all State courts cooperate with owners from any other State who sought to bring runaway bonded African Americans back home. The Upper Canada Government abolished ownership of bonded Africans within its lands, and the French Government abolished the same in the French Colonies. The North Carolina Government outlawed importation of bonded Africans. And, with regard to American marine shippers, the Federal Government, in 1794, forbid outfitting in American ports any ship designed to carry bonded Africans, or the transporting of bonded Africans to any foreign port. But, between 1795 and 1804, British marine shippers would transport 380,993 bonded Africans in 1,283 vessels from stopover ports in England to the Americas and the Caribbean. In 1793, five bonded Africans in Albany, New York, were executed for setting fires, which caused about $250,000 in damage. Efforts to organize a rebellion by African Americans in Point Coupee Parish, Louisiana, in 1795 were broken up by State militia, resulting in the deaths of about 50 resistors and alleged conspirators.

Having concluded the overview of the second George Washington Administration, the narrative history resumes.

The Narrative History Resumes – March 1793

The United States Recognizes the New French Republic

In April 1793, **George Washington** and his Cabinet agreed that the Federal Government would **recognize the new French Republic,** the result of the French Revolutionary's victory, and receive its minister, Edmund Genet. At the time, the new French Republic was engaged in a war with England and Spain, so recognition could have potentially drawn the United States into the war as well. But, Washington's Secretary of State, **Alexander Hamilton**, argued that the United States Government should not question the legitimacy of a foreign government that rested upon the consent of its people. Future administrations would often adopt this policy when faced with revolutions in foreign nations, and the American people would benefit from this degree of isolation from the turmoil that would sweep through Europe in the years ahead.

Although the French Government did not press the United States to declare war against England and Spain, it did demand logistical support and sought covert military support. The French Minister, Edmund Genet, was at the time traveling through the southern States signing up American naval privateers to prey on British marine commerce. **Thomas Jefferson** became alarmed when he learned that Genet had been signing naval privateers and army officers.

Jefferson insisted that the United States was a neutral power and participation in the war by American citizens was prohibited.

But, the revolutionary party of Robespierre swept Genet's party from power. The second new French Government would send J. Fauchet to replace Genet. George Washington would recall his minister to France, Gouverneur Morris, and would replace him with James Monroe, of Virginia. The French Revolution was sparking undercurrents of revolutionary thoughts among certain Americans and was adding to George Washington's concern that the authority of the Federal Government might again be tested. Consequently, Washington would become more dependent on Hamilton and other advocates of a stronger Federal Government.

Disturbed that the limits to Federal power, as defined in the Federal Constitution, were being disregarded, **Thomas Jefferson would resign his Cabinet job in December 1793**.

Anthony Wayne Leads Federal Army West to Defend Against Native Uprisings and to Aid the Chickasaw Nation

As mentioned earlier, in November 1791, the 2,000-man Federal army under Arthur St. Clair, while north of the Ohio River, had suffered a horrific defeat, in which 600 men were killed. Well, since that time, the Federal House and Senate had approved George Washington's request for a new army of 2,500 soldiers to be organized and sent to Native American lands north and west of the Ohio River. **Washington had named Anthony Wayne to lead the new army**. Wayne had recruited his men during the summer of 1792 and moved them down the Ohio, occupying existing Federal forts as they progressed, and finally constructing Fort Greenfield in 1793. There, Wayne and many of his men were spending the 1793-94 winter. About this time, being alerted that the **Chickasaws** along the southern Mississippi River were fearful of a major invasion by Creek Nation warriors, **Secretary of War Henry Knox** directed Anthony Wayne to prepare boats loaded with armaments, ammunition and corn to aid the Chickasaws in defending their people and their towns. He was to send these boats, with ample military guards, down the Mississippi to Chickasaw Bluffs (where Memphis now stands) with this message:

"Brothers, your father, [George] Washington, President of the United States, has understood, through [Governor] William Blount, that you are greatly in want of arms, ammunition and corn, and therefore he has taken the earliest opportunity of proving to you his friendship and the desire of being serviceable to you."

And Wayne was instructed to send a few skilled armory mechanics and tools to help the Chickasaws maintain their weaponry. Spanish authorities complained through diplomatic channels that sending arms to the Chickasaw Nation might be viewed as a warlike act toward the Spanish settlements in Louisiana and West Florida. To these concerns, Secretary of State Thomas Jefferson wrote that he denied any intent to incite the Chickasaws to war, even though "the Creeks have now a second time commenced against us a wanton and unprovoked war; and the present one in the face of a recent treaty, and of the most friendly and charitable offices on our part." On the other hand, the Spanish were arming the **Cherokees** per a September order to the new Governor of Pensacola, Louisiana Colony.

In the Future State of Tennessee, Settlers are in Fights with Cherokees and Creeks

During 1793 Tennessee fighters under **John Sevier** invaded the land of the Cherokees south of the **Watauga** settlements, destroyed many **Cherokee towns** and pushed the Cherokees southward into the Smoky Mountains and beyond. By this action, Cherokees were excluded from the eastern part of the future State of Tennessee, save those living within the Smoky Mountains.

Also, 1793 was an especially dangerous year for Cumberland settlers, for Native American attacks on those settlers were escalating. Current historian John Haywood would name 64 killed, one scalped but surviving and 29 wounded but surviving. Among the January victims was Evan Shelby, the brother of the prominent Watauga settlements leader, Isaac Shelby. During the same attack, which took place near where the Red River flows into the Cumberland, the warriors also killed James Harney and a bonded African American. They stole a number of horses as well. Another attack worthy of mention took place in April. About 200 warriors attacked the station at Greenfield and there killed Jarvis and a bonded African American. "The station was saved by the signal bravery of William Neely, William Wilson and William Hall, who killed 2 [warriors] and wounded several others. Neely and Hall had each lost a father and two brothers by the [Native American warriors]." And James Robertson lost another son to Native American attacks during December 1793. James Randle and John Grimes "were killed by Cherokees of the lower towns, on the waters of the Caney Fork, where they had gone to trap for beavers." John Haywood would also name 20 people, mostly women and children, who were being held captive during 1793 in Cherokee and Creek towns. These attacks were made by Creeks and Cherokees from the lower towns. The **Chickasaws** were at peace, and in fact were receiving corn from the Cumberland settlers to compensate for crop failures in the Chickasaw Nation.

1794

Fighting in Northern Ohio Territory between Anthony Wayne's Calvary and the British and their Native warriors

In mid-February 1794, the Spanish Minister assured United States officials that the King "was satisfied that the [Native Americans] had been the aggressors in their wars with the people of **Georgia**, and that he had transmitted instructions to the governors of Louisiana and Florida to give them no assistance." However, the events of this year would show that the people of the Cumberland settlements were to get no relief from Native American raiding parties.

The situation was different along the Ohio River. By the spring of 1794 **Anthony Wayne** believed that the settlements that bordered the Ohio River were secure, and that he was ready to march north. This is when he received his primary strike force: **1,600 mounted riflemen from the new State of Kentucky**. These men were fast and skilled: "as tough fighters as ever chased" a Native American warrior. Anthony Wayne was about to become known to the Native Americans north of the Ohio River as "The chief who never sleeps."

A few months earlier, during November and December 1793, in the French islands of the eastern Caribbean Sea, the British fleet had been seizing American merchant ships that were helping the French war effort by supplying French operations with foodstuffs such as corn, flour and meal. By the end of these actions, British naval officers would have seized a total of about 300 merchant ships and would have condemned half that number. When news of this ongoing naval action reached the Federal Government in Philadelphia, politicians from the northeastern maritime States, led by **Alexander Hamilton**, demanded a declaration of war against Britain. However, cooler heads prevailed and a thirty-day retaliatory embargo was approved as a more appropriate response. Almost simultaneously, the British Government amended its instructions, permitting food shipments to pass and seizing only contraband of war. **George Washington sent John Jay**, the Chief Justice of the Federal Supreme Court, to London as a Special Minister with instructions **to negotiate a settlement of differences**. Jay would arrive from a position of strength, for both he and the British knew that British forces would be unable to beat back a determined invasion of Canada by Anthony Wayne's western forces.

While **Anthony Wayne** was fortifying the north side of the Ohio River, British officials along the Great Lakes were strengthening fortifications along the south side of the Great Lakes in the vicinity of the British settlement at Detroit. Furthermore, British officials were encouraging leaders of the Native American nations that were situated south of the Great Lakes to defend their land. And, they were freely selling, to those Native American nations, guns and ammunition as well. During February of 1794, the British Governor of what would become Canada, Guy Carleton, also known as Lord Dorchester, delivered a speech to a Delegation from the Native American nations that occupied the land between the Ohio River and the Great Lakes. In that speech, Dorchester encouraged the Delegation to believe that the British Government and the European Americans who lived in what would become Canada would help them defend Native American lands against the steady northward advance of the European Americans who lived along the Ohio River. And these Native American Delegates spread the word throughout the Native nations that the British in Canada would be their allies in the struggle to defend their lands. Furthermore, the Canadian British backed up that promise by building a new fort, **Fort Miamis**, about 100 miles southwest of the **major British base at Detroit**.

George Washington viewed the construction of Fort Miamis as an act of British aggression, so he ordered Wayne to lead his men north to Fort Miamis and destroy the place. American destruction of Fort Miamis might trigger war with Britain, but Washington felt compelled to take that risk. So, during the summer of 1794, Wayne led his army to a position just south of Fort Miamis and built an opposing fort he named **Fort Defiance**.

For a while, the **Chickasaw Nation** seemed determined to fight alongside Wayne's Americans. Sixty Chickasaw warriors passed through Nashville in June on the way north to join Wayne's army, and 100 more would head off to do the same in July. But Chickasaw chiefs would recall these to help defend their Nation from a pending Creek attack. On July 11, George Washington praised Chief Piomingo and lesser Chickasaw chiefs who were at Philadelphia on a diplomatic mission, and he thanked them for reinforcing the Federal army north of the Ohio River. Federal officials promised an annual gift of $3,000 worth of Federal aid. On July 21, Washington gave one of the Chickasaw chiefs a commission as a Captain of Militia. That same day, he delivered a written pledge to respect the boundaries of the Chickasaw Nation.

Although Anthony Wayne received Chickasaw military assistance, he failed to persuade the **Native Americans in the Ohio region** to merely take a position of neutrality. So, near the British fort, Miamis, many warriors established a defensive line among trees that had been felled earlier by a tornado. Seeing this, Wayne decided to attack the Native American warriors prior to laying siege to the British fort. During the attack upon the warriors, which occurred on August 20, Wayne's men forced them to flee their cover among the fallen trees. Many ran toward the British fort with Wayne's mounted Kentucky fighters in hot pursuit, but the British refused to shoot at the Americans or to even open the doors and let the warriors run inside the fort.

Governor Carleton's promises to help the Native Americans defend their land became nothing, for the British were not even willing to open the door and let warriors enter their fort. Therefore, by this decision, the British along the Great Lakes avoided triggering a new war between the United States and Great Britain over control of the Great Lakes region. **The British abandoned Fort Miamis without a fight**.

Cumberland Settlers Attack Cherokee Towns South of the Tennessee River

Shortly after the battle outside Fort Miamis, on September 7, a militia force of 550 men who lived in the **future State of Tennessee** set out to retaliate against the **Cherokee Nation for the many attacks suffered by Cumberland settlers.** A few men were from the Watauga settlements, but most were from the Cumberland settlements. Overall command was given to William Whitley. They marched southeast until they came to the Tennessee River, which at the time was three-quarters of a mile wide. They crossed the river during the early morning hours. After gathering their forces, they marched a short distance to the **Cherokee town of Nickajack**. A smaller town called Running Water was nearby. Because the Cherokees had posted no guards or lookouts:

> The Cumberland men "penetrated into the heart of the Nickajack before they were discovered. Nickajack was a small town inhabited by 200 or 300 men and their families. In the town the army killed a considerable number of warriors. They fired upon the [Cherokees] who took to their canoes to make their escape across the river. Men, women and children, all together, were fired upon by a thick and deadly fire, and many of all descriptions perished in the deathful havoc which it made. In the town were found 2 fresh scalps taken at Cumberland, and several that were hung up in the houses as trophies of war. These 2 towns were the principal crossing-places, for the Creeks, over the Tennessee for war against the Cumberland settlements and Kentucky."

Captives revealed that 60 warriors, Cherokees and Creeks, had passed through Nickajack 9 days previously to attack Cumberland settlements, and, 2 nights previously, a scalp dance had been held at Running Water, which was attended by The Bloody Fellow and John Watts along with other Cherokee chiefs from the lower towns. The Cumberland militia took much Spanish gunpowder and lead from the towns. Retaliation attacks of this nature, although more brutal than the attacks suffered by the settlers, seemed to them to be **the only way to discourage attacks** by Cherokee and Creek warriors.

Meanwhile, Whiskey Distillers are Rebelling in Western Pennsylvania

While Anthony Wayne's men were taking land from Native American nations in what would become the State of Ohio, persistent tax collection efforts by **Federal Revenue agents** were producing a **rebellion among whiskey makers** not far away in western Pennsylvania. Federal officials saw this rebellion as a test of Federal Government power. Apparently, after 3 years of collection efforts, the Federal tax on whiskey was still inciting rebellious behavior among many settlers beyond the Blue Ridge Mountains. The most serious rebellion occurred

156

in September 1794 when 2,000 angry Pennsylvanians threatened to attack a Federal garrison at Pittsburgh. But the protestors avoided bloodshed, choosing instead to march around town protesting the Federal whiskey tax. The Governor of Pennsylvania asked the Federal Government for help.

George Washington responded by asking the governments of Pennsylvania, Virginia and Maryland for 15,000 State militiamen. By the first of September, **12,000 militiamen, under "Light Horse Harry" Lee of Virginia**, and accompanied by Alexander Hamilton, arrived in western Pennsylvania to put down the tax protestors. Eager to prove Federal toughness toward western settlers, Hamilton insisted on rounding up some protest leaders and bringing them to trial. Lee's men arrested 20 protestors who were tried in Philadelphia on charges of treason against the Federal Government. Two of the 20 were found guilty, but escaped death by pardons granted by **George Washington**. This was the first time that a Federal President had used force to put down large-scale public protests by groups opposed to the policies of the Federal Government. And, the action strengthened the authority by which Federal revenue agents could demand payment of excise taxes levied by the Federal Government.

After the protesters were subdued, Washington authorized the maintenance of a 2,000-man militia force in western Pennsylvania as a warning to British authorities while **militiamen under Anthony Wayne were driving Native Americans out of the land that would become the State of Ohio.**

John Jay Treaty Establishes Trading Rules and the Northern Boundary along the Great Lakes

As Special Minister to London, **John Jay signed a treaty** with Britain on November 19 and submitted it to the Washington Administration, which put it before the Federal Senate. Jay's treaty evoked considerable anger from the southern exporting States, because it prohibited transporting molasses, sugar, coffee or cotton in American vessels, either departing seaports in The States or British seaports in the Caribbean. (This is not a misprint: the treaty, as submitted by Jay for ratification did prohibit the transport of the named items by American sailors.) **But the treaty did cede to the Federal Government land south of the Great Lakes upon which the British had previously built fortifications.** It authorized 2 commissions to fix boundaries between British land that would become Canada and the Federal land that would become Federal Territory, and eventually new States. One commission would establish the northwest boundary. Another commission would establish the northeast boundary. Other provisions of the treaty dealt with reimbursements for commercial damage claims.

Cumberland Settlers Continue Suffering from Native Raids

For the year 1794, current historian John Haywood would record the names of 66 Cumberland settlers killed, 12 wounded but surviving and 4 captured by Creek and Cherokee warriors. The Creeks had killed most of them. But, he advises that many more were killed without a surviving record of their demise. For example, on July 6 Isaac Mayfield was killed by [Native Americans] within 5 miles of Nashville. He was standing sentinel for his son-in-law while the latter hoed his corn, and got the first fire at the [warriors], but there being from 12 to 15 of them, and they very near him, he could not escape. Eight balls penetrated his body. He was scalped, a new English bayonet was thrust through his face, and two bloody tomahawks left near his mangled body. He was the sixth person of his name who had been killed or captured by the Creeks or Cherokees." Thomas Bledsoe was killed near his house. "His father, brother, uncle, and cousin had all suffered under the tomahawk and scalping knife." A month later, 50 warriors attacked the families of the Titsworth brothers, Isaac and John, killing 7, and wounding one, while taking 6 prisoners.

Cherokee Chief Bob Benge Killed – Susannah Rescued – A Family Story

During this year of 1794, **tragedy also struck a relative of mine**, yes, an ancestral relative of mine, **Susannah Carmack Livingston**, who was living with her husband, Henry Livingston, near where the Cumberland River flowed out of Kentucky, in what would become Overton County, Tennessee. She had been married only a few weeks when **Bob Benge, a Cherokee chief**, and his warriors set upon the family. The warriors killed one of the men and took Susannah prisoner, but her husband, Henry Livingston, either got away or was away from the place when the attack occurred. Henry joined neighbors in a posse and set out to track down Bob Benge and his band of raiders. Finally, the posse spotted Benge from a point where he was unaware of their presence. At the time Benge happened to be walking beside Susannah, talking to her in English, for he spoke the language rather well. Benge was telling her how he planned to sell her into slavery or force her to become his wife. At that moment a precisely aimed bullet struck Benge from 180 yards away and **Susannah was quickly rescued**. The marksman was Vincent Hobbs, a member of the posse. Later Hobbs would receive a fine gun from the Governor of Virginia as a reward for killing Bob Benge. But, for the moment, Hobbs celebrated by scalping the fallen Cherokee as he lay bleeding to death from the gunshot wound. **Susannah Carmack Livingston was a sister to Margery Carmack Grymes, my 3-greats grandmother**.

1795

United States Sign John Jay Treaty, Less Shipping Restrictions – Now the French are Mad

The Federal Senate struck from John Jay's treaty the restriction that only British ships could transport molasses, sugar, coffee and cotton. Then it considered the balance of the treaty, approving it by a close vote on June 25, 1795. **George Washington signed the treaty** on August 14. On April 30, 1796, the Federal House would appropriate the necessary funds to finance the commissions required to define the boundaries and to arbitrate the commercial claims. The Federal Government had avoided a new war with the British Government and had gained settlement of its northern boundary with what would become Canada. **However, the French Government became immediately furious** that its former ally had signed a treaty with the British Government and retaliated by sending home the American Minister to France, **James Monroe**. This forced George Washington to fill the job with a new man. He chose Thomas Pinckney's brother, Charles. Then, on July 2, the French Navy and privateers would begin **attacking American** marine commerce. So, American marine shippers, having extricated themselves from British attacks, would next suffer French attacks, and those would be more vicious.

Native Nations Agree to Give up Ohio to Western Settlers

In June, in what would become the **State of Ohio**, a great land-transfer Conference was opened at Fort Greenville. During the following several weeks, the Conference was attended by more than 1,100 Representatives from the **Native American nations** that possessed land between the Ohio River and the Great Lakes. Leaders of various Native American nations grudgingly agreed to shift their boundaries westward to vacate a vast region of land west and north of the Ohio River. The land-transfer treaty was consummated on August 3 by the signatures of Federal officials and many Native American chiefs. In exchange for a pledge that European Americans would refrain from settling on remaining Native American land, the Native American chiefs agreed to give the Federal Government uncontested possession of most of the **land that would become the State of Ohio**. About 15 years would pass before Native American warriors would again feel compelled to fight in defense of their shrunken national boundaries.

Tennessee Territory Moves toward Statehood

Representatives to the Territorial Assembly of the Territory South of the Ohio River gathered in late June to call for a census to determine if there was sufficient population to **apply for Tennessee statehood**. And, by the end of July, the wagon road from Knoxville to Nashville was completed. There was also a completed wagon road through the Appalachian Mountains by way of the French Broad River. So, wagons of 2,000 pounds gross weight were able to travel from Georgia, South Carolina, North Carolina and Virginia to Knoxville, and from that town to Nashville. A great migration was beginning and sufficient population to validate Tennessee statehood did seem to be in place or near at hand. And the census, as certified in November, would show the **population to be 77,262 persons**, well above the minimum requirement of 60,000. At that point, Territory Governor William Blount would call for election of Delegates to a **Constitutional Convention** to meet at Knoxville on January 11, 1796.

Land West of Georgia Becomes More Available for Settlement

In 1795, the **Georgia State Government moved to complete the sale of the vast land that lay between its western State line and the Mississippi River**. Ownership disputes in 1789 had prevented the consummation of previous sales contracts, but the newly ratified Eleventh Amendment to the Federal Constitution seemed to clarify this in that it ensured that the Federal Government would not be involved in litigation involving a State Government and citizens from another State or a foreign nation. Four new land companies came forward and contracted to buy, at a price of **1.5 cents per acre**, nearly all the land between the western Georgia State line and the Mississippi River, and between the southern Tennessee Territory border and Spanish West Florida. This included the land previously contracted, but not paid for in 1789. "Prominent men all over [the States] made investments in the various companies, and the buying and selling caused great excitement in many places, including Boston where tidy sums were made in the business."

Thomas Pinckney's Treaty with Spain Sets Southern Boundary and Opens the Port of New Orleans for American Trade

During October, **Thomas Pinckney**, "after a long course of tedious and very protracted negotiation," persuaded the Spanish Government to accept a treaty that confirmed the southern boundary of the United States and **ensured the free navigation of the Mississippi River** all the way into the Gulf of Mexico. **Pinckney, a South Carolinian,** had moved from the job of Minister to England to the job of Envoy Extraordinary to Spain, with the clear mission to persuade the Spanish Government to agree to free navigation of the Mississippi and a proper boundary between the Spanish Colonies and the Territory South of the Ohio River. Many years previously, in 1785, John Jay of New York, as Secretary of Foreign Affairs for the Continental Congress, had, in 1785, been the first man assigned the job of negotiating a treaty with Don Diego Gardoqui, the Spanish ambassador to The States. But, at that time, the Continental Congress was politically weak and western pioneers suspected that John Jay held little enthusiasm for increasing the political and economic power of the vast Ohio-Cumberland-Tennessee-Mississippi region at the expense of the Atlantic region. **John Jay had made no progress**. After the inauguration of George Washington, the job had been handed, in 1792, to two American diplomats who were already living in Europe, but they had made no progress either. Frankly, gaining agreement during those earlier years had been nearly impossible because of the French Revolution and a defensive alliance joining England and Spain. But, in July 1795, Spain had rescinded the alliance with England and signed a peace treaty with France. This placed Spain in a weaker position with regard to defending West Florida and Louisiana against feared aggression by western settlers, who were inclined to take matters into their own hands. To a great extent the military aggressiveness of Tennesseans convinced the **Spanish Government to agree to Pinckney's treaty terms** for land south of the future State of Tennessee. So, Pinckney was able to win the agreement of Gardoqui and consummate the treaty in the same year. The **Spanish-American treaty** was signed at San Lorenzo, Spain, on October 27. The Federal Senate would gladly and unanimously approve it. Pinckney's treaty set the southern boundary of United States territory at 31 degrees latitude, thereby eliminating Spain's claim of north to 32 degrees and 28 minutes; pledged each country to prevent from raiding the other's territory all Native Americans who lived within its respective territories; and allowed American exporters and importers to use the **seaport of New Orleans** via an arrangement termed a "place of deposit." This treaty would prove to be of great economic benefit to settlers in the Ohio, Cumberland and Tennessee valleys.

So, by the summer of 1795, the **Washington Administration** had secured for The United States all the western territory that had been granted by the British Government in the 1783 treaty that had recognized their independence. The Washington Administration had achieved this important goal by the combination of skillful diplomacy in Europe and military assertiveness on the northwestern and the southwestern frontier. And Washington had wisely taken advantage of European military weakness caused by revolutions and wars on that continent.

Chickasaw Nation Repulses Creek Attack – Looks to Better Times

There had been great concern since January over **a potential war between the Creek Nation and the Chickasaw Nation**. In mid-October the **major Creek attack was launched**. "About 1,000 Creeks [came] to break up the Chickasaw Nation. They brought [European American] people with them, and drums and ammunition for a long siege. A great number of them were on horseback." They attacked Big Town, a Chickasaw town defended by 200 Chickasaw warriors. Despite the 5-to-1 Creek advantage, the Chickasaws "put them to the rout," and captured all their blankets, spare clothing, reserve ammunition, kettles and their provisions. The Chickasaws suffered only 7 killed compared to 26 Creeks killed. With negotiating help from William Blount and **James Robertson**, peace was afterward secured between the Creeks and the Chickasaws. The Chickasaws were much better prepared for war.

Some had fought in the Federal army and surely learned much in the process. And, in April, the Washington Administration had delivered to the Chickasaws "500 stands of arms, powder, lead, vermilion, whisky, corn, and other articles" to aid their defense. James Robertson and other Cumberland settlers had traveled to the Chickasaw Nation as well to provide advice and encouragement.

Current historian John Haywood would record the names of Cumberland settlers who suffered under attacks by Creek and Cherokee warriors during 1795. The list was much shorter than in previous years, for peace predominated. Haywood would record only 7 killed, 10 wounded but surviving, and 1 either killed or captured.

1796

Settlers in Tennessee Organized a State Government and Demand Fast Congressional Approval

During January 1796, Delegates gathered at Knoxville to draft a State Constitution to be submitted to the Federal House and Senate as part of their **application for statehood**. **Andrew Jackson, a Delegate from Nashville**, reportedly recommended the name **"Tennessee,"** and it was adopted. The voting requirements written into the Constitution gave almost every man access to the polls. "Any man could vote upon 6 months' residence in a county, a [landowner] upon one day's residence; the owner of 200 acres was eligible to the Legislature, of 500 acres to the governorship." As it adjourned on February 7, the Convention informed the Federal House and Senate that it would consider secession and union with Spain if it did not grant statehood to Tennessee within 49 days. Why the urgency? It was because Tennesseans knew that politicians from Massachusetts and neighboring States would **seek to delay Tennessee statehood** until after the next elections to help ensure that John Adams succeeded George Washington as the next Federal President.

Federal Government Acts to Control Boundaries between Natives and Settlers

In April, the Federal Government enacted legislation that funded Federal trading posts, which were to be set up along the boundaries between Federal Territory land and Native American land. In recognition of Native American genetic susceptibility to alcoholism, these government-operated stores were prohibited from selling whiskey. The following month legislation was adopted that firmly established boundary lines between open Federal Territory, which was available to European American settlers, and prohibited land, which belonged to Native American nations. No European American was allowed to purchase land within any Native American nation. In addition to the $50 Federal trader's license fee, this legislation forced each trader who dealt with Native Americans to purchase a $1,000 bond to guarantee good behavior. By these strengthened laws, the Federal Government was striving to do what the British Government had attempted during colonial days: to draw a boundary line between European American settlements and Native American land. Everyone expected this boundary line to creep westward as more native land was taken, but the intent was to place control of westward expansion in the Federal Government, which would periodically rewrite Federal treaties with the various Native American nations.

New Federal Land Purchase Ordinance Raises Price of Western Land to $1,280 for the minimum 640 Acre Farm Site

In the following month of May, the Federal Government updated fees and procedures for private purchase of land in most of the National Territories. Land that had belonged to the original 13 States, such as Virginia's Kentucky and North Carolina's Tennessee, remained outside of this land sale program. As with the earlier Land Ordinance of 1785, land was to be surveyed in rectangular plots of 640 acres. The price was raised to **$2 per acre**, with one half due upon purchase, and the remainder due the following year. A buyer had to purchase at least **640 acres**. Since buyers had to pay down $640 for the opportunity to build a farm upon virgin land, poor immigrants and poor manufacturing workers were, for the most part, excluded. Typical purchasers were farmers who sold small, established farms east of the mountains and took that money to buy large tracts of virgin land west of the mountains. Under the leadership of Alexander Hamilton, **politicians from the New York-to-Massachusetts region had succeeded in making National Territory land prohibitively expensive for most people**, because they wanted to prevent low-paid manufacturing workers from leaving the employment of industrialists, for that would have driven up manufacturing wages.

Tennessee Granted Statehood

Although the 49-day deadline had passed, the Federal House and Senate granted Tennessee statehood on June 1, 1796. Tennesseans would elect John Sevier as Governor and William Blount and William Cocke as Federal Senators. Politicians from Massachusetts and neighboring States had decided to grant Tennessee statehood before the fall elections. Perhaps the threat to secede and join Spain had scared them a bit. Tennessee statehood increased the number of Senators from Maryland southward to 18, the same number from north of Maryland. So, this new State balanced the power of the northern and southern sections of the nation. **John Sevier** had already been elected Tennessee Governor and William Blount and **William Cocke** had already been named Federal Senators. Soon after statehood was granted, voters in Tennessee elected their State Legislators and their first Federal Representative, who was **Andrew Jackson**, of Nashville. In November, Andrew Jackson would bid Rachel goodbye and set out for Washington City. After the House would adjourn March 1797, Jackson would decline to run for reelection.

President George Washington, of Virginia, Says Farewell, Encourages Advancement of his Vice President, John Adams, of Massachusetts

Sometime in early 1796, **George Washington** had announced his firm intention to retire on March 4, 1797, which would be the end of his second term. Later, he had endorsed his Vice President, **John Adams** of Massachusetts for the job. Fellow Federalists, particularly those from the northern States, enthusiastically concurred. Adams was opposed by Virginia's **Thomas Jefferson**, who enjoyed considerable support from the southern States. Washington issued his farewell address long before his term was complete, so that no one would possibly try to talk him into a third term during the fall election season. Excerpts from his address concerning foreign policy follow:

"Observe good faith and justice towards all nations: cultivate peace and harmony with all. . . Against the insidious wiles of foreign influence, I conjure you to believe me, fellow citizens, the jealousy of a free people ought to be constantly awake, since history and experience prove that foreign influence is one of the most baneful foes of a republican Government. . . The great rule of conduct for us, in regard to foreign Nations, is, in extending our commercial relations, to have with them as little political connection as possible. So far as we have already formed engagements, let them be fulfilled with perfect good faith. Here let us stop."

Bloody African Revolt on Western Hispaniola Kills or Drives Out all Whites – Will Eventually Become an African Race Country

By the end of 1796, **Toussaint L'Ouverture** had made immense progress as the leader of a revolt of bonded African Americans in the large **Caribbean island of Hispaniola**. He had succeeded in making the region's bonded African Americans independent and had assumed the title of French Governor-General, for he was remaining loyal to the Government of France. Ruling over the western half of the island, which was the French-speaking half, he would, over the next 4 years, force some British invasion troops to withdraw and would defeat a rival group of island revolutionaries of mixed African-European descent.

John Adams of Massachusetts is Elected Second President of The United States and Thomas Jefferson, of Virginia, is Elected Vice President

Concurring with the recommendation of retiring President Washington, of Virginia, **John Adams, of Massachusetts, is elected President**. Secretary of State Thomas Jefferson had resigned to campaign for the President's job, but had not been successful.

We now conclude the eight-year era of the George Washington Administration, the administration of the man who shares my ancestry, the important Virginian who led many Nation Builders. Reflect on the accomplishments of Southern families during these eight years.

Southern Families had "Made America" all the way to the Mississippi River in the **new States of Kentucky and Tennessee**. The stage was set to move westward from Georgia toward the settlement of the future States of Alabama and Mississippi. Spanish control over Louisiana, East Florida and West Florida was now weaker. On subsequent pages of this history, Southern families would be moving further westward. During the latter pages, we will see them settling Mexican Texas and creating the vast Republic of Texas.

Chapter 10 — March 1797 to February 1801: The States during the John Adams Administration

Before resuming the narrative history, I have inserted a summary of the 1796 elections and the organization of the John Adams Administration.

A lawyer and a politician, **John Adams of Massachusetts** was elected to succeed George Washington as Federal President. Adams had served under Washington as Vice President the previous 8 years. Like Washington, John Adams was a Federalist. Federalist politicians had defeated Democrat Party candidate Thomas Jefferson of Virginia for the office of President, but had failed to prevent Jefferson from winning the Vice-President job.

Adams was the son of John Adams, a farmer and leather craftsman in Braintree, now Quincy, Massachusetts. Adams' great-great-grandfather, Henry Adams, had immigrated from Somersetshire, England, to Braintree, Massachusetts, a little before 1640. Adams' mother was Susanna Bolyston Adams, supposedly also from the vicinity of Braintree. John and Susanna had 4 children to live to maturity: Abigail who married William Smith (had a successful career in government and political office); John Quincy, a lawyer who had a successful career in diplomatic service and politics and would become the sixth Federal President; Charles, a lawyer who died an alcoholic at age 30; and Thomas, a lawyer in Philadelphia of modest means.

John Adams grew up in Braintree and attended Harvard College, graduating at age 19. He then studied law at a Worcester lawyer's office for 3 years before being admitted to the Massachusetts bar in 1758 at age 23. At the age of 29, Adams married Abigail Smith of Weymouth, Massachusetts. Abigail's father was a minister and her mother was of the prominent Quincy family. Never particularly active in an organized church, Adams professed the religious beliefs of the Unitarian Church.

Adams was a defense lawyer for British troops after they were charged with firing on and killing 3 members of a taunting mob in Boston in 1770 -- a politically unpopular task. His political career began with his election to the Massachusetts Colony Legislature (1770-1774). Next, he was elected to the Continental Congress (1774-1777). The Continental Congress appointed him a member of the Paris peace commission (1778-1779), but he returned home because his personality conflicted with Benjamin Franklin. Next, Adams became a Delegate to the Massachusetts State Constitutional Convention (1779-1780). Then, George Washington appointed Adams Minister to the Netherlands (1780-1782). Then, Adams was asked to rejoin the Paris treaty team (1782-1783), which was in the final stages of negotiations. There, he supported the hardline position requiring Britain to concur that the United States western boundary extended to the Mississippi River. French allies were not permitted to participate in those final treaty negotiations. Next, Adams was appointed Minister to Britain (1785-1788). After returning to The States, Adams was elected the Federation's first Vice President (1789-1797).

Thomas Jefferson had resigned from George Washington's Cabinet to pursue his own election to Federal President. Jefferson campaigned against what he and his supporters considered excessive Federal Government power. Jefferson is considered the founder of the precursor to today's Democratic Party. Aaron Burr of New York was Jefferson's running mate. William DeGregorio would summarize this **most unusual election** as follows:

"The Jeffersonians, so long frustrated with having to mount their opposition to Federalism without appearing to offend the venerable Washington, charged into this, the nation's first real presidential campaign, eager to bloody Adams. Pamphleteers for both sides worked overtime smearing the opposition: Adams was characterized as a despot who longed for American monarchy and distrusted the people. Jefferson, the Federalists charged, was a demagogue, preying on people's fears to further his own political fortunes. Stripped of their excess, the 2 characterizations pointed up the real issues separating the candidates. Adams distrusted the masses. He favored life terms for the Senate as a check on the popularly elected House. Government, he believed, is best left to the pros, the politicians, and the bureaucrats. He vowed to [further strengthen the role of the Federal Government]. Jefferson, on the other hand, advocated [the movement] of power from the Federal Government to the States. He rode the wave of popular fears of insidious Royalism, but he genuinely shared those fears and was not merely preying on them to win an election. In foreign affairs, Adams condemned the French Revolution as mobocracy; Jefferson, while wincing at its excesses, applauded the effort to overthrow the French royal family. Jefferson still saw Britain as America's principal enemy; Adams considered France the greater threat. French Minister to the United States, Pierre Adet, campaigned openly for Jefferson. George Washington made it clear that he preferred Adams as his successor. The endorsement was crucial for Adams in this close election, because many still revered Washington's opinions. The Federal bureaucracy, every important member of which owed his job to Washington, also lined up behind Adams. Alexander Hamilton, although a Federalist, privately opposed Adams, because he was too independent, too unpredictable to control. [Hamilton] therefore hatched a scheme to deny the presidency to both Adams and Jefferson and deliver it to the [candidate for Federalist Vice President], Thomas Pinckney. This maneuver was possible because at that time each elector cast 2 votes without distinguishing which was for President and which was for Vice President. Whoever received the most votes became President; the man with the next highest total became Vice President. By inducing southern States electors to vote for Pinckney and anyone else except Adams, and trusting that loyal Federalists in [Massachusetts and neighboring States] would vote for Adams and Pinckney, Hamilton hoped to make Pinckney President. However, the plan backfired when New Englanders learned of it and deliberately reduce Pinckney's total in the region. Although the effect of Hamilton's plot was to narrow Adams' margin of victory, it also dragged [Federalist candidate] Pinckney down to third place behind [Democrat candidate] Jefferson. Ironically, then, Hamilton indirectly helped his old enemy win the [office of Vice President], a springboard Jefferson [would use] to good advantage 4 years later."

Adams' Cabinet retained some of Washington's men. Timothy Pickering, of Massachusetts, remained as Secretary of State until he was fired for conspiring with Hamilton to subvert Administration policy. John Marshall, of Virginia, served the remaining 2 years. Oliver Wolcott, a lawyer from Connecticut, remained as Secretary of the Treasury until he resigned a few months prior to the end of the Adams Administration, while protesting that Adams had become too soft toward strong Federalism. James McHenry of Maryland remained as Secretary of War until he too was forced out for conspiring with Hamilton. Samuel Dexter of Massachusetts took over the job until he moved to Treasury just prior to the end of the Adams Administration. Charles Lee, a Virginia lawyer, remained as Attorney General and remained loyal to Adams all 4 years. Benjamin Stoddert of Maryland became Navy Secretary, a newly created Cabinet job. Stoddert formalized the United States Marine Corps, expanded the fleet and established shipyards at Norfolk, Portsmouth and Brooklyn.

Federalists slightly increased their domination of the Senate with a 20 to 13 majority and strengthened their control in the House to 58 to 48. During the second 2 years, the Senate remained about the same with a 19 to 13 Federalist majority, but the Federalists gained impressive strength in the House by building their majority to a whopping 64 to 42.

John Adams had less faith in the good intentions of the political majority than perhaps most Americans, as revealed in the following quotation attributed to him. Perhaps Adams foresaw the rise of the Northern States Republican Party (the majority) and its war against the Confederacy (the minority):

> "The people, when they have been unchecked, have been as unjust, tyrannical, brutal, barbarous, and cruel, as any king or senate possessed of uncontrollable power. The majority has eternally, and without one exception, usurped over the rights of the minority."

BIG NEWS: No States were added to the Federation during the Adams Administration.

The more significant events involving African Americans during the 4 years of the John Adams Administration will now be presented. The Georgia State Constitution stipulated the punishment for maiming or killing a bonded African American must be the same as if the victim were a European American. In 1799, the New York State Government established a mandatory program for gradually making bonded African Americans independent (they represented 3.5% of the New York population in 1800). The 1800 census counted 995,022 people of noticeable African descent in America. This represented a 32% increase over the 1790 count, and 19.6% of the total population – a slight increase from the 19.3% recorded ten years previously. Since the 1790 census, the population of **Independent African Americans** had grown by 91% to 61,575 in the southern States and by 70% to 45,835 in the northern States. African Americans represented a barely significant 1.6% of the population of the northeastern States (Massachusetts and neighboring States). Gabriel Prosser, a bonded African American from Henrico County, Virginia, organized a revolt by hundreds of fellow African Americans, but the effort fizzled before it got underway. Virginia authorities captured, tried and hanged about 30 conspirators. Apparently, the successful revolt in Haiti was inspiring occasional foolish efforts in The States. And fear of revolts was encouraging restraints. The South Carolina Government forbid importation of bonded Africans from outside The States, and limited importation from sister States to 2 per owner, but this restriction would be relaxed in 1802. The City of Boston deported 240 independent African Americans who had moved into Massachusetts from sister States. On the other hand, importation of bonded Africans from outside The States into Louisiana was a growing business.

This concludes the summary of the 1796 elections and the organization of the John Adams Administration.

The Narrative History Resumes – March 1797

President John Adams and Diplomatic Efforts

John Adams named a team of 3 ministers to negotiate peace with the **French Government**. The situation in 1797 was very troubling because the French were succeeding at conquering all of western Europe and, under the leadership of Foreign Minister **Charles Maurice de Talleyrand**, were making plans to retake most of North America – the vast heartland between the Appalachian and the Rocky Mountains. The 3 ministers werc **C. C. Pinckney**, **John Marshall** and Elbridge Gerry. Arriving in Paris in October 1797, these men were snubbed by Talleyrand and handed off to 3 French subordinates, Hottenguer, Bellamy and Hauteval, who would be referred to as Messrs. X, Y and Z in later diplomatic reports. The Frenchmen demanded that, before negotiations could begin, the United States Government pay $250,000 in bribes and, also, purchase, with several million dollars, some worthless Dutch bonds. Pinckney, Marshall and Gerry refused and **they eventually gave up** and returned to The States. Meanwhile, the Adams Administration made preparations for war and for suppressing a potential insurrection movement.

Andrew Jackson is briefly in the United States Senate

Andrew Jackson returned to Washington in late November 1797 to fill the **Federal Senate** seat vacated by William Blount. The Senate had impeached Blount during the previous session because of his advocacy of a controversial military venture: the incitement of Creek and Cherokee warriors to join British forces in a conquest of Spain's West Florida. Fellow Senators considered this international intrigue "a high misdemeanor." As he departed Nashville, Jackson wrote to his wife's brother-in-law that he had left Rachel "bathed in tears."

Financial difficulties would prompt Jackson to return to his farm in May 1798 and there submit his resignation from the Federal Senate. He believed he could not afford to sit in the Federal Senate until he had restored his farm and investments to financial health. Toward that goal, Jackson would purchase one of the new cotton engines, called cotton gins for short, and would confirm that the valuable invention did the work of 40 people. He would also build a distillery at his farm and, in partnership with Thomas Watson, would open a mercantile store on the place. But Jackson would not refrain from public life for long. In October, he would accept appointment to the regional **Tennessee Superior Court**. And, he would sit on the Tennessee Supreme Court when he gathered with other Superior Court Judges for that purpose.

1798

Is the Adams Administration Promoting the Massachusetts Culture? – Naturalization Law, Alien Act and Sedition Act

During 1798, the Federal Government enacted 3 laws aimed at suppressing potential insurrection. **The Naturalization Law** reduced the danger from political opposition by newly arrived immigrants. Instead of a 5-year wait to gain citizenship, new immigrants would face a 14-year wait. It was obvious that Federalist political leaders merely wanted to exclude immigrants from the polls as long as possible because the vast majority were inclined to vote for Democratic Party candidates.

The Alien Act permitted the Adams Administration to deport anyone it believed to pose a danger to national interests.

The Sedition Act, in the words of historian Fred Welborn, "made it a high misdemeanor, punishable by fine and imprisonment, for any persons to conspire against [Federal Government laws], or against [Federal Government] officers in the performance of their duties." It allowed Federal officials to fine and imprison 2 or more people gathered in political protest. Furthermore, the Sedition Act stipulated that it was a crime for anyone to write or publish "any false, scandalous and malicious" statements that criticized the Federal Government, the Federal House or Senate or the President. Although an accused person would be able to offer a defense in court, before a jury of his peers, he was prohibited from bringing before the court those Federal officials that had accused him of writing or publishing allegedly criminal statements.

Senators and Representatives who were aligned with the newly emerged **Democratic Party** protested vehemently against all 3 Acts, and flatly declared that the Alien Act and the Sedition Act **violated the Federal Constitution** – obviously in violation of the Bill of Rights Amendments.

House and Senate Establish Mississippi Territory

On April 7, the Federal House and Senate established **Mississippi Territory**.

This action asserted Federal supremacy over State Governments with regard to ownership of western territories. At that time, most of the land in Mississippi Territory belonged to the land companies that had purchased the land from the Georgia State Government in 1795. And much of the stock of these land companies belonged to **wealthy people in Boston**, **New York**, **Philadelphia** and other banking and investment centers in the northeastern States. Negotiators from the Federal Government and the Georgia State Government would agree four years into the future, in 1802, for the Federal Government to pay the Georgia Government **$1,250,000** in compensation for taking the western lands. But, stockholders of the various land companies would insist on much more money than that as compensation for their investments. Investors in land west of Georgia, most of them residing in the northeastern States, would eventually, 12 years later, in 1814, squeeze from the Federal Treasury a payment of **$8,000,000** – over 6 times the payment received by the Georgia State Government.

Adams and Hamilton Differ on French Foreign Policy

President John Adams created an **American Navy Department** and the House and Senate authorized additional funds for the American Navy. Privateers were contracted to capture French armed naval vessels. Increased funding was authorized for the army. The most prominent champion of the military buildup was **Alexander Hamilton**, who, at one point, advocated forming a military alliance and declaring war against France. Hamilton wanted to combine the British and United States navies with a multinational army made up of all North American and South American nations. The objective would be to drive the French out of North America, South America and the Caribbean and then divide the spoils. He figured the British would gain the French Caribbean islands and The States would gain Florida and Louisiana. But John Adams could not be convinced to launch a war with France. He decided to send a new foreign minister to Paris to make another attempt at negotiations. Adams would name William Vans Murray, of Maryland, as Minister to France on February 18, 1799, and later redefined the mission as another team effort by adding Oliver Ellsworth, of Connecticut, and William Davie, of North Carolina. Departure would be delayed for several months by political disputes between the Hamilton forces, which sought war, and the Adams forces, which sought to negotiate. **Napoleon Bonaparte** would be in charge of the French Government by the time this new 3-man Delegation arrived in Paris in March 1800. But, Charles Maurice de Talleyrand would still be Foreign Minister and still busily at work with plans to retake North America between the Appalachian Mountains and the Rocky Mountains.

John Adams made major changes in his Cabinet to rid himself of men eager for war with France. In May 1800, he dismissed his Secretary of War, James McHenry, and his Secretary of State, Timothy Pickering, both being men who had been supporting Alexander Hamilton in his advocacy of an aggressive Federal Government. So, after May of 1800, Adams found it much easier to oppose Hamilton without having to oppose a large percentage of his Cabinet members as well.

Kentucky and Virginia Outlaw Alien and Sedition Acts

By November, the Naturalization, Alien and Sedition Acts were **inciting a revolt in some States**. The **Kentucky State Legislature,** by an almost unanimous vote, declared that the Alien and Sedition Acts violated the Federal Constitution, and were therefore "void and of no force" within the boundaries of Kentucky. Since the Federal Constitution limited the Federal Government's powers to a restricted list, and did not exclude a State from interpreting the constitutionality of a federal law, the political leaders in the Kentucky State Government concluded that their State Government should justifiably interpret the Federal Constitution. Just as any schoolboy of today would conclude after reading the Federal Constitution and those 2 Federal Acts, the Kentucky Legislators found the Alien and Sedition Acts in violation, and thereby void in Kentucky. This was the first major expression of State Sovereignty within the United States. **The Kentucky resolution:**

"Resolved, That the several States composing the United States of America are not united on the principle of unlimited submission to their [Federal] Government; but that, by compact, under the style and title of a Constitution of the United States, and of amendments thereto, they constituted a [Federal] Government for special purposes, delegated to that Government certain definite powers, reserving, each State to itself, the residuary mass of right to their own self-government; and that when-so-ever the [Federal] Government assumes undelegated powers, its acts are unauthoritative, void, and of no force; that to this compact each State acceded as a State, and is an integral party; that this [Federal] Government, created by this compact, was not made the exclusive or final judge of the extent of the powers delegated to itself, since that would have made its discretion, and not the [Federal] Constitution, the measure of its powers; but that, as in all other cases of compact among parties having no common judge, each party has as equal right to judge for itself, as well of infractions as of the mode and measure of redress."

During December, **James Madison** drafted a similar resolution and pushed it through the **Virginia State Legislature**.

1799

Late in the following year, in November 1799, the Kentucky State Legislature passed a second set of resolutions that reaffirmed that the Alien and Sedition Acts were void within the

169

boundaries of that State. And this set of resolutions went further to affirm that a State had the authority to judge the constitutionality of a federal law and declare it void if in violation. The 1799 Kentucky resolutions declared, "a nullification, by those sovereignties, of all unauthorized acts done under color of that instrument, is the rightful remedy." **Nullification!**

This declaration meant that the government of a State, being sovereign, could itself identify any Federal Act that was invalid under the restrictions of the Federal Constitution. And it declared that "nullification," within the boundaries of Kentucky, was the rightful remedy concerning any Federal law judged to be in violation of the Federal Constitution.

A few years into the future politicians in **Massachusetts** and neighboring States would cite the **same State Sovereignty principle** during a political movement aimed at restricting Federal power.

In 1830, the **South Carolina State Government** would find that **excessively high Federal import taxes violated the Federal Constitution**, because, being at such high tax rates, those taxes were designed to economically punish consumers in the agricultural States in order to enrich factory owners in manufacturing States – not to collect revenue for operating the Federal Government.

1800

Adams Administration Arrests Many Writers and Publishers

By early 1800, the **Adams Administration had arrested about 25 writers and publishers** for violations against the Sedition Act. Of these, 10 were convicted – all of these being newspapermen who supported the Democratic Party. Thomas Cooper, one of the 10, was fined $400 and imprisoned for 6 months for criticizing some Adams judicial appointments. Another editor was sentenced for expressing a wish that the wad of a cannon, which had been fired in salute to John Adams, "had struck him in the rear bulge of the breeches." A third was sentenced for writing that John Adams displayed an "unbounded thirst for ridiculous pomp, foolish adulation, and a selfish avarice." But, Adams, Hamilton, and other Federalists would be punished for abusing the liberties assured to every citizen by the Federal Constitution. The Federalist Party would be defeated by the new Democratic Party, and the **Democratic Party's first elected President, Thomas Jefferson, would pardon all who remained in jail because of the Sedition Act.** Under Democrat leadership, the Federal Government would also refund most of the fines. The Federalist Party would thereafter decline into oblivion.

France is Gaining Control Over Vast Louisiana Territory

On September 30, at Paris, France, the 3-man American Delegation, consisting of Oliver Ellsworth, William Vans Murray and William Davie, signed a treaty with the French Government that released the French from any obligations to pay for any war damages to the American Government or to American citizens that had occurred from 1793 through the signing date. In return, the French agreed to formally void all past mutual defense and commercial treaties. **So, the 1800 treaty with France wiped the slate clean, removing all old treaties and claims for war damages**.

The next day, the French Government signed a treaty with the Spanish Government, which forced Spain to cede to France its ownership of Louisiana. That was big! So, the day after the French wiped the slate clean, thereby releasing Americans from future obligations to participate in European wars, she became a dangerous and likely aggressive neighbor to the south and west of Tennessee and Kentucky.

Thomas Jefferson, of Virginia, is Elected President of the United States

The Administration of John Adams of Massachusetts was a **short four-year event** in American history that differed remarkably from the eight years at the helm by Virginian George Washington and the twenty-four subsequent years of four Presidents from Virginia. In all, a Virginian had and would lead the United States for 32 of the first 36 years of its existence. Aaron Burr of New York State was elected Vice President.

The past four-year history did not tell the story of the Nation Builders. Those four years told the story of the Northern Culture and its efforts to block progress by the Nation Builders. **John Adams is now behind us.** Those four years are behind us.

Thomas Jefferson will be successfully pressing forward the goals of the Nation Builders.

Sit back and enjoy this happy and meaningful race forward as "Southern Families Make America."

Chapter 11 — March 1801 to February 1805: The States during the First Thomas Jefferson Administration

Before resuming the narrative history, I have inserted a summary of the 1800 elections and the organization of the first Thomas Jefferson Administration.

Virginia lawyer and politician **Thomas Jefferson, a Democrat,** was elected over incumbent John Adams, who ran for reelection on the Federalist Party ticket. Thomas was the son of Peter Jefferson, a locally prominent farmer, surveyor, militia leader and politician. His mother was Jane Randolph who immigrated to America with her parents as a child. Jefferson was raised on a Virginia farm, but took to school and grew up to practice law. He soon gave priority to politics. He held elected office in the Virginia Colony Legislature, in the First Continental Congress (where he wrote the Declaration of Independence), in the Virginia House of Delegates, as Governor of Virginia during the Defense of Independence, in the Second Continental Congress, as Minister to France, as Federal Secretary of State, and as Vice President under John Adams. He had no military experience. As founder of what was then called the Democratic-Republican Party, Jefferson would become known as the father of the political organization that would become today's Democratic Party. As mentioned previously, I have chosen to call Jefferson's party the "Democratic Party" in this study.

Democrat Representatives in the Federal House, meeting in caucus, chose Jefferson, the undisputed leader of the Party, as its candidate for President. Then they nominated Aaron Burr of New York for Vice President. President John Adams, a lawyer and politician from Massachusetts, was the Federalist Party candidate for reelection. Federalists selected Adams without a formal nominating convention. Charles Cotesworth was the Federalist candidate for Vice President. Adams supporters waged a vicious campaign complete with persecution of the press and religious demagoguery. Jefferson promoted strengthening individual and State rights. George Washington was not on hand to endorse either candidate for he had passed away in 1799. William DeGregorio would summarize this election as follows:

"The campaign waged by the partisan press of both camps was bitter and personal. Federalists were able to blunt the [Democrat] campaign by prosecuting opposition editors under the Sedition Act. Operating under no such [prosecution threat], Federalist campaigners urged voters to choose 'God – and a religious President' over 'Jefferson . . . and no God.' They [alleged] that if Jefferson [were] elected, 'Murder, robbery, rape, adultery and incest will be openly taught and practiced.' Foreign affairs played a lesser role than [they] did in the campaign of 4 years before, because the United States and France had backed away from war by this time, and the rise of Napoleon dampened Jefferson's enthusiasm for France. Rather, the campaign turned on domestic issues, specifically Federal authority versus State rights. Jefferson and James Madison had written the controversial Virginia and Kentucky Resolutions of 1798-1799, which declared the Alien and Sedition Acts unconstitutional in those states. The principle of State nullification of Federal laws did not prevail ultimately, but the resolutions became a rallying point for anti-Federalism and [Democrats]. Adams' defeat was virtually assured in the spring of 1800 when [Democrats] ousted the Federalists in the New York State Legislature. New York went to Adams in 1796, because the Federalist-controlled legislature selected the presidential electors. Now, with [Democrats] in charge, Jeffersonian electors were sure to be chosen. The shift of New York's 12 electoral votes from Adams to Jefferson was enough to tip the election to the [Democrats]."

The electoral vote was a two-way tie: "Jefferson, 73; Burr, 73; Adams, 65. Because Jefferson and Burr received the same number of votes, the election was thrown into the House of Representatives. Even though it had always been clear during the campaign that Jefferson was the presidential candidate and Burr the vice-presidential candidate, the latter refused to concede, thus forcing the issue to a vote in the House. Jefferson and Burr won the majority of electoral votes in 8 States: [from north to south they were: New York, Pennsylvania, Virginia, Kentucky, North Carolina, Tennessee, South Carolina and Georgia]. Adams and Pinckney won the majority of Electors in 7 States: [from north to south they were: New Hampshire, Vermont, Massachusetts, Connecticut, Rhode Island, New Jersey, and Delaware]. Maryland electors were evenly split."

"The House, with each State casting one vote based on the majority of that State's Delegation, took 36 ballots during February 11-17, 1801, to decide the contest in Jefferson's favor. Alexander Hamilton played a key role in bringing Federalist support to Jefferson, whom he considered the lesser of the two evils. In the final tally in the House, Jefferson carried 10 States: [from north to south they were: Vermont, New York, New Jersey, Pennsylvania, Maryland, Virginia, Kentucky, North Carolina, Tennessee, and Georgia. Burr carried 4 States: [from north to south they were: New Hampshire, Massachusetts, Connecticut and Rhode Island]. Delaware and South Carolina cast blank ballots. Jefferson was thus declared President and Burr Vice President. The deadlock prompted [future] passage of the Twelfth Amendment (1804)."

Jefferson had little faith in his Vice President after Aaron Burr sought to usurp the President job, and for good reason. Orphaned in infancy and raised by an uncle, Burr was an unscrupulous New York lawyer and politician of great personal ambition. Disgusted with Burr, Jefferson would recommend George Clinton of New York as his second term Vice President. Even before his VP job concluded, Burr would run unsuccessfully for the Governor of New York.

During the campaign, **Alexander Hamilton** would attack Burr's character. **Aaron Burr would immediately challenge Hamilton to a duel and would kill him on the dueling ground on July 11, 1804**. Indicted for murder, Burr would flee New York State for the Federal Territories. There he would conspire with other ambitious men in a futile attempt to instigate war with Spain, seize the Louisiana Purchase lands and set up a new nation over which he himself would preside. U. S. officials would arrest Burr in 1807, but he would thereafter successfully win a not guilty verdict at his trial. Burr would spend about 5 years in Europe letting the dust settle before returning to New York State. America was especially blessed with a healthy Thomas Jefferson while the dangerous Aaron Burr lurked in the Vice President's quarters.

President Jefferson replaced all but one of the members of John Adam's Cabinet. **James Madison, a lawyer and politician from Virginia, was named Secretary of State**. Samuel Dexter, of Massachusetts, remained briefly as Secretary of the Treasury, until Albert Gallatin, of Pennsylvania, took the position later in the year. A Swiss immigrant, past Federal Representative and past Senator, Gallatin would head up the Treasury Department for 13 years and leave his mark on American history. Henry Dearborn, of Maine, was Secretary of War. Levi Lincoln, of Massachusetts and a lawyer, served as Attorney General until, near the end of Jefferson's first 4 years, John Breckenridge, of Kentucky, replaced him. Robert Smith, an Admiralty lawyer from Maryland, was Secretary of the Navy.

The Democratic Party victory swept huge majorities into both the House and the Senate. Democrats controlled the Senate by 18 versus 14, and they controlled the House by 69 versus 36. The mid-term elections greatly swelled those substantial majorities. The Senate majority increased to 25 versus 9, and the House majority increased to 102 versus 39. Thomas Jefferson was fortunate to be working with a House and Senate firmly controlled by the Democratic Party throughout his first term as President.

Ohio was granted statehood in 1803.

The Twelfth Amendment to the Federal Constitution, which stipulated that electors vote separately for President and Vice President, was ratified in 1804.

The more significant events involving African Americans during the 4 years of the first Thomas Jefferson Administration will now be presented. You will soon be reading about the 1803 treaty with France, by which Louisiana would be purchased. It would obligate the United States to give citizenship to inhabitants and descendants of the people of Louisiana and West Florida whose descent was a combination of African and European. In 1803, the South Carolina Government begin allowing importation of bonded Africans from South America and the Caribbean. Twenty African Americans were convicted of arson in New York City after destroying 11 houses in a planned effort to allegedly destroy the whole city. About 20 bonded African Americans were executed in Georgia, South Carolina and Virginia for poisoning European Americans. The New Jersey Government, in 1804, instituted a program to gradually make independent the bonded African Americans living in that State.

This concludes the overview of the first Thomas Jefferson Administration. The narrative history resumes with a discussion of immigration patterns.

The Narrative History Resumes – March 1801

Democrats and Virginians Begin 24 Year Presidential Run

There was little immigration in the early 1800's, so population growth was primarily through children born to American couples. And none were more enthusiastic for large families than the pioneering parents in the southern States, including Kentucky and Tennessee. Since these people, who were primarily descended from Scots in Scotland and the northern section of Ireland, were fiercely independent and innately adverse to governmental intrusion, they were attracted to the Democratic Party of Thomas Jefferson. And the arrival of Thomas Jefferson to the office of the President in March 4, 1801, was the beginning of a 24-year period of limited Federal Government activity under 3, two-term Democratic Party Presidents, **all of whom were Virginians**.

The Federalist Party becomes Limited to Judicial Influence

Because the Federal Court system was the only remaining power base of the Federalist Party, scheming Federalist Party leaders had arranged, during the last month of the Adams Administration, to revamp and expand the Federal Judicial Court system. John Adams had appointed his Secretary of State, John Marshall, to the job of Chief Justice of the Supreme Court, for Adams was confident that Marshall would be a strong advocate of a powerful Federal Government and a powerful Supreme Court. And, during February, Federalists in the House and Senate had greatly expanded the Federal Courts, relieving the Supreme Court justices of the task of "riding the circuit," and providing spots for 16 new judges. They had also created 42 new Justice of the Peace jobs. So, this action provided 58 new jobs to give out to Federalist Party lawyers. And, just before Thomas Jefferson assumed power, Adams and the Senate had complete appointing men to fill these 58 jobs. One of the Justice of the Peace appointees had been William Marbury, about whom more will be reported shortly.

Adams and Jefferson – Two Very Different Views of Good Government

John Adams did not participate in the inauguration of his successor. "Tired, and in no mood to witness the triumph of his rival," Adams had "called his carriage and **left the city before dawn**." Probably realizing that the Federalist Party was doomed never to regain power, Adams apparently no longer cared about his public image. Apparently, Adams had no desire to listen to his successor pledge to ensure that the Federal Government would respect State sovereignty and individual liberty and reduce taxes on imports. However, Adams would have been pleased to hear Jefferson in his inaugural address also pledge to respect the rights of the minority, including the Federalists, and their rights to publicly criticize the new Administration, thus ending the persecution of political opponents under the outgoing party's Alien and Sedition Acts. On this matter Jefferson pledged:

". . . the minority possess their equal rights, which equal law must protect, and to violate would be oppression. . . But every difference of opinion is not a difference of principle. . . We are all [Democrats], we are all Federalists. If there be any among us who would wish to dissolve this [Federation of States] or to change its republican form, let them stand undisturbed as monuments of the safety with which error of opinion may be tolerated where reason is left free to combat it."

And Jefferson pledged to abide by fundamental democratic principles:

"Equal and exact justice to all men . . . the support of the State governments in all their rights . . . absolute acquiescence in the decisions of the majority . . . the supremacy of the civil over the military authority; economy in the public expense, that labor may be lightly burdened . . . freedom of religion; freedom of the press, and freedom of person under the protection of the habeas corpus, and trial by juries impartially selected. These principles form the bright constellation which has gone before us and guided our steps through an age of revolution and reformation."

The basic difference in the political beliefs of Jefferson and Adams boils down to trusting or not trusting the American voter. Jefferson trusted the voting majority to wisely guide government policy and believed elitism endangered the liberties of the people. Adams distrusted the voting majority and sought to subordinate the voters to elitists. Jefferson believed in a democratic federation of sovereign States. Adams believed in an elitists-controlled federation of subservient states.

The Federal Government is now in the District of Columbia, between Maryland and Virginia

Thomas Jefferson moved into the President's residence in Washington City because, a year earlier, the Federal Government had moved to the **new Federal Capital** on land donated by the States of **Maryland** and **Virginia**. The land on the Virginia side would be returned to that State in 1846, because Federal leaders thought it would not be needed for additional Federal buildings and the Potomac River presented a barrier to integrating and defending the 2 sections. Construction of Federal buildings in the Capital had been financed by contributions by those 2 States and by real estate speculations by Robert Morris and his associates. Charles L'Enfant, a Frenchman, had planned the layout of the city, with the help of George Washington and Thomas Jefferson. William Thornton, an American, and B. H. Latrobe, an Englishman, had designed the Capitol building and James Hoban of South Carolina had designed the President's residence. The President's residence would be painted white in 1812 to cover up fire damage, and would be officially named the "White House" during the term of Theodore Roosevelt. The President's residence stood on a low hill and, a mile away on a larger hill, stood the Capitol building. Between them meandered Goose Creek as it flowed into the Potomac River. The remaining structures were "scattered and unsightly dwellings, stores, and the paraphernalia attendant upon construction." The magnificent tulip popular trees were being rapidly cut down for firewood. There were ample dust, mosquitoes and mud. The streets were not paved. This was not as much an inconvenience as you might think, because the Democratic Party was intent on limiting the power of the Federal Government. The sessions of the House and Senate were brief, so, most of the year, Representatives and Senators remained at home. Wives seldom accompanied them to Washington City. Even Thomas Jefferson would be out of town during most of the summer, primarily at his Virginia mountain home, Monticello.

Napoleon Aims to Retake the Western Half of Hispaniola

During this year of 1801, **Francois Dominique Toussaint L'Ouverture**, the former bonded African American Rebel, consolidated his power over the Spanish half, eastern half, of the **Caribbean island of Hispaniola**. Having succeeded in defeating the Royalists and making independent the bonded African Americans, he had been, since 1796, the French Governor-General over the French half, western half, of the island. And, the formerly bonded African Americans who lived in the French half had been independent for several years. Loyal to the French Government, his army, consisting primarily of African Americans, completed the conquest of the western half of the island. Then, Toussaint declared to be independent the bonded African Americans who lived in that Spanish half of the island. But, not long afterward, **Napoleon Bonaparte** would send a large French army to the island with orders to return its government to the control of a trusted European American governor.

Jefferson Explores Purchase of Louisiana Territory

It was some time in the first weeks of his administration that Thomas Jefferson first learned of unconfirmed rumors that France had acquired Louisiana from Spain in a secret treaty. He would later get confirmation and understand that the treaty had been signed at San Ildefonso on October 1, 1800. Jefferson sought out more definitive information, and as soon as he felt fairly confident that France had obtained **Spain's claim to Louisiana**, he instructed his **diplomat in France, Robert Livingston**, to begin diplomatic discussions with the French Government for the **purchase of New Orleans**. And, if the French Government had also gained ownership of East Florida and West Florida from Spain, Jefferson requested that they be purchased as well. But, of primary importance was the purchase of New Orleans and lower Louisiana. And he instructed his diplomat in Spain, Charles Pinckney, to help facilitate negotiations.

Abuses of the Adams Administration Are Undone

The Jefferson Administration and the Democrat-controlled House and Senate had **inherited a federal debt of $80,000,000 from the 12-year Federalists-Hamilton era**. In spite of the debt, the House and Senate would abolish the Federalist Party's Excise Tax Law, which included a tax on whiskey. Yet, even without that revenue, during the subsequent 8 years, the debt would be paid down to $33,000,000. Democrats rescinded the Federalist law that prevented immigrants from voting until they had lived in The States for 14 years, setting the residency requirement back to 5 years. This voting policy helped the Democrat Party, but more importantly it served to encourage immigration and make new immigrants feel welcome. The Federalists had included an expiration date in the wording of their Alien and Sedition Acts, so the Democrats in the House only had to let the acts expire.

What to do about the Barbary Pirates of Algiers?

Thomas Jefferson was determined to rid the Federal Government and the American people of harassment by the **Barbary pirates of Algiers**, Tripoli and Tunis. Highly organized and in control of the governments of their region, these pirates had, during the 12-year span of the Washington and Adams administrations, enslaved 100 American sailors and extracted about $2,000,000 in tribute from the Federal Government and American families. These pirates had long made a practice of capturing merchant marine ships, taking the cargo, and the crews, and ransoming the crews for all they could get. Back in 1794, the Federal House and Senate had authorized funds to build 6 modern naval warships. These warships – the *Constitution*, *President* and *United States*, with 44 guns each, and the *Chesapeake, Congress* and *Constellation*, with 36 guns each – were, at their completion in 1801, considered the finest in their class anywhere in the world. So, Jefferson and his advisers contemplated how to defeat the Barbary pirates in the most efficient manner.

Protestant Revivals in Kentucky and Tennessee

In August 1801 there was an enormous camp meeting at **Cain Ridge, Kentucky**. It was estimated that as many as **25,000 people attended**. This huge religious revival lasted for 6 days and nights. In fact, American enthusiasm for religion had risen in 1797 and would not return to more normal levels until 1805. And religious enthusiasm was substantially greater west of the Appalachian Mountains than to the east, especially in Kentucky, which was the most heavily populated western State with 220,000 people – one twenty-fifth of the national total. Since Scottish people, whose ancestry went back to Scotland and Northern Ireland, had been a major portion of the pioneers who had settled, and were settling, Kentucky and Tennessee, the Presbyterian Church was the most popular denomination. There were also numerous Methodists and Baptists in those two States.

1802

Napoleon Sends Huge French Military Force to Western Hispaniola – What Might Be Next?

Napoleon Bonaparte had dispatched to the Caribbean island of Hispaniola, 10,000 soldiers and a French fleet, under the command of his brother-in-law V. F. Leclerc. In January, the fleet arrived at the east half of the island, which had been previously wrested from Spanish control by Toussaint L'Ouverture's army. Leclerc's mission was to regain the western half of the island from the control of Toussaint L'Ouverture and then move on to New Orleans and establish French rule over that vast and still-secret acquisition. The French force was welcomed at the eastern half of the island because it was generally controlled by men of European descent. There, Leclerc declared that the French Government had acquired the island from Spain and announced that his force intended to defeat the western-island forces of Toussaint L'Ouverture to enable France to establish control over the whole island.

Then, in October, people living in The States were alerted of future trouble from European domination in the lower Mississippi Valley when the Spanish Government, pretending to still own the region, suspended arrangements that would have continued to facilitate American export-import activity out of the seaport of New Orleans. This export-import activity had been very important to many settlers in western Tennessee and Kentucky, the export volume having averaged over $1,000,000 over each of the previous 4 years. If the Federal Government in Washington City would not force the European power to give them access to New Orleans shipping, many rugged and independent minded men from Tennessee and Kentucky were prepared to form an independent army and conquer the seaport themselves. And Andrew Jackson would gladly lead them. So, Thomas Jefferson followed developments in Hispaniola with worried interest.

1803

Marbury v. Madison and an Overview of the "Principle of Judicial Review"

Although John Adams and the Federalists in the House and Senate had created 16 Federal judge jobs and 42 Justice of the Peace jobs shortly before Thomas Jefferson was inaugurated, not all justice of the peace appointees had received their official commissions before the Adams Administration had concluded. For example, Adams had appointed a Federalist politician, William Marbury, and 3 other Federalists to justice of the peace jobs in the District of Columbia and the Senate had confirmed each. Adams had signed these commissions, and as outgoing Secretary of State, John Marshall had affixed the seal. But, because of a bureaucratic delay, the commission papers had not been delivered to the men. Upon discovering this piece of unfinished business during the first day or so of the Jefferson Administration, Jefferson told his Secretary of State, James Madison, to withhold these commission authorization papers. Marbury and the others had responded by seeking a Federal Supreme Court order demanding delivery of the commission papers. As Supreme Court Chief Justice John Marshall had decided to leverage the Marbury vs. Madison case into a platform for claiming, for the Federal Supreme Court, sole authority to interpret whether or not a Federal law violated the Federal Constitution – in spite of the fact that the Marbury complaint had little relationship to that fundamental issue.

Under Marshall's leadership, the Federal Supreme Court ruled, on February 24, that Marbury was entitled to receive a commission to complete his appointment to the Justice of the Peace job. Then, the decision declared that a portion of the Judiciary Act of 1789, by which the Federal House and Senate had created the original Federal Court structure, that portion being Section 13, was null and void because the Court judged that section to be in violation of the Article III of the Federal Constitution.

I have reviewed John Marshall's decision and both cited documents in search of the "violation" that John Marshall alleged. I find his logic obtuse, and too involved to present in this study. But, we must be aware of the fact that all first year law students in American universities study this case, and are taught to cite it as the basis of "the principle of judicial review." However, this so-called "principle of judicial review" would not result in significant nullification of Federal laws prior to the American Civil War. Today's allegation that the "Marbury v. Madison" decision marked the beginning at the Supreme Court of an assertive policy toward policing Federal legislation seems to me to be a gross exaggeration. This decision was merely a Federalist trick to avoid giving Democrat Thomas Jefferson an order that he could freely ignore and thereby embarrass the Court.

The next decision to nullify a federal law would not take place until 1857 – that would be 54 years later. Then the Court would review the Dred Scott case and hand down a minor nullification, which would actually support State rights.

During the Abe Lincoln Administration the then-dominant Northern States Republican Party would totally ignore and violate rulings handed down by the Supreme Court, because, then, the majority of justices were Democrats. It would not be until Lincoln's Chief Justice appointee, Salmon Chase, would gain control of the Supreme Court that it would begin to gradually and methodically reconstruct the meaning of the Federal Constitution and become a major factor in the lives of individuals and businessmen in America.

But, without question, **Chief Justice John Marshall** would be a strong advocate of increased power within the Federal Government. Marshall's decision in the Marbury vs. Madison case began a process that would 16, years later (after 1819), deny the State sovereignty that had been claimed by the Kentucky State Government and the Virginia State Government when both had passed legislation declaring that the Federal Alien Act and the Federal Sedition Act violated the Federal Constitution, as both obviously did.

The Amazing Story of the Louisiana Purchase

President Thomas Jefferson decided to pursue urgent and forceful diplomacy. He persuaded the Federal Congress to **appropriate $2,000,000** and to support his appointment of **James Monroe as special envoy to aid Robert Livingston, the official American Minister to France.** Monroe sailed for France on March 8, 1803. He carried instructions to offer up to $10,000,000 for the region surrounding New Orleans, plus East Florida and West Florida, if the Florida colonies were available through the French. Monroe was also instructed to value the region around New Orleans at 3 times the value of both Floridas, if he and Livingston were forced to settle for less than everything. Monroe understood that the minimum acceptable French concession would be their agreement to restore American access to import-export business into and out of the seaport of New Orleans, using American ships as well as foreign ships. Although he was authorized to persuade with money, Monroe also planned to persuade by threatening military action. He would argue that the men of western Tennessee and Kentucky would conquer New Orleans, even without help from the Federal Government, if forced to suffer economic deprivation for very long. He would hint that a military alliance with Great Britain would be arranged if the negotiations failed at lease to guarantee access to New Orleans shipping.

But **Napoleon Bonaparte's French Government** would be primarily persuaded to cooperate by reports that the large French army was being devastated in the western half of Hispaniola. "By the tens of thousands French soldiers, Leclerc among them, found graves" in the **island of Santo Domingo**, especially the western half, where they were attempting to re-conquer the people of African descent who controlled that half of the island. Furthermore, the backup expedition that had been organized in the fall of 1802 would be surprisingly ice-bound in Holland until the spring of 1803.

So, during the winter of 1802-1803, **Napoleon Bonaparte** became more determined to **avoid a war over New Orleans** and more eager to get some **badly needed cash** to build up his European military force. He was particularly concerned that Great Britain might gain control of New Orleans anyway. Frankly, he knew that he was unable to defend it. Consequently, on April 11, 1803, Napoleon directed his Minister of Finance, Francois de Barbe-Marbois to offer to sell the complete Louisiana Territory for a minimum of 50,000,000 francs, which amounted to about $12,500,000. Marbois then asked Charles Maurice de Talleyrand to suggest the sale. Soon thereafter Talleyrand "surprised" Robert Livingston by asking him how much money The States would offer for **"the whole of Louisiana."** Startled because his efforts to merely buy New Orleans had not previously been taken seriously, Livingston replied that he believed he could obtain agreement to pay 20,000,000 francs. Talleyrand warned that a number in that range was "too low," but quickly encouraged Livingston to think it over during the night and return to discuss it the next day. Later that day Livingston, James Monroe and probably other advisers gathered and discussed tactics. There was no telegraph then, so Livingston and Monroe were unable to consult with Washington or diplomats in London or Madrid. They had to negotiate based on their personal beliefs about how much money the Federal House and Senate would be willing to appropriate for such a huge purchase. The next day **James Monroe went to Talleyrand** and "negotiations were hurried to a conclusion." A package of 3 treaties was signed on April 30, just 3 weeks after Napoleon made his suggestion and about the time that the French fleet could have sailed out of previously ice-bound Holland, had Napoleon chosen to defend, instead of sell, Louisiana.

The first treaty **ceded Louisiana to The States**. The second established the procedures for paying 60,000,000 francs, which corresponded to **$15,000,000**. The third obligated the Federal Government to assume responsibility to pay the war claims being sought by citizens of The States, particularly owners of marine shipping companies.

Because Napoleon's aggressive military plans needed an infusion of cash, and because African Americans in Santo Domingo, yellow fever and sea ice had defeated his plans to occupy and defend Louisiana, The Federal Government was able to purchase for $15,000,000 "one of the most valuable areas on the earth's surface."

But, **politicians in Massachusetts and neighboring States were consumed with fear** that expansion into Louisiana would destroy any hope that they might again regain control of

180

the Federal Government. Ohio had been granted statehood in February 1803, and its voters would be supporting Jefferson's Democratic Party. They probably reasoned that people from Massachusetts and neighboring States could travel westward, settling the Great Lakes region, and that growth might offset the rising political power of Tennesseans, Kentuckians and ex-Virginians who were moving into the north side of the Ohio River Valley. But they saw no way they could also offset the settlement of Louisiana by farmers expanding out of Virginia, the Carolinas and Georgia.

Politicians in and around Massachusetts wanted a strong Federal Government under their control that would facilitate their economic interests: high import taxes, federal funding of improvements to canals and harbors, and assured profitability of their banking, commercial and marine shipping businesses. The farmers of the southern States wanted a limited, low taxation Federal Government that was primarily involved in expanding the National Territories and defending them from foreign powers.

The farmers of the southern States were Nation Builders. Men in control of politics in and around Massachusetts were of the Northern Culture; they were not Nation Builders.

So, Federal Senators and Representatives from Massachusetts and neighboring States fought approval and funding of the Louisiana Purchase with all the political power they could muster. They struggled vainly to defeat approval by alleging that the Federal Constitution did not permit the Federal Government to acquire national territory by treaty. And, they threatened that, if the purchase were approved, their States would secede from the Federal Government and form a new nation made up of Massachusetts and surrounding States.

But, supporters of the purchase argued that Article II, Section 2 of the Federal Constitution authorized purchase by treaties, and they secured the necessary votes. The treaties were confirmed by the Senate on October 20, and were funded by an appropriation by the House 5 days later.

However, the Spanish flag still flew over New Orleans, because the French Government had never sent officials to take governmental control over what it had secretly obtained from Spain. The Spanish Governor of New Orleans "made gestures that looked like resistance." And Andrew Jackson responded by directing his Tennessee militia "to be in order at a moment's notice to march."

Resistance to an American takeover started to subside when New Orleans officials learned that the Spanish Government, on November 30, had formally transferred Louisiana to the French Government, thereby making official the Spanish cession to France that had been secretly signed on September 31, 1800. **Spanish authorities in New Orleans did not resist** when Federal officials arrived with soldiers and, on December 20, "unfurled the Stars and Stripes in front of the Cabildo at New Orleans. The American flag replaced the French flag and Federal officials, led by James Wilkinson and W. C. C. Claiborne, established temporary Federal military control over all of Louisiana. For all practical purposes, the French had never exercised any control over the Louisiana that they had obtained from Spain.

At the time the Federal Government took over control of Louisiana, the vast region contained about 50,000 European Americans, most of them being of French and Spanish descent and most of them living in and around New Orleans. French was the common language and Catholicism was the common religion. The system of law was Continental "civil law" instead of British "common law."

There was considerable uncertainty about the legal boundary of Louisiana. Napoleon and Talleyrand had dodged the issue, encouraging the new owners to place the boundaries wherever they wanted. When discussing treaty language, Napoleon had advised Talleyrand: "If an obscurity did not already exist it would be perhaps good policy to put one there." The treaty simply said Louisiana was being sold "with the same extend that it now has in the hands of Spain, and that it had when France [had previously] possessed it; and such as it should be after the treaties subsequently entered into between Spain and other states." When Robert Livingston asked Talleyrand for clarification of the boundary he replied: "You have made a noble bargain for yourselves, and I suppose you will make the most of it." The western boundary was understood to go to the continental divide, and the northern boundary was understood to go as far north as the Mississippi River's origin.

Defining the Boundaries of the Vast Louisiana Purchase

A year after taking over "Louisiana," the Jefferson Administration would divide it into two Territories, using 33 degrees latitude as the boundary. The land below was the **Territory of Orleans**. The land above was named the **District of Louisiana**, and was considered part of Indiana Territory.

But, the eastern boundary along the Gulf Coast was in dispute. **Where was the boundary between the Territory of Orleans and West Florida?** "In the more recent Spanish possession, Louisiana included nothing east of the Mississippi River except the Isle of Orleans, which was bound on the north by the Iberville River, just below present-day Baton Rouge. But, when France had previously possessed it, prior to 1763, the Perdido River, which ran south into the Gulf just west of present-day Pensacola, was the eastern boundary." So, rights to the huge stretch of land from the Perdido River to the Mississippi River, about 50 miles north-south by about 230 miles east-west, was uncertain.

So, the two Thomas Jefferson Administrations and the first James Monroe Administration would persistently assert that the Federal Government owned territory eastward to present-day Pensacola, including ownership of the fine harbor site of Mobile Bay.

1804

African Revolt in Western Hispaniola Succeeds – Whites Flee or Suffer Death – Nation of Haiti is established.

On January 1, 1804, African Americans established the independent **nation of Haiti** in the western half of the large Caribbean **Island of Hispaniola**. The revolt by bonded African Americans had begun in 1791 during the turmoil produced by the French Revolution, and had held to various political allegiances during the years that followed. The Revolutionary Government of France had agreed to make the bonded African Americans independent in 1794, and **Toussaint L'Ouverture**, a former bonded African American, had become Governor in 1796. But, Napoleon Bonaparte had dispatched a huge military force in 1802 to regain control of the government of the western part of the island. This force had succeeded in capturing Toussaint L'Ouverture, but had failed to gain control of the population. After the French force had departed, the former bonded African Americans had driven out what remained of the

European American population and established a new independent Nation of people of African descent, which political leaders renamed "Haiti."

An estimated 60,000 people had been killed during the 13-year western Hispaniola conflict. By the way, President Lincoln's war to capture the seceded Southern States would cause 1,000,000 unnecessary deaths, white and black, 17 times the Haitian deaths. By the end of the fighting in western Hispaniola, the African Americans had killed basically all of the European Americans who had not managed to escape. Many European American refugees had escaped to New Orleans and to The States and, during one month, about 1,500 Hispaniola refugees, including bonded African Americans, had been received in Baltimore, Maryland. And these arriving bonded African Americans from Haiti would tell their stories of the revolt on their island and inspire a revolutionary passion within the hearts of a few bonded African Americans in the southern States.

Federal Efforts to Manage the Vast Land Area of the Louisiana Purchase

In February 1804, the Federal Government would establish Fort Stoddert north of Mobile Bay, just above 33 degrees latitude, near the convergence of the Tombigbee River and the Alabama River, to facilitate future occupation of Mobile Bay. At the same time the Federal Government established a customs district for the Mobile area to facilitate import and export trade.

Thomas Jefferson was equally interested in the extent of northwest Louisiana. So, he dispatched an expedition under **Meriwether Lewis and George Clark** to explore the region. Lewis and Clark departed St. Louis for the northwest in May 1804. They paddled up the Missouri River, reaching a Mandan village near present-day Bismarck, North Dakota, where they spent the winter. The next spring, they would continue up the Missouri to its source, then cross the continental divide and walk on to the Columbia River. From there they would proceed on to the Pacific Ocean. They would return by a similar route, arriving back in St. Louis in September 1806. Thomas Jefferson, an avid student of science and geography, would eagerly learn as much as he could about the expedition's findings.

A State Secession Movement in the Northeast and Trouble between Burr and Hamilton

Secessionists in Massachusetts and neighboring States were actively promoting State secession from the Federal Government. Leaders in this movement included Timothy Pickering, Roger Griswold and Oliver Wolcott. But they needed the cooperation of New York State politicians in order to create a federation of seceded States that would be of sufficient size to be viable. So, they were running **Aaron Burr for Governor of New York State**, knowing that, if elected, Burr would help obtain secession of that State as well. With Massachusetts and New York acting together in a secession movement, secessionists figured all States north and east of Pennsylvania would join their movement. Pennsylvania might join in as well.

But, **Alexander Hamilton, of New York, was opposing the secessionists by political maneuvers designed to ensure that Burr lost the New York State election**. And Burr did lose. With **Burr's defeat**, the secessionists would abandon open advocacy of their movement.

Defeated in the election of Governor, Burr responded by challenging Alexander Hamilton to a duel, and Hamilton foolishly accepted the challenge. "On the morning of

July 11, 1804, Hamilton faced Burr at ten paces under the Palisades on the Jersey side of the Hudson." **Burr killed Hamilton and survived to fight another day**.

Yes, politics in New York and New England, the focus of the Northern Culture, was often a bloody affair.

Andrew Jackson is Now Mostly Farming in Middle Tennessee

On the other hand, in the lands of the Southern Culture, politics were not so bloody; **not so bloody in Tennessee**. For relaxation, Andrew Jackson would occasionally stop by the cock-fighting pit near the Nashville Inn, where he roomed when overnighting in town. "Twenty dollars for my Bernadotte! Who'll take me up?" But Andrew Jackson's prized cock was of little financial help. He was suffering intolerable financial difficulties by the summer of 1804.

Seeking solvency, **Andrew Jackson** resigned his job as Superior Court Judge, which he had worked at for 6 years, so he could spend full time managing his farm and other investments. He sold his best farm, with its fine and spacious farmhouse, including an adjourning 640-acre tract that had once belonged to Rachel and her first husband, Lewis Robards. He lamented "I [have] turned myself out of house and home . . . purely to meet my [obligations]." With money derived from this sale he paid off debts and purchased a nearby 640-acre farm, which contained 1,000 peach trees, but only a modest farmhouse. Jackson and his partner, Thomas Watson, relocated their mercantile store to Clover Bottom, about 3 miles from the new farm. The new Jackson farmhouse was very modest, but Rachel was upbeat, for she figured her husband would be able to spend much more time at home.

President Thomas Jefferson is reelected for a Second Term

Of course, Vice President Aaron Burr, of New York, was long gone. **Jefferson, of Virginia, was easily reelected** to a second term and George Clinton, of New York, was elected Vice President.

Chapter 12 — March 1805 to February 1809: The States during the Second Thomas Jefferson Administration

Before resuming the narrative history, I have inserted a summary of the 1804 elections and the organization of the second Thomas Jefferson Administration.

Thomas Jefferson, of Virginia, <u>was reelected President with the support of the</u> **Democratic Party, which he had founded**. George Clinton of New York was elected Vice President.

The Federalist Party had nominated Charles Pinckney, a South Carolina lawyer and politician, to oppose Jefferson. Eight years earlier Pinckney had run for Vice President on the Federalist ticket, which had been headed by John Adams. Although Adams had won the race for President that year, Pinckney had not won the race for Vice President. Why? Because Alexander Hamilton's plot to advance Pinckney's vote total above Adam's vote total had simply backfired. Hamilton's failed plot had permitted Thomas Jefferson, the Democrat candidate for President, to defeat Pinckney for the office of Vice President in the John Adams' Federalist Administration. Pinckney was born in Charleston, South Carolina, but was educated in England, and actually practiced law there before returning to America. He fought with South Carolinians in the Revolution and suffered capture. He was a Delegate to the Constitutional Convention in 1787 and served on a mission to France in 1797. Rufus King of New York was the Federalist candidate for Vice President.

The Federalist Party was in deep trouble in 1804. A faction of the Massachusetts Federalist Party had launched a State Secession Movement, which had weakened the Party as a whole.

Massachusetts would become the motherland of the Exclusionist Movement,[6] which, 50 years later, would enable the sectional Northern States Republican Party to gain control of the Federal Government. In reaction, 7 southern States would seek protection through State secession.

<u>In 1804, however, it was politicians in Massachusetts who were promoting the secession of northeastern States from the Federal Government</u>. DeGregorio would summarize this election as follows:

> **"[Thomas] Jefferson handily checked a feeble challenge from the dying Federalist Party**. The Federalists went into the campaign discredited by radical elements of the party in Massachusetts, the so-called Essex Junto, which sought to escape the effects of Jeffersonian democracy by seceding from the [Federation]. Junto leaders hoped to enlist neighboring States in forming a New England Confederacy. The movement failed. With the outcome never in doubt, the presidential campaign was lackluster. In addition to his traditional [southern States] base of support, Jefferson made significant inroads in once solidly Federalist New England. Die-hard Federalists managed to mount a significant challenge to Jefferson only in Connecticut, Delaware and Maryland."

---

[6] The writer has defined as the "Exclusionist Movement," the passion in the Northern States to exclude bonded African Americans (slaves) from the Western Territories north and west of Missouri and Texas. He classifies their advocacy, "Exclusionism."

Jefferson won the electoral vote by 162 to 14. **Jefferson carried 15 states**. From north to south they were: New Hampshire, Vermont, Massachusetts, Rhode Island, New York, New Jersey, Pennsylvania, Maryland, Ohio, Virginia, Kentucky, North Carolina, Tennessee, South Carolina and Georgia. Pinckney carried only Connecticut and Delaware.

Jefferson retained much of his Cabinet. **James Madison**, a lawyer and politician from Virginia, remained as **Secretary of State**. Albert Gallatin, of Pennsylvania, remained as Secretary of the Treasury. Henry Dearborn, of Maine, remained as Secretary of War. John Breckenridge, of Kentucky, served as Attorney General for only 2 years, for he died in that office. Caesar Rodney, of Delaware, served the remainder of the term and was actively involved in bringing **Aaron Burr** to trial for **treason**. When lawyers won Burr's release through technicalities involving the Federal Constitution, Rodney worked actively to broaden the legal definition of treason to include conspiracy. Robert Smith, an Admiralty lawyer from Maryland, remained as Secretary of the Navy.

Democrats strengthened their huge Senate majority a bit more to 27 versus 7, and their huge House majority swelled further to 116 versus 25. The midterm elections added even a little more Democrat dominance. The Senate majority became 28 versus 6, and the House majority became 118 versus 24.

Representative George Campbell, of Tennessee, would praise Thomas Jefferson in 1807 with these words: "So long as virtue, wisdom and patriotism continue to be revered in the world, so long will his character remain a distinguished monument of the triumph of liberty and the rights of man over despotism and aristocracy, around which the sons of freedom will rejoice to rally." In 1826 James Madison would praise Jefferson with these words: "He lives and will live in the memory and gratitude of the wise and good, as a luminary of science, as a votary of liberty, as a model of patriotism, and as a benefactor of human kind."

The more significant events involving African Americans during the 4 years of the second Thomas Jefferson Administration will now be presented. The Virginia Government stipulated that all bonded African Americans who were made independent after May 1, 1806, had to leave the State, thereby making it much more difficult for an owner to ensure a successful outcome if he made a bonded person independent. In accordance with the Federal Constitution, the Federal Government stipulated that no bonded Africans could be imported into The States after December 31, 1807, and imposed a fine of $800 for taking ownership of an illegal importee and $20,000 for equipping a ship for transporting bonded Africans. But smuggling would continue to bring in bonded Africans (I have no figures on how many were smuggled into The States from 1808 to 1860). The importation of bonded Africans being outlawed in The States, the British Government cooperated by outlawing the transport of bonded Africans by the British merchant marine.

This concludes the overview of the second Thomas Jefferson Administration. The narrative history resumes with first attention going to Andrew Jackson's middle Tennessee horse racing activities.

The Narrative History Resumes – March 1805

The Horse in America

Andrew Jackson and horses shared a common historical trait. **Both were Nation Builders**. Six hundred years previously, the horse had made possible the building of the largest nation ever created upon this planet: the Mongol empire of the Great Khans of eastern Asia. Genghis Khan had forged a huge nation that conquered northern China and western Asia. The Mongol empire had been expanded by his sons and grandsons to stretch from Korea on the Pacific to Ukraine in Western Europe. And the Mongol empire had not been a fleeting event, for it survived for centuries. This conquest and the governance over such a large expanse of territory had been made possible by the horse and the superior horsemanship of the Mongol people. So, a little attention to horses and the breeding of racehorses seems appropriate.

During the spring of 1805, Andrew Jackson expanded his sizable investment in horses. At the **Hartsville, Tennessee, racetrack**, Greyhound had beaten Jackson's prize horse, Indian Queen, as well as a competitive horse, Truxton, which Jackson admired. Truxton's owner, having lost on his bets, was in desperate need of cash, and Jackson figured he could somehow scrape up enough money to buy the handsome stallion, **Truxton**. Jackson knew horses, and had confidence in that knowledge. Truxton was a big bay horse that "stood fifteen hands and three inches high, was beautifully formed and had white hind feet." Truxton was "got by imported Diome out of Nancy Coleman, in the stable of Thomas Goode, Chesterfield County, Virginia." The pedigree looked impressive and Jackson figured he could improve Truxton's endurance and speed with exceptionally hard training. **Jackson bought Truxton** in an exchange of assets valued at **$1,500** and arranged for a rigorous training program. "Jackson's training methods were severe. He worked a horse to the limit of endurance, but somehow implanted in him a will to win, a circumstance, which, as much as anything, epitomizes the character and [would elucidate] the singular attainments of Andrew Jackson." Jackson bet $6,500 on Truxton, which was considered an underdog, and was gratified to see Truxton first to finish. The winnings greatly helped Jackson restore his financial health. He used part of the winnings **to buy Greyhound** and add him to the Jackson racing stable. In the fall races at Clover Bottom, Greyhound would be a winner and further established Jackson "in the first file of western turfmen."

Now horse racing in middle Tennessee was not an altogether peaceful sport, as the story of Joseph Erwin and his son-in-law Charles Dickinson will reveal. Erwin challenged all owners of racehorses to race against his horse Tanner at Clover Bottom (near Andrew Jackson's farm) during the fall racing season. And Erwin pledged a purse of $5,000 to the winner. Andrew Jackson took up the challenge and, on race day, saw his horse Greyhound defeat Erwin's horse, Tanner. Erwin, who also owned a famous stallion, Ploughboy, sought revenge against Jackson's stable by challenging to race Ploughboy against Jackson's stallion, Truxton. **Erwin and his son-in-law Charles Dickinson** put up $2,000 and pledged a forfeit fine of $800. But, on the day Ploughboy and Truxton were to race, Ploughboy came up lame and Erwin and Dickinson chose to forfeit, each paying Jackson $400. When Erwin and Dickinson offered Jackson notes with distance maturity dates, the latter protested he needed at least half of the payment in current notes. Dickinson then agreed to make his notes to Jackson current. It seems many financial obligations were transacted using notes and barter, for bank money was rather scarce. This detail is important because a dispute over these notes would feed passions that would later result in a **deadly duel between Andrew Jackson and Charles Dickinson.**

Americans Invade Tripoli and Force a Stop to Pirate Attacks

In June, the Federal Government completed a treaty with the Tripoli Government, which secured its pledge to **desist in pirate actions** against American marine commerce. A 400-man

American land assault force, with the support of 3 American warships, had marched 500 miles from Alexandria into Tripoli and there captured the Tripolian town of Derne, thereby encouraging the Tripolian government to agree to the treaty. The Federal Government agreed to pay $60,000 as ransom money to gain the release of the men captured from the *Philadelphia*, plus additional presents. This arrangement would prevent the Tripoli pirates **from preying on American shippers for 7 years**. Then, in 1812, the war with Great Britain would entice them to resume pirate assaults.

It would be 1815 before the Federal Government would put a final stop to Tripoli pirate attacks. In that year the American Navy, under Stephen Decatur would sail to Tripoli and, by threatening a devastating cannon siege, would force that nation to desist preying on the American merchant marine. Therefore 1815 would be the year that the Federal Government would quit paying tribute to pirates.

British Navy Crushes French and Spanish Fleet at Trafalgar – Destroying Napoleon's Hopes for Regaining Power in the New World

On October 21, the **British fleet**, under the command of **Horatio Nelson**, destroyed the combined **French** and **Spanish fleet** off **Trafalgar** in one of history's most significant sea battles. The destruction of the French and Spanish navy was so complete that **Napoleon Bonaparte's French Government would never be able to challenge British naval supremacy**. And the people living in The States were surely glad that Napoleon had no means of invading Louisiana in hopes of getting her back. Unable to wage war at sea, Napoleon directed his army toward Eastern Europe. His forces would crush Austria by December.

1806

Andrew Jackson -- A Horse Race and a Duel

Andrew Jackson had been training Truxton at an intense pace and hoped he would be victorious over Joseph Erwin's Ploughboy in a race to be held at **Clover Bottom** on April 3, 1806. Erwin's son-in-law, Charles Dickinson, was also eager to see Ploughboy defeat Truxton. The race was billed to be "the greatest and most interesting race ever run in the western country." The winning horse had to win two of three heats of 2 miles distance. On race day, Jackson looked over the gathering crowd of spectators and thought it "the largest concourse of people I ever saw assembled, unless in an army." But the Jackson men were worried about Truxton, for the hard training had produced "**a serious hurt to his thigh**, which occasioned it to swell very much." Jackson's inner circle of supporters and trainers recommended that he pay the forfeit fine and postpone the race. Then "Jackson went over his horse again, minutely, spoke to him [and] stroked his nose." Men observed that Jackson talked to a horse and looked in its eyes as if he were addressing a man. At that point, Jackson concluded that his horse was able and announced that Truxton would run. But the injury restricted the betting on Truxton to only $10,000. In the first heat Truxton "slipped into the lead, held it, increased it, and passed the finish line going away." But "a front leg had gone lame" and the shoe "had sprung and lay across the foot." Most thought Truxton would slow severely during the second heat. "A hard-beating rain came as the horses returned to the post. The drum tapped. Through the April downpour, the crowd saw the long bony body of Jackson's bay glide ahead of Ploughboy with effortless ease," winning by 60 yards at the finish line.

Joseph Erwin was greatly disappointed over his horse's defeat. And his son-in-law, Charles Dickinson, who was on a business trip to New Orleans at the time, was practicing with his dueling pistols.

Dickinson was a well-educated and ambitious 28-year-old lawyer. The feud between Jackson and Dickinson was founded in disputes over the soundness of Dickinson's $400 forfeit note, over Dickinson's political ambitions, and over his ridicule of the legality of Jackson's marriage to Rachel. And much of the quarrel had been public, climaxing in Dickinson's attack advertisement published in the local paper, which concluded by calling Jackson "a worthless scoundrel, a poltroon and a coward." Them were fighting words!

Andrew Jackson felt obligated to **challenge Dickinson to a duel** in spite of his knowledge that Dickinson was fast and deadly accurate with a dueling pistol. Dickinson eagerly agreed to duel. The parties met just over the State line in Kentucky beside the Red River as dawn broke on May 30. These 2 lawyers were to face each other at a distance of 24 feet "with their pistols down perpendicularly." When John Overton, a fellow lawyer and Jackson's good friend, hollered out "fire," they were to shoot at each other with intent to kill. Each pistol was loaded with a one-ounce 70-caliber ball. Dickinson had a reputation of being "a snap shot." It was told that, "at the word of command and firing apparently without aim, he could put 4 balls in a mark 24 feet away, each ball touching another." On the other hand, "Jackson was neither a quick shot, nor an especially good one for the western country. He had decided not to compete with Dickinson for the first fire. He expected to be hit, perhaps badly. But he counted on the resources of his will to sustain him until he could aim deliberately and shoot to kill, if it were the last act of his life."

Fire! Dickinson "fired almost instantly," delivering a **bullet into Jackson's chest** at or near his heart. "For an instant he thought himself dying, but, fighting for self-command, slowly he raised his pistol" and took careful aim. Dickinson backed off the line blurting out "My God! Have I missed him?" Overton raised his pistol and commanded: **"Back to the mark, sir!"** Dickinson folded his arms across his chest and stood at the line. **Jackson fired and Dickinson fell to the ground, mortally wounded.**

Jackson would recover, but he would carry the one-ounce ball in his chest the rest of his life. **It had barely missed his heart.** Apparently the rather broad coat Jackson was wearing tricked Dickinson into misjudging the location of the heart within Jackson's tall and lean frame. An inch of two to the right and history would have been changed. Upon hearing the news Rachel "fell to her knees weeping. 'Oh, God have pity on the poor wife.'" Have "pity on the babe in her womb." Such was the tragedy of settling feuds with dueling pistols.

Andrew Jackson Helps Block Aaron Burr's Scheme

On November 3, **Aaron Burr visited Nashville and persuaded Andrew Jackson to build and provision five flatboats** at Clover Bottom for a payment of $3,500. The boats were to be dispatched down the Cumberland to be received by Burr at the Ohio River. And on that same day, unknown to Jackson at the time, a United States District Attorney "petitioned the Federal Court at Frankfort, Kentucky, to **arrest Aaron Burr** for **treason**." But Burr would elude conviction in Kentucky. About a week after Burr's receipt of his order for five provisioned flatboats, a young man from New York State stopped at Jackson's house with a letter of introduction and asked to spend the night. Jackson had never met the man, but became

189

interested when he began revealing that he was headed for New Orleans to help in a scheme to divide the nation. Jackson asked the New Yorker "how they would effect it. He replied by seizing New Orleans and the bank, shutting down the port, conquering Mexico, and uniting the western part of the union [of States] to the conquered country." And the New Yorker further explained that the military force would consist of Federal troops led by James Wilkinson. And, Jackson surmised that Aaron Burr was involved as well, for the young man stated that his information had come from Samuel Swartwout, of New York, who Jackson knew to be as associate of Burr. Jackson immediately wrote letters warning officials of the danger. To Burr, he warned that, unless the accusations were proved to be false, "no other intimacy was to exist between us." To Tennessee's senator in Washington, Daniel Smith, he warned of a scheme, "in concert with Spain, to seize New Orleans and Louisiana and attempt to divide the union [of States]." Jackson assured President Thomas Jefferson of his readiness to lead troops to defeat such a scheme if necessary.

Andrew Jackson wrote **William Claiborne, the governor of Louisiana**, warning him to put New Orleans "in a state of defense" and "keep a watchful eye on [James Wilkinson]." And, he added, "I love my country and government. I hate [Spaniards]. I would delight to see Mexico reduced, but I will die in the last ditch before I would . . . see the [union of States] disunited."

Meanwhile, **James Wilkinson decided to betray Burr** and seek extra compensation from the **Spanish**. You see, in addition to his federal salary as military commander of the region, Wilkinson was also receiving from the Spanish Government an **annual $2,000 salary as spy number 13**. Wilkinson wrote a letter to Thomas Jefferson detailing **Burr's scheme to seize Louisiana**. At the same time, he sent a letter to the Spanish Government in Mexico City warning them of Burr's scheme to seize Spanish lands to the west, and adding a suggestion that they reward him with a special bonus of $110,000. Upon receiving the letter from Wilkinson, **President Thomas Jefferson** issued, on November 26, a proclamation warning of a military conspiracy "against the dominion of Spain.

Prior to news of the president's proclamation arriving at Nashville, on December 17, **Aaron Burr showed up at Jackson's house**, but Rachel declined to invite him to stay. He lodged at nearby Clover Bottom tavern and conned Jackson and some associates into believing that he was involved in a legitimate undertaking by producing a "blank commission signed by [Thomas] Jefferson." Burr asked for two provisioned flatboats and Jackson agreed. But Jackson sent Rachel's nephew Stockley Hays on one of the boats with a secret letter for Claiborne. Conveniently, the Hays lad needed to go to New Orleans anyway to attend school. Burr departed with the two flatboats at dawn on December 22. A few days later news arrived at Nashville that Thomas Jefferson had issued a proclamation warning of Burr's treasonable scheme.

1807

Burr and Wilkinson Scheme Fails

Burr and Wilkinson failed miserably to mount a revolutionary force of significant size. In January the Federal Army captured Burr's 60 revolutionaries and his 12 boats at Natchez, Mississippi Territory, but Burr had already slipped away in disguise. He was captured a few days later a few miles short of Spanish Florida.

190

The revolutionary group in the northeastern States disbanded. Politicians in the northeastern States would launch no further campaigns to counteract the loss of Federal political power that had been produced by the acquisition of Louisiana.

Their next major political fight to limit national growth would focus on withholding an invitation to the nation of Texas to become a State. Failing at that, they would later attempt to block the taking of land from Mexico. Burr would be tried, but be only found guilty of a high misdemeanor. Afterward he would flee the country. **Wilkinson** would convince President James Madison that he was neither a traitor nor a Spanish spy and would **retain his job as commander of Federal forces in Louisiana**. Knowledge that Wilkinson controlled the defense of New Orleans would greatly worry Andrew Jackson during the upcoming war with Britain.

President Thomas Jefferson keeps America out of Napoleon's War in Europe

Napoleon Bonaparte's French forces had completed the conquest of Prussia by October 1806. In November 1806, Bonaparte had instituted a complete blockade of import-export trade with the British Isles by closing all continental seaports to British merchant vessels. Then, in July 1807, the French army forced Russia to accept French domination. **At that point, only Great Britain stood in the way of complete French domination of Europe.**

In November, the British Government expanded its enforcement of a blockade of Continental seaports, "proclaiming a blockade of ports from which British vessels were excluded, and requiring all neutral vessels going to such ports to stop in a British port, pay a tax, and secure a license before proceeding." The next month **Napoleon's French Government responded with the Milan Decree**, which gave privateers the rights to prizes upon capturing "any vessel, of whatever nation, which obeyed British rules, traded with her or her colonies, or submitted to examination by a British warship."

Owners of merchant marine shipping companies in The States were thereby placed in a difficult position. The European war had swelled trade and profits since 1803, but the British rules would cut into profits and the encouragement of privateers would produce occasional total losses of ship, cargo and seamen. In 1803, domestic exported goods had totaled $42,210,000 and foreign goods re-exported had totaled $13,590,000. That had increased in 1805 to $42,390,000 and $53,180,000 and in 1807 to $48,700,000 and $59,640,000. But seamen working on American merchant ships suffered another danger as well – **British impressments**.

British defense against Napoleon's war machine was particularly dangerous for merchant marine sailors and sailors on British warships. To escape the dangers of war many had deserted the British merchant marine and the British Navy and taken jobs as sailors in the American merchant marine. Jobs were plentiful because war-induced growth had produced a need to hire about 4,000 new sailors each year. About 2,000 of those hired had been **deserting British seamen**. The British Navy had responded by stopping and searching American merchant ships and taking away men who appeared to be probable British deserters. But it was often hard to distinguish between American and British men, because so many looked and talked alike.

The Jefferson Administration responded by issuing identification papers to legitimate American sailors for them to present to British naval officers when confronted with a British search. But many American sailors sold their papers to desperate British deserters, thereby causing many British officers to suspect that other presented papers were fraudulent. The

British were seizing about 1,000 American merchant seamen each year, a process termed **"impressment."** By the end of the Napoleonic Wars about 20,000 British sailors would desert and take jobs in the American merchant marine and the British would impress about 10,000 men from American merchant vessels. But British naval officers were very poor at identifying British deserters, because it is believed that about 90 percent of impressed men were not British citizens and thereby illegally seized. **Since most American merchant seamen were from the coastal region stretching from Baltimore to Boston, the political outcry was most intense in the States of that region.** And owners of merchant marine companies, who were losing ships and cargoes to privateers, further encouraged political protests over British impressments.

1808

The British versus Napoleon, the Embargo Act, Smuggling and the Impressment of Sailboat Crewmen

In spite of the protests and calls for military action to rescue impressed sailors and to defend merchant ships, Thomas Jefferson had been most anxious to keep The States out of the horrific war that Napoleon was waging across Europe. So, the Jefferson Administration had opted to send a diplomatic team to London while pressuring the British Government by announcing that the importation of certain British goods would be disallowed after November 15, 1806. But this approach had been far too meek to persuade the British Government. So, the Federal Congress had passed an **Embargo Act**, to take effect at the beginning of 1808, which "forbade the clearance of all vessels bound for foreign ports." This approach was designed to prevent commerce with England and France either directly or through intermediate seaports. This meant the owners of merchant shipping companies could only legally transport cargo along the coast between Boston and New Orleans. But, the amount of goods requiring shipping between American ports represented a tonnage far below the capacity of their ships and crews. So, many owners would **resort to illegal smuggling**, often directing their vessels to intermediate seaports in the Caribbean. And there would be considerable smuggling to seaports in Canada and Florida. "It was the law-abiding ship-owners, whose vessels were caught at home by the act, who were hardest hit. Commerce for them was ruined. Business that was associated with foreign commerce suffered greatly as well. Goods rotted in warehouses and merchants took heavy losses, while many [farmers] found the market for their surplus cotton, rice, meat, and tobacco destroyed." So, by removing American ships from the European theater, Thomas Jefferson would succeed in keeping The States from becoming involved in Napoleon's War, but he was doing so at great political expense.

1809

Northeast States Experience Protests over the Embargo Act, but Federalist Political Gains are Limited

Owners of shipping companies, out-of-work seamen, owners of import-export businesses, bankers and farmers growing products for export had become angry with Thomas Jefferson and his Democratic Party over the loss of business and jobs as a result of the January 1808 Embargo Act. And Federalist Party politicians were exploiting the political unrest sufficiently to gain control of the **State Governments of Massachusetts** and her neighbors. Many Federalists from the region were advocating enacting State laws to nullify the Embargo Act, claiming that

States were sovereign and had the power of nullification. **Some of these politicians were even advocating State secession.** Some were calling for a regional political convention of several States to nullify the embargo. But 3 days prior to the end of President Jefferson's second term, and with his blessing, Democrats, who overwhelmingly controlled the Federal House and Senate, inhibited the resurrection of the Federalist Party by reducing the scope of the Embargo Act to cover only marine commerce with Britain and France. Shortly thereafter, President Thomas Jefferson retired to his beautiful mountain home, Monticello. Although he had, for a time, given the Federalist Party an exploitable political issue, he retired with The States at peace. **The States were not entangled in Napoleon's horrific European war.**

James Madison, of Virginia, is elected to his First Presidential Term

James Madison, of Virginia, received 70 percent of the Electoral vote. George Clinton of New York State won election as Vice President. From the outset, Federalists knew they were beaten. President Madison would continue into a second term as President.

Chapter 13 — March 1809 to February 1813: The States During the First James Madison Administration

Before resuming the narrative history, I have inserted a summary of the 1808 elections and the organization of the First James Madison Administration.

Virginia lawyer and politician James Madison, a Democrat who served as Secretary of State during Thomas Jefferson's two administrations, was elected President over Federalist candidate Charles Pinckney of South Carolina. James Madison was the son of a prosperous Virginia farmer, James Madison, Sr. The senior Madison had fought in the Defense of Independence and held local political offices. Madison's mother Nelly was the daughter of a prominent Virginia farmer and tobacco merchant. **Through his family, Madison acquired an agricultural orientation**. For many years a bachelor, Madison married the widow Dolly Payne Todd, of Philadelphia when he was 43. When Dolly was still a young girl, her father had converted to the Quaker religion, sold his Virginia farm (at the same time making his bonded African Americans independent) and moved the family to Philadelphia, where he went bankrupt as a starch manufacturer. Four years prior to marrying Madison, Dolly had married a Philadelphia lawyer who, after only 3 years of marriage, had died of yellow fever, leaving her with one son.

Madison finished his education at Princeton in 1772 and studied law afterward. Always of frail health, Madison did not fight in the Defense of Independence. Madison was a Delegate to the Virginia Convention in 1776; a member of the Virginia House of Delegates (1776-1777); a member of the Virginia Council of State (1778-1779); a member — in fact the youngest member at age 29 – of the Continental Congress (1780-1783); again a member of the Virginia House of Delegates (1784-1786); a Delegate to the Annapolis Convention (1786); a Delegate to the Constitutional Convention (1787) where his immense contribution won him recognition as the "Father of the U. S. Constitution;" co-author, with Alexander Hamilton and John Jay, of *The Federalist Papers*, which promoted a strong Federal Government structure; Representative from Virginia (1789-1797); again a member of the Virginia House of Delegates (1799-1800), and finally, Secretary of State in the Jefferson Administrations (1801-1809).

Thomas Jefferson could have had the Democratic Party nomination for a third term, but wishing to follow Washington's example of only 2 terms, **Jefferson had endorsed his Secretary of State, James Madison**. Some southern States Democrat Representatives in the Federal House supported James Monroe of Virginia because he favored a less-powerful Federal Government than did Madison. Some northern States Democrat Representatives supported George Clinton of New York hoping thereby to make a northern State man President. Knowing that they were beaten, many Representatives who favored Monroe boycotted the Democratic Party Caucus, which gave Madison an overwhelming victory on the first ballot: Madison, 83; Monroe, 3; Clinton, 3. George Clinton was nominated for Vice President.

The Federalist Party again nominated Charles Pinckney of South Carolina for President and Rufus King of New York for Vice President.

Vice President Clinton, of New York, would be disloyal to Madison, for he would permit the continuance of the sectional conflict sparked 8 years previously by Aaron Burr, also of New York, and just 4 years previously by the Essex Junto, of Massachusetts. DeGregorio would summarize this election as follows:

"Madison was vulnerable on just one issue – the [Embargo Act of 1808]. It had failed to persuade Britain and France to respect the neutral rights of American ships at sea while at the same time severely damaging [the Federation's] economy. Federalists roundly criticized Secretary of State Madison for advocating the embargo as a means of building up domestic manufactures at the expense of those whose livelihood depended on foreign trade. The unpopularity of the embargo revitalized the Federalist Party, particularly in the [northeastern States], but the sentiment was insufficient to overcome the [Democratic Party] majority that had become entrenched during the Jefferson Administration. President Jefferson played a key role in wooing back Monroe's followers to support the Party's nominee. Immediately after the nominating caucus, old-line [Democrats] denounced Madison as 'unfit to fill the office of President in the present juncture of our affairs.' But, in the end, the [southern and western States] went solidly for Madison. George Clinton, even though he accepted the [Democrat Party] Vice President nomination, criticized the caucus nominating process and allowed his supporters to campaign for him for President. A viable [candidate for President] only in his home State, he won 6 of New York's 19 electoral votes."

Madison won by a wide margin, carrying 70% of the electoral vote, which was **Madison, 122, Pinckney 47, and Clinton, 6**. Sweeping every large State, Madison won the majority of electoral votes in 12 States. From north to south Madison's States were: Vermont, New York, New Jersey, Pennsylvania, Maryland, Ohio, Virginia, Kentucky, North Carolina, Tennessee, South Carolina and Georgia. Pinckney won the majority in only 5 States, the small ones: Massachusetts, New Hampshire, Connecticut, Rhode Island and Delaware.

Madison moved Jefferson's Navy Secretary, Robert Smith, of Maryland, to the office of Secretary of State to appease political antagonists, but was not satisfied with Smith's performance in the job. After 2 years, Madison appointed his nomination rival, **James Monroe**, **of Virginia**, **to serve as Secretary of State** for the remainder of his first term. Later on, James Monroe would become President himself. Albert Gallatin was retained as Secretary of the Treasury. William Eustis, of Massachusetts, served as Secretary of War, but was dismissed after taking the blame for early defeats in the War of 1812. John Armstrong, of New York, replaced Eustis as War Secretary. Caesar Rodney, of Delaware, was retained as Attorney General, but was replaced in 1811 by William Pinckney, of Maryland, because of criticism that Rodney spent too much time moonlighting with his private law practice. Paul Hamilton, of South Carolina, was appointed Secretary of the Navy but was replaced in 1813 by William Jones, of Pennsylvania, because of personal problems with alcoholism.

The huge Democratic Party majority remained unchanged in the Senate (28 versus 6), but by gaining 24 House seats, the Federalists had chipped away at the huge Democratic Party majority in that body (94 versus 48). The mid-term elections strengthened the Democratic Party majorities. The Senate strengthened to 30 versus 6 and the House strengthened to 108 versus 36. Thomas Jefferson had led the Democratic Party to quick dominance with the start of his Administration and James Madison was similarly blessed with huge majorities in the House and Senate.

Louisiana was granted statehood in 1812.

The more significant events involving African Americans during the four years of the First James Madison Administration will now be presented. The 1810 census counted 1,304,151 people of noticeable African descent. This represented a 31% increase over the 1800 count, and 19.2% of the total population, a slight decrease from the 19.6% recorded in 1800. Since the 1800 census, the population of **independent African Americans** had **grown by 58%**, to 97,284, in the **Southern States**, and had grown by **66%** to, 76,086, in the **North**. African Americans represented a barely significant 1.5% of the population of the northeastern States (Massachusetts and neighboring States). Independent African American men had been permitted to vote in Maryland, but the State Government withdrew the right in 1810. In 1811, over 400 bonded African Americans revolted in St. Charles Parish and St. John the Baptist Parish near New Orleans, Louisiana. In that conflict, only a few European Americans were killed, but militia killed about 70 of the rebellious African Americans while putting down the uprising. The Delaware Government prohibited independent African Americans from moving into the State. During the **War of 1812**, African Americans comprised about one sixth of the seamen of the Federal Navy, and Georgia, North Carolina and Louisiana permitted some independent African Americans to serve in the respective State militia. The Tennessee Government outlawed the importation of bonded African Americans from the sister States. In 1812, the Illinois Territory Legislature forbade further settlement by independent African Americans.

This concludes the overview of the first James Madison Administration. The narrative history resumes with first attention going to the American merchant marine problem.

The Narrative History Resumes – March 1809

Non-Intercourse Act Remains a Big Problem for the American Merchant Marine

On June 10, 1809, about 600 American merchant marine ships set sail for Great Britain, with crews and owners joyfully celebrating what they believed to be the British Government's acceptance of the Federal Government's repeal of the British section of its Non-Intercourse Act. But, the seamen were soon disappointed because the British Government rejected the offer for peaceful trade and Napoleon's French Government took advantage of the situation as it **"seized still more American ships in French ports."**

1810

Federal House and Senate Repeal the Non-Intercourse Act

On May 1, 1810, the Federal House and Senate **repealed the Non-Intercourse Act**, thereby permitting the American merchant marine to go anywhere in the world. The language of the Act was intended to coerce Britain and France to repeal their restrictions: "If either France or England should remove its restrictions upon American trade, [The States] would resume non-intercourse against the other – unless the other followed the lead of its rival within 3 months."

The Far West Florida Revolt

On September 23, rebels, numbering about 75, under the command of **Philemon Thomas**, captured the sparsely guarded Spanish fort, San Carlos, at **Baton Rouge** in Spanish West Florida Territory. It was a successful attack. Thomas raised a flag and declared that small part of Spanish West Florida was to be the independent **Republic of West Florida**. This commenced the "West Florida Rebellion," which would succeed in seizing the Spanish land between the Mississippi River and the Pearl River. **The Spanish would never get it back!**

On October 27, **President James Madison proclaimed** that the Republic of West Florida "**should be taken**." Louisiana Territory Governor William Claiborne, who had been born in Virginia, received a directive from President Madison to send troops to the Republic of West Florida and seize it for the United States. Claiborne, a Nation Builder, did just that. The leaders of Spanish West Florida, located at its capital, Saint Francisville, quickly acquiesced. On December 10, the land of this short-lived "Republic" **became part of Louisiana Territory**.

Philemon Thomas celebrated **a job well done**! Philemon Thomas had been born in Virginia, fought in the American Revolution, moved west to Kentucky, and then migrated to Spanish West Florida. In fact, many settlers living in Spanish West Florida had migrated down there from the Southern States! **Philemon Thomas was among the many, many Nation Builder leaders who "Made America."**

Napoleon Still Making Trouble for Americans

Meanwhile, in Europe, **Napoleon Bonaparte tricked James Madison** into believing that he was opening French ports to the American merchant marine. Falling for the trap, Madison proclaimed, on November 2, that the Federal Government would subject Great Britain to the Non-Intercourse Act if its government failed to repeal its Orders of Council within 3 months. Since 1807, the Orders of Council had forbidden "neutral coasting trade between all enemy ports, [proclaimed] a blockade of all ports from which British vessels were excluded, and [required] all neutral vessels going to such ports to stop in a British port, pay a tax, and secure a license before proceeding." Napoleon had responded with the **Milan Decree**, which declared a good prize of any vessel, of any nation, that obeyed the British Orders of Council. So, trade with Europe was dangerous and expensive for the American merchant marine, even though The States were not taking sides in the European war.

1811

Andrew Jackson has a Good Year at Clover Bottom in Middle Tennessee

It was a good year for **Andrew Jackson**. He had sold his racetrack at Clover Bottom to the Nashville Jockey Club before the fall 1811 racing season began. Over the previous 5 years he had "gradually depleted" his debts by applying earnings from his farm and racing stable. **His prized stallion, Truxton**, "had won more than $20,000 in race winnings and stud fees" and the offspring were "becoming famous." One of the offspring was a promising colt, Decatur. But Jackson's racing fortunes were about to reverse. Jesse Haynie's 3-year-old chestnut mare, **Maria**, beat Decatur and won all 6 of the races in which she was entered. During the next several years Maria would consistently win. Years later, when asked about great disappointments in his life, Jackson would answer "Nothing that I can remember, except Haynie's Maria. I could not beat her." No one else would be able to beat her either, for the chestnut mare would never lose a race, not even a heat – amazing.

197

During 1811, War Fever is on the Rise in America

The year 1811 marked a major change in United States Federal politics. The Federal House and Senate convened a month early, on November 2, 1810. Nearly half the members were new, many of the newcomers being from southern and western States. The new Representatives were eager to declare war on Great Britain, France, or both, because they had grievances against Great Britain for aiding Native Americans within reach of the Great Lakes and they had grievances against France for disrupting trade with Europe. Among the new Representatives were **Henry Clay** and Richard Johnson, of Kentucky, **Felix Grundy**, of Tennessee, and **John Calhoun** and Langdon Cheves, of South Carolina. New Representatives joined with returning Representatives of similar mind to take control of the House, electing as Speaker the newcomer Henry Clay, of Kentucky. The great majority of Representatives from the frontier and southern States favored war, for these Nation Builders figured they could expand the National Territories during a war with Great Britain, or France, or both. On the other hand, almost all Representatives from America's seaport regions were strongly opposed to war even though their seamen and shipping company owners were suffering great hardship at the hands of Great Britain and France.

Representatives who favored war were eager to defeat the Native American nations that stood in the way of western and southern expansion, to take Canada from Great Britain, and to take Florida and Mobile Bay from Spain. And they viewed war as the best tactic for taking land from European and Native American nations, and eradicating raids by Native American warriors. So, the pretense for war was rooted in French and British trade prohibitions and British impressments of American seamen. **But the objective of war was taking more land and pacifying the frontier**. And this contradiction between pretense and objective would drastically limit the military success of the Federal Army, the various State militias, and the Federal Navy.

Shawnee Nation is Next to fall to American Westward Migration

Out west, it looked as if the lands of the Shawnee Nation would be the next to be seized among those north of the Ohio River. This greatly worried 2 key leaders of the **Shawnee Nation**, the brothers **Prophet and Tecumseh**. The 1809 Treaty of Fort Wayne, by taking 3,000,000 acres, had pushed the frontier to near the Wabash River, and the Shawnee felt their land would be included in the next seizure. Although Prophet had been a respected Shawnee leader for many years, William Harrison, the Governor of Indiana Territory, feared Tecumseh more, for Tecumseh was a moral leader and skillful at encouraging unification of Native Americans from many nations.

In 1808, Tecumseh and Prophet had established a Shawnee town not far from where Tippecanoe Creek flows into the Wabash River, named it Prophet's Town and made it their headquarters. "A man himself of splendid character, Tecumseh deplored the terrible demoralization [that] the [European American] man's whiskey and diseases had wrought" upon his people. And Tecumseh's moral leadership had worried Harrison most of all, for he fretted over reports that the Shawnee warriors were not drinking whiskey, since whiskey was far more debilitating to a Native than to a European.

During the latter half of 1811, **Tecumseh was traveling through the southern Native American nations**, encouraging political leaders and warriors to join in a unified assault on the European American's frontier. And he and Prophet were working closely with British authorities in Canada to gain their support as well. Tecumseh envisioned a powerful, rejuvenated, well-armed

Native American federation whose warriors would be capable of forcing the Federal Government to negotiate permanent frontier boundaries.

With the new House and Senate in session back in Washington City, and with the capable Tecumseh away in the southern nations, **Indiana Territory Governor William Harrison** decided the time was right **to attack Prophet's Town**. So, he gathered 1,000 militiamen and, on November 7, met a large force of Shawnee defenders not far from Prophet's Town. After 2 hours of fighting, the warriors retreated and Harrison's force was able to destroy most of Prophet's Town the following day. When news of the destruction of Prophet's Town reached Washington City, war advocates in the House and Senate felt their movement was gaining momentum.

1812

The United States Seize the Remainder of Spanish West Florida

On May 14, by a unilateral act of the House and Senate, the Federal Government declared that the remainder of Spanish West Florida was being seized and made a part of the National Territories of the United States.

I suppose this "seizure" was within the House and Senate's constitutional power to "declare war." This declaration involved the land between the Pearl River and the Perdido River. The main feature was Mobile Bay. As you recall, as previously reported, the land between the Pearl River and the Mississippi River had been seized in 1810.

This declaration extended Alabama Territory and Mississippi Territory to the Gulf of Mexico!

War Fever Erupts with Declaration of War against Great Britain

On June 1, President James Madison sent a message to the House and Senate recommending a declaration of war with Great Britain.

He "assigned as principal grievances: impressments, interference with trade, and incitement of [Native Americans] to hostility." Madison purposely ignored the fact that Representatives from New York, New Jersey, Massachusetts, and her neighboring New England States were opposed to war, even though those States "had furnished most of the seamen and three-fourths of the ships of commerce," which had so suffered from impressments.

Political leaders and financial leaders from this northeastern region feared loss of voting power in the Federal Government if America expanded westward. **They were not Nation Builders.** They figured it better to continue to suffer trade restrictions and hope for better times. Anyway, Napoleon's France had been more disruptive than had been Great Britain, so those Representatives thought that France was the more appropriate object of an American declaration of war. The war bill was debated passionately. Some advocated **war with Great Britain** while others advocated **war with France**.

The declaration of war against Great Britain passed the house by a vote of 79 to 49. All Representatives from Ohio, Kentucky, Tennessee, South Carolina and Georgia voted for war. New York Representatives voted 2 for war, 11 against. Massachusetts Representatives voted 6 for war and 8 against. All Representatives from Connecticut, Rhode Island and Delaware voted against war. The northeast lost the vote; the rest of America was in.

Tennessean **Billy Philips** was outside the Capitol building sitting **in the saddle atop Truxton** awaiting news of the vote. When the vote total was announced, Philips was **off at a gallop to inform Andrew Jackson** and the people of Nashville. Nine days, 860 miles and 3 mountain ranges later, Philips and Truxton would arrive in Nashville with news that the Federal House had voted for war with Great Britain.

At the conclusion of voting in the Federal House, debate over a declaration of war began in the Senate. A motion in the Senate to instead declare war on France lost by 2 votes. France was spared because Frenchmen had impressed few seamen, and, since 1805, there had been no significant French Navy to bother American coasts. "More significantly, she had no territory to entice expansionists," like America's Nation Builders. After war with France was voted down, the declaration of war against Great Britain cleared the Senate by a vote of 19 to 13. I have been unable to locate the Senate vote by State, but assume it followed the sectional pattern displayed in the House. **President Madison signed the war bill on June 18**.

In spite of the sectional opposition to war, most advocates expressed great confidence in quick victory. The conquest of Upper Canada and Lower Canada – the primary objective of the war – seemed rather easy, given that the population of The States was 15 to 20 times the population of those British provinces, and the British had only about 4,500 regular British soldiers defending their province. Back in March, John Calhoun had assured that, "in 4 weeks from the time a declaration of war is heard on the frontier, the whole of Upper Canada and a part of Lower Canada will be in our power." And, with war declared, Thomas Jefferson wrote: "The acquisition of Canada this year as far as Quebec will be a mere matter of marching."

Billy Phillips and Truxton rushed into Nashville. Upon learning the news, Andrew Jackson offered James Madison "his military division of 2,500 trained men for instantaneous service and promised to have them before Quebec in 90 days." And William Blount, Governor of Tennessee, endorsed Jackson's proposal with the promise: "He can most certainly do so." But Madison and the Federal War Department **would not accept Jackson's offer**, and succeeding events would demonstrate the error in that decision.

Napoleon's Army Enters Russia

Six days after the Federal Government declared war on Great Britain, **Napoleon Bonaparte's 600,000-man French army** crossed the Niemen River and entered Russia. Napoleon was intent on the conquest of Russia, a feat that had previously been accomplished only once: by the cold-adapted Mongols and their trustworthy horses. The success or failure of Napoleon's military venture would greatly impact the American war with Great Britain. If Napoleon's army succeeded in conquering Russia, then the prospects were bright for its conquest of Great Britain. But, if the Russians defeated Napoleon's army, then the British would probably succeed in defending the British Isles as well.

Just what is the New War in America All About?

The people living in the northern States were rather timid about risking their lives in an attempt to conquer Upper Canada and Lower Canada, considered the major objective of the war. But, Federal soldiers north of the Ohio River had already been attacking a British fort. Yes, even before the Federal Government declared war on Great Britain, about 1,500 Federal soldiers under William Hull had been advancing north toward Detroit from their base in Dayton, Ohio. They aimed to drive British forces from Fort Malden, which guarded the opposite side of the Detroit

River between Lake Erie and Lake St. Clair. Hull's Federal force crossed the Detroit River in July and advanced toward Fort Malden. <u>The fort was guarded by 1,000 British soldiers and 1,000 Native American warriors, who were loyal to</u> **Tecumseh**, <u>the Shawnee Chief, and it was</u> **commanded by Isaac Brock**. Hull found the country surprisingly hostile. He encountered many ex-Americans who had settled in Upper Canada after losing their property during the defense of American Independence. These people still hated independence-minded American's, and had no intention of accepting statehood under the Federal Government. <u>Fearful of defeat by the British-Native American alliance, Hull ordered that his federal force retreat to Detroit. The forces of Brock and Tecumseh followed, laid siege on Detroit and demanded Hull's surrender.</u> **William Hull surrendered his federal force of 2,000 men on August 15**.

The British Navy Dominates the Atlantic Coast

The British navy dominated the western North Atlantic Ocean with 97 warships, including 11 ships-of-the-line, and 34 frigates. The British were blockading commercial shipping in and out of seaports from New York to Georgia. <u>But the</u> **British were allowing shipping into and out of Massachusetts** <u>and neighboring States because the British Government was</u> **purposely encouraging treason** <u>among political and commercial leaders in those New England States</u>. And, treason there was rampant, for the region would "[prosper] from foreign trade during most of the war." Although New England held more than half of the Federation's silver and gold coin, little of it would be invested in Federal war bonds, even less than would be loaned to the enemy, Great Britain. <u>This British encouragement of treason in Massachusetts and neighboring States would extend to April 1814.</u>

Unable to challenge the powerful British naval force, the American navy had to resort to preying on isolated smaller British warships, military transports and commercial shipping. <u>The only warships capable of scaring the British Navy were the 3 new 44-gun frigates:</u> *Constitution*, *President* and *United States*. They were the only American warships of this class, but "they were sturdy and fast, and were superior to vessels of corresponding rank in the British navy."

The first notable American victory during 1812 was the result of a British commander's foolish challenge. James Dacres, the commander of the British frigate *Guerriere*, sought to avenge the 1811 defeat of the British sloop-of-war *Little Belt*, by the American crew of the frigate *President*. So, he challenged any American warship to a duel. Isaac Hull, commander of the frigate *Constitution*, accepted the challenge and the 2 warships met off Sandy Hook on August 19. "Half an hour later the *Guerriere* was a ruined hulk, and 79 of her crew were dead or wounded." Other British Navy commanders would find themselves involved in one-on-one sea battles during 1812. In October the American crew aboard the sloop-of-war *Wasp* would defeat the *Frolic*, killing or wounding all but 20 of the British crew. A week later the American crew of the frigate *United States* would overwhelm the *Macedonian*, capture her and bring her into port. In December the American crew of the frigate *Constitution* would defeat the *Java*. <u>So, American sailors were diligent at seeking one-on-one encounters and avoiding fights with a British fleet of warships.</u>

British Commander Isaac Brock was back in the vicinity of Niagara Falls by September. There, his forces stood in opposition to an American force of 6,000 men, almost all of them New York State militia under the command of Stephen Van Rensselaer. In mid-October Rensselaer ordered his militia to cross the Niagara River and attack Brock's British force. Almost all of the militia refused to follow Rensselaer's order. The few who did cross the river and fight were quickly repulsed. Their only accomplishment was killing the British commander, Isaac Brock. A similar result befell Henry Dearborn, who commanded State militia on a mission to conquer Montreal. When Dearborn's men reached the border between New York State and Lower Canada, his men likewise refused the order to advance across the border. Obviously, the men of New York State and neighboring States were unwilling to risk their lives for the conquest of Upper Canada and Lower Canada.

Andrew Jackson Knows What this War is All About – He Takes Command of the Tennessee Militia

Turning our attention to Tennessee, we observe that **Andrew Jackson was disgusted** over military failures along the Great Lakes, and confident that, **if his Tennessee militia** were permitted to go to war, the outcome would be much different. He had finally gained the opportunity to prove the assertion. In mid-December **2,500 Tennessee fighting men gathered at Nashville** to answer Andrew Jackson's call for 1,500 militiamen to reinforce New Orleans or to occupy the remainder of Spanish West Florida, including Mobile Bay. After a long wait Jackson had finally received orders in October to mobilize his Tennessee militia. Jackson did not know which mission his men would eventually be assigned. The Federal House and Senate had voted to seize the remainder of Spanish West Florida in May, but no military force had yet entered the region to consummate the act. And Jackson was especially eager to fulfill that role.

The October order to mobilize Tennessee militia had been issued from Washington City to **Tennessee Governor William Blount**, strangely bypassing Andrew Jackson. Perhaps Jackson had been bypassed because Secretary of War William Eustis, of Massachusetts, feared Jackson's independent spirit and political potential. Eustis had been Secretary of War since the beginning of the James Madison Administration, but was being dismissed about this time because of repeated failures to seize Upper Canada and Lower Canada. And Eustis was surely consumed by mixed allegiances. Although James Madison was his boss, Eustis' State was trading with the enemy and firmly against supporting the invasion of Upper Canada or Lower Canada.

So, Eustis' War Department was instructing Jackson to gather his militia and put it **under the overall command of James Wilkinson**, commander of Federal forces at New Orleans. Under Wilkinson's oversight, Jackson would be unlikely to gain recognition that could be used to future political advantage. Now, Jackson had long suspected that **Wilkinson was a Spanish spy**, or at least a man prone to commit treason when opportunity presented itself. But he had promised Blount that he would accept orders from Wilkinson, if that were necessary to see his militia activated.

"From every quarter of Middle Tennessee they came, by companies, by platoons, by ones and twos, with horse and on foot, in dark-blue and nut-brown homespun and in buckskin hunting shirts. . . These men had been reared with arms in their hands and they came with rifles." Jackson had recommended rifled weapons because bullets from smooth-bored guns did not "carry straight." **The War Department accepted 2,070 militiamen, to be under Jackson, and the rest were sent home.**

Andrew Jackson and His Tennessee Militia wait at Natchez, Mississippi

Andrew Jackson's militiamen departed Nashville for Natchez, Mississippi Territory, on January 7, 1813. The cavalry took the Natchez Trace and the infantry took flatboats down the Cumberland, Ohio and Mississippi rivers. At Natchez they would await further orders for their deployment. Throughout the month of February, **they would wait!**

America Builds a Navy, just for the Great Lakes

Meanwhile, enthused over American warship dueling success, the Federal House and Senate, in January 1813, funded construction of 6 large frigates and 4 larger, 74-gun vessels. When completed, these warships would greatly expand the power of the American Navy. However, none would be completed before the conclusion of the war with Great Britain. At the same time British Navy commanders positioned their warships near the harbors where American warships were anchored and would thereafter effectively prevent the American warships from leaving port. There would be no more foolish, one-on-one naval duels capable of producing glorious American victories. Yes, those large ocean-going warships would not be available for several years.

But, victory by sailors on new Great Lakes warships was attainable. In fact, by the winter of 1812-1813, **Oliver Perry** and his men seemed to be the only threat to continued British control of Upper Canada. Perry was at Lake Erie overseeing the construction of a fleet of American warships. While men sawed lumber from trees felled in the area and hauled it to the shipwrights, other men were hauling cordage, sails, guns, hardware and ammunition from Philadelphia and Washington City. They were building warships in the wilderness.

President James Madison is reelected to a Second Term

President James Madison, of Virginia, was **reelected** for a second term in office.

Chapter 14 – March 1813 to February 1817: The States during the Second James Madison Administration

Before resuming the narrative history, I have inserted a summary of the 1812 elections and the organization of the second James Madison Administration.

James Madison was easily re-elected to a second term. His opponent was independent candidate DeWitt Clinton of New York. DeWitt Clinton was a nephew of George Clinton, who had been previously elected as Madison's Vice President. A graduate of Columbia College and a lawyer by trade, DeWitt Clinton was a successful New York politician. Like his uncle, George Clinton, DeWitt had been a member of the Democratic Party. Prior to his run for President, DeWitt Clinton had been elected to the New York State Legislature, to the New York City mayor's office, and to the Federal Senate. But sectional politics was a stronger force than party politics in the northeastern States, so Federalists and Democrats had teamed up to support DeWitt Clinton in an attempt to defeat the Virginian, James Madison. The movement started in May 1812 when Democrat State Legislators in New York ditched Madison and nominated DeWitt Clinton for President. To enable independent candidate Clinton to have a clear shot at Madison, the Federalist Party decided to abstain from nominating a man for President at its national convention, which was held in New York in September. Federalists only nominated Jared Ingersoll of Pennsylvania for Vice President.

DeGregorio would summarize Madison's election as follows:

"**The War of 1812 dominated the campaign**. Because the United States suffered early defeats in the [Great Lakes Region], Clinton supporters blasted the President for incompetence in directing the war effort, a war Federalists denounced as groundless. Madison campaigners defended the war as necessary to establish American neutral rights. Clinton sought to appeal to hawks and doves alike. 'No canvas for the Presidency was ever less creditable than that of DeWitt Clinton in 1812,' wrote historian Henry Adams, who accused the candidate of duplicity in 'seeking war votes for the reason that he favored more vigorous prosecution of the war; asking support of peace [Democrats] because Madison had plunged the country into war without preparations; [while] bargaining for Federalist votes as the price of bringing about a peace.' The [southern States and western States] again gave Madison a majority. Even some Federalists rallied around the President because of the war. Opposition to Madison was strongest in [Massachusetts and neighboring States]."

Madison won the electoral vote by 128 to 89. Madison won the majority of electoral votes in 11 States – from north to south they were: Vermont, Pennsylvania, Ohio, Maryland, Virginia, Kentucky, North Carolina, Tennessee, South Carolina, Georgia and Louisiana. Clinton won the majority of electoral votes in 7 States – from north to south they were: New Hampshire, Massachusetts, Rhode Island, Connecticut, New York, New Jersey and Delaware.

James Madison retained much of the Cabinet from his first Administration. **He retained James Monroe, of Virginia, as Secretary of State**. Later James Monroe would become President himself. Alexander Dallas, of Pennsylvania, remained as Secretary of the Treasury until 1816. In that year he played a major role in creating the Second Bank of the United States. William Crawford, of Georgia, was moved from Secretary of War to replace Dallas in 1816. John Armstrong, of New York, who remained a short time as Secretary of War, was forced to resign over the failure of the American expedition to Montreal and the British destruction of Washington City. **James Monroe covered the War slot** for a few months until Madison placed William Crawford in charge of the War Department. Crawford moved to Treasury near the end of Madison's second term, leaving the War Secretary slot vacant. William Pinckney, of Maryland, remained as Attorney General until 1814, when he resigned to serve in the military. Richard Rush, of Pennsylvania, held the Attorney General job for the remainder of Madison's second term. William Jones, of Pennsylvania, remained as Secretary of the Navy until 1815, at which time he was replaced by Benjamin Crowninshield, of Massachusetts.

The Democratic Party retained huge majorities in both the Senate and the House throughout Madison's second term. The Democrat margin in the Senate narrowed only slightly to 27 versus 9. Its margin in the House narrowed more significantly to 112 versus 68. The midterm elections showed little change. The Democrat Senate margin narrowed a bit to 25 versus 11 while its House margin widened a bit to 117 versus 65. As in his first term, James Madison was fortunate to be working with a House and Senate firmly controlled by his own party throughout his second term as President.

Indiana was granted statehood in 1816.

James Madison was concerned about the importance of keeping American citizens truthfully informed in a democratic society, because intelligent behavior – such as voting for well-meaning candidates and going to war for the right reasons – required truthful knowledge of history and current events of local, regional and national importance. He was aware that clever but dishonorable politicians could gain power in a democracy by disseminating deceptive information through politically controlled newspapers and educational media. Of this concern Madison said:

"A popular Government without popular information, or the means of acquiring it, is but a prologue to a farce or a tragedy; or, perhaps both. Knowledge will forever govern ignorance; and a people who mean to be their own Governors, must arm themselves with the power which knowledge gives."

James Madison had foreseen the tragedy that would be perpetrated upon the American people only 4 decades into the future — the era of the rise of the Northern States Republican Party and the Secession of Southern States — the time when **one million Americans would die unnecessary deaths**. [7]

The more significant events involving African Americans during the 4 years of the second James Madison Administration will now be presented. African Americans constituted between 10% and 25% of the sailors under Oliver Perry, the glorious team that won the crucial battles for control of Lake Erie. And a large portion of the crew of the American warship *Chesapeake* was African American. Over 450 African Americans and 150 Santo Domingoans of African descent fought with Andrew Jackson's forces at New Orleans. But in 1814 the Louisiana Government began prohibiting independent African Americans from moving into the State, although it did set up a police corps made up of independent African Americans. When the British abandoned Fort Blount on the Apalachicola Bay in East Florida in 1815, about 300

---

[7] For the history of those future years, read the author's history, *Bloodstains, An Epic History of the Politics that Produced and Sustained the American Civil War*, Volume 2, The Demagogues, available on Amazon.

runaway bonded African Americans from Georgia took possession and began expeditions into Georgia to harass European Americans and bring back other bonded African Americans. This fort was overrun a year later by Federal troops, and about 270 runaway African Americans were killed. The Kentucky Government banned bringing bonded African Americans into the State to be sold. **The American Colonization Society was founded in Washington City**. I will be calling this important organization the American Deportation Society, for the aim was to "rid our country of a useless and pernicious, if not dangerous, portion of its population," the independent African Americans. The Georgia Government began paying for the support of old or infirm bonded African Americans whenever the owner failed to provide support, and it demanded reimbursement by the owner. The Georgia Government also forbade bringing bonded African Americans into the State for sale. This law was in effect from 1816 to 1824. The South Carolina Government instituted a similar law, which was in effect from 1816 to 1818.

This concludes the overview of the second James Madison Administration. The narrative history resumes with discussion of Andrew Jackson's dilemma.

The Narrative History Resumes – March 1813

Andrew Jackson's Tennessee Militia return to Tennessee as Ordered by the War Department

Around the first of March, **Andrew Jackson received orders to dismiss** the Middle Tennessee militiamen right there in Natchez, Mississippi Territory. **Secretary of War John Armstrong, of New York State, had issued the order.** Armstrong had taken over the War Department from William Eustis of Massachusetts, who James Monroe had dismissed for poor performance. Like Eustis, Armstrong perhaps had conflicting allegiances. His boss, James Madison, wanted vigorous prosecution of the war, but militiamen from his State, New York, were unwilling to obey orders to merely cross into Upper Canada. When James Wilkinson sent men to Natchez to recruit many of Jackson's men into the Federal Army, Jackson discouraged contact with the recruiters. He refused to abandon his men, for many of them were still boys. He notified Armstrong that he had led these young men from Middle Tennessee and would take them back, at his own expense if necessary. And if the War Department did not provide rations, he said they would eat the horses along the way. More anxious to get rid of Jackson than to recruit his men, Wilkinson sent rations for 20 days from New Orleans. Jackson gave his 3 horses to sick men and walked all the way back, encouraging everyone along the way. **Concerning Jackson, one fellow exclaimed, "He's tough."** Another replied, "Tough as Hickory." From that day forward, Andrew Jackson would be known as '"Old Hickory."

We now Introduce Sam Houston of Future Texas Fame.

It is now time to introduce Sam Houston, among America's most noteworthy Nation Builders. On March 24 at Maryville, in eastern Tennessee, a rather rebellious **young man of 20 years age volunteered to join the Federal Army. His name was Sam Houston**. Houston was unusual in many ways. Although he had, over recent months, done well as a local schoolteacher, for 3 of his teenage years **he had lived with Cherokees** on an island in the Tennessee River.

In his teenage years, his residence among the Cherokees had met with the approval of **Oo-loo-te-ka, an important Cherokee Chief**. Oo-loo-te-ka, who would later also take the name John Jolly, was the younger brother of Tah-lhon-tusky, who had been the first Cherokee Chief to lead his clan west to present-day Oklahoma. During 1807, Return Meigs, the Federal Agent to the Cherokee Nation, had persuaded 4 Chiefs – Black Fox, The Glass, Tah-lhon-tusky and Oo-loo-te-ka – to advocate before the National Cherokee Council that the whole Nation move west into present-day Oklahoma, to land that had been purchased from France 4 years previously. But an influential and prosperous Chief, The Ridge, had persuaded the Council to vote against moving and to expel the Black Fox, The Glass and Tah-lhon-tusky from the Council as punishment for advocating a move so disrespectful of Cherokee ancestors. Disgraced, Tah-lhon-tusky seceded from the Nation and moved west with his clan to the White River in present-day eastern Oklahoma. Sequoyah, who later created a Cherokee alphabet and system for writing the Cherokee language, was a nephew to Tah-lhon-tusky and Oo-loo-te-ka.

Sam Houston's disapproving brothers had failed to convince him to come back home and help with the family farm. Sam apparently detested farming. On the other hand, **he loved to read books** and reveled in Greek mythology, reading a translation of the *Iliad* so many times that he could recite much of it from memory. And he had loved the carefree life among the Cherokees, and they had seemed to love his presence as well. He best friends were John and James Rogers, two Cherokee youths of partial Scottish descent. **Chief Oo-loo-te-ka considered Sam an adopted son and gave him the Cherokee name, "The Raven."**

Houston's father, also named Sam, had fought in the Defense of Independence, rising to a Captain in Morgan's Rifle Brigade, "the most celebrated corps in the Continental Army." And Sam, the father, had remained in the Army afterward, making that his career. Descended from Scots out of the northern section of Ireland, the original Houston immigrant had arrived in 1730 and settled in the Valley of Virginia. He had inherited the family farm and had married Elizabeth Paxton, likewise **descended from Scots** out of the northern section of Ireland, and from a prosperous Valley of Virginia family. Although Sam loved to read, he had been a poor student as a youth, preferring his father's library to the classroom.

After Sam's father's death in 1806, Elizabeth, who was then 50 years old, had sold the Virginia farm, paid off considerable debt, and moved with Sam and his 5 brothers to **eastern Tennessee** to create a new farm near some Houston cousins who had lived in the region for many years.

Sam's mother Elizabeth did not oppose his entering the Army. Her late husband had fought the British and Sam could do the same. She slipped a gold ring on Sam's finger and, as Sam would recall many years later, admonished him with these words:

> "My son, take this musket and never disgrace it: for remember, I had rather all my sons should fill one honorable grave than that one of them should turn his back to save a life. Go, and remember, too, that while the door of my cabin is open to brave men, it is eternally shut against cowards."

Federal Military Takes Control of Mobile Bay in Spanish West Florida

Andrew Jackson had hardly seen his militiamen safely back to Middle Tennessee when **James Wilkinson led a military force into Mobile Bay and seized the remainder of Spanish West Florida**. As previously mentioned, the Federal Government had declared on May 14, 1812, that the remainder of Spanish West Florida was annexed to the National Territories. This was the land between the Pearl River and the Perdido River. But no military action had been taken during the ensuing 11 months. So, during April 1813, Wilkinson's men seized the Spanish territory without a fight "after bluffing out the garrison at Mobile." Andrew Jackson had hoped to take a part in taking this Spanish land, but it appears that his men were not needed. Perhaps Jackson's presence at Natchez had forced Wilkinson to stop procrastinating and take the desired military action. In any event, after Wilkinson's men completed the seizure at Mobile, **only East Florida remained in Spanish hands**. Its boundaries match the boundaries of today's state of Florida. The Spanish Governor of East Florida was headquartered at Pensacola.

Andrew Jackson is William Carroll's second in the latter's Duel with Jesse Benton

During the middle of July, Andrew Jackson became involved in a duel between 2 men. The challenger was Jesse Benton, the brother of Thomas Benton, who was an officer in the Middle Tennessee militia and, during the trip to Natchez, was one of Jackson's aides-de-camp. The defendant was William Carroll, the brigade inspector during the militia trip to Natchez. The cause of the quarrel is obscure, but it must have been the result of a controversy during the militia trip to Natchez. Actually, the challenge was originally leveled by Littleton Johnston, another officer in the militia, but Carroll had refused to accept that challenge, "on the ground that Johnston was not a gentleman." It was at that point that Jesse Benton had proffered his challenge. Carroll had felt obligated to accept the second challenge and asked Andrew Jackson to be his second. **Jackson's attempt to ameliorate the quarrel came to naught**. The duel took place with Benton getting off the first shot, but missing Carroll. At that point Benton turned his back on Carroll, bent over and presented his buttocks as his least vulnerable body part. Carroll obliged by pumping a shot of lead into Benton's proffered part, "which did far more injury to the spirit than to the flesh." You will soon see what gives significance to this sadly amusing story.

Creek Nation Launches Bloody War in Mississippi Territory

On August 30, **warriors of the Creek Nation**, **commanded by William Weatherford**, launched a **surprise attack on Fort Mims in Mississippi Territory** and **killed about 180 settlers and 70 Louisiana militiamen**. At about the same time, Weatherford's warriors probably **killed about 250 more settlers in the region**. As previously reported, two years earlier, during October 1811, Tecumseh, the Shawnee Chief, had been traveling through the Creek Nation, encouraging warriors to join northern nations in a coordinated attack on the advancing Americans. And, Weatherford and many Creek warriors had been persuaded to embrace Tecumseh's agenda. News of Federal defeats along the Canadian border had more recently convinced Creeks that they were capable of driving European American settlers from Mississippi Territory.

Although a major Creek leader, **William Weatherford was only one-eight Native American.** The Creeks called him Red Eagle. He was the son of a Scottish trader, Charles Weatherford, and a half-sister of Alexander McGillivray. McGillivray, until his death in 1793, had been for many years the powerful and prosperous leader of the Creek Nation. McGillivray was the son of a Scottish trader, Lachlan McGillivray and Sehoy Marchand. Sehoy Marchand was the daughter of a French military commander, Louis Marchand, and a Creek woman. So, William Weatherford was one-eighth Creek and seven-eighths European.

Fort Mims was "the fortified residence of Samuel Mims," a man of considerable wealth by frontier standards, whose ancestry was half European and half Creek. But Mims' allegiance was to the European American settlers, not the Creek Nation. His was the largest fortified structure in the region. Seventy Louisiana militiamen, under Daniel Beasley, had taken refuge at the fort along with many nearby settlers, as they had all sought protection from the Creek warriors.

Just before News Arrives of the Creek Massacre at Fort Mims, Jackson is Involved in a Gun Fight in Nashville

Five days after the massacre at Fort Mims, **Jesse Benton and his brother**, **Thomas Benton**, arrived in Nashville and went into the City Hotel. You will recall these brothers being mentioned during the return from Natchez. Each brother wore 2 single-shot pistols. At about the same time Andrew Jackson, John Coffee and Stockley Hays arrived at the Nashville Inn, which was diagonally across the Court House Square. News of the massacre had not yet reached the town. Jackson, Coffee and Hays were armed and Jackson also carried a riding whip. Returning from a trip to the post office, Jackson encountered Thomas Benton in front of the City Hotel. Raising his whip Jackson challenged: "Now, defend yourself you damned rascal!" Thomas Benton reached for his pistol, but Jackson was first with his pistol at Thomas Benton's chest. Thomas Benton backed down a hall toward the Hotel's rear porch. **At this point, his brother, Jesse Benton, shot Jackson from behind.** Jackson fell forward, discharging his pistol, but only grazing Thomas Benton. Thomas Benton fired his 2 pistols at Jackson as he was falling and Jesse Benton rushed toward Jackson to shoot him again. But a bystander shielded Jackson. John Coffee came upon the scene firing. He missed Thomas Benton, but managed to club him with the butt of his pistol. Hays sprang at Jesse Benton with a sword cane, but it broke upon a coat button. Hays kept coming with a knife, and Jesse Benton pressed his second pistol against Hays chest, but it failed to fire.

Apparently, Thomas Benton's 2 pistol shots had missed. But **Andrew Jackson almost bled to death from Jesse Benton's bullet**. The bullet had "shattered" his left shoulder and become "embedded against the upper bone of that arm." Physicians recommended amputating the arm, but Jackson insisted **"I'll keep my arm."** Shortly afterward Nashville received the news of the horrible massacre at Fort Mims.

Oliver Perry Leads Americans in Heroic Victory on the Great Lakes

Meanwhile, the war with Great Britain continued along the Great Lakes. On September 10, The States finally won a significant victory in the drive to conquer Upper Canada. This effort did not require a large army – just a core force of determined sailors under the command of the brilliant **Oliver Perry, of Rhode Island**. Under Perry's oversight, the Americans had constructed 10 warships on a tributary of Lake Erie, launching them into the main part of the lake on August 4. Then Perry's force defeated the British fleet at Put-in-Bay on September 10. Unable to defend against Perry's fleet, **the British decided to evacuate Detroit and Malden**. This made the retaking of Detroit much easier for American ground forces. So, forces under William Harrison invaded Ontario, and at the Battle of the Thames, defeated the smaller British force that had remained, as well as the allied Native American forces, which were led by Tecumseh. This put the Lake Erie region firmly under the control of the Americans. Of his remarkable victory, Oliver Perry said, "We have met the enemy and they are ours!"

Northeastern Federalist Obstruct the War Efforts of the Nation Builders

In spite of the victory by Perry's sailors, State secession advocates among Federalist politicians were gaining control of the Massachusetts State Government and the governments of neighboring States. Marine shipping and import-export businesses in the region were making big profits because <u>the British had intentionally omitted the northeastern States from</u> <u>its blockade of the American coast</u>. Obviously, the British blockade policy was designed to encourage a State Secession political movement in Massachusetts and neighboring States, and the plan was working quite well. Divide and conquer. During 1813, secession-leaning Federalists would control all of the State governments in and around Massachusetts. In Massachusetts and neighboring States, Federalist Party politicians wanted a strong Federal Government only if they could exercise significant political influence over that government. So it would be with grave fear that they would observe Nation Builders in Tennessee and Kentucky using the war to expand the Federation westward, southward and northward. They recognized that, for most of the Federation's people, the war was primarily an effort to expand the United States. Successful national expansion would mean that politicians in Massachusetts and neighboring States would have no hope of exercising future political influence over an enlarged Federal Government, considering the small size of Massachusetts and neighboring States. So, retaining big profits from British trade was not the primary issue moving these Federalist politicians toward State secession.

The Northeastern Culture was simply opposed to Nation Building.

<u>Opposition to the war among the people of New York, Massachusetts and neighboring States</u> <u>made it easy for</u> **James Wilkinson to fumble his mission to conquer Montreal**. <u>He had a force</u> <u>of 2,000 men under his command and the support of another army under Wade Hampton, of South</u> <u>Carolina.</u> Like Andrew Jackson, Hampton distrusted Wilkinson's loyalty and hated him "cordially." Nevertheless, he was committed to support Wilkinson in the conquest of Montreal. But, after Wilkinson's 2,000 men were beaten back by 800 Canadians at Chrysler's Farm, Hampton realized that his force, which was advancing by a different route, would be too small to conquer Montreal alone. So, he and his men retreated to winter quarters as well. **Wilkinson would be fired for his failure to attack Montreal.**

Although Seriously Wounded, Jackson leads Tennessee Militia against Weatherford's Creeks

<u>Meanwhile,</u> **in Middle Tennessee, John Coffee immediately called up his cavalry upon hearing news of the massacre at Fort Mims** – <u>even before the news reached Washington</u> <u>City. Governor William Blount quickly authorized a Tennessee militia of 2,500 men.</u>

From his bed, too weak from his wound and loss of blood, Andrew Jackson alleged, "The health of your general is restored." And, he promised that he would "command in person." Jackson dispatched spies into the Creek Nation and sent emissaries to Creeks who had remained friendly and had refused to follow William Weatherford. Furthermore, Jackson sent emissaries to the Cherokee Nation and the Choctaw Nation seeking the support in forcing Weatherford's Creeks to seek peace. On October 11, Jackson, "a haggard man with an arm in a sling," broke camp and led his militiamen from Fayetteville southward toward the Creek Nation. Coffee and his cavalry were already camped at Ditto's Landing on the Tennessee River, just below the settlement of Huntsville, in present-day Alabama. Jackson moved his men downstream to the southern-most tip of the Tennessee River, and there some of them built a defensive supply fortress named Fort Deposit. Other militiamen cut a road across the Raccoon Mountains to the Ten Islands of the Coosa River, which was 50 miles farther south. It took them only 6 days. There, Jackson directed the building of **another fortress, Fort Strother**, from which he would launch attacks on Creek towns. But the provision contractors were behind schedule, the supplies arrival dates were uncertain, and the men were getting very hungry. On the other hand, Jackson expected military help, for his militiamen were not the only forces gathering to attack Weatherford's Creeks. Militia units from Georgia, Louisiana and Mississippi Territory were expected.

The Creek town of **Tallushatchee** was 13 miles away from Fort Strother. It contained 200 warriors who were loyal to Weatherford. John Coffee led 1,000 men against the town on November 13. While only losing 5 killed and 51 wounded, Coffee's men killed all the warriors and captured 84 women and children. **David Crockett**, of later Alamo fame, who was among Coffee's men, would report, "We shot them like dogs." Upon hearing the news, Jackson dispatched a report exclaiming, "We have retaliated for Fort Mims."

After considering the overwhelming defeat of fellow Creeks at Tallushatchee and Jackson's likely reinforcement by Cherokee warriors and other militia units, Creek leaders in the town of **Talladega** decided to defy Weatherford's call for all Creeks to join together in waging war against the European Americans. In response, 1,000 Weatherford warriors put the fortified town of Talladega under siege. A Talladega runner arrived in Andrew Jackson's camp on November 7 and pleaded for help in liberating his town. Jackson's response was immediate. Talladega was across the Coosa River, 30 miles toward the south. Jackson's men "deployed for battle on November 9." Although many warriors managed to flee during the fight to liberate Talladega, Jackson's men managed to kill 300. Jackson's loss was only 15 dead and 87 wounded. But hunger was still Jackson's main enemy. Finally, at the time that many of the men were mutinying, provisions finally arrived: 150 beeves and nine wagonloads of flour.

On December 10, most of Andrew Jackson's militiamen chose to return to their homes in Middle Tennessee. They had joined up one year previously, had marched with Jackson to Natchez and back, and, although at home for several months afterward, believed that their one-year obligation was concluded. It would take time for Jackson to rebuild his militia. Meanwhile, the Georgia militia was in retreat after its fight with Weatherford's warriors. The Louisiana militia and the Mississippi militia had "accomplished little." Many Creeks were emboldened by these signs of weakness, enabling Weatherford to double the size of his warrior force. Surely worried, Jackson must have been wondering if his Cherokee allies would stick by him. On December 12, William Cocke arrived with 1,450 East Tennessee militiamen: "as fine-looking troops as you ever saw." But Jackson dismissed them upon learning that their tour of duty would conclude in just 10 days.

1814

Jackson and Sam Houston at the Battle of Horseshoe Bend

Governor William Blount advised Andrew Jackson to gather John Coffee's cavalry and retreat to Tennessee. But, Jackson warned that a retreat would "add 5,000 wavering Choctaws, Cherokees and hitherto friendly Creeks to Weatherford's cause." **Jackson's force dwindled to a mere 130 men before 800 fresh recruits arrived from Tennessee** on or about December 16. Jackson immediately ordered an advance toward Talladega, camping there on December 18. Jackson and his men were accompanied by 200 Cherokee warriors. Jackson took his men farther south toward Weatherford's stronghold at the section of the Tallapossa River called **Horseshoe Bend**. During the night of January 21, Creek warriors attacked in force. The battle continued into the morning before the Creeks finally withdrew.

Jackson was thankful that his Cherokee warriors "had done well in the battle." It was basically a draw, but would be reported in Tennessee as a victory and the news would stimulate recruitment. Jackson's men buried the dead, including a Jackson kinsman, Alexander Donaldson, made litters from the hides of dead horses, and retreated northward toward Fort Strother with their wounded. Weatherford's warriors, "noiseless, invisible, a part of the leafless landscape of winter, crept alongside" the retreating militiamen. They attacked Jackson's men as they crossed Enotachopco Creek and inflicted considerable damage, in spite of Jackson's efforts to plan and direct a defense for the perilous crossing. The sole cannon was almost lost. It was untrue, but Tennessee newspapers hailed this battle as a victory as well, in their attempts to encourage recruitment. **Jackson desperately needed more men.**

By February 21, Andrew Jackson was expressing solid confidence. **A new Tennessee militia force of 5,000 men had arrived.** Although "hastily raised and poorly equipped," they could be trained and were present in ample numbers. Furthermore, the Thirty-Ninth Federal Infantry, complete with young **Sam Houston**, had arrived to serve under Jackson's command. These men were disciplined and trained and capable of setting a good example for the other militiamen. On February 21, Jackson wrote, "[the Federal infantry] will give strength to my arm and quell mutiny." Four days later he wrote, "With the continuation of the smiles of fortune I shall soon put an end to the Creek war." **And Jackson had the services of 500 Cherokee cavalry**, 100 friendly Creek warriors and a few Cowetas warriors as well. Obviously, **William Weatherford's warriors were in grave danger**. Weatherford's headquarters was at To-ho-pe-ka, the town located in the Horseshoe Bend section of the Tallapoosa River.

As dawn broke on March 27, it was apparent that Jackson was at To-ho-pe-ka with 2,000 infantrymen plus the aforementioned Cherokee and friendly Creek warriors. Weatherford's force of 1,000 Creek warriors defended the place behind protective breastworks, protected behind piles of pine logs. Cannon balls and grape shot proved ineffective. It would be necessary to storm the defensive structure.

Weatherford's warriors had positioned a fleet of canoes to provide a retreat across the river, should they need them. Realizing a need to remove the canoes, **The Ridge led his Cherokee warriors** as they swam the river while Creeks poured on musket fire, as they drove the Creek pickets back to their breastworks, and as they removed the canoes to the opposite bank.

Then Jackson ordered 1,000 of his men to make a line to charge upon command and warned the men that anyone observed retreating without cause would be shot. Meanwhile, he permitted the Creeks to evacuate the women and children. That completed, the order was given for the massive charge.

"Major Lemuel Montgomery of the Thirty-Ninth Regiment was the first man on the works. He reeled back dead." **Sam Houston was the second man upon the ramparts.** "Waving his sword he leaped down among the [Creek warriors] on the other side." **Houston's platoon** "scrambled after its leader." There was a hard fight on the rampart, but it was overrun. **Houston received an arrow into his thigh**, which a fellow soldier pulled out with great difficulty, thereby making the wound worse. This forced Houston to retreat in search of a surgeon to stop the extensive bleeding. The Creek warriors retreated in small bands into the rugged terrain behind the rampart, where 20 battles raged at once. [Houston would later write],

"Arrows, and spears, and balls were flying, [and] swords and tomahawks [were] gleaming in the sun."

The Creek warriors refused offers to accept surrender. When Creeks fled toward the river where the canoes had been, **The Ridge led his Cherokee warriors into the river where they fought the Creeks hand-to-hand**. "With his sword [The Ridge] killed one [Creek] and left the sword jutting up in another. He took the knife from a third and butchered him with it. In all, in the bloodied water, he slaughtered 6 Creeks before his passion ebbed and he was left standing in the river among his men, satisfied."

Eventually, only a small band of defenders remained. They were "entrenched in a covered redoubt at the bottom of a ravine. Andrew Jackson's demand for surrender was refused. **Sam Houston**, by this time bandaged up, volunteered his platoon to charge the "portholes, which bristled with arrows and rifle barrels." When his men hesitated, **Houston grabbed a musket and charged forward**:

> **"Five yards from the redoubt [he] stopped and leveled his piece. He received a volley from the portholes. One ball shattered his right arm. Another smashed his right shoulder. His musket fell to the ground and his command took cover. [He] tried to rally his men [but] they failed him and alone he climbed back up the ravine under fire and collapsed when he reached the top."**

Applying more intelligence to the challenge, Jackson then ordered the redoubt set fire with flaming arrows. The Creeks had fought to the last man. Jackson would write Rachel, "The carnage was dreadful."

The count of dead Creeks was 557 on land and about 350 in the river. Perhaps 100 had escaped, including Menawa, the local Chief, who had disguised himself as a dead squaw. Andrew Jackson's European American force had suffered 32 dead and 99 wounded. His Native American force had suffered 23 dead and 47 wounded.

But, apparently by chance, **William Weatherford was not present that day**. So, Jackson's force moved south toward the Hickory Ground at the junction of the Coosa River and the Tallapoosa River, where reports suggested that Weatherford was rallying a remnant of Creek warriors. Fort Toulouse was situated at this strategic spot. But, when Jackson's men arrived, the Creek warriors fled, and the Federal flag was easily flown over the fort, which was renamed Fort Jackson. But where was William Weatherford?

"I am Bill Weatherford." Weatherford had walked into the fort unarmed, and "bare to the waist, his buckskin breeches and moccasins badly worn." Weatherford, Jackson and his aide, John Reid, walked into the tent and talked. Reid would later write up an account of the conversation. Weatherford announced, **"I am come to give myself up**. I can oppose you no longer. I have done you much injury. I should have done you more . . . [but] my warriors are killed. . . I am in your power. Dispose of me as you please." But Jackson countered that, since Weatherford had walked into the fort on his own accord, he was not a captive. He replied, "I would gladly save you and your nation, but you do not even ask to be saved. If you think you can contend against me in battle, go and head your warriors." But Weatherford lamented, "There was a time when I . . . could have answered you. . . I could animate my warriors to battle; but I cannot animate the dead." He only requested that Jackson help feed the women and children who had fled to the woods. "They never did any harm. But kill me, if the [European Americans] want it done."

Jackson poured Weatherford a cup of brandy and promised to help the women and children. Weatherford promised to encourage the remaining Creek braves to be peaceful. They shook hands. **Then, William Weatherford "strode from the ruined fort in which his mother had been born – vanishing from the view of the astonished soldiery, and from history."**

Of Weatherford, John Reid would write, "He possessed all the manliness of sentiment – all the heroism of soul, all the comprehension of intellect calculated to make an able commander." And, as previously reported, Weatherford was only one-eight Creek, the remaining ancestry being European American. He and his warriors had been persuaded to war by the great Shawnee Chief, Tecumseh, and by reports of British victories along the Great Lakes. But he had greatly underestimated the power and resolve of Andrew Jackson and his Tennessee militia.

Tennesseans were different. Andrew Jackson and Sam Houston were Nation Builders!

Sam Houston would almost die from the surgery that would later be performed to remove the ball from his shoulder. He would receive further treatment in New York in 1816. But the shoulder would never completely heal, and the wound received in the rather foolish charge of the final Creek redoubt would impair the use of that arm for the rest of his life. But Houston would be promoted to Second Lieutenant during his recovery. Elizabeth Houston had no reason to question her son's bravery.

Jackson Replaces Wilkerson as Federal Military Commander over Tennessee and Territories of Louisiana and Mississippi

On May 28, the Federal **Secretary of War, John Armstrong**, of New York State, **gave Andrew Jackson** the job that **had been held by James Wilkinson**. We say goodbye to Wilkinson:

> You will recall that James Wilkinson had been forced to resign in disgrace after inept leadership during the assault on Montreal. Wilkinson would twice survive courts martial over charges that he was also a paid Spanish spy. Then, James Wilkinson, former spy for Spain, would move to Mexico. He would die there in 1825. Of this traitor it would be said, "he never won a battle or lost a court martial."

In his new job, Jackson commanded the Seventh Federal Military District, comprising Tennessee, Louisiana and Mississippi Territory. Secretary of War James Armstrong did not worry about Jackson gaining any additional political prestige with the new job because southern Native Americans were expected to be peaceful and British forces were not expected to launch a southern attack. So, Armstrong instructed Jackson to retain a small militia of only 1,000 soldiers.

Jackson Forces Creek Nation to Cede 23,000,000 Acres

Under the threat of "destruction," all chiefs of the Creek Nation gathered at Fort Jackson to sign over land to the Federal Government. Jackson demanded about half of

the **"ancient Creek domain" – 23,000,000 acres.** The vast territory amounted to one-fifth of the present State of Georgia plus three-fifths of the present State of Alabama. William Weatherford had only persuaded a part of the Creek Nation to join him in war, but land was also demanded of the Creeks who had refused to follow Weatherford into war. Treating friend and foe alike, Jackson was building a nation, and wanted to ensure that no Creeks lived near Georgia or Tennessee or Spanish Florida. And he was providing for a safe settler route between Middle Tennessee and Mobile on the Gulf of Mexico. **On August 9, a land cession treaty was signed by 36 Creek chiefs.** Weatherford's warriors had been supported by only one of the chiefs present at the signing. Weatherford's other supporting chiefs had refused to come to the fort.

With Napoleon Out of the Way, Great Britain Launches Attacks on America

Meanwhile, Great Britain was finally gearing up to win the war in North America. Napoleon had been removed from the top position in the French Government on April 13, and this French political development had made the British Government more confident of British security in Europe. Consequently, the British Government had decided to send to Lower Canada and Upper Canada all veteran troops needed to secure those possessions and to force The States to accept favorable peace terms. In July, just before the British regulars arrived in Lower Canada, American forces under Jacob Brown and Winfield Scott had fought fierce but indecisive battles in upstate New York. Shortly afterward, **the British commander, George Prevost, had at his command 30,000 British regular troops**.

By the way, Prevost had little trouble feeding this large force, for, as he wrote on August 27, "Two thirds of the army [was being] **supplied with beef by American contractors, principally of Vermont and New York**." We clearly see that many in Vermont and New York were opposed to the Nation Builders.

Such observations concerning American attitudes toward the war encouraged Prevost to invade New York State along the Lake Champlain route with troops and boats during August. His boats encountered sailors on 13 small American warships commanded by Thomas Macdonough. Although the two naval forces were rather evenly matched in size and firepower, the **American fleet defeated** the British fleet, forcing the British to retreat to the north end of the lake. Prevost withdrew his British troops as well, thereby eliminating the threat of a British conquest of upstate New York.

British burn the new capital buildings at Washington, D. C.

Simultaneous with the British advance down Lake Champlain, a combined sea-and-land British force under Robert Ross advanced up the Chesapeake Bay toward the new Federal capital at Washington City. The British force consisted of more than 20 vessels and a force of 4,000 regular British soldiers. A smaller American fleet of vessels and 5,000 to 6,000 green militiamen, all under **Joshua Barney**, opposed the British advance (at this time John Armstrong of New York State was Secretary of War). **The American defenders retreated and then fled, leaving the Federal capital, with its new Federal buildings, for the British to burn on August 24.**

After destroying Washington City, the British headed for **Baltimore**, Maryland. **Defenders at Baltimore succeeded in turning back the British force and in killing Ross, its commander. During the defense of Baltimore, Francis Key, of Maryland composed text of the** *Star-*

Spangled Banner, which would become the Federation's national anthem. Concluding that the conquest of Baltimore would not be worth the cost in British killed and wounded, the **invasion force withdrew** from the Chesapeake region.

Great Britain's Major Objective is the Conquest of Louisiana

Meanwhile, "the most formidable military expedition the New World had ever seen moved toward its secret rendezvous at Jamaica." This was the main British thrust, the attacks in New York and Washington City being more diversionary in nature. From the Jamaica military base, the British planned "to subjugate" Louisiana and conquer the Federal Territories below Tennessee and along the Mississippi River, hopefully all the way to St. Louis. Planning for the attack had probably begun in London while James Wilkinson commanded the defense of Louisiana and Mississippi Territory, and with the knowledge that Wilkinson was Spanish spy Number 13, incompetent as a commander of fighting men, and unwilling to mount a vigorous defense. But, soon afterward, Wilkinson had been transferred north to attempt the conquest of Montreal. London planners hoped he would be reassigned to New Orleans, but would soon learn that he had been fired. Their grand plan for southwestern conquest would have been rather easy, if opposed by Wilkinson and Secretary of War John Armstrong, of New York State. But that was not to be, for **James Monroe would make sure that the men standing in the way of this massive British assault force would be comprised mostly of Tennesseans, and that the force would be commanded by Andrew Jackson.** London military planners knew of Jackson's success at fighting Native Americans and, from their failed attempt to recolonize The States, they had learned that **Tennesseans were the most fearsome fighting men on the North American continent.**

So, as the weeks transpired, London planners became less optimistic. **Eventually, they would advise British peace negotiators to obtain a no-win peace treaty**, probably as a contingency against failure of their southern Mississippi Valley invasion plan. They probably reasoned that, if the Southern military plan succeeded, they would break the treaty.

British promote Currency Chaos in Ploy to Divide and Retake America

By the fall of 1814, silver and gold coin was extremely scarce outside of Massachusetts and neighboring States. As mentioned before, the British partial-embargo tactic was designed to benefit Massachusetts and neighboring States in hopes of encouraging a State Secession movement. The British war tactic also made bankers and commercial men in those States **increasingly wealthy** and concentrated the Federation's supply of gold and silver coin in that region. Furthermore, the British embargo was preventing farmers, especially southern States cotton farmers, from shipping their crops and receiving payment. By fall of 1814, every bank that operated outside of Massachusetts and neighboring States suspended payments in gold and silver coin. The economy of most of the nation therefore suffered greatly because it was forced to **rely entirely on paper money**, and much of the paper money in circulation was **fraudulent**. During the suspension of gold and silver coin issuance, revenue received by the Federal Government alone contained $5,000,000 in counterfeit paper.

British Seek Coalition with Louisiana Pirates

Louisiana pirates enter the picture at this point. On the Louisiana coast a powerful band of pirates, under **Jean Lafitte**, occupied formidable fortifications at their headquarters base at **Barataria Bay**. For many years, these men had been attacking Spanish shipping and selling their booty in New Orleans, thereby participating in the region's economy. Hoping to enlist the allegiance of these pirates, British emissaries arrived at Barataria Bay aboard the *Sophie* on September 3 and proposed to Lafitte: "I call upon you, with your brave followers, to enter into the service of Great Britain, in which you shall have the rank of Captain." And they warned him that, if he refused, he would be considered their enemy. Coyly, **Lafitte responded:** "If you grant me fifteen days . . . to put my affairs in order . . . I will be entirely at your disposal." Anticipating Lafitte's cooperation, the emissaries sailed off the following day to join the *Hermes*, the *Carron* and the *Childers* in an attack of Fort Bowyer, which protected Mobile Bay.

President Madison is close to a Nervous Breakdown, so Virginian James Monroe begins Directing the War Effort

Finding the Federal buildings in ashes upon returning to the new Capital along the Potomac River, **President James Madison directed the Federal Government to set up temporary headquarters in Philadelphia**. And Madison decided to fire his Secretary of War, John Armstrong, of New York, and to **add Secretary of War to James Monroe's duties as Secretary of State.**

Recognizing that President James Madison "was on the verge of nervous prostration," James Monroe simply "took charge."

Monroe wanted to "wage war as it had not been waged before," but the Federal Treasury had no money, which had forced an end to Federal military recruitment, and political and business leaders in Massachusetts and neighboring States were advocating State secession. "**In the blackest hour since Valley Forge, James Monroe** pinned his hope for deliverance on emergency measures for **raising money**, Federal conscription for **enlisting soldiers**, and on **Andrew Jackson**. Madison found $100,000 to place at the Southern Commander's disposal and [he] validated levies for troops, adding Kentucky and Georgia to the territory from which [Jackson] could draw." Meanwhile, **Andrew Jackson, the Southern Commander, had moved down to Mobile** and established his military base there, using the forts at that region to advantage.

British Seek Coalition with the Creek Nation

To augment the British southern assault plan, agents had persisted at inciting Native Americans to go to war against European American settlements along the Gulf Coast. Shortly before the signing of Jackson's land cession treaty with the Creeks, a British force under Edward Nicholls had seized Pensacola and attempted to raise an army of Native Americans, Spaniards and Frenchmen. Nicholls would later reveal the plan:

> "The British would occupy Pensacola as a base, then seize the mouth of the Mississippi and Mobile, and, marching on Baton Rouge, cut off New Orleans from above and below. [Bonded African Americans] were counted on to join the [African American] regiments of Jamaica and help was expected from the Louisiana [men who were of significant African descent]."

Jackson Prepares to Defend the Gulf Coast from British Attack

John Coffee arrived from Middle Tennessee during September with 1,800 cavalrymen, each with a horse and a rifle, giving Jackson greater "confidence." Coffee asserted that "every one of my [men] wants to get within fair buck-range of a [British soldier]." Upon discovering that British forces were occupying Pensacola with Spanish consent, Jackson, without seeking orders from Washington, took his men east and **invaded Spanish Florida**. He was before **Pensacola with 3,700 men** on November 6. Jackson's force captured the town and **secured surrender** by the Spanish authority, Commandant Manrique. That night, the **British abandoned Fort Barrancas**, blowing it up as they left to sail off in their warships, which were anchored offshore. The seizure of Pensacola put an end to Nicholls' efforts to raise a British-led force within that region and "it ruined British prestige among the die-hard Creeks and Seminoles. Deserted by allies who had promised so much, [those Natives] fled destitute into the Florida wilderness." Jackson and his men left Pensacola shortly afterward to **reinforce Mobile**.

The entrance to Mobile Bay was guarded by Fort Bowyer. Having overseen considerable strengthening work, Andrew Jackson was confident that the fort could hold off a major attack. Yet, he worried in mid-September when the 4 British warships, *Sophie*, *Hermes*, *Carron* and *Childers*, attacked Fort Bowyer with offshore cannon and a landed force of marines and Native American warriors. Andrew Jackson was at Mobile at the time, unable to personally direct the defense. But the fort held, the land assault never gained momentum, and the British were forced to blow up the disabled *Hermes* before abandoning their efforts.

From his headquarters in Mobile, Andrew Jackson was directing military preparations for **defending New Orleans** and **Baton Rouge**. Under Jackson's orders, William Claiborne was raising a local militia, Federal officials were shipping arms down the Mississippi River, and William McRae was directing the strengthening of area forts. Arthur Hayne was inspecting progress and sending reports to Jackson. Overall command was entrusted to James Winchester, who had begun his military career in Jackson's Middle Tennessee militia. John Coffee's Middle Tennessee cavalry was stationed at Baton Rouge, where they awaited Kentucky militiamen and newly mustered militia from Tennessee. Jackson left Mobile Bay for New Orleans on November 22. He rightly figured the British would soon be directly attacking New Orleans.

British Armada Leaves Jamaica for New Orleans

On November 27, the huge British armada set sail from Negril Bay, Jamaica. The fleet of 50 ships carried 10,000 seamen, 1,500 marines, and 9,600 soldiers. Part of the armada consisted of the British force that had previously burned Washington City. It seems that the officers' wives were excited over expectations that they would soon be a prominent part of New Orleans social life. **Yes, the fleet was bound for New Orleans. British commander John Keane** had decided to invade New Orleans directly instead of taking Mobile Bay and marching overland to the Mississippi River. Having failed to take Fort Bowyer in September and aware of the pace of Jackson's military buildup, Keane figured the sooner his men arrived at New Orleans the better. Five days earlier Jackson had made the right decision to leave Mobile Bay for New Orleans. **Jackson entered New Orleans on December 1.**

"New Orleans lies about 105 miles from the mouths of the Mississippi River... The whole [delta] region is seamlessly patterned and webbed by streams and sloughs and lakes, which in 1814 afforded no less than 6 definable approaches to the environs of the city." Jackson found New Orleans "an opulent and commercial town," whose inhabitants were softened by the habits . . . of wealth." So, he knew his Tennesseans would be more important than any local group of men. Jackson set many of these Tennessee men to work felling trees to block the smaller waterways that gave access to the city.

British Ships Land Troops East of New Orleans

Nine days after Andrew Jackson arrived in New Orleans, on December 10, the **British armada arrived** outside of the mouth of Lake Borgne and "anchored off the white beaches of Ship and Cat Islands," which are located about 12 miles off the coast of present-day Gulfport, Mississippi. Apparently, the water was too shallow to sail any farther toward New Orleans from the east. Except for being spotted by Thomas Jones and his small fleet of 5 gunboats, they had managed to arrive "with a degree of secrecy that has not favored another modern military expedition." Apparently, people in the region felt no loyalty to report what a few surely were witnessing. There were about 50 ships, ranging from the "huge *Tonnant*" to small gun-brigs. Troops descended ladders and boarded light craft to seek out the 5 American gunboats and to make landfall. The men were seasoned fighters. Among the men were 4 regiments that had burned Washington City and threatened Baltimore. A brigade of Wellington's veterans had come directly from defeating Napoleon's armies in Spain. The Ninety-Third Highlanders had come from action at the Cape of Good Hope. And 2 regiments from the Caribbean, mostly Jamaican African Americans, were among the invaders. In addition, there were trains of artillery, a rocket brigade, sappers and engineers.

The first order of business was to destroy the 5 American gunboats and the 82 Americans who manned them. The British accomplished this with a force of 1,200 men who rowed their little rowboats 36 miles to find the gunboats "becalmed and unable to maneuver." Although Jones had managed to send word to Jackson that some British warships had arrived, Jackson would get no further information about the size of the fleet or the subsequent landing operations.

Meanwhile, Leaders in the Northeast States advocate Secession again

Meanwhile, secessionist-minded Federalist Party men in Massachusetts and neighboring States were moving their State Secession agenda forward. On December 9, Representative **Daniel Webster, of New Hampshire**, had argued against a proposed Federal draft law and had threatened that New Hampshire and like-minded States would nullify such a law within their boundaries. He had called the proposed Federal military draft "unconstitutional and illegal." And, by warning that it "ought to be prevented by a resort to other measures which are both [permitted by the Federal Constitution] and legal," Webster had threatened to void the law through State nullification. Politicians were also cowed by the British occupation of several seaport towns in present-day Maine. A few days after Webster's speech, on December 15, secession-minded Federalist Party politicians from Massachusetts, Connecticut, Rhode Island, New Hampshire and Vermont **gathered at Hartford, Connecticut to secretly debate State secession** versus less drastic expressions of State sovereignty. The Delegates from Massachusetts, Connecticut and Rhode Island were official representatives of their respective State Governments, but the Delegates from New Hampshire and Vermont were attending unofficially. During this time span, "some Federalist orators and many newspapers boldly proposed that [Massachusetts and neighboring States] secede from the [Federation] and establish an independent republic." Although proponents of immediate State Secession were numerous, the majority would advocate, instead, demanding a weaker Federal Government, reduced political power for the southern States and strengthened State rights. **Northeastern**

Secessionists were stupid; if their states had seceded and created a northeast nation, the British would have conquered it and added it to British Canada. Their actions defy logic!

British Troop Landings Continue

Down on the Louisiana Gulf coast, for 6 days and nights British seamen rowed small boats, taking soldiers from the fleet of warships eastward to landfall at Pea Island, which was located where the Pearl River empties into the north shore of Lake Borgne, about 30 miles from the old city. "Some of the crews were at the oars 4 days without relief." It was cold and rainy on the swampy land where they disembarked, and "many of the Jamaican [African Americans] died of exposure." But the whole operation was completed in secrecy.

Meanwhile, on December 15, Andrew Jackson and the people of New Orleans received news of the defeat of the 5 American gunboats in Lake Borgne. Although they did not know where the British were going to attack, most of the people of New Orleans were terrified and a general panic was building. To maintain control, Jackson proclaimed martial law, prohibiting anyone from leaving the city and imposing a 9 pm curfew. He dispatched a **message to John Coffee and his cavalrymen at Baton Rouge**: "You must not sleep until you reach me." He sent **dispatches to Billy Carroll, whose 3,000 Tennessee militiamen** had been traveling toward New Orleans by water for 2 months. Although coming by slow transit, Carroll's men had overtaken a federal shipment of 1,100 muskets, which Carroll's gunsmiths were putting in good repair, while militiamen fabricated "50,000 cartridges in the best manner, each containing a musket ball and 3 buckshot." Jackson also sent dispatches to speed the arrival of Thomas Hinds' **Mississippi Dragoons** and John Thomas' **Kentucky militia**.

Louisiana Pirates Decide to Fight Alongside Jackson

Good news: pirate leader Jean Lafitte had decided to refuse to support the British invasion. But, the pirates of Barataria were not yet participating in the defense of New Orleans. Authorities had jailed some Baratarians, including Dominique You, Lafitte's "most celebrated" sea captain. Some legislators had attempted to pass a bill to free them, but their effort failed. Then Judge Dominick Hall of the United States District Court had been petitioned. He asked for and obtained a legislative resolution, and promptly freed You and the other jailed Baratarians. **Jean Laffite's men** having been freed, the pirate captain immediately came to New Orleans and offered his and their military services to Andrew Jackson. William Claiborne recorded the event with the following words: "Mr. Lafitte solicited for himself and for all Baratarians the honor of serving under our banners, that they might have an opportunity of proving that, if they had infringed the revenue laws, yet none were more ready than they to defend the country." And Claiborne added, "Persuaded that the assistance of these men could not fail of being very useful, [Andrew Jackson] accepted their offers." Jackson was especially enthusiastic about using the Baratarians' expertise with artillery and **gaining the use of their cannons**.

British Army Advances Toward New Orleans – Jackson is ready

At this time, Captain Spencer of the British Navy and Captain Peddie of the British Army were cruising the coast of Lake Borgne, searching for a bayou to facilitate moving inland, especially with cannon. On December 18, they spotted a fishing village manned by Spanish and Portuguese fishermen and obtained their cooperation. Using the fisherman as guides, Spencer and Peddie rode in boats up the Bayou Bienvenue, took the Mayou Mazant branch and arrived that night at fields where they saw Gabriel de Villere's farmhouse ahead in the distance, and the Mississippi River to the left. Their presence went undetected. Furthermore, fallen trees had not impaired access due to failure to carry out Jackson's order in this particular stream. Two days later, John Coffee's Tennessee cavalry arrived at New Orleans. Later the same day, William Carroll's 3,000 Tennessee militiamen arrived. Still Jackson did not know that British soldiers were advancing on New Orleans by way of the Bayou Bienvenue and de Villere's farm.

On December 22, a British force of 2,080 men, with 2 cannons, trudged through swamp and cypress bogs toward Gabriel de Villere's farmhouse. They encountered a small contingent of pickets placed near the fishing village by Andrew Jackson's organization, but succeeded in capturing all of these men. Under questioning these captives reported that Jackson had 12,000 to 15,000 men in and around New Orleans, a number in agreement with what had been reported by emissaries Jackson had sent to inquire about prisoners taken during the destruction of the 5 American gunboats.

This British force advanced onto **Gabriel de Villere's** farm the following morning and captured de Villere. The commander, John Keane, could have marched his men 4 miles farther and attacked New Orleans, but, fearful of encountering 12,000 to 15,000 soldiers, he decided to wait for a reinforcement of 3,000 British troops, which was expected the next day. Fortunately, **de Villere managed to escape rather soon** after his capture and send the alarm to Jackson, which was received at 2 o'clock in the afternoon. "By the Eternal, they will not sleep on our soil! . . . We must fight them tonight."

The Battle of New Orleans

Three hours later Jackson had 2,167 men, two cannon and the schooner *Carolina* alongside the Mississippi River at the Rodriquez Canal, which was 2 miles from the British position and an excellent defensive location. All was silent, and the British did not know Jackson's men were there. By 6:30 pm Jackson's men had crossed the canal and quietly advanced to within 500 yards of the British while the Carolina had drifted downstream at the same pace. All was ready, and at seven thirty the Carolina opened fire with its cannon and the British mustered to combat what they believed to be only the threat of the warship. Thirty minutes later, according to plan, **Jackson's men attacked with fury**. At midnight the British retreated to beyond cannon range and the battlefield became strangely quiet.

Learning from prisoners that 3,000 British reinforcements were due to arrive at that time, Jackson decided to retreat to behind the Rodriquez Canal and establish a defensive line at that location, although it was only "a dry grass-grown ditch 20 feet wide and about 4 feet deep." During this first battle the Americans had lost 24 killed, 111 wounded and 74 taken prisoner. The British had lost 46 killed, 167 wounded and 64 taken prisoner.

The next morning, after the arrival of British reinforcements, the force numbered 4,703 able-bodied men plus officers. So, Jackson had made an excellent choice when he had decided to quickly gather available men and attack that first night. **Behind the Rodriquez Canal, Jackson's men worked feverishly digging defensive earthworks.**

Since July, American-British Negotiations had been Underway in Ghent and a December 24ᵗʰ draft Treaty was signed

The commanders of the armies at New Orleans did not realize that a breakthrough was developing at the negotiating table in Europe. **Five American ministers**, including John Quincy Adams of Massachusetts and Henry Clay of Kentucky, **had been in Great Britain negotiating with British ministers since July**. The British had wanted peace, but before agreeing to terms, they had wanted to wait and see if their forces could conquer Louisiana and the lower Mississippi Valley. When negotiations had begun on August 8, widely conflicting demands had been presented. The British had wanted land in Maine, control of the Great Lakes, and considerable land in what would become Michigan, Wisconsin and the northern half of Ohio, Indiana, and Illinois. And the British had wanted the right to navigate the Mississippi River. Furthermore, the British had refused to consider changes in maritime trade policy or a policy change regarding impressments of sailors. The Americans had wanted an end to impressments of sailors, fishing rights off the coast of Newfoundland and possession of all of Upper Canada and Lower Canada, if they could get it. However, the British position had softened considerably a few weeks later when news had arrived describing American success on the Great Lakes and Lake Champlain. And news of the subsequent British retreat from Baltimore had caused their negotiators to be even more compliant. Furthermore, with the spy James Wilkinson no longer in charge of Louisiana defenses, **British worried that Andrew Jackson and his Tennesseans might successfully defend the region.** Too often defeated by Tennesseans and Kentuckians, the British had become much less confident about military success at New Orleans. **Perhaps, they figured that initiating a nobody-wins treaty might be a good insurance policy.** Anyway, the treaty would not be ratified before the outcome in Louisiana was known. So, all that remained was for the chief American negotiators, John Adams and Henry Clay, to drop demands for Upper Canada and Lower Canada and agree upon reasonable American demands. Adams insisted on fishing rights and Clay insisted on barring the British from the Mississippi River. But both wanted a quick settlement before the British became emboldened by the State Secession Movement in Adams' home State of Massachusetts and in neighboring States. **John Adams** was in an awkward position because, while the leaders of his State Government were advocating seceding from the Federal Government, as a Minister representing the Federal Government, he was responsible for negotiating an international peace treaty. The next day would be Christmas and both sides wanted to settle.

So, while a major battle was being fought on the outskirts of New Orleans, American and British negotiators at **Ghent** closed in on the draft of a deal both could support. **In fact, they did reach agreement on Christmas Eve, December 24, 1814.** The treaty contained no significant changes in relations between the nations. No land changed hands. The British did not agree to any changes in maritime policies. **The British lost nothing. The Americans lost nothing. The Native Americans lost almost everything.** Because they had aligned with the British, American settlers on the frontier would feel even more justified than before in continuing to take Native American land while driving Native American nations farther west and further toward extinction. The draft treaty would be forwarded to the British Parliament and to the Federal Senate.

The Battle of New Orleans Continues

Three days after the draft treaty signing, on December 27, British cannon succeeded in blowing up the *Carolina*, but another American battleship, the *Louisiana*, was saved. The next day the British launched their second infantry attack. Jackson's line had been reinforced considerably by that time. The British "opened with Congreve rockets, a new and terrifying, but seldom fatal, bit of pyrotechnics." The 10 British cannon opened fire. Then the British infantry begin its broad advance. Artillerymen aboard the *Louisiana* and at batteries spaced along the Rodriquez Canal defensive line played a major role in turning back this attack. For 3 days and nights the British prepared for a third attack. They hauled in more cannon from the far-off British fleet. Then, under cover of darkness, 17 British cannons were advanced to shell the Rodriquez Canal defensive line.

1815

British Continue to Attack of Jackson's defenders

The following morning, January 1, 1815, a hard-fought artillery duel commenced, but the **British never gained an advantage** over Jackson's defenders.

Meanwhile, in the Northeast, State Secession Advocates Continued their Schemes

State secession talk was building to a climax in Massachusetts and neighboring States as the Hartford Convention concluded its business on January 5. Secessionists were numerous among the Delegates, but insufficient in number to control the Convention. Delegates had approved resolutions demanding revisions to war policy and demanding new Amendments to the Federal Constitution. A proposed Amendment had been approved that would eliminate the bonded African American population in computing seats in the Federal House and Electoral College. Another had been approved that would limit a President to one term in office and prohibit election to President of a man from the State of the sitting President. A majority of the Convention had also approved a nonsensical resolution, which advocated that each State plan to defend itself, using its own militia, paid for with Federal funding. The Convention named 3 Delegates to travel to the temporary Federal Capital at Philadelphia and present the demands to the Federal Government. And the Convention set a date to reconvene to take more drastic action if its demands were not met. **Stupidity among these Northeastern fools is confirming the fact the "Southern Families Made America."**

A Decisive Day in the Battle of New Orleans – British Hear a "Don't Ever Mess with Me Again" Message Loud and Clear

Far to the southwest, in Louisiana, United States Nation Builders were fighting the biggest battle of the war. The defenders behind the Rodriquez Canal defensive line were especially tense during the first hours of January 8, because a massive British attack was anticipated at or before dawn. Andrew Jackson began inspecting his men at 1 am. He began at the Mississippi River where a bastion was defended by Beale's City Rifles and the Federal Seventh Infantry. Battery Number One was next; then more Federal Seventh Infantry, followed by Battery Number 2, manned by *Carolina* sailors. Plauche's Uniformed Companies were next; then Battery Number 3, the Baratarians' battery.

Joking with Dominique You, Jackson pretended to complain, "That smells like better coffee than we can get. Smuggle it?" "Maybe so, General." You teased as he poured Jackson a cup. "I wish I had 500 such devils," Jackson mused.

Then Jackson inspected Lacoste's African Americans, Daquin's African Americans, Battery Number 4, Crawley's men, the Forty-Fourth Federal Infantry, Battery Number 5, Perry's men, Battery Number 6, Spotts' men, Carroll's division of Tennessee militia, Battery Number 7, Battery Number 8, and then, trailing off into the cypress swamp, John Coffee's Tennessee cavalrymen, dismounted. **Jackson had a total of 5,172 men on the defensive line.**

It included some Kentucky militiamen who had arrived 2 days previously, most without rifles. Dismayed to see 2,380 militiamen with only 700 rifles, Jackson had barked, "I have never seen a Kentuckian without a gun and a pack of cards and a bottle of whisky in my life!"

Jackson also had 550 Louisiana militiamen, under David Morgan, defending the opposite bank of the Mississippi River. Having observed British soldiers dragging rowboats overland to the Mississippi, Jackson worried if Morgan had enough men. So, he sent him 500 newly arrived Kentuckians, but only 170 of them had rifles or muskets.

As the first light of dawn arrived, fog shrouded the battlefield, preventing Jackson's men from observing the advancing British soldiers. Then "a breeze broke ragged patches in the fog. . . They were immediately in front, not more than 650 yards away and headed straight for the point behind which Jackson had massed his reserve.

"Jackson never forgot the sight that met his eyes. A heavy frost had embossed the cane stubble with silver. Across this shining carpet moved a field of red tunics latticed by white cross-belts, and a pulsing hedge of bayonets that gave an impression of infinity."

Within a few seconds Jackson's artillerymen opened fire. The first rank of Carroll's and Coffee's Tennesseans took aim just above the beltplate of a British soldier. "Fire!" The first rank stepped down to reload as the second rank stepped up and took aim. "Fire!" The second rank stepped down to reload as the third rank stepped up and took aim. "Fire!" **And on it went as British soldiers fell by the hundreds.** The British commander, John Keane, ordered the Ninety-Third Highlanders, a famous Scottish regiment of at least 6-feet tall men, to lead the second charge. "Give these to my wife," the Highlander commander asked as he went forward to lead his men. The Highlanders "stumbled" forward, sidestepping their dying and the dead from the first attack. The battlefield was strewed with the dead, dying and wounded. The top British battlefield Commander, Keane, was dying, and subordinate commanders Parkenham, Gibbs and Dale were dead. Eventually survivors retreated.

Jackson's men ceased firing at 8:30. Jackson looked out over the battlefield and saw a sight he would later describe: "I never had so grand and awful an idea of the insurrection as . . . [when] I saw . . . more than 500 Britons emerging from the heaps of their dead comrades, all over the plain rising up, and . . . coming forward . . . as prisoners."

Jackson's men had inflicted those enormous losses upon the British while suffering only 7 killed and 6 wounded! The British had suffered over 2,000 killed and wounded.

That brief morning battle remains today **"the most decisive victory ever won by an American army over a foreign foe."**

Across the river, British soldiers under William Thornton were making much better progress against Daniel Patterson's defenders. In fact, Patterson's artillerymen were forced to spike their cannon and retreat. But the disastrous defeat suffered by the British on Jackson's side of the river persuaded Thornton's men to give up and cross back over the river to join their defeated comrades.

Badly Beaten, British Troops Retreat to their Ships and Sail Away

There was no more fighting! Andrew Jackson felt no need to risk the lives of his men with attacks. Ten days later the British, after making elaborate preparations to guard their escape route, retreated the 5 miles back through the marshy ground, boarded small boats, rowed back to their warships, and sailed away. The 2-year blockade of the port of New Orleans was no longer a threat and **vast stockpiles of cotton would soon be on their way to Massachusetts, Great Britain and Europe.**

The Aftermath of the Battle of New Orleans

Delegates bearing the **resolutions of the Hartford Convention**, on their way from Connecticut to the temporary capital at Philadelphia, were in Baltimore, Maryland, when news of the New Orleans victory first arrived. Realizing how foolish their resolutions would appear, they would meekly deliver their documents and return home. Nothing more came of their campaign to weaken the Federal Government. The Northeast would not try to stop progress by the Nation Builders until after emigration swelled the population of the North sufficiently to empower the Northern States Republican Party.

On February 21, the people of New Orleans would receive news of the draft treaty signing at Ghent, but **Jackson would maintain military rule until March 13,** when he would receive official orders from the Federal War Department. On that day he would dismiss his men and rescind martial law.

Overwhelming British naval superiority in the Atlantic and Gulf had forced American warships to lie at anchor in protected American ports since the end of 1812. Most of the damage inflicted on British marine commerce had been the result of attacks by American privateers. During the war, 526 private warships had attempted attacks on British shipping. Although the British had eventually captured nearly half of these American privateers, the **privateers had succeeded in taking 1,344 prizes**, far more than the 165 prizes that had been taken by the Federal Navy.

When British leaders at home received news of the defeat of the invasion armada at New Orleans, they were thankful that they had pursued the contingency plan and agreed, on December 24, to peace without political changes.

And the defeat by Andrew Jackson's forces would dramatically persuade the British Government to never ever again go to war against the United States.

The magnitude of the victory would make American frontiersmen more confident that they were in control of their own destiny and would signal a shift of political power from the coastal States to the frontier States. After a few years, the victory would elevate Andrew Jackson to the office of President.

The Ghent Peace Treaty and the victory at New Orleans **instantly stopped the State Secession Movement in Massachusetts and neighboring States**. Politicians in those States would struggle to find issues capable of elevating their declining political power. Their first political response was to ignore Andrew Jackson's demonstrated superb military leadership and, instead, praise God for the victory at New Orleans. Accordingly, the Massachusetts Legislature approved a resolution that did just that.

A littler earlier, on February 27, the Federal House and Senate had directed the Navy to sell or mothball all warships operating in the Great Lakes, save what was needed to enforce import and domestic revenue laws. When ministers would sign a naval limitation agreement in April 1817, this disarmament program would become official and binding for both The States and Great Britain. That agreement would limit each nation to 3 Great Lakes warships, each with only one cannon. The following year, 1818, the boundary between Federal land and Upper Canada land would be established from Lake of the Woods to 49 degrees latitude, then westward to the Rocky Mountain continental divide. Beyond the continental divide, the land named Oregon would be open for the following 10 years to settlers from both Upper Canada and The States. After the 10-year joint control period, negotiations were planned for drawing the western boundary from the continental divide to the Pacific Ocean.

Summer of 1815

It is now the summer of 1815. **You are arriving at a mini-climax in our *Southern Families Made America* history**. This is the point when the Federalist Party lost its residual power and when the politicians of Massachusetts and surrounding States lost hope of ever winning control of the Federal Government. Controlling political power was moving to States located west of the Appalachian Mountains. The Democratic Party was becoming even more dominant. For 22 years (1793-1815) immigration had been below earlier levels, causing the American population to become primarily native-born. Big families on frontier farms had been the main source of population growth, but after 1815 immigration would increase and expanding immigration would gradually, but dramatically, alter United States Federal politics.

For Decades Going Forward, America's Nation Builders Will be advancing Their Goals

The mountain has been climbed! Nation Builders, atop those mountains now gaze out to the rivers, the plains and the distant mountains and see no troublesome impediment to the future westward migration by Southern Families. Fathers gladly tell sons, **"Go west, young man."** And, those sons would go west, take young wives along, settle, have children and, twenty to twenty-five years later, tell those sons. "Go west, young man." **Our history continues to reveal the facts substantiating our truthful history: SOUTHERN FAMILIES DID MAKE AMERICA!**

1816

The Second National Bank of the United States is created

We now proceed with our history.

When the Federal House and Senate had convened in December 1815, a major legislative priority had been to fix the Federation's banking system, which had been so badly damaged by unpatriotic and greedy bankers in Massachusetts and neighboring States. On January 8, 1816, Representative **John Calhoun of South Carolina** introduced to the House a bill to establish a new National Bank of the United States. As mentioned earlier, problems with the previous National Bank had caused the House and Senate to refuse to renew its charter in 1811. But the grave abuses inflicted upon most of the people by bankers in Massachusetts and neighboring States had produced an outcry for renewed involvement in Banking by the Federal Government. The Speaker of the House, Henry Clay of Kentucky, firmly supported Calhoun's bank bill, as did most other Democrats from agricultural States. Speaking for bankers in Massachusetts and neighboring States, Representative Daniel Webster, of New Hampshire, said he was firmly opposed to the new National Bank because, he alleged, "such a bank was unnecessary and might become dangerous." But opposition was futile. The bill chartering the **Second National Bank of the United States** passed the House in March, the Senate shortly thereafter, and received James Madison's signature on April 10.

Stock in the new bank would be widely distributed among 31,334 individuals, a truly remarkable number. But, although Massachusetts and neighboring States contained most of the gold and silver coin and much of the fluid assets of the Federation, only one-ninth of the stock would be held by individuals in that region. Apparently, most financially successful people in that region would be encouraging the new National Bank to fail.

With Peace Established, How Heavily should America Tax Imports?

A year earlier, in June 1815, a new trade treaty between The States and Great Britain had taken effect. This treaty permitted foreign merchant ships to carry goods to and from The States. The resulting competition from European merchant ships was driving down shipping prices and idling some of the merchant fleet belonging to owners in Boston, New York and other seaport cities. Since peacetime conditions were boosting the European economy, demand for American exports was rising dramatically. Exports of cotton, tobacco, rice, wheat and corn was boosting the farm economy of producing States. But, the competition from European marine shippers was depressing the economy in Massachusetts and neighboring States.

During the war with Great Britain, manufacturing industries in Massachusetts, New York, Pennsylvania and intervening States had received a boost from reduced competition and heightened domestic demand, but, since then, they continually pleaded that they were unable to match the prices being offered for imported goods coming from Europe. Since 1789, the prices charged by these manufacturers had been subsidized by Federal import taxes on manufactured goods. The Federal Import Tax had risen to 12.5% by 1812, and then was doubled to 25% during the war with Great Britain. **But the 25% tax was scheduled to revert to 12.5% in January 1816.**

Although voters who benefited from a profitable domestic manufacturing industry were a rather small minority, leading Democrats in the Federal House decided in March to propose to double import taxes to the war-time rate of 25% to permit domestic manufacturers to raise their prices. In the spirit of reducing American dependence on imports from Europe, **a majority of Democrats decided to support a 25% import tax bill** unselfishly introduced by William Lowndes of South Carolina. Representatives John Calhoun of South Carolina and Henry Clay of Kentucky provided strong leadership in advocating passage. These men were willing to subject the people of their States to higher prices for manufactured goods in hopes such sacrifice would result in sectional harmony and an expanded domestic manufacturing capacity for the Federation as a whole. Strangely, Representative Daniel Webster of New Hampshire argued against increasing import taxes. Using the textile industry as his basis for argument, Webster decried the evils of industrial-age manufacturing and urged fellow Representatives to change course and discourage bringing more European-style manufacturing jobs to The States. **The 25% import tax bill passed the House with support from all sections of the Federation.** The tax would become effective on April 27.

Yet, even with this tax, imports would far exceed exports. During 1816 imports would be more than $150,000,000, but exports would total only $64,700,000. Although the percentage of Representatives from Pennsylvania through Massachusetts who favored passage exceeded the percentage favoring passage among Representatives from the remaining States, the wide support throughout the Federation was rather amazing. **The Nation Builders were kind and considerate of others!**

Within a few years a bitter sectional political fight would center on this issue of subsidizing manufacturing industries through high import taxes. In fact, owners of manufacturing, shipping and commercial businesses would become the major financial supporters of the Sectionalism that would empower the Republican Party as it would arise in the Northern States in the 1850's.

1817

The New Second Bank of the United States Demands Payment in Gold and Silver Coin

The new Second Bank of the United States opened for business in January 1817, and 19 branches would be in operation within a few months. In the month following the opening of the Bank, the Federal Government required that all taxes and fees be paid in gold and silver coin. This requirement would soon force all banks within the Federation to resume exchanging gold and silver coin for paper money.

James Monroe, of Virginia, is Elected President

In a landslide victory Democrat James Monroe, of Virginia, won 84 percent of the vote, trouncing Rufus King of New York State. The Federalist Party was falling apart. Another political issue was needed to elevate the Northeastern States to political power in Washington City. Northern States political agitators would be searching for something useful.

Chapter 15 — March 1817 to February 1821: The States during the First James Monroe Administration

Let us take time out from the narrative history to study an overview of the first James Monroe Administration.

A soldier and politician, James Monroe, of Virginia, a Democrat, was elected President over Federalist candidate Rufus King of New York. Under James Madison, Monroe had been Secretary of State, and at a crucial time also Acting Secretary of War. Born in 1758 in Westmoreland County, Virginia, James was the oldest son of Virginia farmer and carpenter Spence Monroe, and great-grandson of Andrew Monroe, who had come to Virginia from England in 1648. James Monroe's mother, Elizabeth Jones Monroe, was born in Virginia of Welsh heritage.

James left his studies at the College of William and Mary at age 18 to fight in the Continental Army. At age 24, he entered Virginia politics and continued in government work with few interruptions for the remainder of his life. At age 27, he married Elizabeth Kortright of New York City. Elizabeth was the daughter of Loyalist merchant and British army officer Laurence Kortright, who lost much of his fortune during the Defense of Independence. James and Elizabeth had 2 daughters to live to maturity.

Monroe never received a college degree, but furthered his knowledge by studying law under Thomas Jefferson for 3 years. He was admitted to the Virginia bar in 1786, but practiced law for only 4 years. Monroe was a member of the Virginia Assembly (1782-1783); a member of the Continental Congress (1783-1786); a Federal Senator (1790-1794); Minister to France (1794-1796); Governor of Virginia (1799-1802); Special Envoy to Paris to help negotiate the Louisiana Purchase (1803); Minister to Great Britain (1803-1807); Governor of Virginia (January-March 1811); Secretary of State (1811-1817), and Secretary of War (1814-1815).

Monroe received the endorsement of both former President Thomas Jefferson and retiring President James Madison, but Democrat supporters of Secretary of War William Crawford of Georgia made a major bid to end Virginia's domination of the office of President with the Georgian. Although Democrat Representatives from New York were particularly keen on derailing Madison with Crawford, when all the Representatives gathered for the Democrat Caucus, Monroe was chosen over Crawford by a fairly close 65-54 vote.

Governor Daniel Tompkins, of New York, was nominated for Vice President. Tompkins had been Governor of New York during the War of 1812 and, displaying immense patriotism, had chosen personally to finance the military effort to defend New York State when a defiant State Legislature had refused to appropriate supplemental money for the State militia. For years thereafter, subsequent New York State Legislatures would refuse to reimburse Tompkins, and he would fight bankruptcy until the Federal House and Senate would finally bail him out in 1824.

Monroe's opponent was Federalist Rufus King, a New York lawyer. King had represented Massachusetts in the Continental Congress (1784-1787) where he had advocated a strong central government. Eager to keep African Americans out of the new northwestern lands that would become Ohio, Indiana, Illinois, Michigan and Wisconsin, King had led the drive to ban bonded African Americans from National Territory north of the Ohio River. After moving to New York, King had been elected to the Federal Senate (1789-1796). He had been Minister to Britain (1796-

1803), again a Federal Senator from New York, and twice a Federalist Vice President candidate teamed with Charles Pinckney.

King was among the last Federalists to cling to power in the Federal Senate. In fact, the Federalist Party was so weak it decided against nominating a formal candidate, but supported King's race informally. John Howard of Maryland was the principal Federalist candidate for Vice President. After his defeat in the race for President, King was very active in promoting a program to gradually deport African Americans to Africa or South America. King's proposal included monetary compensation for owners of bonded African Americans who were being prepared for deportation.

William DeGregorio would describe the election:

> **"Monroe's nomination was tantamount to election, for the Federalist Party was moribund after the War of 1812.** The Party's opposition to the war had accelerated its decline. A few die-hard partisans rehashed Monroe's diplomatic failure abroad, but candidate King put up only token opposition. Monroe's supporters did little campaigning, preferring to sit on their commanding lead until the election."

Monroe won by a wide margin, carrying 84% of the electoral vote: Monroe 183, versus King 34. Monroe won the majority of electoral votes in 16 States; from north to south they were: New Hampshire, Vermont, Rhode Island, New York, New Jersey, Pennsylvania, Maryland, Ohio, Indiana, Virginia, Kentucky, North Carolina, Tennessee, South Carolina, Georgia and Louisiana. King won 3 small northeastern States: Massachusetts, Connecticut and Delaware.

John Quincy Adams, son of the second President, John Adams, a lawyer and a Federalist politician from Massachusetts, was appointed Secretary of State, even though King had carried Massachusetts in the election. William Crawford, of Georgia, continued as Secretary of the Treasury, in spite of the failed attempt by Monroe's political opponents in the Democratic Party to derail his nomination by promoting Crawford for President. **John Calhoun, of South Carolina, was Secretary of War.** Richard Rush, of Pennsylvania, continued as Attorney General until 1817, at that point being replaced by William Wirt, of Virginia. Benjamin Crowninshield remained as Secretary of the Navy until 1819, at that point being replaced by Smith Thompson, of New York.

The Democratic Party retained huge majorities over the Federalist Party in both the Senate and the House during Monroe's first term. Democrats improved their domination in the Senate to **34 versus 10**, and increased their large margin in the House to a whopping **141 versus 42.** In the mid-term elections, Democrat strength grew further in the Senate to 35 versus 7, and grew even more in the House to 156 versus 27.

Rapid growth and a pleasant political atmosphere produced 4 new States – 2 from the northern region and 2 from the southern region.

Mississippi was granted statehood in 1817.

Illinois was accepted in 1818.

Alabama was accepted in 1819.

Maine, after being carved away from Massachusetts, was accepted in 1820 (a ploy to acquire two more senators for New England).

The more significant events involving African Americans during the 4 years of the first James Monroe Administration will now be presented. The Mississippi Constitution, drafted by Joseph Davis, "required an owner to care for his [bonded African Americans] and refrain from injuring them under penalty of having them sold by the State. It also provided for jury trial for a [bonded African American] in a capital case." The New York State Government enacted a law in 1817 that required that adult bonded African Americans living in the State must become independent in 1827, except for those who were younger than 28 years. That gave each owner 10 years to prepare his or her bonded African Americans for independence or to sell them to a southern State owner. The North Carolina Government stipulated that the murder of a bonded African American was homicide to be treated by law enforcement in a manner similar to the murder of a European American; and, in 1820, a white person would be executed for the murder of a bonded African American in North Carolina. The Missouri Territory Legislature decreed that a person knowingly stealing a bonded African American or selling an independent African American into bondage was to be hanged. The New Jersey Government outlawed selling bonded African Americans to anyone from outside the State. The Connecticut Government stopped allowing independent African American men the right to vote. The Alabama Constitution required that the murder or maiming of a bonded African American was a crime to be prosecuted as if the victim was a European American, except in cases of insurrection. As a precaution against organized revolt, the Missouri Government made it illegal for African Americans to assemble or for bonded African Americans to receive instruction about how to read and write.

The 1820 census counted 1,758,632 people of noticeable African descent. This represented a 35% increase over the 1810 count, and 17.5% of the total population, a major decrease from the 19.2% recorded in 1810. Since the 1810 census, the **population of independent African Americans** had grown by **34% to 130,487** in the **Southern** States and by **30% to 99,133** in the **North**. African Americans represented a barely significant 1.3% of the population of the New England States (Massachusetts and neighboring States).

In conjunction with the statehood bill for Missouri, which became a State in 1820, the Federal House and Senate passed legislation that promised to exclude bonded African Americans from all future States north of 36 degrees and 30 minutes (north of the Kansas-Missouri border). Territories south of 36 degrees and 30 minutes were to choose or exclude bonded African Americans based of a vote by territory settlers upon application for statehood. The Missouri Constitution stipulated that bonded African Americans be given the same rights for trial by jury, and be subjected to the same criminal code as white people.

Maine, which was carved out of Massachusetts in 1820, stipulated that the few African Americans living in the State would attend the same schools as the European American children, thereby saving the cost of separate schools for the extremely small African American population (3 in every 1,000 students). The New Jersey Government instituted a voluntary program for making bonded African Americans independent. The New Jersey population of bonded African Americans would dwindle as follows: 1820 (7,557), 1830 (2,254), 1840 (674), 1850 (236), and 1860 (0).

This concludes the overview of the first James Monroe Administration. The narrative history resumes with first attention going to Jefferson Davis who, at the tender age of 9 years, is away at boarding school in Kentucky.

The Narrative History Resumes

1817

Sam Houston and the Cherokee Nation

During the winter of late 1817, **Sam Houston,** while still somewhat recovering from the severe wounds he had received when charging the Creek redoubt at Horseshoe Bend, was temporarily detached from the Federal Army while he **worked a Federal job as Subagent to the Cherokee Nation.** His assignment was to renew Government requests that the Cherokee people move west into present-day Oklahoma. Considering his teenage experience living with Chief Oo-loo-te-ka's clan, Houston was clearly well qualified for the job. First, he requisitioned blankets, kettles, beaver traps and rifles to carry out past promises, which the Federal Government had been remiss in fulfilling in a timely manner. Most Cherokee clans were not persuaded by Houston's appeal that they all move out west to Indian Territory (approximately equal to present-day Oklahoma State). But Houston did succeed in persuading Chief Oo-loo-te-ka's clan to go. And, he saw to it that "generous" Federal funding was provided for the move.

Oo-loo-te-ka's brother, **Chief Tah-lhon-tusky,** had moved to present-day Oklahoma with his clan 10 years previously. At this time, Tah-lhon-tusky and his delegation were traveling from Indian Territory through Tennessee on his way to Washington City, hoping to convince the Monroe Administration that he had seceded from the Cherokee Nation upon his departure for the west 10 years previously, and was entitled to Federal payments for the land he had given up in Tennessee.

Mississippi Statehood

On December 10, 1817, Mississippi was admitted into the Union as a State.

1818

Sam Houston and Tah-lhon-tusky in Washington

Sam Houston met the Tah-lhon-tusky Delegation when it arrived in Knoxville, Tennessee, and he traveled with them the rest of the way to Washington City. Secretary of War John Calhoun was one of the officials with whom they met. Although Houston thought it a miserable offering, Tah-lhon-tusky seemed satisfied with Federal gifts of seed corn and personal items, and prepared to return homeward. But Houston became furious when Calhoun privately reprimanded him for having arrived at his office with the Tah-lhon-tusky Delegation, while being dressed in Cherokee clothes instead of a proper army officer's uniform.

Secretary Calhoun then accused Houston of helping men who had been smuggling bonded African Americans from Spanish Florida into Tennessee. Houston explained that he had discovered the smuggling gang in Tennessee and had "broken up its activities without asking for instructions" from his superiors. Calhoun suspected Houston was telling the truth, and with the help of an investigation supported by Calhoun and James Monroe, he was vindicated. The accusation against Houston was traced to politicians who were attempting to cover up the smuggling activity. Houston was furious that no Federal action would be taken against the smugglers or their political supporters.

Sam Houston submitted his immediate resignation, dated March 1, 1818: "Sir, you will please accept this as my resignation to take effective from this date." He then returned to Knoxville with the Tah-lhon-tusky Delegation and bid farewell to them. He also bid farewell to Oo-loo-te-ka's clan of 340 Cherokees, which departed down the Tennessee River on well-provisioned flat boats. Each of the 109 warriors had "a good new rifle." Oo-loo-te-ka's clan would live near Chief Tah-lhon-tusky's clan in present-day Oklahoma. **Then, Houston, 25 years old, headed west for Nashville to begin a new career**.

Edmund Ruffin of Virginia -- A Farmer and a Self-made Soil Scientist

Edmund Ruffin, of the Tidewater region of Virginia, had just about given up in his attempts to return his farmland to the fertility that it had provided during its first years of agricultural production. By the end of the second war with Great Britain, 1815, the fertility of the Virginia farms that lay east of the mountains had so badly deteriorated and western land had become so attractive, that many farmers were giving up on the eastern Virginia soil, selling out and moving to western States and National Territories. The wonderful Ruffin history follows.

The same problem plagued farmers in eastern Maryland and the piedmont and coastal regions of the Carolinas. Much farmland was no longer being worked, for there was no profit in attempting it. **Soil infertility "cursed the land."** Typically, farms were "worn out, washed and gullied, so that scarcely an acre could be found in a place fit for cultivation." Travelers through the region observed "dreary and uncultivated wastes, a barren and exhausted soil, half clothed [African Americans], lean and hungry stock, a puny race of horses, a scarcity of provender, houses falling in decay, and fences wind shaken and dilapidated." Population was declining and desperate Virginia farmers were cutting work-forces, selling many of their bonded African Americans to farmers in Kentucky, Tennessee, Mississippi and Louisiana where soils were fertile and workers were needed for cotton cultivation. Over 388,000 Virginians had left their native State.

Ruffin had diligently tried the recommendations of soil specialists, John Binns and John Taylor, who advocated fertilizers and crop rotation. But, nitrogen-producing legumes, such as clover, refused to grow on his land, and manure, a good source of nitrogen, seemed to make matters worse. Ruffin despaired of selling his large farm at Coggin's Point, Virginia, because, in his words, "there was scarcely a [farmer] in my neighborhood . . . who did not desire to sell his land," and sales that were being made were "at half of the then very low estimated value." Ruffin had "drained his better swamp lands only to find their yields, after 3 years of good crops, so reduced as to necessitate abandonment." Ruffin was seriously considering joining the herds of Virginians who were continually moving west.

Then, in 1817, Edmund Ruffin, by chance, saw a copy of Humphry Davy's publication, *Elements of Agricultural Chemistry*, which had been published 4 years previously. Davy was Professor of Chemistry at the Royal Institution in London. Though completely ignorant of chemical science or even its terminology, Ruffin as "struck by a statement to the effect that sterile soils containing 'the salt of iron, or any acid matter . . . may be ameliorated by the application of quick-lime'." Ruffin had observed that his infertile land could still support sorrel and pine and that there was no limestone present. So, although he did not suspect his was a problem with salt of iron, he was hopeful that the root cause might be the same: acid soil. His farm contained deposits of marl, a hard, clay-like soil containing fossilized seashells. And he understood that marl was a source of lime. He made some crude measurements of his soil's acidity, which gave inconclusive results, but he decided to proceed anyway and conduct a field trial.

During February 1818, shortly after Edmund Ruffin's twenty-fourth birthday, his bonded African Americans **dug about 200 bushels of calcareous marl** from pits opened in his lower farmland and spread it "over a few acres of newly-cleared, but poor, ridge land." Shortly afterward, they planted the test field in corn. Ruffin would notice improved plant vitality immediately and would measure an **increased yield of 40 percent**. Yield improvements would increase further in subsequent crops. "A new era in the agricultural history of the region had dawned." Edmund Ruffin would present his findings to the county agricultural society in October. He would expand his application of calcareous marl throughout his farm, and by that method, restore the soils original fertility. He would refine chemical testing for soil acidity and establish targets to be met.

In 1822, he would share his findings with farmers throughout the United States by **publishing a technical paper in the *American Farmer*.** He would eventually expand his technical paper to 242 pages and publish it in 1833 as a book titled, *An Essay on Calcareous Manures.*

At the end of the century a Federal agricultural expert would praise Ruffin's contribution as "the most thorough piece of work on a special agricultural subject ever published in the English language." American farmers would fight acid soil by application of calcareous marl or pulverized limestone. That would be a first step, "to be followed by the wider production and use of barnyard manures, the rotation of crops, the building of covered drains, the growing of clover and cowpeas [and] better plowing."

Edmund Ruffin would become known as the father of soil chemistry in America. With the possible exception of the cotton gin, which Eli Whitney had invented in 1793, no other man would make a greater contribution to the prosperity of the southern States, where acid soils were such a widespread problem and where the economy was so dependent on agriculture.

Andrew Jackson Leads Federals and Militia into Spanish East Florida and Enforces the United States Claim

Meanwhile, Andrew Jackson was asserting Federal claims to Spanish East Florida. On February 13, 1818, Andrew Jackson was camped with 200 cavalrymen near Hartford, Georgia. They were on a mission to invade Spanish East Florida. A few weeks earlier, on December 26, Secretary of War John Calhoun, of South Carolina, had directed Jackson to take personal charge of the military campaign and "adopt the necessary measures to [conclude] . . . [the] conflict." Soon thereafter Jackson had revealed his recommended plan to President James Monroe in a January 6, 1818 letter:

> "The whole of East Florida [should be] seized and . . . this can be done without implicating the [Federal] Government. . . Let it be signified to me through any channel . . . that the possession of [Spanish East Florida] would be desirable . . . and in 60 days it will be accomplished."

President Monroe and Secretary Calhoun seemed to concur. They encouraged Jackson to take whatever military action he thought proper. And they well knew that Jackson was a Nation Builder. Calhoun advised, "Jackson is vested with full power to conduct the war as he may think best." Monroe advised, "The movement . . . against the Seminoles . . . will bring you on a theater where you may possibly have other services to perform." Asserting, "Great interests are at issue," President Monroe further encouraged Jackson to press forward "until our cause is carried triumphantly through." Both men knew that their "cause" was the acquisition of all the land of Spanish East Florida. And both men had figured that aggressive military action soon would encourage the Spanish Government to accept a future offer to purchase the colony.

It is necessary to go back two years and present some history:

During the previous 2 years, Andrew Jackson had relied on an experienced military leader, Edmund Gaines, to lead Federal soldiers in campaigns designed to maintain order along the border with Spanish East Florida.

In fact, during 1816, Gaines had led soldiers 60 miles into East Florida and destroyed Negro Fort, which had been built and stocked with arms by the British during the war of 1812. The British had left a huge stockpile of 3,000 muskets and rifles and 1,000 barrels of gunpowder. Runaway bonded African Americans and Seminole and Creek Native Americans had taken over this fortress and its armaments and were threatening to spread rebellion among the bonded African Americans of Georgia and beyond – a rebellion similar to the bloody Haitian revolt of 1791.

On March 9, 1819, Jackson and his 200 Tennessee cavalrymen had arrived at Fort Scott, near the Florida border. There he had taken command of 800 Federal soldiers and 900 Georgia militiamen. Jackson's military force had marched 60 miles into Spanish East Florida and occupied Negro Fort on March 15. Jackson's men had not killed many Seminoles, Creeks or runaway bonded African Americans, for all had fled. Jackson and his men had then marched to the town of St. Marks, where stood a stone Spanish fort where the Spanish commandant controlled a supply of muskets and rifles. There, Jackson had arrested Alexander Arbuthnot, a Scotsman and merchant who operated out of Nassau in the Bahamas. Jackson and his men had then trudged 107 miles through the jungle to the Suwannee River and the village of Chief Boleck. There, the Native Americans had fled, but Jackson had arrested Robert Ambrister, an Englishman in the Royal Colonial Marines. Returning to St. Marks, Jackson had arranged for both captives to be tried in a field military court. Arbuthnot had been found guilty of "exciting [Native Americans] to war, spying, and giving aid to the enemy." Ambrister had been found guilty of "assuming command of [Native Americans] in . . . war with the United States." Both had been promptly executed. Jackson and his men had then returned to Negro Fort and renamed it Fort Gadsden.

On May 5, 1818, **Andrew Jackson wrote John Calhoun** that he planned to invade the panhandle region of Florida and **"probably take Pensacola."** Two days later, long before the letter arrived in Washington City, Jackson and his men marched to Pensacola, invested the town and, on May 28, the town surrendered. The next day, "in the most sweeping exemplification of imperial powers, [Jackson] seized the royal archives, appointed one of his colonels Military and Civil Governor, and declared in force the 'revenue laws of the United States.'" The next

235

day he "departed for Tennessee." Mission accomplished. Now, Jackson reasoned, let the diplomats untangle the mess and pressure Spain to sell us Spanish East Florida.

The Spanish Government created a stir in Washington City when its Minister, Don Louis de Onis asserted, "In the name of the King, my master, I demand a prompt restitution of St. Mark's, Pensacola, Barrancas, and all other places wrested by [Andrew] Jackson from the Crown of Spain. I demand . . . indemnity for all injuries and losses, and the punishment of [Jackson]."

For several days James Monroe's Cabinet debated the situation. Then they agreed to order a military retreat from Spanish Florida and depend on successful purchase negotiations. Secretary of State John Adams was earnestly negotiating with the Spanish Minister. Among the words of a 20-page letter that Secretary of State John Adams wrote to the Spanish Government is found a forceful warning: **Spain must properly defend Florida "or cede to the United States** a province of which she retains nothing but the nominal possession." **In other words: defend it or give it up!**

Andrew Jackson, Sam Houston, Nashville, Politics and Race Horses

Upon returning from Spanish East Florida, Andrew Jackson settled down again at his **Hermitage** farm near Nashville. But he no longer bred racehorses. By this time, he had sold off his stable of racehorses, all except the noble Truxton. And Truxton continued to earn money as a prized stud. Jackson was simply too often called out of town to give proper attention to racehorses. Furthermore, he had given up any hope of beating Jesse Haynie's Maria. Cotton prices were firming and he was processing his crop through his new cotton gin and arranging shipping directly to a New Orleans broker to cut out middlemen.

And, 1818 was the year that Sam Houston gained entrance into the Tennessee Bar and set up his office in Nashville. He was 25 years old. Fortunately, Houston had recovered from the rather severe wounds receive in the war with William Weatherford's Creek warriors. In a few years Houston would successfully run for the Federal House. **Houston and Jackson were becoming good friends.** They would often talk over current events in the late afternoons at the bar in the Nashville Inn. The friendship would be valuable to Houston, for in a few years, Jackson would praise Houston as "a truly noble-minded fellow" and recommend him for election to the Federal House.

Illinois Statehood

On December 3, 1818, Illinois became a State. Like Ohio and Indiana, people of the Southern Culture were very common in southern Illinois, most of those coming north out of Kentucky. So, the land on the north side of the Ohio River was now made up of three States, all the way west to the Mississippi River.

1819

Spain Gives Up on Florida and Sells the Remainder to the United States – From Mississippi to Georgia the Southern Shore Becomes American Land

The British Government had become upset over the execution of Alexander Arbuthnot and Robert Ambrister during the invasion Andrew Jackson had led into Spanish East Florida. The British demanded that Jackson be punished as a war criminal. The Federal House took up the issue in January and heated debate followed. **But Jackson supporters rallied to defeat all resolutions demanding that he be censured**.

Perhaps this House support of Jackson during this British censure controversy persuaded the Spanish Government to believe that its Florida colony would be seized if not sold. Take the money and run! **The Spanish Government did just that on February 22, 1819, signing a treaty ceding Florida to the United States for a purchase price of $5,000,000.**

Andrew Jackson and James Monroe had demonstrated again their basic commitment to Nation Building. This was a time of remarkably friendly sectional political feelings between the Northern Culture and the Southern Culture. Even the most prominent politician from Massachusetts, John Adams, played an important supportive role.

The United States now owned Florida Territory.

Federal Supreme Court uses McCulloch versus Maryland to Expand Federal Power

During 1819, the **Federal Supreme Court**, under the leadership of **Chief Justice John Marshall, of Virginia**, made major advances in expanding the power of the Federal Government over the governments of the individual States. A case, decided on March 6, called McCulloch versus Maryland, asked if a State government, such as that of Maryland, was empowered to levy a tax on bank notes issued by The Second Bank of the United States, whether at Philadelphia or at a branch office, such as Baltimore. The lawyers for Maryland argued that the States were sovereign except where specific powers were delegated to the Federal Government by the Federal Constitution. Therefore, Maryland could rightfully tax the banknotes, even though the bank, a private corporation, had been chartered by the Federal Government. The Bank's lawyers argued that, being chartered by the Federal Government, its banknotes could not be taxed by a State. Under Marshall's leadership the Supreme Court used this case to assert greater power for the Federal Government and reduced sovereignty for the State governments. The Court ruled that a state government could not tax the banknotes, but could tax the bank's physical property within the State and the interest earned on the banknotes. With regard to State sovereignty, Marshall, in the majority report, said:

"The powers delegated to the state sovereignties were to be exercised by [the people], not by a distinct and independent sovereignty, created by [the people]. To the formation of a league, such as was the Confederation [Government], the state sovereignties were certainly competent. But when, 'in order to form a more perfect union,' it was deemed necessary to change this alliance into an effective [Federal] Government, possessing great and sovereign powers, and acting directly on the people, the necessity of referring it to the people, and of deriving its powers directly from them, was felt and acknowledged by all. The [Federal Government], then (whatever may be the influence of this fact on the case), is, emphatically and truly, a government of the people. In form and in substance it emanates from them. Its powers are granted by them, and are to be exercised directly on them, and for their benefit."

Alabama Statehood

On December 14, 1819, Alabama was granted statehood. This completed the Southern States map between the Atlantic Ocean and the Mississippi River, except for Florida, which would be a Southern Territory for a long time.

1820

President James Monroe, Democrat of Virginia, is Reelected, Receiving 230 of the 231 Votes

The concept in America of political parties in presidential elections lay dormant during 1820 as **James Monroe was reelected to a second term without opposition.** The Federalist Party named no candidate. **This was an "Era of Good Feelings."**

Massachusetts Divides into Two States: Massachusetts and Maine

On March 15, 1820, Southern Culture political leaders granted a gift to the Northern Culture. They allowed Massachusetts to divide itself into two states. The western half remained as Massachusetts. The northeastern half became the State of Maine, complete with two new senators.

Please remember that, before the election of Abraham Lincoln, West Virginia was within the State of Virginia. Then, Virginia contained 67,005 square miles, far more than the 50,012 square miles within Maine, plus Massachusetts, plus Connecticut, plus Rhode Island. So, permission to divide Massachusetts into two states was clearly an 1820 gift from kind-hearted Southern people, **a gift from America's Nation Builders.**

Chapter 16 — March 1821 to February 1825: The States during the Second James Monroe Administration

It is time to interrupt the narrative history in order to present an overview of the second James Monroe Administration.

James Monroe was unopposed for reelection. His re-nomination by the Democratic Party was so certain that few Representatives in the House showed up at the Democratic Caucus to vote. Rather than record only a handful of votes, the Caucus declined to make a formal nomination. So, President James Monroe of Virginia and Vice President Daniel Tompkins of New York became de facto candidates for reelection. The Federalist Party named no opponent. William DeGregorio would summarize Monroe's reelection as follows:

"With the incumbent President standing unopposed for reelection, of course, there was no campaign. Not since George Washington had a President enjoyed such broad-based support. Even former President John Adams, a pillar of the Federalist Party, came out of retirement to stand as a Monroe elector in Massachusetts. It was indeed an 'Era of Good Feelings.' Only 1 of the 231 Electors voted against Monroe. That was Federalist Governor William Plumer of New Hampshire, who couldn't resist the opportunity to strike a blow at the Virginian. He voted for John Quincy Adams."

Taking 230 of 231 votes, Monroe won the majority of all electoral votes in all 24 States; from north to south they were: Maine, New Hampshire, Vermont, Massachusetts, Rhode Island, Connecticut, New York, New Jersey, Pennsylvania, Ohio, Indiana, Illinois, Delaware, Maryland, Missouri, Virginia, Kentucky, North Carolina, Tennessee, South Carolina, Georgia, Alabama and Mississippi.

Monroe retained much of the Cabinet from his first administration. John Quincy Adams, of Massachusetts, the son of the second President, John Adams, a lawyer and a Federalist politician, remained as Secretary of State. William Crawford, of Georgia, continued as Secretary of the Treasury. John Calhoun, of South Carolina, remained as Secretary of War. William Wirt, of Virginia, continued as Attorney General. Smith Thompson, of New York, remained as Secretary of the Navy until 1819, when he took a seat on the Federal Supreme Court. He was replaced by Samuel Southard, of New Jersey.

The Democratic Party retained huge majorities over the Federalist Party in both the Senate and the House during Monroe's second term. **Democrats increased their domination to an incredible 44-to-4 advantage in the Senate, and their huge House margin gained a little to 158 versus 25**. In the mid-term elections, Democrat Party strength held in the Senate at 44 versus 4, and grew even further in the House to 187 versus 26.

Missouri was granted statehood in 1821.

James Monroe was President during the most remarkably harmonious period in American history. Five States were added to the Federation during his two 4-year terms. His Democratic Party held almost 90% of the seats in the House and Senate. He was admired by his Secretary of State, John Quincy Adams, of Massachusetts, and by his Secretary of War, John Calhoun, of South Carolina, two men who would figure prominently in the divisive politics that would surface 5 years after Monroe stepped down and would produce war 30 years later. Of Monroe, John Quincy Adams said:

239

"There behold him for a term of 8 years, strengthening his country for defense by a system of combined fortifications, military and naval, sustaining her rights, her dignity and honor abroad; soothing her dissention, and conciliating her acerbities at home; controlling by a firm though peaceful policy the hostile spirit of the European Alliance against republican South America; extorting, by the mild compulsion of reason, the shores of the Pacific from the stipulated acknowledgment of Spain; and leading back the imperial autocrat of the North, to his lawful boundaries, from his hastily asserted dominion over the Southern Ocean. Thus, strengthening and consolidating the federative edifice of his country's [Federation], till he was entitled to say, like [Augustus] Caesar of his imperial city, that he had found her built of brick and left her constructed of marble."

Of Monroe, John Calhoun said:

"Though not brilliant, few men were his equals in wisdom, firmness and devotion to the [Federation]. He was a wonderful intellectual patience; and could above all men, that I ever knew, when called on to decide an important point, hold the subject immovably fixed under his attention, until he had mastered it in all of its relations. It was mainly to this admirable quality that he owed his highly accurate judgment. I have known many much more rapid in reaching a conclusion, but few with a certainty so unerring."

Monroe held the office of President during a period of great western expansion, and he was comfortable with an expansion policy that occupied more and more Native American land. He believed that this was just in the eyes of God, for he once said:

"The earth was given to mankind to support the greatest number of which it is capable, and no tribe or people have a right to withhold from the wants of others more than is necessary for their own support and comfort."

Monroe had seen the creation of essentially a one-party government and, viewing the beneficial harmony throughout the Federation, he saw it as both "good" and uniquely "American." He once said:

"Surely our government may get on and prosper without the existence of parties. I have always considered their existence as the curse of the [Federation], of which we had sufficient proof, more especially in the late war. Besides, how keep them alive, and in action? The causes which exist in other countries do not here. We have no distinct orders."

The more significant events involving African Americans during the 4 years of the second James Monroe Administration will now be presented. The Ohio Supreme Court decided that African Americans who were of 75% European descent had all the same "rights, privileges and duties" as European Americans. The revised New York State Constitution continued to permit independent African American men to vote, but instituted more rigorous requirements of property and residence. The Maine Government voided marriage between a European American and a person of full or partial African or Native American descent. The Tennessee Government likewise prohibited marriage between a European American and an African American. The American Deportation Society purchased land at Cape Mesurado on the western African coast for a new homeland for African Americans who were willing to be deported. This new land was called Liberia. Denmark Vesey, an independent African American in Charleston, South Carolina, set up an extensive secret organization with the object of seizing "arsenals, guardhouses, powder magazines, and naval stores," and killing all the area

European Americans. But, that vast conspiracy was found out, and authorities arrested 130 alleged conspirators and executed 35. In reaction, the South Carolina Government enacted laws limiting freedom of assembly among African Americans and prohibiting the teaching of reading and writing. And, citing the same concerns, the Mississippi Government prohibited gatherings of more than 5 African Americans. The Rhode Island Government withdrew the right to vote of the less than 1,000 African American men who lived in the State. A mob of between 400 and 500 European Americans gathered in Providence, Rhode Island, in 1824 and destroyed a section of town where Africa Americans lived. The Ohio Legislature voted to encourage deportation of African Americans to Africa. That same year, the Spanish Government made independent the bonded African Americans living in Central America.

This concludes the overview of the second James Monroe Administration. The narrative history resumes with first attention going to the Federalism agenda of Chief Justice John Marshall.

The Narrative History Resumes – March 1821

The Federal Supreme Court assumes Yet More Power

During 1821, the **Federal Supreme Court**, under the leadership of **Chief Justice John Marshall, of Virginia,** claimed for the Federal Government **increased power over judging State laws**. The case used for this claim, called Cohen versus Virginia, involved a complaint by "persons named Cohen" against a Virginia State law that "prohibited the sale of tickets for lotteries that were operating under other laws than her own." It seems that the Cohens were selling lottery tickets in the northern part of Virginia for a lottery that the Federal Government was running in Washington City and the surrounding Federal District. A Virginia State court had fined the Cohens for selling the tickets on Virginia soil and the Cohens had appealed all the way to the Federal Supreme Court. John Marshall used this case to claim greater power for the Federal Government.

During the months preceding this case, the governments of several other States, including those of Pennsylvania, Ohio, Indiana, Illinois and Tennessee, were warning they planned to defy the movement to grant the Federal Government greater power by rulings based on the "implied" meaning of the Federal Constitution. Virginia and these other State governments were insisting on a literal reading of the Federal Constitution, especially the Tenth Amendment:

"The powers not delegated to the [Federal Government] by the [Federal] Constitution, nor prohibited by it to the States, are reserved to the States respectively, or to the people."

And, they were insisting that "or to the people" was not a legitimate basis for giving the Federal Government, through implication, greater power. And, neither was there justification, through implication, in "to form a more perfect union," of any other clauses in the Preamble section of the Federal Constitution. Thomas Jefferson called the justices on the Federal Supreme Court, the majority of which were of the discredited Federalist Party, "a subtle corps of sappers and miners constantly working underground to undermine our confederate fabric." And, Jefferson's words make sense even today, when we observed that one of the few rights left to a state is the right to regulate lotteries and other forms of gambling within its borders.

241

The Spanish Treaty Ceding Florida finally arrives – Andrew and Rachel Jackson oversee Document Transfer at Pensacola

The Spanish Government had taken its own good time in ratifying the **treaty for the purchase of Spanish East and West Florida at a price of $5,000,000. Andrew Jackson and his wife Rachel were at Pensacola** during the spring of 1821. Government negotiators had signed the draft treaty in February 1819, but 2 years had transpired without receipt of the ratified copy from Spain. Talk of another invasion of Florida was gaining momentum, and Andrew Jackson was a proponent of such action. But, finally, in February 1821, Francisco Dionisio Vives, the Spanish Minister, arrived in Washington City with the ratified treaty. James Monroe had already asked Jackson to oversee the establishment of a Florida Territory Government. After thinking it over for several days, Jackson had accepted the appointment in a letter from his farm near Nashville, provided that he could "resign as soon as the [Territory] Government is organized." His wife, Rachel had accompanied him to Pensacola:

> "From her balcony Rachel saw the American and Spanish troops facing each other in front of the Government House with flag and staff between them." She saw her husband call on the Spanish Governor of West Florida, Don Jose Callava. "In a few moments they descended the broad steps together. . . The dignitaries passed between the lines of troops who raised their arms to salute. The Fourth [Federal] Infantry band began The Star Spangled Banner and the royal standard of Spain fluttered to half-mast. . . The Stars and Stripes were raised to a level with it. Aboard the *Hornet* in the bay boomed the first of 21 guns, after which the Spanish flag came down and the American [flag] went up."

Although Callava governed only what was left of Spanish West Florida, this ceremony also applied to the acquisition of Spanish East Florida, the government of which was headquartered on the Atlantic coast at St. Augustine. The Federal acquisition of the Spanish Floridas was encouraging a settlement rush by Americans. Rachel observed, "The vessels are daily coming in loaded with people." By fall, Andrew Jackson would believe that he had a working Territory Government in place in what had been Spanish East Florida and Spanish West Florida. **So, on October 5, Jackson would write James Monroe reporting that his assignment was completed, and notifying him that he and Rachel were going home to Hermitage farm.**

The Nation Builders and Sam Houston

Nation Builders, Southern families predominating, had expanded the United States to the Great Plains and to the Gulf Coast. They had secured a favorable boundary along the Great Lakes. They had arranged for joint British-American settlement of Oregon Territory, with a date set to establish a final far-west boundary with Upper Canada. Now Nation Builders were focused on the acquisition of vast Texas, presently part of Mexico. And Sam Houston would be equal to the task of leading such an effort. Sam Houston and Andrew Jackson were very good friends. Jackson probably saw in Houston the same youthful, confident, frontier fighting fire that had propelled him from the Carolinas into Tennessee Territory. Sam often dined with Andrew and Rachel at Hermitage farm. Sam would represent Tennessee in the Federal House (1823-1827) and he would be Governor of Tennessee (1827-1829). Then, in 1833, Sam would go to Texas, and, 2 years later, he would lead Texas revolutionaries in their fight to wrest that vast land from Spanish control. Sam Houston was an observant student of Andrew Jackson – every bit the Nation Builder.

1822

Andrew Jackson Buys Farm near Florence, Alabama

During June, **Andrew Jackson** made an inspection trip to an Alabama farm, which he had purchased from Felix Grundy a few months previously. Called **Melton's Bluff**, the farm was where Mill Creek entered the Tennessee River near Florence, Alabama. The farm contained "a good orchard, several excellent springs and a distillery."

To live on and work the farm, Jackson had **purchased 60 bonded African Americans** "from a former river pirate" who had managed them more often with whippings than with kindness. Jackson had hired Egbert Harris to oversee the 60 bonded African Americans and manage the newly purchased farm. Jackson realized that these slaves had been abused by the previous owner's management methods, and, when advised that one of the bonded African Americans, Gilbert, had run away, Jackson had written his overseer, Egbert Harris, advising his management philosophy: "you know my disposition, and as far as lenity can be extended to these unfortunate [people], I wish to do so; subordination must be obtained first, and then good treatment." For many years Jackson had maintained good morale at his farm outside Nashville, which he called Hermitage, through "good treatment" and a caring attitude, and had seldom felt forced to apply harsh discipline to any of the 100 bonded African Americans who lived on, and worked on, his Hermitage farm. "He called [them] "the family;" and relations between the bonded and the free were marked with instances of genuine and reciprocal attachment." But it was difficult to find an overseer who was skilled in managing people.

Upon arriving at his Melton's Bluff farm, Jackson was informed that 3 more bonded African Americans had run away. He took charge of the manhunt, and all 4 runaways were captured. Jackson wrote: "although I hate chains, I was compelled to place 2 of them in irons" for a while. Jackson spent 2 weeks at the Melton's Bluff farm working to improve organization and morale and in defining work he wanted accomplished over the ensuing months.

Campaign Begins to Elect Andrew Jackson to the Office of Federal President

The following month, the **Tennessee House of Representatives**, meeting at the Capitol in Murfreesboro, **endorsed Andrew Jackson to succeed James Monroe as Federal President.** The State Senate concurred in an August 3 vote. Of course, many politicians across the Federation wanted to derail the campaign to nominate Andrew Jackson for President. Many in the northwest preferred Henry Clay. Many in the northeast preferred John Quincy Adams. And many in the southeast preferred William Crawford.

1823

Attempt to Get Jackson out of the country fails

By the first week of 1823, politicians opposed to nominating Andrew Jackson for President had apparently persuaded James Monroe to be helpful to their cause, for Monroe agreed to get Jackson out of the country by offering him the **Minister to Mexico job**. Anyway, there was no other person in the Federation more qualified to handle the job, for in Mexico City, Jackson

243

could represent Federal Government interests in what would become the future acquisition of Mexican Texas. The Federal Senate approved the appointment. But, talking it over with Rachel at Hermitage farm, Andrew **declined to accept the job**.

Sam Houston is now a Prominent Nashville Lawyer

By 1823, **Sam Houston was a prominent Nashville lawyer,** involved in regional political activities and admired by Tennessee Governor Billy Carroll, and by Andrew Jackson. Voters liked Houston as well. He ran for the Federal House seat for the Nashville area, and he won the race without opposition. He would go to Washington City when the next session would convene in December. Because he was elected to complete the second year of a vacant seat, Houston would stand for reelection in 1824; and he would win that election as well.

Andrew Jackson is Elected Senator from Tennessee

The Tennessee Legislature convened on October 1. A major task was to elect a Federal Senator. State Representatives from East Tennessee counties favored returning John Williams to the Federal Senate, but Representatives from Middle Tennessee counties favored dumping Williams in favor of Andrew Jackson. David Crockett, of future Alamo fame, led a successful fight to rush the vote, figuring that would favor Williams' election. But 7 Legislators abandoned Williams and voted for Jackson, ensuring his **election to the Federal Senate.**

Upon hearing news of his election, Jackson sat down and wrote John Coffee: "I have been elected [Federal] Senator, a circumstance which I regret more than any other in my life." The thought of leaving Rachel here at Hermitage farm "fills me, as well as her, with much regret." In November, **Jackson and John Eaton, the other Senator from Tennessee**, rode to Washington City on horseback. Jackson's most important vote would be his agreement with Henry Clay to raise import taxes to enable domestic manufacturers to raise their prices. Jackson was not yet concerned about the economic problems that would derive from high import taxes – taxes so high they would reduce imports sufficiently to reduce overall Federal revenue at the same time they protected abnormally high prices for manufacturer goods. **And Sam Houston would support Jackson's political agenda from his seat in the House.**

1824

Steamboats and a Ruling by the Federal Supreme Court declaring that it can Oversee Legal Issues Concerning Interstate Commerce

Robert Fulton had demonstrated the usefulness of steam-powered riverboats, he and a partner, Robert Livingston, had won a monopoly from the State of New York to build and operate a steamboat passenger service within the State. And this monopoly had been extended to include trips across the Hudson River to the opposite bank, which was New Jersey. Thomas Gibbons had begun operating a few steamboat ferries in violation of the State monopoly and, as a key employee, Cornelius Vanderbilt, later to become immensely wealthy, had designed for Gibbons the *Bellona*, and was running it between New Jersey and Manhattan, evading police as best he could. But the State hauled Gibbons into court and the case progressed to the Federal Supreme Court.

Defenders of State sovereignty rallied around the State of New York in public debate, even though the case seemed clearly a matter of interstate commerce and therefore a matter for the

Federal Government. This presented Chief Justice John Marshall an easy opportunity to issue a ruling that strengthened the Federal Government claim of jurisdiction over interstate commerce.

So it was during 1824 that the **Federal Supreme Court**, under the leadership of **Chief Justice John Marshall** of Virginia, ruled, in a case called "Gibbons versus Ogden," **that regulations involving interstate commerce** were the province of the Federal Government. But, Marshall went further, for the Court's decision alleged, **"The power to regulate commerce was not limited to state lines but extended to commerce wherever found."** This part of the decision was clearly beyond the intent of the Federal Constitution. And, it was that part of Marshall's decision that drew heavy criticism from Democratic Party political leaders.

Federal Supreme Court Gives the Second Bank of the United States more Independence from State Influence

Three weeks later the Federal Supreme Court issued a decision further insulating branches of the **Second Bank of the United States** from oversight or taxation by the various State governments. The Ohio State Government had levied a tax on the bank branch that was located in Ohio. Bank officers had refused to pay the tax. The State Government had retaliated by authorizing the State Treasurer to seize bank funds to cover the tax. Federal authorities had retaliated by arresting the State Treasurer. The trial of the State Treasurer had progressed in Federal courts to the Supreme Court. And, the Federal Supreme Court, under the leadership of John Marshall of Virginia, ruled "against the defendants," because the operative Ohio State law was judged "repugnant to the [Federal] Constitution," and was judged to furnish "no authority to those who took, or those who received, the money for which this suit was instituted."

So, this ruling placed the Federal Government more firmly in control of taxation of, and regulation over, the Second Bank of the United States, **which it had chartered and given a monopoly with regard to all of the Federal Government's banking business.** And, this ruling further drew criticism from defenders of State sovereignty, for many Americans believed a "strict construction" of the Federal Constitution was intended by the founders of the Federal Government and was best for the Federation. Clearly, this case involved no hidden political agenda concerning bonded African Americans, for the action had taken place in Ohio.

John Quincy Adams, of Massachusetts, Defeats Andrew Jackson, of Tennessee for Office of President

The string of consecutive Federal Presidents from Virginia was coming to a close. People were moving west and Democrats believed that a westerner was right for the next office of President. But the vote was split between western candidates and John Quincy Adams, of Massachusetts, **allowing Adams to win the office of President with only 32 percent of the votes.**

Chapter 17 — March 1825 to February 1829: The States during the John Quincy Adams Administration

We now temporarily leave the narrative history to study an overview of the John Quincy Adams Administration.

President John Quincy Adams was the son of George Washington's Vice President and his successor, John Adams, of Massachusetts. Like his father, John Quincy Adams advanced from Vice President (under a Virginian) to President. The Federalist Party was too weak to nominate a candidate.

Because the **Democratic** Party so dominated American politics, it **splintered into 4 candidates**: **Andrew Jackson of Tennessee, John Quincy Adams of Massachusetts, Henry Clay of Kentucky**, and **William Crawford of Georgia**. Andrew Jackson won the most Electoral College votes, but not a majority, and that **forced the election into the House of Representatives**. Clay and Adams supporters teamed up to squeak out a majority for Adams. **Adams became President with 32% of the popular vote**. By that splintering of the race for President, Adams, of Massachusetts, brought the long and successful string of Presidents from Virginia to a conclusion.

John Quincy Adams was descended from early **Puritan Separatist settlers of Massachusetts.** His father was John Adams, who had been George Washington's Vice President for 8 years and President for 4 years. His mother was Abigail Smith Adams. Born in 1767 in Braintree, now Quincy, Massachusetts, the parents sent their son John Quincy to Europe at age 10 for his education and to get him away from the fighting for Independence, which was then raging about the newly independent northeastern States. Eight years later, long after the British surrender at Yorktown, John Quincy returned to Massachusetts and entered Harvard to complete his last 2 years of college. Graduating in 1787 (second among 51 graduates), Adams followed in his father's footsteps by studying law at a Massachusetts law firm. Adams was admitted to the Massachusetts bar in 1790. He was 23 years old. According to William DeGregorio, "Adams opened a law office in Boston but attracted few clients."

President George Washington appointed John Quincy (his Vice-President's son) to be Minister to Holland from 1794 to 1797. The appointment made sense because John Quincy, although still quite young, was bright and had learned French and Dutch while away at school in Europe during the Defense of Independence. While in England, John Quincy met an English lady, Louisa Johnson, and fell in love. Louisa's parents were Joshua Johnson, an American merchant, and Catherine Johnson, an Englishwoman. Louisa had grown up in London and Nantes, France, where her family had taken refuge during the Defense of American Independence. A short while later, Louisa's father would be bankrupt and happy that his brother-in-law, President John Adams, was able to appoint him Federal Director of Stamps. During John Quincy's 4 years as President, Louisa would have difficulty fitting in as First Lady. According to William DeGregorio, "As First Lady she became reclusive and depressed."

President John Adams appointed John Quincy to be Minister to Prussia from 1791 to 1801. Returning to Massachusetts in 1801, John Quincy won election to the Massachusetts State Senate the following year. Shortly thereafter he ran as the Federalist candidate for the Federal House, but was defeated. Next, he ran on the Federalist ticket for the Federal Senate seat for Massachusetts. This time Adams won and held a seat from 1803 to 1808.

Adams often supported President Jefferson during his Senate years. In fact, every Federalist member of the House and the Senate voted against the Louisiana Purchase – except for John Quincy Adams! John Quincy Adams's support for the Louisiana Purchase, his support on that occasion for the cause of America's Nation Builders, infuriated the Massachusetts Legislature and it **refused to reelect John Quincy to the Federal Senate** after his first term was finished.

However, President James Madison rewarded Adams with appointment as Minister of Russia (1809-1814). Next, Madison assigned Adams to lead the 5-man American Delegation to negotiate a peace agreement with Great Britain, ending the War of 1812. President Madison subsequently appointed Adams Minister to Great Britain (1815-1817). With excellent credentials in foreign diplomatic service, President James Monroe selected Adams to serve in his Cabinet as Secretary of State.

The Democratic Party had become so powerful, and the Federalist Party so weak that the nominating process for President deteriorated into a contest among 4 regional favorites. President James Monroe's "Era of Good Feelings" was deteriorating into Sectionalism. This election was perhaps the beginning of a rising passion for Sectionalism in American politics, which would give rise to the Northern States Republican Party during the 1950s and, 35 years later, culminate in the secession of Southern States and a war that would result in one million unnecessary America deaths, both White and Black.

Firstly, the Democratic Party caucus met on February 14, 1824, but less than a third attended. Those attending voted overwhelmingly to endorse Treasury Secretary William Crawford of Georgia for President. Secondly, the Kentucky Legislature nominated Federal Representative Henry Clay of Kentucky for President. Thirdly, on June 10, the Massachusetts Legislature nominated John Quincy Adams for President and other neighboring legislatures soon followed. Fourthly, the Tennessee Legislature nominated Andrew Jackson for President. None of these men actually ran on a political party ticket. William DeGregorio would summarize the campaign:

"The campaign turned on sectional rivalries and the strong personalities of the 4 candidates. Adams's apparent aloofness and formal manner compared unfavorably with Jackson's down-home style. All 4 candidates supported in varying degrees a protective tariff. A Federal program of internal improvements also had wide appeal. [The status of African Americans] had not yet become a divisive issue. Adams enjoyed the solid support of his home base of [Massachusetts and neighboring States,] and the manufacturing interests. He also had a large following in New York; among those campaigning for him there was 27-year-old Thurlow Weed, later a political boss in the Whig Party, and then in the Republican Party. Jackson and Crawford drew from the [southern States]; Jackson and Clay divided the [western States]."

Jackson won the popular vote, beating out Adams by a full 10%. The popular vote was **Jackson, 152,933 (42%)**; Adams, 115,696 (32%); Clay, 47,136 (13%), and Crawford, 46,979 (13%). Jackson also won the electoral vote, beating out Adams by 6%. The electoral vote was Jackson, 99 (38%); Adams, 84 (32%); Crawford, 41 (16%), and **Clay, 37 (14%).** Jackson won the majority of electoral votes in 11 States: from north to south they were New Jersey, Pennsylvania, Indiana, Illinois, Maryland, North Carolina, Tennessee, South Carolina, Alabama, Mississippi and Louisiana. Adams won the majority of electoral votes in 7 States: from north to south they were Maine, New Hampshire, Vermont, Massachusetts, Connecticut,

Rhode Island, and New York. Crawford won the majority of electoral votes in 3 States: from north to south they were Delaware, Virginia and Georgia. Clay won the majority of electoral votes in 3 States: from north to south they were Ohio, Missouri and Kentucky.

John Calhoun of South Carolina won the election for Vice President <u>over 5 other candidates. Calhoun received a clear majority of 70% of the votes of the 261 Electors.</u>

<u>When the Electoral College met, the electors could not agree on a candidate. Neither Crawford's people nor Clay's people would unite behind Jackson, the plurality winner. Therefore, the election was thrown into the House of Representatives.</u>

Crawford's people could have won the election for Jackson, but chose silence instead. Representatives from Illinois, Maryland and Missouri disobeyed the wishes of their voters, who had chosen Jackson, and instead voted for Adams. Adams needed 13 States to win. That's all he got, but it was enough. Politicians maneuvering to negotiate deals for second and third ballot votes never got that chance, because the Adam's people succeeded in putting together a winning combination on the first ballot.

William DeGregorio would tell the story of how the Adams and Clay supporters teamed up in the House of Representatives to win the election for Adams:

> "Because none of the 4 [candidates for President] received a majority of the electoral vote, the election was thrown into the House of Representatives. In accordance with the Twelfth Amendment to the Constitution, the House was directed to choose the President from the top 3 electoral vote getters; thus, Henry Clay was dropped from consideration. **Clay thereupon supported Adams.** <u>On February 9, 1825, the House, with each State casting one vote based on the majority of its Delegation, elected Adams President on the first ballot with the barest majority.</u> Adams carried 13 States – the 7 States he had won in November [(Maine, New Hampshire, Vermont, Rhode Island, Massachusetts, Connecticut, and New York)], the 3 States that had gone to Clay [(Ohio, Missouri and Kentucky)] plus Illinois, Maryland, and Louisiana (former Jackson States). Jackson held on to just 7 States – New Jersey, Pennsylvania, Indiana, Tennessee, South Carolina, Alabama and Mississippi. Crawford carried 4 States – his original 3 [(Delaware, Virginia and Georgia)] plus North Carolina, a former Jackson State."

<u>President Adams awarded candidate</u> **Henry Clay, of Kentucky, the job of Secretary of State** <u>in recognition of his decisive support of him in the House of Representatives balloting for President.</u> Of that obvious deal making, William DeGregorio would write, "Clay's support of Adams over fellow-westerner Jackson in the House [balloting for President], and President Adams' prompt appointment of Clay as Secretary of State smacked of a political deal to Andrew Jackson and his followers. Although both Clay and Adams denied any collusion, the persistent charge of a 'corrupt bargain' dogged the [Adams] Administration."

Native Americans had good reason to fear the new Secretary of State, especially after he said he was comfortable with his expectation that the Native American nations to the west would eventually be exterminated. <u>Of Native Americans, Secretary of State Henry Clay said:</u>

> <u>"I believe they are destined to extinction. Although I would not use or countenance inhumanity towards them, I do not think them, as a race, worth preserving. . . Their disappearance from the human family will be no great loss to the world."</u>

John Adams made Richard Rush, of Pennsylvania, his Treasury Secretary. He had been Attorney General under President James Madison, as well as under President James Monroe. James Barbour, of Virginia, was Secretary of War until 1828. Adams sent Barbour, a long-time advocate of State rights, to be Minister to Great Britain in 1828. Then, Adams appointed Peter Porter, of New York, to the War Secretary job for the remainder of his Administration. William Wirt, of Virginia, remained as Attorney General. Samuel Southard, of New Jersey, remained as Secretary of the Navy.

Party alignments were so blurred, that it is not possible to classify Federal Representatives and Senators as "Democrats" or "Federalists." Instead, they must be classified as "supportive of the Administration" or "opposed to the Administration." During the first 2 years of the Adams Administration supporters enjoyed an advantage in the Senate of 26 versus 20. Supporters also enjoyed an advantage in the House of 105 versus 97. Supportive majorities increased slightly at mid-term. In the second two-year span, the Senate supporters enjoyed an advantage of 28 versus 20, and, in the House, it was 119 versus 94.

The more significant events involving African Americans during the 4 years of the John Quincy Adams Administration will now be presented. A 1826 study of the prisons of Massachusetts, New York and Pennsylvania showed vastly higher incarceration rates for African Americans than for European Americans. African Americans "in Massachusetts made up 1/74th of the population and 1/6th of the prisoners; in New York State, 1/35th of the population and 1/4th of the prisoners, and in Pennsylvania, 1/34th of the population and 1/3rd of the prisoners." In Maryland an imprisoned independent African American, upon release, was given $30 and banished from the State. The North Carolina Government forbade independent African Americans from moving into the State. About 10,000 adult bonded African Americans living in New York State became independent in 1827, in accordance with the law passed 10 years previously. African Americans who wished to live in Michigan Territory had to post a sizable money bond to guarantee good behavior. Florida Territory restricted voting to European American men.

This concludes the overview of the John Quincy Adams Administration. The narrative history resumes.

The Narrative History Resumes – March 1825

Adams, of Massachusetts, is President, but Support Solidifies for Another Run for the Office by Andrew Jackson, of Tennessee

Interest in Andrew Jackson as a candidate for President was growing across the Federation, and was being facilitated by a team of 3 Tennessee political supporters whom Jackson called his "literary bureau." It consisted of fellow Tennessee Senator John Eaton, Representative Sam Houston and Judge Jacob Isacks, of Winchester. "They enjoyed themselves and contributed to a great many newspapers. Sometimes the same man, using different names, would carry on both sides of a controversy. Sam Houston is believed also to have written, '*A Civil and Military History of Andrew Jackson*, by an American Army Officer,' which in 1825 [was among that era's] flood of Jackson literature."

Freemason Party? – What a Crazy Political Notion That Was!

During September 1826, the destruction of a book while it was being printed, and the disappearance of the book's author shortly thereafter, would launch an amazing political movement across the northern States. This movement would be aimed at forming a political party through which aspiring politicians believed they could win elections against the very popular Democratic Party. The Federalist Party had become so weak by 1826 that its members were desperate for another political basis for challenging the popular Democrats. Perhaps, never before and never since has so much political activity devolved from so little substance. What little substance there was came from a book by William Morgan, which reported on the secret ceremonies of the Free and Accepted Masons, a widespread fraternal society of men. Members of the Order were called Freemasons for short.

Free and Accepted Mason societies had grown out of the stonemason guilds of Europe and the British Isles, which were common during medieval times. Members within a community group gathered to form a "lodge," and several lodges joined together to form a "grand lodge." The first grand lodge that conformed to this practice had been the one formed in London on June 24, 1717. The first lodge to appear in The States had been the Philadelphia Lodge, which appeared in 1730, followed by the Boston Lodge, which appeared in 1733. Masonic lodges were common in The States, both north and south, by the time that printer's shop was destroyed in 1826. To join a lodge, a man had to be invited by an existing member and be accepted for membership by a vote of the members – much like today's college fraternities and quite a few golf-oriented country clubs. Members had to profess faith in God, and Protestants, Catholics and Jews were admitted. The purpose of the lodge was "to enable men to meet in harmony, to promote friendship, and to be charitable." Today, about 3,000,000 Americans are freemasons. Masonic lodges of today sponsor several subsidiary groups which bear familiar names: the Shriners for men, the Order of the Eastern Star for couples, the Order of De Molay for boys, and the Order of Job's Daughters and the Order of Rainbow for girls. Just like politically-minded members of a prestigious college fraternity can influence campus politics, and just like members of a prestigious country club can influence mutually beneficial business activity as well as politics, it is obvious that members of Masonic lodges in 1826 were able to similarly benefit each other by being together in the group. And, being a secret society, the membership list was secret and the public at large did not know who was and who was not a member.

The destroyed book's author, William Morgan, was "an itinerant stonecutter and bricklayer" in Batavia, New York, who was "contentious and fond of strong drink." He had been a member of the local Masonic Lodge, but had "quarreled" with other members and had thereafter "thirsted for revenge." To that end Morgan, who was apparently unusually literate for a man of his trade, wrote a book in which he reported the Masonic secret "rites and oaths" that he had previously sworn to keep to himself. Morgan titled his book, *Illustrations of Masonry*, and went looking for a publisher. Thurlow Weed, the well-known politician and newspaper publisher in Rochester, New York, turned Morgan down. But Morgan later succeeded in getting publication underway in Batavia. What was reported in Morgan's book was not preserved for history because 5 masked men broke into the print shop while the book was being printed. The 5 men clubbed the owner of the print shop and destroyed the papers and the plates.

In a parallel action, on September 11, Morgan was arrested in Batavia and taken to Canandaigua, where he was booked on a charge of stealing clothing from an innkeeper. He was released, then rearrested the next day and fined $2.69. He spent the night in jail. Then he paid his fine and left the jail. However, some men seized Morgan later that day, threw him into a carriage and drove him rapidly toward Fort Niagara. Morgan was never seen again. Nor was his body ever found. Five Masons were accused of breaking into the print shop and of killing Morgan. "The evidence seemed to indicate" that the 5 men "had taken [Morgan] out onto Lake Ontario and drowned him." The 5 Masons were all prominent men in Canandaigua. The judge who presided over the trial was a Mason, too. The jury voted for minor punishment: 3 were declared innocent and the other 2 were sentenced to a few months in jail. Over the next 2 years, other Canandaigua Masons would be accused of collusion in the kidnapping, but none would ever be convicted.

This destruction of a rather ordinary man's book and his likely murder would fuel a powerful political movement all across the northern States, which would be aimed at defeating Democratic Party candidates at the polls – in spite of the fact that there was no connection between the "secret rites and oaths" reported in Morgan's book and local, State or National political issues. With Thurlow Weed at the forefront, a political party would be organized in New York State based on opposition to members of Masonic lodges. Of New York State men voting in the fall 1827 elections, 33,000 would mark their ballots for the new party's gubernatorial candidate. The party would call itself the "Anti-Mason" Party, but that name will be translated in my study, for I have pledged to not name any political movement solely on the basis of what its advocates say they are against. Instead, the name that I will use must indicate what its advocates say they are for. From this point forward the **"Anti-Mason" Party** will be referred to as the **"Open-Leagues" Party**.

1827

Nashville Replaces Murfreesboro as Tennessee's State Capital

By 1827, Nashville had replaced Murfreesboro as Tennessee's capital, but it remained a frontier town. Nashville's population was about 5,000, of which about 1,000 were bonded African Americans. The courthouse dominated the center of the square, atop the bluff and near the site of the wooden fort where James Robertson and his pioneers had fought off Native American warriors. The Nashville Inn occupied one side of the square while the City Hotel occupied the other. Democrats patronized the Nashville Inn. Sam Houston lived in the Nashville Inn and, along with Andrew Jackson, frequented the cockfights in the adjacent vacant lot.

Sam Houston Elected Governor of Tennessee

Sam Houston was elected in August to follow Billy Carroll as the next Governor of Tennessee. He would be 35 years old when inaugurated in the spring of 1828. Houston won by a vote of 44,426 to 33,410 over opposition candidate Newton Cannon. **Billy Carroll had served 3 consecutive terms as Governor** and was unable to run again for reelection according to the Tennessee Constitution. Carroll and Andrew Jackson expected to elect Houston for one term, and then resubmit Carroll to the voters for a subsequent string of 3 more terms. As a victorious commander of Tennessee cavalrymen and as a successful Governor, Carroll remained very popular among the voters.

At this point **James K. Polk, of Columbia, Tennessee,** gained important recognition, since Andrew Jackson also admired Polk. With support from Carroll and Jackson, **Polk won election to Houston's vacated seat in the Federal House. And Polk would eventually become one of America's most important Presidents.**

251

Benjamin Lundy, Lloyd Garrison and the Rise of Abolitionism as a Political Movement Aimed Against the Southern States

Benjamin Lundy hosted a meeting of Boston ministers on March 17. He hoped to win their support for organizing a local Abolition-Deportation society. Lundy, 39, had been born a Quaker in Sandwich, New Jersey. As a youth he had apprenticed to a saddle-maker in Wheeling, Virginia. Afterward, he had moved a few miles across the Ohio River to Mount Pleasant, Ohio, where, in 1815, he had formed that State's first Abolition-Deportation society.

There, in 1821, he had begun the publication of one of the first Abolition-Deportation newspapers, *The Genius of Universal Emancipation.* "As a Quaker, Lundy inherited a long tradition of uncompromising resistance to [African American bonding], a tradition that emphasized the moral wrong of [owning African Americans] and reduced the problem to the dimension of individual conscience. The opinions of the Quakers were not always moderate and inoffensive. Their belief in the immediacy of the Holy Spirit and their trust in the informed conscience freed them from institutional prejudices and the need to compromise. Lundy's forebears had bequeathed to him a concern with personal worthiness and soul-searching, an unyielding hostility to [African American bonding], the militant views and blunt language of Christian zealots." **Lundy had a solution, which was to make bonded African Americans independent and then deport them.** He had or would travel to Haiti, Canada and Texas to evaluate those regions for deportation destinations. His favorite destination was Haiti.

The ministers who attended Lundy's meeting in Boston refused to become involved in the startup of a local Abolition-Deportation society.

But a young man was in attendance and, as the meeting broke up, this man impressed Lundy with his passion for Abolition and his capacity for vituperation, for wordy and vehement verbal abuse. The man's name was Lloyd Garrison.

Lloyd Garrison, 22, had been born in Newburyport, Massachusetts, his parents having just emigrated from Nova Scotia. His mother Fanny was a devout Baptist and his father Joseph was an easy-going seaman. When Joseph had been home from the sea the couple rather tolerated each other as Fanny had strived to convert Joseph to devout Baptist Christianity, and Joseph had strived to have some fun at the local taverns. This incompatibility had come to a crisis point in 1808, when Lloyd was near 3 years old. Joseph had walked out and never returned. "Lloyd [had grown] up in extreme poverty; without the help of devoted friends Fanny Garrison would never have been able to provide even the necessities for her family." And Lloyd [had grown] up under the stern direction of a fervent Baptist mother and without the positive male guidance of a father. Fanny had moved her family to Baltimore, Maryland, in 1815, when Lloyd was 10, where she and the children had worked in a shoe factory. The next year Lloyd had returned to Newburyport, boarded with an uncle and received the last of his formal education.

Then, as Lloyd approached his thirteenth birthday, he had been apprenticed to the editor of the *Newburyport Herald* for 7 years, and during these years he had boarded with his employer. He had learned the printing trade as he set type and did other production and cleanup jobs. And I expect he had also done some proofreading. Adopting the politics of his employer, Lloyd had embraced the ideals of the Federalist Party. Soon after completing his apprenticeship at the age of 20, Lloyd had taken over a struggling secondary Newburyport newspaper, renamed it the *Free Press* and revealed that it staunchly supported the Federalist Party. After 6 months, the paper had failed and Lloyd had moved to Boston. That was December 1826.

By January 1828, Lloyd Garrison had become editor of the *National Philanthropist*, a struggling newspaper, which Nathaniel White had just purchased. This paper was highly moralistic and advocated Christian behavior throughout society and political life. It opposed drinking alcoholic beverages. And it demanded Christian morality of political leaders: "It is due to our principles, our civil, social and moral institutions, that men whose characters are notoriously bad should be deprived of the control of our political destines." Being an impressionable newcomer to Boston, his social attitudes were shaped by Unitarian preachers, advocates of various religious crusades, advocates for various social causes, advocates within the peace movement, advocates for the prohibition of alcoholic beverages, advocates for a strict observance of Sunday, and so forth. His religious, social and political attitudes and his style of rhetoric were greatly influenced by Lyman Beecher and other Boston social, religious and political activists.

It was at this point that Lloyd Garrison met Benjamin Lundy. In his struggling newspaper, the *National Philanthropist*, Lloyd Garrison promptly praised Benjamin Lundy. "He called Lundy's publication, *The Genius of Universal Emancipation*, 'the bravest and best attempt in the history of newspaper publications'." He praised the American Deportation Society, which was a national effort to deport independent African Americans to Africa. But he praised Lundy's efforts to encourage African American emigration to Haiti with the greatest enthusiasm. "He noted that over 1,000 [independent African Americans] had already been sent back to Africa while over 7,000 were now established in Haiti."

Impressed with Benjamin Lundy's "unconquerable spirit," Lloyd Garrison decided to join Lundy's crusade for Abolition and Deportation. "Henceforth [African American bonding] took precedence over all the other moral causes." In July Garrison would resign his editor's job in Boston and take a job in Bennington, Vermont, as editor of a political newspaper that would become a Whig Party advocate. This would primarily be an organ of the Quincy Adams for President Campaign. In Bennington, while doing his duty to advocate Quincy Adams and oppose Andrew Jackson, Garrison would pursue his main passion, which was to agitate for Abolition and Deportation. While at Bennington, he would sponsor a statewide petition to prohibit the buying and selling of African Americans in Washington City. It would carry 2,352 signatures and be presented on the floor of the Federal House on January 26, 1829. That same month Garrison would meet with Lundy. In the post-presidential-election environment, Garrison's Vermont newspaper would have no future, so he agreed to take over from Lundy the job of resident editor of Lundy's Ohio Abolition and Deportation newspaper, *The Genius of Universal Emancipation*."

Anti-Mason Parties Organize in New York and Pennsylvania

The Open-Leagues Party in New York State, founded on opposition to members of Masonic Lodges, grew further in 1828, and the political movement spilled over into other northern States. New York State voters would cast 70,000 votes for the Open-Leagues Party candidate for Governor, over twice the vote count recorded the previous year. This party, became significant in Pennsylvania during 1828. A few Open-Leagues Party newspapers were started in Pennsylvania, and hopeful politicians with no immediate prospects for recognition in the dominant Democratic Party joined with the Open-Leagues people.

1829

Governor Sam Houston, 36, Marries Eliza Allen, 18

On January 22, 1829, Tennessee Governor Sam Houston married Eliza Allen at Gallatin, not far from Nashville. Sam had known Eliza and her family for 5 years, but she had only recently attained marriageable age. She was 18 years old. Her father was a prosperous Middle Tennessee farmer. He had commanded volunteers in the War of 1812 and had been to Washington City as a Representative in the Federal House. <u>Sam was almost 36 years old.</u>

Closing a Brief John Quincy Adams Four-year Term; Democrats Elect Andrew Jackson, Long-term Democrat of Tennessee, as the Next Federal President

John Quincy Adams of Massachusetts failed to win reelection. In a basically two-way contest against **Andrew Jackson**, Democrat of Tennessee, Adams received far less votes than did his Democratic opponent. **Yes, like his father, John Adams, son John Quincy failed to win re-election.** Political strength in the growing country was rapidly moving westward. <u>Tennessee was the foremost symbol of America's westward expansion.</u> **Andrew Jackson was America's unchallenged Nation Building leader!**

Chapter 18 — March 1829 to February 1833: The States during the First Andrew Jackson Administration

We briefly leave the narrative history in order to present an overview of the first Andrew Jackson Administration.

John Quincy Adams failed to win reelection to a second term as President, for **Andrew Jackson of Tennessee would not be denied a second time.** In a 4-way contest 4 years earlier, Jackson had gathered 42% of the popular vote versus Adams' 32% – but an Adams-Clay combination had wrestled away that apparent victory in a House of Representatives showdown. Now, Jackson cleanly out-polled Adams, 55% versus 42% in an essentially 2-way contest. Adams' father had similarly failed to win reelection 28 years previously. Every southern States President – Washington, Jefferson, Madison and Monroe – had won reelection, but both northern States Presidents – the father-son Adams team – had failed to win reelection. **John Quincy Adams was so angry he even refused to attend Jackson's inauguration.**

Andrew Jackson was the son of Scottish emigrants from Northern Ireland. His 2 brothers were born in County Antrim, Ireland. Andrew was born about 2 years after his parents arrived in America and settled near the border between North Carolina and South Carolina, on land near or within the Waxhaw Nation. Andrew's father had injured himself lifting a log and died about 2 weeks before the birth. Jackson relatives helped his mother with raising the 3 boys.

Jackson was born not far from where I live in Charlotte, North Carolina. When a younger man, I occasionally bicycled over the land of Andrew's birth, but do not know exactly where it took place. In fact, historians are not sure if the birth occurred in North Carolina or in South Carolina. Andrew claimed to be born in South Carolina. Carolinians resettle the question annually with a high school football game. If the Union County, North Carolina, high school wins, the Jackson bust resides in their courthouse for the next 12 months. If the Lancaster County, South Carolina, high school wins, Lancaster has it for 12 months.

The Jackson's were fierce supporters of the Defense of Independence. At 13 Jackson, along with his older brother, joined the Continental Army. Andrew served as a mounted messenger and participated in the Battle of Hanging Rock in August 1780. The Jackson boys were surprised by a British officer in April 1781, an event that further swelled their hatred for the British. The British officer demanded that Andrew Jackson clean his boots. Jackson refused. Then the officer struck him with his sword cutting Andrew's hand to the bone and slicing open his scalp. That scalp wound would leave a prominent scar that would mark Jackson for life. Without even dressing the wounds, the British officer forced the boys to march to a prisoner-of-war camp 40 miles away where they subsisted on bread and water until they were fortunate to be released in a prisoner exchange just 2 weeks later. Jackson would be the last President to have fought in the Defense of Independence and the only President to have been a prisoner of war.

While the Jackson boys were serving in the Continental Army, their mother Elizabeth traveled to Charleston to nurse the captured American soldiers languishing on British prisoner-of-war ships anchored in Charleston harbor. While nursing those poor men she contracted cholera and that patriotic lady died in Charleston, leaving her patriotic son Andrew an orphan at the age of 14.

During Andrew Jackson's childhood his mother Elizabeth had encouraged him to gain an education. From age 8 to 13 he had received a basic classical education under local instructors.

He was already reading well at age 9 and, in 1776, had read aloud the Declaration of Independence for folks in the region who had never learned to read. Andrew's grandfather, who had died in Ireland, had left him enough money to finance a good education and a solid start in life, but Andrew chose the role of the shortsighted and rebellious teenager – that is until the money ran out – for he squandered his inheritance gambling and carousing in Charleston. Perhaps Elizabeth's death had shaken Andrew's determination to become successful. So, Andrew had to learn the importance of character and perseverance the hard way. Determined again to be successful, Andrew returned to the Waxhaw region, near Charlotte, North Carolina, and spent a year teaching school. Next, he moved to Salisbury, North Carolina, and studied law for two and a half years under local lawyers. **In 1787, at age 20, Andrew Jackson was admitted to the North Carolina bar. A year later he moved to what would become Nashville, where he served as public prosecutor for what was then the Western District of North Carolina.**

In August 1791, **Andrew Jackson married Rachel Donelson Robards at Natchez**, then in Spanish West Florida and later in the State of Mississippi, mistakenly believing that Rachel's divorce was final. Upon learning that Rachel's divorce from her first husband had not been finalized until after the marriage at Natchez, the couple properly remarried in Nashville, Tennessee, in January 1794. Rachel was the daughter of Colonel John Donelson, and Rachel Stockley Donelson. Jackson's political opponents unmercifully slandered Andrew and Rachel, for, technically speaking, living out of wedlock for two and a half years. The slanderous attacks would peak during Jackson's second race for President, and would contribute – so Andrew believed – to Rachel's sudden and tragic death in December 1828. Andrew would vow at Rachel's funeral, "In the presence of this dear saint, I can and do forgive all my enemies. But those vile wretches who have slandered her must look to God for mercy."

Jackson began his political career in 1796, at age 29, as a Delegate to the 1796 Tennessee Constitutional Convention. He immediately won election as Tennessee's first Representative to the Federal House (1796-1797). Soon thereafter, the Tennessee State Legislature elected Jackson to the Federal Senate (1797-1798). That post was quickly followed by his election by the Tennessee State Legislature to the position of Tennessee Superior Court Justice (1798-1804).

In 1812, Tennessee's Governor appointed Jackson Major General of Federal Volunteers. The following year a major faction within the Creek Nation attacked and killed 250 European Americans at Fort Mims in what is now Alabama. In October, Jackson led 2,500 Tennessee volunteers southward to confront the militant faction. The next month, at Talladega, Jackson's men defeated a force of 1,000 Creeks, killing 300 and driving off the remainder. In March of the following year – after allowing the women and children to safely evacuate – Jackson's men subdued the Creek warriors at Horseshoe Bend. Two months later, Jackson was promoted to Major General in the Federal Army. In the aftermath, Jackson forced the Creek Nation to cede to the United States a vast amount of land that would become a major portion of the State of Alabama.

During 1814, Jackson moved to secure the Federation's southeast border with Spanish Florida. He led a combined militia and Federal force into Spanish Florida and took command of Pensacola. He strengthened defenses at Mobile Bay, and there a British attack was successfully repulsed. Then, he marched with his men to New Orleans to help with and oversee the defense of that city, which he quickly strengthened. He received reinforcements from Tennessee. His men were ready when, on January 8, 1815, a huge British force advanced toward the New Orleans defensive line in the early morning fog. His defenders laid down a withering barrage of rifle and cannon fire. More than 2,000 British soldiers were killed within a short time. The remainder surrendered. **Jackson's forces only lost 6 killed and 7 wounded. The British Government would never again consider becoming engaged in a war with the United States.**

Andrew Jackson ran against President John Quincy Adams, who sought a second term. William DeGregorio would describe the nominations and the election:

"Within months after the inauguration of John Quincy Adams in 1825, the Tennessee Legislature re-nominated Jackson for President, thus setting the stage for a rematch between these two very different politicians 3 years hence. No nominating caucus was held. Jackson accepted the incumbent Vice President, John Calhoun, as his running mate. Jackson's supporters called themselves Democrats, thus marking the evolution of Jefferson's [party] into the modern Democratic Party."

"President John Quincy Adams of Massachusetts was re-nominated on the endorsement of State legislatures and partisan rallies. No nominating caucus was held. Adams accepted Richard Rush of Pennsylvania as his [running mate for Vice President]. Adams supporters called themselves National Republicans, antecedents of the Whig [Party] and later the Republican [Party]."

"The campaign turned more on personality than on issues. Both men supported, in varying degrees, a protective tariff and a program of internal improvements. The contest pitted the erudite, experienced, reserved John Quincy Adams against a national war hero whose humble origins stood him in good stead with the swelling ranks of frontier settlers and manual laborers. For many Americans, Jackson embodied the democratic spirit that was anathema to the eastern [families that were wealthy and well established]."

The Jackson-Calhoun ticket was the rare exception in which the candidate for President and the candidate for Vice President were both from a southern State. Andrew Jackson won by a comfortable margin, carrying 56% of the popular vote to 44% for Adams. **The electoral vote was 178 for Jackson versus 83 for Adams.** Jackson won the majority of electoral votes in 15 States. From north to south Jackson's States were: New York, Pennsylvania, Ohio, Indiana, Illinois, Missouri, Virginia, Kentucky, North Carolina, Tennessee, South Carolina, Georgia, Alabama, Mississippi, and Louisiana. All of Jackson's States were of large size with substantial farm populations. Adams won the majority of electoral votes in 9 States. From north to south Adams' States were: Maine, New Hampshire, Vermont, Rhode Island, Massachusetts, Connecticut, New Jersey, Delaware, and Maryland. All of Adams' States were north of Washington City, eastern, small and under the influence of substantial manufacturing interests.

John Calhoun, of South Carolina, was elected Vice-President by 171 electoral votes, versus 83 for Richard Rush of Pennsylvania, and 7 for William Smith, also of South Carolina.

Andrew Jackson appointed Martin Van Buren, of New York, as Secretary of State. Van Buren would follow Jackson as President 8 years later. Holding the job from 1829 to 1831, Van Buren was replaced by Edward Livingston, of Louisiana. Samuel Ingham, of Pennsylvania, was appointed Treasury Secretary and held the office from 1829 to 1831. He was replaced by Louis McLane, of Delaware. John Eaton, of Tennessee, was appointed Secretary of War and held that job from 1829 to 1831. He was replaced by Lewis Cass, of Michigan. John Branch, of North Carolina, was appointed Navy Secretary and worked the job from 1829 to 1831. He was replaced by Levi Woodbury, of New Hampshire. William Barry, of Kentucky, was appointed Postmaster General.

John Berrien, of Georgia, was appointed Attorney General and held the job from 1829 to 1831. He was **replaced by Roger Taney, of Maryland**. Jackson would later appoint **Roger Taney to the Federal Supreme Court. Roger Taney would replace John Marshall as Chief Justice** upon the latter's death. In that key office, as Chief Justice, Taney would figure in the sectional politics that would give birth to the Republican Party and would oppose the invasion of the Confederacy and the imprisonment of dissidents. But Abe Lincoln would simply ignore Roger Taney and the decisions of the Supreme Court.

Jackson's Democratic Party controlled both the House of Representatives and the Senate. The Democrats held a 26 to 22 majority in the Senate and a large 139 to 74 majority in the House. The mid-term elections changed these majorities slightly. During the second half of his first term, Democrats held 25 Senate seats versus 23 other seats and Democrats held 141 seats in the House versus 72 other seats.

The National Republican Party (this was not the Northern States Political Party of Abraham Lincoln) was a new political organization that stood opposed to the Democratic Party.

Two notable quotations shed light upon Andrew Jackson's strong belief in the need to protect the common man against oppression from the influential and wealthy, or from government itself:

In 1821, Jackson said, "I ... believe ... that just laws can make no distinction of privilege between the rich and poor, and that when men of high standing attempt to trample upon the rights of the weak, they are the fittest objects for example and punishment. In general, the great can protect themselves, but the poor and humble, require the arm and shield of the law."

As President, in 1832, Jackson said, "Distinctions in society will always exist under every just government. Equality of talents, of education, or of wealth cannot be produced by human institutions. In the full enjoyment of the gifts of Heaven and the fruits of superior industry, economy, and virtue, every man is equally entitled to protection by law; but when the laws undertake to add to these natural and just advantages artificial distinction . . . to make the rich richer and the potent more powerful, the humble members of society – the farmers, mechanics, and laborers – who have neither the time nor the means of securing like favors to themselves, have a right to complain of the injustice of their Government."

The more significant events involving African Americans during the 4 years of the first Andrew Jackson Administration will now be presented. In 1829, the Illinois Government required independent African Americans entering the State to carry certified proof of independence and to purchase a sizable money bond guaranteeing good behavior. The Indiana Government did likewise in 1831. A riot in Cincinnati, Ohio, in 1829 "caused 1,200 [independent African Americans] to leave the city for Canada." There was also a major riot in Philadelphia against independent African Americans. The Massachusetts Legislature endorsed the program of the American Deportation Society. Ohio excluded African American children from the public schools. Illinois forbade marriage between African Americans and European Americans. The Mississippi Government provided the same welfare support for the children of poor independent African Americans as for poor European Americans. African American bonding was abolished in Mexico in 1830, but was permitted to continue in the region known as Mexican Texas. The 1830 census counted 2,300,031 people of noticeable African descent. This represented a 31% increase over the 1820 count, and 18.0% of the total population, greater than the 17.5% increase recorded in 1820. Since the 1820 census, the population of **independent African Americans had grown** by 34% to **175,074 in the Southern States** and by 39% to **137,529 in the Northern States**. African Americans represented a barely significant 1.1% of the population of the northeastern States (Massachusetts and neighboring States) and of Michigan.

Statistics at about this time showed that many independent African Americans living in Louisiana "owned large sugar and cotton [farms worked by bonded African Americans], had prosperous businesses, practiced many professions and trades, [and] educated their children both in private schools and by private teachers," and some also sent their children to schools in the northern States and France. About 750 independent African Americans in New Orleans owned bonded African Americans, the largest number owned by one individual being 32. Typically, these Louisianans were of less than 50% African descent. European Americans forced about 200 independent African Americans to leave Portsmouth, Ohio. In 1830, the Louisiana Government demanded that all independent African Americans who had moved into the State since 1825 leave the State. **By 1831 the American Deportation Society had sent 1,420 voluntary deportees to Africa.**

Mob action against African Americans in Providence, Rhode Island, resulted in the death of 4 European Americans. The Indiana Government required African Americans moving into the State to purchase bonds guaranteeing good conduct. The Mississippi Government, in 1831, stipulated that all independent African Americans had to leave the State, but census records showed a population of 519 in 1830 and 1,366 in 1840. In 1832, 200 independent African Americans left New York State for Trinidad, a rare incidence of African Americans leaving The States without help from the American Deportation Society.

In 1831, in Southampton County, Virginia, Nat Turner led a major assault by his bonded African American gang against European American families. In those attacks, Turner's gang of about 30 bonded African Americans murdered 55 European Americans: 13 men, 14 women and 28 children. A huge force of 3,000 militiamen from Virginia and North Carolina rounded up the perpetrators, killing about 100 African Americans in the process. A Virginia court tried 51 captives and executed 17, including Turner. **The murder rampage by Turner's gang was a major factor in moving politicians in the southern States to place more strict restrictions on permitting African Americans to assemble or receive instruction in reading and writing.**

This concludes the overview of the first Andrew Jackson Administration. The narrative history resumes.

The Narrative History Resumes – March 1829

Among American History's Most Remarkable and Important Events, Sam Houston Resigns the Tennessee Governor's Office and Heads West

It seems that Billy Carroll would have to compete with Sam Houston to become the next Governor of Tennessee. As I had mentioned earlier, Carroll had been Governor for 3 terms –

the maximum allowed by the Tennessee Constitution – and had figured that Houston would step down after a year, opening the way for a Carroll return.

Houston had grown to like the job of Governor of Tennessee and saw in his widespread popularity an opportunity to win reelection to a second term. Sam and Eliza Houston had been married only a few weeks when the pressures of the Governor's job and the reelection campaign were often taking him away from home. This apparently troubled the marriage, **for in mid-April 1829 Eliza gathered her things and moved back to her parent's home in Gallatin.** The couple had been married only 3 months. It would become a permanent separation.

The marriage breakup would crush Sam. Sam would never publicly reveal his understanding of the reason for the breakup, but would strongly refute any inference that his wife had behaved dishonorably. Feeling emotionally unable to handle the Governor's job, **Sam promptly resigned the Governor's Office on April 16.** He penned a letter to William Hall, Speaker of the Tennessee State Senate: "Sir, it has become my duty to resign the office of [Governor] of the State, and to place in your hands the authority and responsibility, which on such an event, devolves on you by the provisions of the Constitution [of the State of Tennessee]." To the multitude of inquirers, he would reply that it was "painful" but a "private matter."

On April 22, Sam retreated to his room in the Nashville Inn and burned many letters. The next morning. he left with a procession of friends, walked down to the Cumberland River landing and stepped onto the packet, *Red Rover*. **Houston was headed west to spend time with old Cherokee friends.**

Sam Houston Settles among Old Cherokee Friends

Sam Houston arrived at Chief Oo-loo-te-ka's Cherokee village in June. There was a warm greeting: "My son 11 winters have passed since we met. . . I have heard you were a great chief among your people. . . I have heard that a dark cloud has fallen on the [European American] path you were walking. . . I am glad of it – it was done by the Great Spirit. . . We are in trouble and the Great Spirit has sent you to us to give us counsel. . . My wigwam is yours – **my home is yours – my people are yours – rest with us**." The wigwam was on "the crest of a knoll that separated the Arkansas River from the Illinois River in present-day eastern Oklahoma.

Houston would often reveal to friends in later years that, "when he laid himself down to sleep that night, he felt like a weary wanderer returned at last to his father's house." And he saw many friends from that island in the Tennessee River where he had spent several teenage years among Oo-loo-te-ka's Cherokee people. Oo-loo-te-ka's brother, Chief Tah-lhon-tusky, had led the first Cherokee migration to present-day Oklahoma in 1809 and Oo-loo-te-ka had followed with his clan in 1818. Since then, Tah-lhon-tusky had died and left Oo-loo-te-ka with sole leadership responsibility. There had been frequent fighting with the Osage and the Pawnee, and the Comanche threatened from their lands further west. Those were plains Native Americans who were less civilized that the Native Americans from the southeastern quarter of North America, who had mixed farming, hunting and gathering in a more settled lifestyle, and had learned much from association with European Americans. Furthermore, not far to the east,

Arkansas Territory was growing in population and within a few years it would seek statehood. The western Cherokee lands might well be next.

So, Oo-loo-te-ka viewed Houston's return as an opportunity to seek better times and organize a defense against European American advancement. Ordering the slaughter of many beeves, Oo-loo-te-ka celebrated with a huge feast, for he was personally a prosperous man. He had about a dozen servants, a large farm and over 500 head of cattle. He entertained guests generously and fed them well. Houston cast aside his western clothes and dressed like a prosperous Cherokee. He shaved his face, save a small mustache and goatee. He plaited his hair and put on a "white doeskin shirt, brilliantly worked with beads." He wore "leggings of elaborately ornamented yellow leather extended to his thighs." He put upon his head either a "circlet of feathers" or a "turban of figured silk." If the evening was cool, he threw a brightly colored blanket over his shoulders. He was again a son of Oo-loo-te-ka, and his friends again called him by his Cherokee name, **"The Raven."**

> "The tall and commanding figure of The Raven moved through a gallery of tall, commanding men, saluting the elders with deference, embracing the younger ones with whom he had hunted and played as a [teenager] on Oo-loo-te-ka's island. He flattered his former sweethearts on their good looks, their pretty shawls and the aptitude of their children. The Cherokees were a lively and warm-hearted [people], fond of colors and dearly loving of a fete such as this. Groups laughed and sang and strolled about the shady grove on the bluff, the vivid reds and yellows of their garments flinging animated patterns against the foliage. An army of dogs bedeviled the [bonded African Americans] who did the cooking. Tethered horses switched flies and ate grass."

On the other hand, President Andrew Jackson felt personal sorrow over Sam Houston's personal troubles, while at the same time he, along with other Washington City politicians, were fearful that the capable Sam Houston might confound Federal efforts to gain Texas from the independent nation of Mexico. Upon hearing the news of his friend's resignation, Andrew had written Sam, "Oh, what a reverse of fortune! Oh, how unstable are human affairs!"

Since the conclusion of Oo-loo-te-ka's celebration feast, Sam Houston had been investigating the region with an eye toward helping his friends in any way that he could. He had joined a band of Cherokees on a 100-mile horseback trip up the Arkansas River Valley and the Six Bull River Valley, into Osage country and conferred with Auguste Chouteau, a well-educated and prosperous French trader. His father had been one of the founders of St. Louis, and Auguste had been one of the founders of the Santa Fe Trail. He lived in a large log house beside a "beautiful clear river" in a "pleasant country" that resembled "park land." He owned bonded African Americans and had one wife in St. Louis and 2 wives in Osage country. Osage political leaders followed his advice without question. He was the most influential man "beyond the frontier, south of the Missouri River." Houston became friends with this powerful man and would enjoy visiting his home.

Cantonment Gibson, a federal military outpost near the mouth of the Six Bull River, was located about midway between Oo-loo-te-ka's clan and Auguste Chouteau's establishment. It would become a permanent outpost and be renamed Fort Gibson. **Matthew Arbuckle** was the commanding officer. Houston spent 2 weeks at Cantonment Gibson and established himself as a potential mediator on behalf of the Cherokee people. The American Fur Company was stationed about 6 miles away where the Verdigris, Six Bull and Arkansas rivers joined. A Federal agent to the Osage Nation was stationed there as well. This was a gathering place for Osage, and Creeks who had moved west out of Alabama. It was a tempestuous time. European Americans in Arkansas Territory were threatening to organize a militia and move against the Native American nations to their west. Creeks were appealing to Houston for help. A number of Cherokees were seeking a military alliance among Creeks, Osage, Choctaws, Shawnees and Delawares that was designed to attack the Pawnees and Comanche to their west. Realizing that Houston was very influential, Arbuckle relied heavily on him to maintain the peace. At a war dance held on July 7, Houston persuaded the war parties to delay their attack for 15 days. During those 15 days, Houston, Arbuckle and supportive Chiefs soothed the war talk and brought peace to the region. Then, Houston traveled eastward to Fort Smith in Arkansas Territory and there met with a western branch of the Choctaw Nation and "won the lifelong friendship of the Choctaws." **Within the span of 8 weeks, "The Raven had thrust himself into a position of leadership over 7,000 [Native Americans] who controlled the country from Missouri to Texas and westward to the Great Plains."**

We catch up on the American Deportation Society

While Sam Houston was applying his immense practical knowledge to help Native Americans on the western frontier, 23-year-old **Lloyd Garrison**, without any practical knowledge of his subject, was railing in Boston against African American bonding. He was the featured speaker at the July 4 gathering of the American Deportation Society at Boston's Park Street Church. I have previously related that Garrison was a newspaperman, with experience in Massachusetts and Vermont, who had become a fervent Abolitionist about 15 months previously, after he had begun to work with one of the nation's leading Deportationists, Benjamin Lundy. Being fervent about Abolition and lukewarm about Deportation, Garrison was rather out of step with his audience. But Garrison had been looking forward to his first opportunity to deliver a significant public address and had prepared a 2-hour speech. But first, I should describe the American Colonization Society, which I have renamed the American Deportation Society to more accurately depict its agenda.

The American Deportation Society "symbolized the confusion of American thinking on [African American bonding] before 1830." Members believed that the typical American of pure or mostly African descent was born with less capacity for intelligence than the typical American of European descent, that this deficiency was of major proportions and, if all bonded African Americans were made independent, then it would be "impossible for both races to live together. The only solution lay in educating the [African American], preparing him for self-government, and then returning him to his native Africa." Furthermore, the Society believed it essential that African Americans understand and accept the Christian faith prior to departing for Africa. And, it looked forward to these deportees disseminating "the blessings of knowledge and freedom on a continent that [at the time] contained 150,000,000 people who were degraded by "idolatry, superstition and ignorance." Toward that end, the society encouraged public social programs that taught the necessary coping skills to independent African Americans; and, concerning bonded African Americans, the society encouraged owners to treat them with humanity and likewise teach the coping skills that would eventually be needed upon deportation to Africa. The American Deportation Society had been established on January 1, 1817, as a national organization. Nine States were represented in the leadership. **Bushrod Washington** was its first president, and **Henry Clay** was one of the vice presidents.

The society had received some funding from the Federal Congress and, in 1822, had purchased land in western Africa and there had founded a colony they had named "Liberia." The tally at the end of the following year, 1823, would show it had **deported 1,420 African Americans** to the fledgling African nation. At this point, Society spending would amount to $75 per deportee, far less than the cost of purchasing the typical bonded African American.   Most had come from the southern States, with 580 coming from Virginia and 400 coming from North Carolina. **But deportation was not very popular with African Americans. Between one in 4 and one in 6 deportees were dying during the voyage or within a year after arriving in Africa** – a death rate that was almost as bad as the poor survival experience of the first settlers in Virginia and Massachusetts Bay. It had quickly become obvious that living in Africa was hazardous even to immigrants who were of African descent. Knowledge of how to cope in The States was poor preparation for successfully coping in Africa. And the vast majority of independent African Americans refused to accept free deportation passage. Bonded African Americans were generally opposed to deportation as well, and very few agreed to accept the occasional owner's offer to make him or her independent if he or she would afterward accept deportation to Africa. This was the situation when Lloyd Garrison stepped forward to deliver his address to the Society.

Lloyd Garrison Prefers to Agitate for Abolition

Lloyd Garrison spoke little of Deportation and much of Abolition. He warned, "I will despair of the [Federation of States] while [African American bonding] exists therein. . . our destruction is not only possible but almost certain." But he alleged "the fault [would not be] ours if a separation [of the States] eventually takes place." He further alleged that the preamble of the Declaration of Independence had been intended to assure African Americans of the same political rights as bestowed upon European Americans, but that had obviously never been the practice. "In view of it, I am ashamed of my country, I am sick of our unmeaning declaration in praise of liberty and equality, of our hypocritical cant about the unalienable rights of man." He alleged that Christianity, as described in the Holy Bible, was opposed to bonding one person to another and carefully selected passages to seemingly support that position, while omitting reference to the many passages that acknowledged the practice and merely encouraged the owner to treat the bonded person with kindness.

Garrison's goal was to make all bonded African Americans independent and to allow them and future generations to remain in The States. The fundamental Baptist theology he had learned during childhood from his mother was evident in his rhetoric. "He closed his two-hour performance with an appeal to the churches. 'Let them pour out their supplications to Heaven in behalf of the [bonded African American]. Prayer is omnipotent: its breath can melt the adamantine rocks; its touch can break the stoutest chains'." Garrison's speech was "dutifully reported" in Boston's *National Philanthropist*, but it made little impression on the ministers or the politically active men in the city. Garrison would soon leave Boston to work alongside Benjamin Lundy in Baltimore, Maryland.

Benjamin Lundy had moved himself and his newspaper from Ohio to the major seaport city of Baltimore to be in the mist of the Deportation action. As junior editor, Lloyd Garrison would write for, and help edit, Lundy's newspaper, the *Genius of Universal Emancipation*. Soon after arriving in Baltimore and moving into a boarding house operated by 2 Quaker ladies, the Lundy and Garrison would agree to courteously disagree. Lundy remained committed to deporting African Americans to Africa and Haiti. Garrison opposed this agenda, preferring instead to advocate making bonded African Americans immediately independent and permitting them to remain in The States. But, despite this fundamental difference in opinion, Lundy agreed to follow through with his offer to involve Garrison in his newspaper. He told Garrison, "Thee may put thy initials on thy articles, and I will put my initials to mine, and each will bear his own burden." To this generous and understanding offer Garrison replied, "Very well, that will answer, and I will be able to free my soul."

Sam Houston Almost Dies of Malaria

Meanwhile, out on the frontier, Sam Houston's helpfulness to the Cherokees and other Native Americans would soon be interrupted by sickness. **Sam was stricken by malaria in August.** He lay on a mat of corn shucks in a log hut in Oo-loo-te-ka's village. "His limbs trembled, his skin was yellow and hot to touch. He was burning with a malarial fever, which had reached a stage that was usually fatal." But under the care of Cherokee nurses and medicine men he would survive. On September 19, he would answer a letter received from Andrew Jackson. "I am very feeble from a long spell of fever . . . but I thank my God that I am again cheered by the hope of renewed health."

The Abolitionism Movement Grows

During September, Benjamin Lundy and Lloyd Garrison began publishing Lundy's Abolitionist newspaper. *Genius of Universal Emancipation,* in Baltimore. "Lundy launched a series of articles on Haiti describing in radiant terms the condition of the [deportees who had already arrived there]." And, Garrison launched a series of articles denouncing the aims of the American Deportation Society. Garrison attacked the society head-on. Instead of Deportation, Garrison advocated: 1) immediately make bonded African Americans independent, 2) because making them independent is right, there can be no quibbling about delaying the event, 3) once independent, and with supportive training, African Americans will learn to prosper and live peaceful lives, and 4) no societal organization has the right to coerce African Americans to accept Deportation.

Garrison Biographer John Thomas would condense this prevalent Abolitionist dogma to a few lucid sentences:

"First and most important, never explain, only denounce. Second, "inculcate a sense of guilt, collective and individual, by emphasizing the barbarity of African American bonding." Third, "stress the disparity between American [ideals] and American practice." Fourth, "spare neither the [northern States] or the [southern States] in your censures." Fifth, "chide the people for their failure to [vote against continuing African American bonding]." And sixth, "reprobate the lack of Christian zeal in the American churches and denounce the ministers responsible for this moral laxity."

Officially, Sam Houston Becomes a Cherokee Citizen

During October, the Federal Government dispensed a large Cherokee annuity payment to the western Cherokees. It was paid in paper money, instead of gold and silver coin, so traders, who had come to sell merchandise to the Cherokees, found that most Cherokees would give up their paper money for merchandise that was worth very little. Perhaps the most successful seller was Sam Houston who had recovered sufficiently from malaria to accumulate $66,000. I do not know what Houston sold for that much paper money, but it appears that the Cherokee leadership viewed his actions favorably.

When Federal agents attempted to gain control over the merchants operating in the region, the Cherokee leadership came to the rescue by making Houston a citizen of the Cherokee Nation. This was the reason that, **on October 21, Sam Houston became the first European American to be granted citizenship in the Cherokee Nation**, per the following proclamation:

> "Whereas, an order has been published by the [Federal Agent for] the Cherokee Nation requesting all [European Americans] who reside in the Nation . . . to comply with certain rules. . . Now, be it known . . . that Samuel Houston, late of the State of Tennessee, has been residing in the [Cherokee] Nation for some time past and . . . In consideration of his former acquaintance with; and services rendered the [Native Americans], and . . . our confidence in his integrity, and talents . . . We do . . . irrevocably grant him forever, all the rights, privileges and immunities, of a citizen of the Cherokee Nation . . . as though he was a native-born Cherokee."

1830

Sam Houston Takes Cherokee Tiana Rogers to be His Wife

During the summer, Sam Houston took a Cherokee wife, a widow named Tiana Rogers. He had not yet been granted a divorce from Eliza back in Tennessee, but understandably felt that she had no right to abandon him and, as punishment, forever prevent him from enjoying marriage. He was a Cherokee citizen and felt comfortable taking Tiana as a wife within the loose legal rules of Cherokee marriage. **He had known Tiana as a teenager at Oo-loo-te-ka's island village in the Tennessee River.** She was the half-sister to his best friends of that era, John and James Rogers. She had been previously married to David Gentry, whose fate is unknown. Tiana was of prominent Cherokee linage. Her half-brother, Captain John would succeed Oo-loo-te-ka as First Chief of the Nation. And Captain John's grandson would become the last First Chief of the Nation. Tiana's nephew, 3 generations removed, would be the world-famous entertainer, Will Rogers. Sam Houston had constructed his own wigwam "near the Neosho River, a little above Cantonment Gibson, and 30 miles from [Oo-loo-te-ka's wigwam]." He would build a "large log house and set out an apple orchard. There he would live in style, transacting his affairs and entertaining his friends."

1831

A Wealthy New York City Merchant Finances Lloyd Garrison's publishing of the *Liberator* Newspaper in Boston

On January 1, 1831, William Lloyd Garrison began publishing his own anti-slavery newspaper, *The Liberator*, in Boston, Massachusetts. Arthur Tappan, a wealthy New York City merchant, was contributing money to Garrison, making possible his new anti-slavery newspaper. Without Tappan's financial support, Garrison might not have ever made a success of his anti-slavery propaganda publication passion.

A native of Northampton, Massachusetts, 45-year-old **Arthur Tappan** was a wealthy New York City merchant who, in conjunction with his brother, Lewis, had operated their silk importing business since 1826. He was dutifully religious and a thrifty businessman. By 1830, he was contributing much of the profits from his business income to a wide variety of social and religious causes. And, by late 1930, he had added the militant Abolition movement to his list of benefactors, giving priority to Garrison's new newspaper, *The Liberator*.

William Lloyd Garrison had also won over several important people in Boston, particularly at a speech he delivered 6 weeks prior to the launch of *The Liberator*. **Lyman Beecher** thought Garrison too militant and uncompromising, but others in attendance, including Arthur Tappan's brother and business partner Lewis Tappan, were favorably impressed. Biographer John Thomas would consider the speech "a masterpiece of destructive argument." **And Garrison announced his militant intent on January 1, 1831 in the first issue of *The Liberator*:**

"I will be as harsh as truth, and as uncompromising as justice. On this subject, I do not wish to think, or speak, or write, with moderation. No! No! Tell a man whose house is on fire to give a moderate alarm; tell him to moderately rescue his wife from the hands of the ravisher; tell the mother to gradually extricate her babe from the fire into which it has fallen; but urge me not to use moderation in a cause like the present. I am in earnest – I will not equivocate – I will not excuse – I will not retreat a single inch – and I will be heard."

Although he would have been among bonded African Americans and their owners – the relationship of his interest – if he had remained in Baltimore, Maryland, he had chosen to relocate to Boston. Apparently, he had recognized that he would be constantly fighting opposition if he were to publish his newspaper in Maryland. He had considered Washington City and Philadelphia as the home for his endeavor, but had settled on Boston.

Garrison chose to publish in Boston because so many politically influential and potentially enthusiastic Abolitionists lived there. *The Liberator* **would be published for 35 years and would be the most important militant Abolitionist newspaper in the United States. It would not be a local newspaper, for it would be mailed throughout the northern States.**

Meanwhile, Benjamin Lundy had given up on his Deportationist newspaper, the *Genius of Universal Emancipation*, partly because Arthur Tappan had stopped giving him money.

In Southside Virginia, Nat Turner begins Plotting to Mass-Murder White People

As **Nat Turner, a bonded African American and self-styled preacher,** watched an eclipse of the sun from Southampton County, Virginia, he concluded that it represented a sign from God that the time had come to launch a terrorist crusade against the region's European American population. The eclipse occurred on February 12, 1831, but Nat needed more time to gather his terrorist gang. He had been secretly striving toward a terrorist crusade since 1828. Nat was unusually intelligent and adept at reading and writing. Since childhood, Nat had harbored the belief that he had been born to accomplish some immense task for God and for the bonded African American population. His religion was a mix of African influences learned from his mother and others and the Christianity he had learned from the European American population. He claimed to spend much time in prayer searching for instructions from God. His third owner, Thomas Moore, had died in 1828 and the widow, Sally had married Joseph Travis, a carriage maker, in October 1829. Travis had hired a supervisor, F. Johnson, to manage the farm on which Nat lived and worked, and Travis and Johnson had allowed Nat to come and go when his tasks were done. Nat "could travel about Southampton County and into neighboring counties on weekends and to more distant places during the holiday seasons. It was reported he traveled as [far] as Richmond." With this freedom of movement, Nat had preached to bonded African Americans all over the county, gained recognition of what he claimed to be his special conduit to God, won acceptance of his leadership, and prepared followers to respond positively when the time came to reveal his terrorist agenda. He was gathering a small team of 4 bonded men who he knew he could influence, but even they were ignorant of his intent.

Nat Turner Launches a Long Night of Mass Murders

From the farm where he lived and worked in Southampton County, Virginia, Nat Turner figured that the unusual sun, a solar eclipse that he observed on February 12, 1831, was a sign from God that he should commence with his terrorist attacks. During the six months following the solar eclipse Nat had been working on his terrorism plan, had gathered a small group of subordinates, and was looking for such a sign from the Heavens by which he might justify his launch. **Then, on August 13, the sun looked strange, like the sign from God that Nat was looking for**. Of the sun that day, a newspaperman wrote:

> The sun rose with "a pale greenish tint, which soon gave place to curlean blue, and this also a silvery white . . . In the afternoon it appeared as an immense circular plane of polished silver, and to the naked eye there was exhibited upon its surface an appearance that was termed a 'black spot.' The sun shone with a dull, gloomy light, and the atmosphere was moist and hazy."

The next day, Sunday, Nat Turner preached before a large gathering of bonded African Americans at Barnes' Methodist Church and indirectly appealed to militancy. "Nat gained many sympathizers [that] day, and they signified their willingness to cooperate with him by wearing around their necks red bandanna handkerchiefs." Convinced it was time to act, Nat told the 4 men on his leadership team to meet him 7 days later, on Sunday afternoon, August 21.

Nat Turner met with 4 trusted bonded African Americans at a camp in the woods about 3 pm that Sunday afternoon. The men were Hark; who was, like Nat, owned by Joseph Travis; Nelson, who was owned by Jacob Williams; Sam, owned by Nathaniel Francis, and Henry, owned by Richard Porter. They feasted on pork and brandy until 2 hours past dusk. Nat disclosed his plan for terrorist murders of nearby European American families and alleged that, as they progressed, volunteers and armaments would join them in sufficient numbers to make possible many military victories. **Nat insisted that no White family member should be spared death until his gang had grown into a formidable army**.

Their killing would include all women and children, even the babies. They would kill as many families as possible that very night while the victims slept in their beds. Two additional bonded African American men had joined them at the camp, so the force numbered 7 men.

The 7 terrorists set out toward their first family killing about 10 pm that Sunday night. The first killing would be the Joseph Travis family, which owned Nat and Hark. Nat's gang next went to the home of Mrs. P. Reese, murdered her in her bed, and then murdered her son

William and the farm supervisor, James Barmer. It was sunrise when the gang reached the home of a widow, Elizabeth Turner. They shot the supervisor, Hartwell Peebles, while visiting the brandy still and killed Mrs. Turner and Mrs. Newsome in the farmhouse. <u>By this time, Nat had gained more recruits, 9 of them on horses.</u> The walking members of the gang went to the home of Henry Bryant and killed him, his wife, their child and his wife's mother, while the mounted members went to the home of Catherine Whitehead, a widow, where they killed Mrs. Whitehead, her son Richard, her daughter Margaret, plus "3 daughters and a child receiving its morning bath at the hands of a loving grandmother."

<u>By this time the news of the terrorist attacks was advancing ahead of Nat's gang, and many potential victims were fleeing.</u> <u>Many bonded African Americans were helping their owner's families to safe hiding places.</u> The gang killed Trajan Doyle, but his bonded African American, Hugh, managed to reach Doyle's family and help them safely hide. At the Nathaniel Francis farm, Nat's gang killed the supervisor, Henry Doyle, two boys and Mrs. John Williams and her child. Jeff, the bonded African American foreman at Peter Edwards' farm, had hidden the Edwards family in the woods before Nat's gang arrived, so all Nat gained was the recruitment of 5 bonded African American terrorist volunteers (Jeff would apprehend these 5 volunteers upon their later return, and they would be "shot by the enraged neighbors.")

When Nat's gang reached the Barrow farmhouse, John Barrow put up a stiff fight with several firearms but was overcome and killed. Lucy, a bonded African American servant girl attempted to detain Mrs. Barrow so she could be killed as well, but Easter, an older bonded African American woman, intervened and managed to get Mrs. Barrow away to safety (Lucy would later stand trial and be executed). The gang killed George Vaughan as he approached the Barrow house. <u>When the gang reached the Newit Harris farmhouse they found no European Americans there, for all were away or safely hidden by bonded African American servants.</u> But Nat's gang continued their practice of drinking brandy and smashing furniture. "There was brandy in abundance, and barrels of the beverage were rolled into the yard and an end knocked out of each." It was 9 or 10 am.

Nat told his terrorist gang to next murder the Levi Waller family and the children at their boarding school. <u>They set out toward the Waller place, with Nat in the rear of the gang as usual. The mounted terrorists were in the lead and Nat followed on foot.</u> **With one exception, "Nat never arrived at the scene of slaughter until the murders had been committed."** <u>Then, upon his arrival, he "viewed the mangled bodies as they lay, in silent satisfaction, and immediately started in quest of other victims."</u> At the Waller's home and boarding school Nat's gang killed Mrs. Waller and 10 children.

Next, the gang arrived at the William Williams home where they killed both parents and two boys. The gang next went to the Jacob Williams farm where they killed Mrs. Williams, her 3 children, Edwin Drewry, and the wife of the farm's supervisor and her 2 children. The gang's next stop was the home of the widow Rebecca Vaughan. They killed Mrs. Vaughan, a niece, one son and the supervisor of the farm. **By this time Nat's terrorist gang numbered "50 or 60, all mounted and armed with guns, axes, swords and clubs."**

<u>Nat Turner's gang next went to the James Parker farmhouse.</u> All the European Americans had previously fled, so the gang entertained themselves with brandy sweetened with loafsugar.

"Groggy and unconcerned with the progress of the [terrorism campaign], many [gang] members lay down under the shade of the trees to slumber."

Nat managed to rally his gang and send them on the road again, but they immediately encountered the first armed band of European American fighting men. This was a force of about 20 Southampton County militiamen armed with shotguns, who had been seeking out Nat's gang for several hours. **The militiamen killed several of Nat's gang and scattered the rest without suffering any deaths themselves.** Most of the gang fled toward their homes hoping to blend into the farm population and escape identification. Nat fled with a remnant of his gang of terrorists.

Nat's remnant, which numbered about 20 camped together and moved out before daylight on Tuesday to attack the large farm of Simon Blunt, who owned about 64 bonded African Americans. Blunt was expecting the attack and had gathered his bonded African Americans together Monday evening, had warned of the futility of Nat's terrorism and had told each to decide to join the terrorists or defend the farm. All of them had agreed to defend the farm. Six European Americans armed with 6 guns and plenty of powder, and 64 bonded African Americans armed with "grubbing hoes, pitch forks, axes and clubs" waited through the night in the farmhouse and adjacent outbuildings. Shortly before dawn, Nat's gang advanced on the main house toward the front door. Some of Nat's gang were killed in the first volley and Nat's most important assistant, Hark, was seriously wounded. As Nat's gang began its retreat, it was rushed by Blunts' bonded African Americans, who captured several wounded terrorists, including Hark. Nat fled with a remnant.

A bit later, the gang was attacked by cavalrymen freshly arrived from Greenville County. Their attack killed several terrorists including Will Francis, the axe-wielding murderer of more victims than any other gang member. Nat and two survivors of the attack hid in the woods, while the other survivors fled, most with plans to return to their respective farms and deny involvement.

After nightfall, Nat went his own way so he could hide out alone. Nat's terrorist gang had killed 13 men, 14 women and 28 children.

As soon as news of the terrorist attacks reached neighboring counties, militiamen gathered to stand guard in their counties and to help Southampton County subdue the terrorists. About 3,000 armed militiamen were either in the vicinity of the Southampton County murders or on their way, but none had arrived before the gang's dispersal at James Parker's farm on Monday afternoon. The first militia companies from neighboring counties – Greenville and Sussex, Virginia, and Hertford, North Carolina – arrived by Tuesday. This overwhelming military force quickly suppressed any remaining yearning to commit terrorist murders. But these 3,000 men were not a police force trained to patiently sort the guilty from among the innocent and bring the suspects to jail. They were quick to execute any man or woman on the spot if he or she acted suspicious or someone accused him or her of participating. It must have been a fine opportunity for a bonded African American to get rid of a person he or she did not like. Of these 3,000 militiamen, only one would lose his life in the action. Militiamen killed perhaps 100 bonded African Americans in the field on suspicion of involvement, but an accurate account is not available to history, for records were not kept.

Nat would hide out alone and doggedly avoid capture for several weeks. But 3 leaders in his terrorist gang, Hark, Sam and Dred, were promptly brought in to stand trial. The Southampton County Court convened on Wednesday, August 31 to begin trials for the people who had been captured and brought to jail. The Court tried 51 African American captives: 5 independent men, 1 bonded woman, 4 bonded boys and 41 bonded men. Sixteen were convicted and sentenced to death, and 7 were convicted of lesser involvement and sold to a distant owner far from Virginia.

Nat Turner Captured, Tried and Convicted

Meanwhile, Nat Turner remained in hiding. He was hiding under some brush in a hole he had dug along a fencerow in a field. He could trust no one to help him. His only weapon was a sword. On October 30, he was captured by Benjamin Phipps and brought to jail. He was tried in county court by the county's 6 justices. He made no effort to win acquittal. **Nat Turner was executed** accordingly and his body was given to medical research so there would be no grave to enhance martyrdom and inspire future terrorists.

Southern Whites Feel Compelled to Restrict Future Movements and Gatherings and Reading Opportunities among Blacks

Concerned citizens and politicians in Virginia and other southern States recognized that Nat Turner and four of the terrorists had been preachers, often addressing gatherings of African Americans at African American churches. This suggested it would be prudent to limit such gatherings of African Americans and, instead, bring African Americans to the churches attended by European Americans. Others expressed concerns about continuing to teach the brighter bonded African Americans to read and write, especially considering the growing access to inciting literature and newspapers being disseminated by Abolition groups in the northern States. Most dangerous to peace and harmony would be William Lloyd Garrisons' newspaper, *The Liberator*, which would be expanding to a wide circulation as the years passed. Many pointed out that it would be prudent to restrict gatherings of bonded African Americans beyond the farms on which they lived and worked, whether such gatherings were social, religious or sporting games like baseball. Concerns were also expressed about the likelihood that independent African Americans might instigate future terrorist attacks, since one-tenth of the group captured and tried on charges of terrorism were men who were independent. For the most part, independent African Americans were intelligent and had ready access to travel. So, many advocated laws to make it more difficult for an owner to make independent one or more of his bonded African Americans.

Therefore, in Virginia, teaching a bonded African American to read and write became illegal and an African American Church had to be overseen by a White preacher. Sadly, throughout the southern States, the quality of life available to African Americans would degrade significantly as a result of Nat Turner's terrorist attacks in Southampton County, Virginia. For example, within a few months, the North Carolina Legislature would enact laws "prohibiting any [African American, bonded or independent,] from preaching upon the pain of 39 lashes, and the death penalty was allowed for [African Americans] disseminating [Abolitionist] propaganda. Teaching of reading and writing to [bonded African Americans] also was forbidden."

Sam Houston Returns Briefly to East Tennessee

Sam Houston, upon receiving news in August 1831 that his mother was dying, left his Cherokee wife, Tiana, at their log house beside the Neosho River and headed east to Tennessee. During September, he was in East Tennessee at his mother's bedside in her Baker's Creek Valley home. He was there when she passed on.

Sam Houston then returned briefly to his Cherokee home and sat with the Cherokee National Council. Houston departed in December for Washington City.

1832

Sam Houston Finds New Purpose for his Life

Sam Houston, while in Washington became enraged by William Stanbery's March 31 verbal attack upon the floor of the Federal House. Stanbery, a Representative from Ohio, accused Houston of complicity in Federal bribery: "Was not the late Secretary of War removed because of his attempt fraudulently to give [Sam] Houston the contract for [Native American] rations?" Now it seems that Stanbery and Houston had never met. Upon learning about Stanbery's attack, Houston went to the House foyer in a rage, but Representative James Polk of Tennessee "hustled him out into the fresh air." Houston then dispatched Representative Cave Johnson, of Tennessee, to Stanbery with a challenge to duel. Stanbery declined to reply to the challenge.

On the evening of April 13, a friend pointed out Stanbery, whereupon Houston walked over to him. "Are you Mr. Stanbery?" Houston inquired. "Yes, sir," came the reply. "Then you are a damned rascal," Houston shouted as he beat the surprised man upon the head with a hickory cane:

> "Stanbery was almost as large a man as Houston. He threw up his hands. "Oh don't!" he cried, but Houston continued to rain blows and Stanbery turned . . . to run. Houston leaped on his opponent's back and dragged him down. The 2 rolled on the pavement, Stanbery yelling for help. Houston could not hold and punch at the same time, his right arm having been useless in such emergencies since the battle of [Horseshoe Bend]. Stanbery managed to draw one of his pistols. He pressed it against Houston's chest [and fired] . . . But the charge did not explode, and Houston tore the weapon from Stanbery's grasp. Houston stood up, landed a few more licks with the cane and, as a finishing touch, lifted [Stanbery's] feet in the air and [struck him in the genitals]."

William Stanbery, with help from Speaker Andrew Stevenson, **won a 145-to-25 vote to have Sam Houston arrested** and brought before the Federal House on an assault charge. Stanbery and Stevenson won the vote despite James Polk's assertion that the House would be exceeding its authority by taking powers from the Judicial Branch of the Federal Government.

The escalation of a street brawl into a major legislative debate infuriated President Andrew Jackson, who sent for Houston. Houston went over to the President's house. He would later report that he "had never seen [Andrew] Jackson in such a temper." Looking at Houston's buckskin coat, Jackson asked if he had more appropriate clothes. When Houston replied that he did not, Jackson tossed him some money and told him to "dress like a gentleman and buck up his defense." Houston listened. He "went to a tailor and obtained 'a coat of the finest material, reaching to my knees, trousers in harmony of color and the latest style in cut, with a white satin vest to match'."

The House trial of Sam Houston lasted several days. It was well attended and was the talk of the town. On May 7, Houston took the floor to conclude the arguments for the defense. "Every seat on the floor was filled and chairs had been placed in the aisles to accommodate the privileged overflow. A solid bank of men pressed against the colonnaded semicircle of wall. For 2 hours, there had been no room in the galleries, where the diplomatic corps, gay with ribbons, the Army, the Navy and [the socially prominent] were authentically represented."

"Mr. Speaker, arraigned for the first time of my life on a charge of violating the laws of my country, I feel all that embarrassment which my peculiar situation is calculated to inspire. I disclaim, utterly, every motive unworthy of an honorable man. . . [I am] willing to be held to my responsibility. All I demand is that my actions may be pursued to the motives which gave them birth."

Junius Booth, **of Baltimore**, the great Shakespearean actor, and a friend of Houston's, listened with trained ears at the skill with which Houston made his delivery. **Francis Scott Key**, **of Maryland**, who had written America's *National Anthem*, sat on the front row, enraptured. Houston inserted poetry:

> "'I seek no sympathies, nor need;
> The thorns, which I have reaped, are of the tree
> I planted; they have torn me, and I bleed'."

Amid applause, a bouquet of flowers fell at his feet and a woman's voice came down from the balcony:

"I had rather be Sam Houston in a dungeon than Stanbery on a throne!"

Houston picked up the flowers and bowed over them with the perfect sense of timing we associate with skillful stage actors. He continued: more skillful and grand argument, more poetry, then, as he looked at the American Flag, he entered upon his close.

"So long as that proud emblem . . . shall wave in the Hall of American legislators, so long shall it cast its sacred protection over the personal rights of every American citizen. Sir, when you shall have destroyed the pride of American character, you will have destroyed the brightest jewel that Heaven ever made. You will have drained the purest and holiest drop which visits the hearts of your sages in council and heroes in the field and . . . these massy columns, with yonder lofty dome will sink into one crumbling ruin. . .

"But, Sir, so long as that flag shall bear aloft its glittering stars . . . so long I trust, shall the rights of American citizens be preserved safe and unimpaired – till discord shall wreck the spheres – the grand march of time shall cease – and not one fragment of all creation be left to chafe the bosom of eternity's waves."

Sam Houston had spoken – the frontiersman who loved books of classic literature – who loved the simple life among the Cherokee people as much as life in a frontier town – a past Federal Representative and State Governor – a man as fearless on the battlefield as in the courtroom – every inch an exceptional leader of men. That man had spoken! **Junius Booth** "plowed through the crowd and embraced his old friend. **'Houston, take my laurels'!"**

For 4 days the House debated "discharge" versus "reprimand." In spite of James Polk's arguments for "discharge," the final vote went against Houston 106 to 89. But that only meant that Speaker Andrew Stevenson was ordered to repeat the charge before Houston and conclude with, "I do reprimand you accordingly." The Speaker's reprimand meant nothing!

The inconsequential nature of the reprimand further maddened William Stanbery. He obtained a criminal assault charge in the local court and won a jury judgment for a $500 fine. But that did not really matter.

This episode is important to our study only because of how it affected Houston. It seems the excitement and hubbub cleansed Houston of the melancholy that had attended his moods since Eliza had left him to live again with her parents. At that time, he had sought solitude among his Cherokee friends, and, despite being thrust into Cherokee politics, that solitude had been healing. Later, his mother's death had perhaps renewed a compulsion to make more of his life. Finally, the admiration he had won upon the House floor during his defense had renewed his confidence and strengthened a conviction that his life was intended for greater purposes.

Sam Houston would soon turn his eyes toward Mexican Texas and there he would seek a new leadership role. As if he was symbolizing his return to the world of European Americans, Houston gave Andrew Jackson an elaborate Cherokee ceremonial costume, and he gave Eliza's engagement ring to Jackson's daughter-in-law. A House Committee would eventually absolve Houston of "all imputation of fraud." Later in life, Houston would explain what had happened:

> "I was dying out and had they taken me before a Justice of the Peace and fined me $10, it would have killed me; but they gave me a national tribunal for a theater, and that set me up again."

Before concluding this account, I need to say more about Houston's friend, Junius Booth. Thirty-three years into the future, this famous actor's son, **John Wilkes Booth** – also an accomplished Shakespearean actor – would add the name Abraham Lincoln to the horribly long list of Americans who would be killed in the Northern States Republican Party's military invasion of the Seceded States, a four-year war that resulted in one million unnecessary American deaths. John Wilkes Booth would add President Lincoln to the war death total.

Sam Houston prepares to Emigrate to Mexican Texas – Crosses the Red River

Sam Houston was quietly making arrangements to go to Mexican Texas to discover in what way he could assume a leadership role in the emerging Texas Independence Movement. He had traveled to New York City to solicit funds. The New Yorkers had been "sympathetic, but not so quick to part with their money. Eastern financiers had recently made heavy investments in [Mexican] Texas lands and a revolution was something that required reflection."

But President Andrew Jackson was downright encouraging, loaning Houston $500 to help his cause. And, to speed him on his journey, Jackson "concocted a confidential [Federal] mission to [Mexican] Texas under a United States passport." So, at some time during the summer, Houston quietly departed Washington City. He traveled through Tennessee, quietly discussing plans for Texas among men he could trust.

From Nashville, Houston went up to Cincinnati to meet with friends who had expressed interest in Texas, but would discover extreme hostility among the intellectuals of that city. Attending a play as a featured member of the audience on July 20, he was mocked and howled down so severely that the actors would be forced to cancel their play, but "Houston and his friends [would succeed] in leaving the theater without injury." Houston felt the hatred of Cincinnati intellectuals. Leaving Cincinnati, Houston picked up his passport at Cantonment Gibson and then spent 3 months making discrete arrangements to move on into Mexican Texas.

On December 1, Sam Houston crossed the Red River, which marks the southern boundary of present-day Oklahoma, and entered Mexican Texas.

He had left his Cherokee wife Tiana behind at their log cabin on the Neosho River, with its fields and 2 bonded African Americans. He was not destined to return to her. Sam had suffered the loss of his first wife Eliza when she suddenly left him to return to her parent's home. Now it was Tiana's turn to witness Sam leaving her. There was no reason for Eliza to leave Sam. There was no way that Tiana, of exceptional Cherokee heritage, could leave her people and move to Mexican Texas with Sam.

Catching Up on Mexican History and how it affects her Territory of Mexican Texas

Here is a brief history affecting Mexican Texas, beginning in 1821. The region called Mexican Texas was a major part of the Mexican State of Coahuila. The State Capitol was Saltillo, which was a little over 100 miles southwest of the Rio Grande River town of Laredo, and today remains in Mexico. According to a previous diplomatic agreement made during the purchase of Florida from Spain, which had been consummated in 1821, the United States Government, under President John Adams of Massachusetts, had pledged to recognize Spanish Mexico as starting at the Sabine River. The Sabine River, as it runs southward from Logansport to the Gulf at Port Arthur, constitutes the eastern boundary between present-day Texas and Louisiana.

Of course, Mexico had been New Spain for centuries. Then, successive revolutions and insurrections had transformed her into an independent nation, sometimes under a dictatorship and sometimes under a republican form of government. Miguel Hidalgo had led an unsuccessful revolt against Spanish authority in 1810. It was a large campaign involving at least 60,000 troops, but this effort had met a final defeat at Guadalajara in 1811. Jose Morelos had led a renewed rebellion in 1813. After Morelos had been captured and executed in 1815, Vicente Guerrero had picked up the pieces and continued the revolt. He had joined forces with another revolutionary leader, Iturbide, and together they had led revolutionaries to a successful victory. Iturbide had established himself as Emperor of Mexico, holding on to absolute power. Iturbide had been Emperor when Andrew Jackson had refused James Monroe's appointment as Minister Plenipotentiary to Mexico.

Just prior to and during Iturbide's reign, Moses Austin had received permission from the Mexican Government to bring settlers from the United States and establish English-speaking settlements in Texas. The Mexican Government hoped that immigrants from The States, once settled on the Mexican Texas frontier, would be politically loyal to Mexico and constitute a buffer between central Mexico and the United States. At that time, within the boundaries of present-day Texas, there was very little Spanish population. There were only 3 significant Spanish settlements: San Antonio, Goliad and Nacogdoches. **Moses Austin** began with 300 settlers. When he died shortly thereafter, in 1821, his son, **Stephen Austin**, continued the work of establishing new English-speaking settlements. Stephen would be overseeing considerable growth beyond his father's initial group of immigrants. The early Austin settlements were San Felipe and Washington, on the Brazos River, and Columbus on the Lower Colorado River.

Iturbide was deposed in a military *coup d'etat* in 1823. At that point, a republican form of government was proclaimed, with Guadalupe Victoria as President. A Constitution was established in 1824. This Constitution empowered the Catholic Church to be the sole State Church. Many of Stephen Austin's settlers went through the motions of joining the Catholic Church to avoid political persecution. Mexican politicians sorted themselves into the Conservative Party and the Liberal Party. Conservative politicians favored a powerful Central Government and Catholic domination over educational facilities. Liberal politicians favored State rights and a less powerful Central Government, limits on the power of the Catholic Church and its influence over education, and expanded social liberties.

The **Liberal Party under Vicente Guerrero gained control** of the Central Government in 1829. His government decreed that bonded African Americans (and, where they existed, bonded Native Americans) be immediately made independent. This had presented difficulties to Stephen Austin's settlers, some of whom owned bonded African Americans. It had also presented similar difficulties to new settlers from the southern States who had come into Texas without Austin's guidance.

That was the situation when Anthony Butler, a courier for President Andrew Jackson, arrived in Mexico City with instructions to the United States Minister to Mexico, Joel Poinsett. The instructions directed Poinsett to press the Mexican Government to sell Texas to the United States for $5,000,000. Mexican leaders, shocked by the offer, had then considered the United States as an even larger threat than before. They began to more earnestly question the policy of inviting United States citizens to immigrate to Mexican Texas in hopes that would strengthen defense of the region. They feared the opposite political consequence. They realized that forcing Catholicism on settlers from The States worked against winning their allegiance. And they had seen problems with accepting immigrants who wanted to bring in bonded African Americans.

So, in 1830, the Central Government closed the border, prohibiting further immigration from the United States. But the Mexican Government had no effective way to enforce the ban on immigration.

In 1831, **Anastasio Bustamante led a Conservative-backed military *coup d'etat*,** killed Vicente Guerrero and established a military regime. Revolt had been following revolt during this period, and, in the latest episode, Antonio Lopez de Santa Anna was leading a revolt by the Liberal Party. Nevertheless, **Stephen Austin was remaining faithful** to the Mexican Government, attempting to work with whoever was in power at the time. During this period the Mexican ban on immigration by United States citizens remained in place, but it was essentially impossible to enforce in remote Texas, especially in eastern Texas.

By 1832 the English-speaking population of Texas was about 20,000 people. The major wagon road across Texas was El Camino Real, which ran west-south-west from the Sabine

River to the Rio Grande River. It ran through San Augustine, Nacogdoches, Bastrop and San Antonio, ending at De Rio.

Two months prior to Sam Houston crossing the Red River and entering Texas, a political convention was held at San Felipe, a Stephen Austin town, with the object of petitioning the Central Government in Mexico City to authorize splitting the vast State of Coahuila along the Rio Grande River, so that Texas could be a State unto itself. Delegates also petitioned to lift the prohibition against further immigration from the United States. Delegates pledged allegiance to Mexico and "denied any desire for independence." There would soon be considerable optimism that Santa Anna and the Liberal Party would set Mexico on the path toward a limited Central Government with substantial State rights. But these hopes would fade. Santa Anna would be the key political and military leader of Mexican forces during the upcoming Texas Revolution and the later War between Mexico and the United States.

1833

President Andrew Jackson is Re-elected for a Second Term as President of the United States

Andrew Jackson, Democrat of Tennessee, easily defeated Henry Clay, National Republican of Kentucky, in the race for President. The popular vote was 55.0 percent for Jackson versus 42.2 percent for Clay. The National Republican Party (this is not the Republican Party created in the Northern States in the 1850's), whose strength lay in the northern states, had realized it must run a candidate from a Southern State to have a chance of winning the office of President.

Chapter 19 — March 1833 to February 1837: The States during the Second Andrew Jackson Administration

We briefly leave the narrative history in order to present an overview of the second Andrew Jackson Administration.

Andrew Jackson easily won reelection to a second term as President. Two parties had arisen to oppose Jackson's Democrats. One opposition party, termed the National Republican Party, chose Henry Clay, of Kentucky, as their standard bearer. The other opposition party, the Open-Leagues Party, nominated William Wirt of Maryland.

The South Carolina State Legislature, exercising its power to "appoint" Electors according to the Federal Constitution, assumed an independent attitude in which it might not endorse the candidate receiving the most votes in the State. The Nullification fight by South Carolinians put many in opposition to all 3 candidates, and the Legislature hoped it could broker a deal on reducing Federal import taxes if the election was close.

William DeGregorio would summarize the nominations for President:

"In this the first [election for President] in which candidates were chosen at national party conventions, Democrats met at Baltimore in May, 1832 to endorse Jackson for reelection. Although there was substantial opposition within the Party to Jackson's choice of Martin Van Buren of New York as his running mate, Delegates nevertheless nominated him for Vice President by an overwhelming margin. The Convention adopted a rule requiring a two-thirds majority to nominate a candidate; it [would remain] in force at Democratic conventions until 1936."

"A candidate [for President] in 1824, Clay emerged the [major] leader of the anti-Jackson forces. He was nominated for President at a convention of "National Republicans" in Baltimore in December 1831. [This upstart "National Republican Party" would not be associated with the Northern States Republican Party of Abraham Lincoln.] John Sergeant of Pennsylvania was nominated for Vice President. [The Open-Leagues Party, at a convention in Baltimore, nominated William Wirt of Maryland.]"

DeGregorio would then summarize the election campaign:

"The dominant issue was the fate of the Bank of the United States. Clay charged that in destroying the bank Jackson not only hurt the moneyed interests but also threatened the financial security of small borrowers. Most common people applauded Jackson's attack on the bank, long a symbol of special privilege and manipulation. Clay supporters, denouncing Jackson for instituting the spoils system and for his liberal use of the veto to thwart the will of [the House and Senate], dubbed the President King Andrew I. The Democratic press painted Clay as a dissolute gambler. The [western and southern States] continued to support Jackson overwhelmingly, and he improved his standing in New England. [Open-Leaguers opposed] Jackson, himself a Mason, and in some States collaborated with Clay supporters."

Jackson won the popular vote by 55.0%, versus 42.4% for Clay and 2.6% for Wirt. Jackson won the electoral vote by a huge majority: 219, versus 49 for Clay, 11 for John Floyd (the South Carolina vote), and 7 for Wirt. Jackson won the majority of electoral votes in 16 States – from north to south they were: Maine, New Hampshire, New York, New Jersey, Ohio, Indiana, Illinois, Pennsylvania, Virginia, Missouri, North Carolina, Tennessee, Georgia,

Alabama, Mississippi, and Louisiana. Clay won the majority of electoral votes in 6 States – from north to south they were: Massachusetts, Connecticut, Rhode Island, Delaware, Maryland and Kentucky. The Electors selected by the South Carolina State Legislature cast their 11 votes for John Floyd. William Wirt won Vermont.

Jackson's running mate, Martin Van Buren, of New York, was elected Vice President by 189 electoral votes, versus 49 for Sergeant and 48 split among 3 other candidates.

Because Treasury Secretary Louis McLane, of Delaware, refused Jackson's order to transfer Federal deposits from the Second Bank of the United States to State banks, Andrew Jackson transferred him to Secretary of State. Holding that job from 1833 to 1834, McLane was replaced by John Forsyth, of Georgia, who would be retained in the next administration as well. William Duane, of Pennsylvania, was appointed Treasury Secretary. Because Duane also refused the President's order to transfer Federal deposits from the Second Bank of the United States to State banks, he was replaced in September 1833 by Levi Woodbury, of New Hampshire, who Jackson transferred from the Navy Secretary's post. In Woodbury, Jackson had finally found a man who would support him in his campaign against the Second Bank of the United States. Woodbury would be retained in the next administration as well. Lewis Cass, of Michigan, was retained as Secretary of War. Benjamin Butler, of New York, was appointed Attorney General. Butler would be retained in the next administration. Levi Woodbury had been retained as Navy Secretary until he was transferred to the Treasury job in 1834. Mahlon Dickerson, of New Jersey, replaced Woodbury as Navy Secretary and was retained in the next administration as well. William Barry, of Kentucky, was retained as Postmaster General until he was replaced in 1835 by Amos Kendall, of Kentucky. Kendall was retained by the next administration.

Jackson's Democratic Party controlled the House of Representatives, but was dependent on the support of independent Senators to control the Senate. **Democrat seats in the Senate dropped** from 25 to 20, and National Republican seats dropped from 21 to 20. At the same time, seats held by others rose from 2 to 8. So, these 8 held the balance of power. On the other hand, **in the House the Democrat margin swelled slightly** to 147 seats, versus 53 seats controlled by the Open-Leagues Party and 60 seats controlled by independent Representatives. The National Republican Party that had advanced Henry Clay for the Presidency was not in control of the minority organization in the House.

The mid-term elections changed these majorities slightly and gave rise to the Whig Party. The National Republican Party had died, and from its ashes had risen the Whig Party. All Senators and Representatives then chose to be identified as either a Democrat or a Whig. During the second half of Jackson's second term, Democrats held 27 Senate seats versus 25 Whig seats. None were classified as "other." Democrats held 145 seats in the House versus 98 Whig seats. Here as well, none were classified as "other."

Arkansas was admitted as a State in 1836. Bonded African Americans were permitted to live in Arkansas.

Michigan was admitted as a State in 1837.

The more significant events involving African Americans during the 4 years of the second Andrew Jackson Administration will now be presented. The Virginia Government established a Deportation Board to encourage voluntary deportation to Africa. **The British Government**

began a program in 1833 to make independent bonded people of African descent – most lived in the Caribbean islands. **Owners were paid** 20,000,000 pounds sterling to prepare 800,000 bonded people to be independent. Farm workers were to be independent in 7 years and house workers were to be independent in 5 years. The exception was Antigua, where all were made independent immediately. Significant mob fights between European Americans and independent African Americans occurred during 1834 in Philadelphia and Columbia, Pennsylvania; in Trenton, Southwark, Lancaster and Bloomfield, New Jersey, and in Rochester, New York. More mob fights occurred the following year in Philadelphia and Washington City. The revised New Jersey Constitution denied the vote to independent African American men. **Henry Blair, of Maryland, an African American, was granted a patent for a corn harvester.** In 1834, the British Government decreed that bonded African Jamaicans were to be independent. Although an insignificant number of African Americans lived in Michigan, the State Constitution denied the vote to African American men. The North Carolina Constitution was amended to deny the vote to African American men; this meant that perhaps 1,000 men, who had previously met the property requirement and been eligible to vote, were no longer eligible.

This concludes the overview of the second Andrew Jackson Administration.

At this point, Southern Families have Made America as far as the eastern boundary of Mexican Texas. **So, let us shift our attention to Mexican Texas.** There, we will learn how American settlers who had immigrated to this vast land, Mexican Texas, in a few short years, will win it from Mexico and established an independent nation, The Republic of Texas.

Chapter 20 — Sam Houston and the Nation Builders Gain Mexican Texas

The Narrative History Resumes – March 1833

Sam Houston is Rapidly Emerging as a Leader in Mexican Texas

As you recall, Sam Houston had crossed the Red River and entered Mexican Texas on December 1, 1832. Since then, Houston had traveled about 1,000 miles through Texas, including a trip down to San Antonio, discussed political policy with **Stephen Austin** and grappled with passions at politically turbulent **Nacogdoches**, which ranged upward to rabid Texas nationalism. **He had written Andrew Jackson** in February to report widespread eagerness for Texas Statehood within a law-abiding Mexican Republic. But, if political lawlessness were to continue, Houston had predicted, there would be widespread eagerness for Texas Nationhood, and he had predicted that Mexico would be too weak to militarily deny such an ambition.

Then two events occurred in Mexico on April 1, 1833:

The Liberal Party, having forcibly ousted President Anastasio Bustamante, inaugurated its leader, Antonio Lopez de Santa Anna as the new President of Mexico. Since the Liberal Party publicly advocated a limited Central Government and substantial State rights, Texas felt even more eager to seek Statehood within Mexico.

On the same day Mexican Texas politicians convene a Second Texas Statehood Convention at San Felipe, the town that Stephen Austin had founded. Although Sam Houston had only been in Texas 4 months, he had been immediately recognized as a potentially important leader, and voters in the town of Nacogdoches had accordingly elected him to be a Delegate at the Convention. As had been the object of the previous San Felipe Convention in October 1832, this Convention denied any intent toward Texas nationalism and professed to only be seeking a division of the Mexican State of Coahuila along the Rio Grande River so that Texas could become a Mexican State unto itself. Toward that goal **Sam Houston wrote a draft Texas State Constitution,** which the Convention adopted as its recommendation, with some revisions by others. On another subject, Houston won approval of his resolution to prohibit encroachments on Native American lands. The Convention **elected Stephen Austin** to take the resolutions and proposed State Constitution to Mexico City and to **submit them to President Santa Anna**.

British Government Decides to Pay Owners of African Slaves to Transition Them to Freedom

On August 29, the British Government enacted legislation that began the process of preparing bonded African Americans for independence in all the British colonies where they lived. Most of the people covered by the legislation lived in the Caribbean region, so the legislation was named the **"West India Emancipation Act."** Public pressure to enact such legislation had been growing rapidly for the previous 3 years. Unlike the chaotic, politically-charged and war-ravaged land into which southern States African Americans would be made independent in 1865, the Caribbean African Americans were prepared for independence by their owners, who were in general cooperative.

The British Act gave the owners of bonded African Americans compensation of 20,000,000 pounds sterling in Government money to finance preparing for independence the 800,000 bonded African Americans who lived in the British West Indies. This amounted to 25 pounds sterling per person. The Act declared immediately independent all children younger than 6 years and all that would be born in the future. Bonded African Americans who worked as domestic servants would become independent after 5 years, and all who performed farm work would become independent after 7 years. The plan would work rather well because British political activists and government leaders had sat down together and worked out a reasonable plan that considered the welfare of people who would become newly independent.

This type of cooperation between political activists and government officials would never occur in the United States because the American Abolition and Exclusion movements would be forever focused on political advantage, rarely on what was best for the African American. In short, the African American in The States would be generally nothing more than a pawn in a large-scale political chess game.

And we must remember that there was one major legal difference in the two governments: the British Government in London had the political authority to regulate bonded people of African descent throughout the Empire, but the American Federal Government did not, **for that issue was controlled by the individual States.**

Mexican Government Throws Stephen Austin in Jail in Mexico City

Meanwhile, in Mexico, during the latter part of this year, 1833, President Antonio Lopez de Santa Anna ordered that Stephen Austin be seized and thrown into a Mexico City jail. **Stephen Austin was a political prisoner.** He had arrived in Mexico City during July and had submitted to Santa Anna the resolutions of the Second San Felipe Convention, including the proposed Texas State Constitution that Sam Houston had drafted. He had asked that they be given serious consideration, and he had advocated Texas statehood within Mexico with understandable hopefulness. But, Austin had become despondent after Santa Anna had procrastinated and avoided taking any action for many weeks. So, he had headed north only to be seized and imprisoned.

Meanwhile, Sam Houston had established himself in Nacogdoches as a lawyer in the Mexican Court of Judge Juan Mora. He apparently had little difficulty working in the Mexican courts even though he was not a citizen of the nation. He went through the motions of joining the Catholic Church to ensure continued acceptance. His main client was the Galveston Bay and Texas Land Company, which was led by Anthony Dey, a New York City banker. It represented the "entry of big business and politics into the unsettling affairs of Texas." It was funded by stock sold to select investors and land script sold to regular investors; however, "the land script was a fraud."

1834

Sam Houston Visits President Andrew Jackson in Washington

During the fall, Sam Houston was back east in Washington City. Undoubtedly, he found an opportunity to **confer with Andrew Jackson** and talk over the latter's frustration over Anthony Butler's failure to convince President Santa Anna to sell Texas to the United States for $5,000,000. And they probably discussed Stephen Austin's imprisonment in Mexico City.

But Houston also spent time on more enjoyable pursuits, such as engaging in theatrical recitation with his friend Junius Booth and entertaining a young cousin with extemporaneous poetry. <u>Then on another occasion Houston met a young girl from Virginia, Narcissa Hamilton, a cousin he had not seen for many years. "Do you remember me," she asked? Sam took a few moments to compose a verse in her honor:</u>

> "Remember thee?
> Yes, lovely girl;
> While faithful memory holds its seat,
> Till this warm heart in dust is laid,
> And this wild pulse shall cease to beat,
> No matter where my bark be tossed
> On Life's tumultuous, stormy sea;
> My anchor gone, my rudder lost,
> Still, cousin, I will think of thee."

Immensely impressed, Narcissa would "treasure" those few lines till her dying day.

During his eastern visit, Sam Houston traveled to Baltimore, Philadelphia and then to New York City, where he held business meetings with officials of the Galveston Bay and Texas Land Company.

Mexican President Santa Anna Assumes Dictatorial Rule – Stephen Austin Advises: "War is Our Only Course"

Far away in Mexico City, President Santa Anna was destroying the Liberal Party's ideals of a limited Central Government and substantial State rights. And he was setting himself up as a dictator. He had authorized Stephen Austin's release from prison, but that was not conciliation toward the people of Texas. By military force, Santa Anna had forced the State of Zacatecas to accept his dictatorship and had ordered his brother-in-law Martin Cos to lead an army into Texas to ensure obedience there. But the army had not yet arrived.

Then, on September 1, Stephen Austin arrived in Texas. In addition to time spent in a Mexico City prison, he had also spent months in various parts of the city studying the political situation. He had concluded that hope was lost for a constitutional Mexican Republic based on a limited Central Government and substantial State rights. Austin's course was set, and he advised Texans of it: **"War is our only course."**

Sam Houston was already making plans to wage war. The Committee of Vigilance and Safety at Nacogdoches had appointed Houston to be "Commander-in-Chief of the forces" for that region of Texas with the object being "to sustain the principles of the Mexican Constitution of 1824," which had guaranteed a Mexican Republic with a limited Central Government and substantial State rights. Houston had raised money for expenses by selling some Red River land and was issuing appeals for military recruits: "War is our only alternative! . . . Volunteers are invited to join our ranks with a good rifle and 100 rounds of ammunition." He published an appeal for volunteers in a New Orleans newspaper: "Volunteers from the United States will . . . receive liberal bounties of land. . . Come with a good rifle, and come soon."

Texas English-speaking leaders convened in San Felipe on November 3 to weigh making another appeal for a separate State of Texas within Mexico, versus a Declaration of Independence from Mexico. **At this time, Antonio Lopez de Santa Anna's army, under the command of his brother-in-law Martin Cos, had entered San Antonio,** intending to make that its base for suppressing revolutionary activity. But **Stephen Austin's fighters were preparing to put San Antonio under siege.** Although many wanted to postpone the San Felipe Conference and help in the siege of San Antonio, Delegate Sam Houston advocated holding the meeting as planned, for he believed political action was just as important as military action.

Most immigrants from the United States favored declaring independence from Mexico, but a very prominent leader of the Mexican Liberal Party, **Lorenzo de Zavala**, was present at the San Felipe meeting and Houston figured it was wise to make one more attempt at declaring Texas to be a separate State within Mexico under the structure of the Mexican Constitution of 1824, which had guaranteed a limited Central Government and substantial State rights. Zavala had held many important offices in past governments, including "Governor, Senator, Cabinet officer and Minister to France." A "hero of the revolution that had won freedom from Spain," Zavala had "repudiated Santa Anna and fled to Texas." Would Santa Anna give up his dictatorship and honor that Constitution? Like Stephen Austin, Houston thought not. But Houston wanted to keep the support of important Mexicans like Zavala. So, Delegates agreed to declare a separate **Mexican State of Texas**. They wrote a Mexican Texas State Constitution and organized a State of Texas civil administration under Governor Henry Smith and a legislative body called the General Council. Stephen Austin and 2 other men were directed to attempt to borrow $1,000,000 from the United States. **Delegates elected Sam Houston to be Commander-in-Chief of Texas State Armies.**

And Sam Houston was making fine progress in his efforts to recruit volunteer soldiers from the United States. A company of volunteers was organized in New Orleans. And men formed up in Georgia, Mississippi, Tennessee, and Kentucky. Men were coming from New York State, being helped along with financing arranged by Henry Swartwout. And some men were even coming from Cincinnati, Ohio.

Sam Houston was not present at the San Antonio siege lines when impatient New-Mexican-State fighters decided to charge the 1,400-man Mexican army under Martin Cos. Houston had advised the Texans on the siege line to wait until artillery arrived. Houston was away working on longer-range military issues, while the commander of the siege force, Edward Burleson, was directing his men to wait for artillery. But, the men on the siege line were "tired of waiting." Then, in early December a fellow soldier, Ben Milam challenged, **"Who'll go into [San Antonio] with old Ben Milam?"** He got his answer when 301 men stepped forward. Fearlessly facing Mexican artillery fire, they stormed the town. Milam was killed. But, after 5 days of fighting, **Cos and his 1,400-man army was forced to surrender.** The Texans permitted the Mexican force to retreat to south of the Rio Grande River with the promise that they would never again bear arms against Texas.

With the withdrawal of this Mexican army, Texas was free of any military presence that was answerable to the Santa Anna Government in Mexico City. Many Texans thought this victory meant that Texas had succeeded in gaining significant independence, whether as a Mexican State or as the Republic of Texas. But Houston was rather certain that Santa Anna would return with a more massive army. He continued his efforts to build a formidable army to defend the sovereignty of Texas, whether as a State within a limited Mexican Central Government or as a nation unto itself. He cautioned Texans that, by March 1, 1836, "we must meet the enemy with an army worthy of our cause." Praising "our countrymen in the field," who have "presented an example worthy of imitation," he encouraged "the brave to rally to the standard."

1836

Santa Anna's Mexican Army Arrives Early

Sam Houston had been wrong about needing, by March 1, a strengthened Texas Army to meet Antonio Lopez de Santa Anna's Mexican Army. He needed his Texas Army in January. The capable Santa Anna had marched his larger Mexican army into Texas during the dead of winter, before Houston was prepared to meet him. Santa Anna's men were headed for San Antonio. Upon receiving word that Santa Anna was in Texas leading a large Mexican force toward San Antonio, Houston dispatched **James Bowie** "with instructions to 'demolish . . . the fortifications . . . remove all the cannon . . . blow up the Alamo and abandon the place.'"

The Alamo was a Franciscan mission building that had been modified into a fortress. Houston believed it more of a trap than a useful fortress from which to fight. Houston had not personally gone to San Antonio to take command of the defensive force because he had needed to deal with a problem controlling his army on the south Texas coast. A sizable portion of Texas fighting men had been gathering to invade Mexico, south of the Rio Grande River, and loot the town of Matamoras. Houston had been struggling to redirect these men away from an aggressive agenda and back into a defensive posture.

The Alamo Siege and the Texas Independence Convention

The Texas Independence Convention opened at Washington, Texas on March 1. Delegates were eager to work fast, for the town had received a desperate message 2 days earlier from **William Travis**, commander of the approximately **200 besieged San Antonio defenders who were trapped inside The Alamo:**

". . . am besieged by 1,000 or more of the Mexicans under Santa Anna. I have sustained a continual bombardment and cannonade for 24 hours and have not lost a man. [Santa Anna] has demanded a surrender at discretion, otherwise, the garrison are to be put to the sword. . . [But] I shall never surrender or retreat. Then, I call on you in the name of Liberty, of patriotism and everything dear to the American character, to come to our aid with all dispatch. [Santa Anna] is receiving reinforcements daily, and [his army] will no doubt increase to 3,000 or 4,000 [men] in 4 or 5 days. If this [plea for help] is neglected, I am determined to sustain myself as long as possible. . . Victory or Death!"

Sam Houston was surely furious at James Bowie for having not carried out his order to salvage the cannon and destroy The Alamo. Now his fear that the place represented a trap was becoming a reality. Since Santa Anna's agents had been attempting to enlist Native American warriors in the Mexican campaign to subdue the Texas Independence movement, Houston had been away in the Cherokee Nation during February seeking to assure The Bowl and other Cherokee leaders that their interest would be honored by an independent Texas. So he had not made a trip to San Antonio, and was now occupied as a Delegate from Refugio at the Convention in Washington, Texas

The Texas Independence Convention worked at lightning speed, day and night. **Delegates wrote a Declaration of Independence**, not for an independent State within Mexico, but for an independent **Republic of Texas**. Complete separation from Mexico had become the aim. **It was approved unanimously and signed on March 2.** Of the signers, "11 were natives of Virginia, 9 of Tennessee, 9 of North Carolina, 5 of Kentucky, 4 of South Carolina, 4 of Georgia, 3 of Mexico, 2 of Pennsylvania, 2 of New York, and one each of Massachusetts, New Jersey, Ireland, Scotland, England and Canada. The birthplaces of 3 are not obtainable." Almost three-fourths of the signers were from the major "Nation Building" States of Virginia, North Carolina, Tennessee, Kentucky, South Carolina and Georgia. For her role in support of "Nation Building," **Tennessee would become known as the Volunteer State.** Delegates elected Houston Commander-in-Chief of the Armies of the Republic.

Sam Houston "Commander and Chief of the Republic"

While other Delegates remained at the Convention to create a National Government, Houston headed off to gather up the dispersed Texas army and confront Santa Anna. But Houston would be too late to help the brave defenders of the Alamo.

Santa Anna's army overran The Alamo on March 6 and killed all of the defenders – about 200 men. Among the dead were William Travis and James Bowie, both of Georgia, and David Crockett of Tennessee. No men were allowed to surrender.

Sam Houston was intent on defeating the Mexican army that was under the direct command of Antonio Lopez de Santa Anna, which was the middle army of the 3 Mexican armies that were moving through Texas, destroying the Independence Movement. Antonio Gaona's Mexican army was moving northeast from San Antonio. Santa Anna's Mexican army was moving east from San Antonio, never far from Houston's force. And Jose Urrea's Mexican army was moving north from Matamoras following the contour of the Gulf Coast. Since returning to Texas, Mexican forces had been ruthlessly victorious.

In addition to killing all defenders at The Alamo, Mexican dragoons under Urrea had destroyed Independence soldiers under Francis Johnson at San Patrico on February 27 and destroyed Independence soldiers under James Grant at Aqua Dulce on March 7. These dragoons then destroyed Independence soldiers under King at Refugio on March 16. Most recently, at Goliad, Urrea's dragoons defeated 390 stubborn Texas soldiers under James Fannin, killing every man in that unit. **Santa Anna and his generals did not take prisoners.** If they were able, they killed every Independence fighter they encountered.

So, Texas independence fighters knew that every battle was a fight to the death. And men worried about their families, especially as they daily witnessed many women and children fleeing toward the east in wagons, on horseback and on foot. Under such perils, Houston struggled mightily to curb desertions and shore up military morale. For several weeks he had been retreating before the Mexican Armies in a manner reminiscent of Nathaniel Greene's highly successful strategy in North Carolina during the American defense of Independence.

Then, on April 15, just when Santa Anna probably figured that Houston would direct his army to take the east-north-east road to Nacogdoches and the safety of Louisiana, Houston instead directed his men to take the southeast road toward Harrisburg, for he was intent on intercepting Santa Anna's army and engaging in battle. Marching rapidly, covering 55 miles in only two and a half days, Houston's army arrived to find Harrisburg in ashes, but learned that Texas Government officials had fled to Galveston Island "in the nick of time," thwarting Santa Anna's goal of capturing or killing these political leaders.

At this time, Houston's men were closing in on Santa Anna's army. A battle was near at hand, but Santa Anna was not fully aware of that fact. Houston's men advanced another 10 miles to the Rio San Jacinto River. Houston had recently received 2 cannon, a gift from supporters in Cincinnati, Ohio. But lacking anti-personnel grape shot, he had directed the camp blacksmith to cut up horseshoes to improvise a grape shot effect. The cannon and the improvised grape shot would be ready when Houston would direct his men to a narrow band of woods that bordered Buffalo Bayou all the way until it joined the San Jacinto River, where a ferry was positioned to transport travelers across to the small village of Lynchburg. Houston planned to surprise Santa Anna as his men approached the ferry landing. It was the morning of April 20.

"Trust in God and Fear Not! – "And Remember the Alamo!"

Sam Houston addressed his men at daybreak to prepare them for the battle expected later in the day:

286

"Victory is certain!"

"Trust in God and fear not!

And, Remember the Alamo!

Remember the Alamo!"

Houston knew his men were ready **when they roared back, "Remember the Alamo!"** Then, Houston led his men (slightly over 800 in number, of which 53 were cavalry) closer to the ferry landing and positioned them for battle.

Later in the day Santa Anna's advanced skirmishers approached with one Mexican cannon and columns of infantry behind them.

Houston's 2 Texas cannon were loaded with horseshoe shot as each man took aim at a Mexican soldier. Houston's artillerymen had never made a practice firing of the improvised horseshoe shot, for gunpowder was too scarce. But, amazingly, the first shot disabled the Mexican gun carriage making it mostly ineffective. Carefully aiming, the Texans fired their rifles with telling effect. The battle continued for a while, but **Santa Anna called his men back to make camp**. He was expecting reinforcements soon.

Houston did not attack immediately the next morning, allowing time for 540 Mexican soldiers to arrive, which were commanded by Martin Cos. This brought Santa Anna's force to about 1,350 men, compared to Houston's force of just over 800 men. At this point Santa Anna was not worried about an attack by Houston's men. Except for the fight the previous day all he had seen of Houston's leadership was retreat, retreat, retreat. **Houston had the proud Santa Anna just where he wanted him!**

Sam Houston was patient. He sent men to cut down the bridge across Vince's Bayou – one less escape route. He wanted the Mexicans to feel safe from any attack on that particular day. He wanted many of them to settle down to their naps. As the afternoon wore on Houston quietly prepared his men for a furious attack. At 4 o'clock "he lifted his sword."

Emerging from the woods, everyone rapidly advanced through the grass toward the Mexican line, which was defined by rather fragile breastwork. The Texans held their fire until they reached within 20 yards of the Mexican breastworks. **Houston signaled with his hat and the cannon blasted away a section of the breastwork as the infantrymen fired their rifles and raced forward with their hunting knives drawn for action. "Remember the Alamo!"**

"They swept over the torn barricade as if it had not been there. Shouts and yells and the pounding of hoofs smote their ears. Through key-holes in the pungent wall of smoke they saw gray-clad figures, with chin-straps awry, running back, kneeling and firing, and running back – toward some tents where greater masses of men were veering this way and that. The Texans pursued them. The pungent wall melted; the firing was not so heavy now as the Texans were using their knives and the bayonets of [captured] Mexican guns. The surprise lacked nothing.

Santa Anna had thought Houston would not, could not, attack. In his carpeted marquee, he was enjoying a siesta when a drowsy sentinel on the barricade [caught sight of] the Texan advance. Cos's men were sleeping because of their previous night's march.

Cavalrymen were riding bareback to and from water. Others were cooking and cutting wood. Arms were stacked."

"Santa Anna rushed from his tent commanding everyone to lie down. A moment later he vaulted on a black horse and disappeared." Juan Almonte led about 400 Mexicans on a retreat, but they would eventually surrender. Mexicans "plunged into the swamp and scattered over the prairie," some pleading, "Me no Alamo." When some Mexican cavalry fled toward Vince's Bayou, "Texans rushed them down a vertical bank. A hundred men and a hundred horses, inextricably tangled, perished in the water. . . **The battle proper lasted perhaps 20 minutes. The rest was in remembrance of the Alamo.** This pursuit and slaughter continued into the night."

Texan Independence casualties were only 6 killed and 24 wounded. **One of the wounded was Sam Houston, whose right leg had been "shattered above the ankle."** The Texans claimed Mexican casualties were 630 killed, 208 wounded and 730 taken prisoner, the wounded also being counted among the prisoners.

After Surgeon Ewing attended to the shattered leg, Houston wrote a brief letter to Andrew Jackson and sent it on its way by express rider. The next day some Texans found Santa Anna sitting on a stump near the destroyed bridge over Vince's Bayou. He was disguised in a blue cotton smock and red felt slippers, clothing he would claim to have found "in a deserted house."

The prisoner, Santa Anna, was brought to Sam Houston, who was "lying on a blanket under an oak tree his eyes closed and his face drawn with pain" from his wound. "I am General Antonio Lopez de Santa Anna, President of Mexico, Commander-in-Chief of the Army of Operations. **I place myself at the disposal of the brave General Houston."** Houston's Spanish was ragged, but he comprehended well enough.

"General Santa Anna! Ah, indeed! Take a seat, General. I am glad to see you, take a seat!" Houston asked Lorenzo Zavala, Jr., the son of the renowned Mexican Liberal Party leader, to help with translation. Speaking to Zavala, Santa Anna pleaded that Houston "may consider himself born to no common destiny, who had conquered [me,] the Napoleon of the West; and it now remains for him to be generous to the vanquished." Houston coldly answered, "You should have remembered that at the Alamo."

But Houston decided to treat Santa Anna with respect and give him some comforts as a captive. And, he would not order the execution of Cos for having violated the parole he had pledged at San Antonio. **Houston aimed to keep Santa Anna captive for a while, during which time he expected to obtain a pledge from the Mexican Government to accept the Republic of Texas as a separate and independent nation.**

Houston would receive surgery on his wound at New Orleans in June and would recover the use of his right leg.

With Santa Anna a captive and the middle Mexican army destroyed, the western army, under Antonio Gaona, accepted Santa Anna's order, issued from captivity, to retreat out of Texas. And the coastal army, under Jose Urrea did likewise. Militarily, the independent Republic of Texas had been established, and it was time for political leaders to establish the associated government.

Nation Builders were building the Republic of Texas!

288

Sam Houston's letter to President Andrew Jackson reached the White House as fast as the horses ridden by express riders could take it. Jackson was still recovering from a severe illness. Yet, he was jubilant upon reading the letter. The man delivering the letter would write: "I never saw a man more delighted. . . He read the dispatch . . . exclaiming over and over as though talking to himself, 'Yes, that is his writing. I know it well. That is Sam Houston's writing.' . . . [Jackson] ordered a map . . . and tried to locate San Jacinto. He passed his fingers excitedly over the map. . . 'It must be here. . . No, it is over there.'"

Jackson realized that Sam Houston had won a victory greater than his earlier victory at New Orleans, for at New Orleans he had skillfully stood a defensive line, while at San Jacinto his friend had attacked with glorious effectiveness. The victory inspired many Americans to have faith in the Republic of Texas and to support the fledgling government with money and men. But support of the Republic of Texas was the result of many personal efforts, for the United States Government was officially neutral on the matter.

The Provisional Texas President, David Burnet, called for nation-wide elections to formally elect a President and Legislators for the Republic of Texas Government and to ratify the Texas Constitution. Three men were running for President: Henry Smith, a previous Provisional President, Sam Houston and Stephen Austin.

Stephen Austin was ill. The pioneering effort by Moses and Stephen Austin had begun American immigration into Spanish Texas and had sheltered immigrants through the perils of frequently changing governments in Mexico City. But, before his death in December, Austin would see elected the first officials of the new government of the Republic of Texas.

On September 5, Texas voters elected Sam Houston President by a vote of 5,119 for Houston versus 742 for Smith and 587 for Austin. Voters ratified the Texas Constitution. Houston was sworn into office on October 22, 1836. The European American population of the vast Republic of Texas, a country larger then than the present-day State of Texas, was about 30,000, but enthusiastic emigrants were arriving from the United States daily.

Antonio Lopez de Santa Anna remained a prisoner, but his willingness to recognize the Republic of Texas was improving, as was the ability of Texans to defend their new nation.

Chapter 21 — 1836 to 1846: The Republic of Texas under President Sam Houston

Although the Mexican government in New Mexico refused to officially recognize the Republic of Texas as an independent nation, separate from Mexico, it would never attempt to attack it militarily in a serious attempt to conquer it. Leaders in Mexico City knew that their nation was far too weak to take back its former Texan land.

From the creation of the Republic of Texas in 1836 through to its merger with the United States as a state in 1846, the Republic of Texas was a successful nation under the leadership of Presidents Sam Houston (1836-38 and 1841-44), Mirabeau Lamar (1838-41), and Anson Jones (1844-46).

One day prior to finishing his second term, on March 3, 1837, United States President Andrew Jackson officially recognized the Republic of Texas as an independent nation and appointed Alcée La Branche American charge d'affaires to the new nation.

Sam Houston's first term as President of the Republic went smoothly, considering that the nation was newly formed. Those years were successful and peaceful, with many more immigrants arriving from the United States, mostly from the South.

Back East, President Andrew Jackson's second term is over, but Democrats retain power

The Southern States great Nation Builder, Andrew Jackson, of Tennessee, had performed his last tour of duty. On March 4, 1837, President Jackson turned his office of 8 years duration over to Vice President Martin Van Buren, of New York State. Democrats retained power. Jackson had recommended his Vice President for the office of President. Job well done! Andrew Jackson was happily retiring to the Hermitage, near Nashville, Tennessee.

In 1834, opposition to the Democrat Party had coalesced around a new party, named the "Whig Party." But the new Whig Party was unable to defeat the seasoned and proven leader, Martin Van Buren, of New York State. President Van Buren would retain many of Jackson's Cabinet. Democrat majority in the Federal Senate strengthen, but, in the House, if fell by 37 seats to just one seat. Following the mid-term elections, Democrat majorities in the Senate and House were firm.

Chapter 22 — 1836 to 1846: The Republic of Texas under President Mirabeau Lamar – 1838-1841

Mirabeau Lamar was the Republic's second president. He was inaugurated on December 1, 1838. David Burnet was Vice-President. Several weeks later, in his first formal address to the Texas Congress, President Lamar advocated immediate action to drive Cherokee and Comanche Native Americans from their lands within the Republic of Texas. That advocacy infuriated Sam Houston! Lamar began his term of office with a government cash reserve of $1.4 million. **When his presidency would conclude in 1841, the Republic would be almost $7 million in debt**.

After spending a few months in the Republic, Sam Houston went east to visit several places in America. At one point in May 1839, Sam was in Mobile, Alabama meeting with William Bledsoe to encourage him to invest in the Republic of Texas. And, following the meeting Mr. Bledsoe invited Sam to come home with him to visit his family. The Bledsoe home was a stately southern mansion named Spring Hill. Mrs. Bledsoe was hosting a strawberry festival on the spacious lawn and the weather was splendid. Sam was strolling through the rose garden with the younger 18-year-old daughter when her 20-year-old half-sister came by with a dish of strawberries.

"General Houston, my sister Miss Margaret Lea." General Houston politely bowed very low, saying "I am charmed." Sam thought Margaret Lea the most beautiful young lady he had ever seen. Margaret had been in New Orleans when the people received General Houston following the Texas military victory over Santa Anna at San Jacinto. So impressed, Margaret had thereafter hoped to someday meet "this romantic man." Well, that day at home during the Bledsoe strawberry festival on the lawn, she had met him. And the event would change the lives of both.

Soon afterward, Sam Houston was near Nashville, Tennessee, **at the Hermitage visiting Andrew Jackson**. From there he visited a cousin, Judge Wallace, in Maryville. Sam then left Maryville, for **Alabama**. He wanted to visit William Bledsoe and his family again; and see Margaret Lea again, we must assume. Sam further explained to William Bledsoe the attractive investment opportunities that abounded in the Republic of Texas. And Sam was especially interested in encouraging the beautiful Margaret Lea's mother to come to Texas, too. Mrs. Lea, a widow and a sharp business woman, realized that going to Texas with William Bledsoe might be profitable. So, Mr. Bledsoe and Mrs. Lea agreed to visit Texas and learn about investment opportunities. And Margaret was eager to go to Texas, too. **See saw herself as Sam Houston's future wife.**

When Sam Houston arrived back in Texas, he was infuriated over President Lamar's action against the Cherokees. **President Lamar had ordered a Texas militia to drive a small band of Cherokees from Texas soil a little south of Red River**. The Cherokees had fought back but, in the face of defeat, **their leader**, **The Bowl**, had directed survivors to flee north, leave Texas and "nurse their wounds in Oo-loo-te-ka's wigwams." The Bowl, 84 years old, had explained, "I stay. I am an old man. I die here." The Bowl had died, holding the sword in his hand that Sam Houston had given him years ago. In a speech at Nacogdoches, Sam Houston trounced the actions of President Lamar's militia and declared that The Bowl was a better man than any of the murderers in Lamar's militia.

Houston was mad at President Lamar for many other mismanagement failures. By late summer, 1839, Texas paper money had heavily depreciated and "coin was disappearing from circulation."

On September 25, 1839, France granted official recognition of the Republic of Texas. French Minister Monsieur de Saligny came to the Republic of Texas to represent France. There was much talk of a French loan to strengthen the declining Texas financial situation. But Saligny saw much trouble in the Lamar administration. France refused to provide a loan.

Sam Houston found time to write frequent "impassioned letters" to **Miss Margaret Lea in Alabama.** Anticipating the financial investment trip to the Republic of Texas that Miss Lea's mother and her son-in-law, Mr. Bledsoe, had promised to make when Sam had visited their Alabama home, Sam was encouraging Margaret to come with them. Sam was earnest! He wrote to Margaret encouraging her to come and to marry him! In return mail, Sam read Margaret's letter promising to come with her mother and Mr. Bledsoe, naming the arrival date and the vessel they would take to Galveston. Sam and friends were at the Galveston dock when the vessel arrived, shooting a greeting cannon. Bad news: "General Houston," said **Mrs. Nancy Lea**, a Baptist minister's widow, "my daughter is in Alabama. She goes forth in the world to marry no man. The one who receives her hand will receive it in my home and not elsewhere." Mr. Bledsoe and Mrs. Lea invested in some Texas land and returned home.

Plan B!

One month after Mr. Bledsoe and Mrs. Lea left Texas Sam Houston was on his way to Alabama. **The wedding between Sam Houston and Margaret Lee took place in Mrs. Lea's home, the home where Margaret had been born and raised, in Marion, Alabama.** On May 9, 1840, amid the music of violins the two were married. **"As quickly as possible, General Houston and his bride sailed for Galveston where guns proclaimed" the hero of the Republic of Texas had acquired a beautiful young bride.**

On June 19, 1841, President Mirabeau Lamar's combination-merchant-and-military expedition left Kennedy's Fort near Austin, Republic of Texas, on **a mission to Santa Fe** on the far western edge of land claimed by the Republic government to be part of its territory. This territory was part of Mexican Texas before settlers from America fought for and won their independence from Mexico. Former President Sam Houston and the Texas Congress had been content to let the Santa Fe region be free of Republic rule until some later time in the future when the population of Anglo settlers substantially increased. Lamar's Santa Fe Expedition featured several merchants and 21 oxen-drawn wagons carrying about $200,000 worth of merchandise that those merchants hoped to trade with people of the Santa Fe area, most of them being Native American and the remainder being Mexican. A military force of **320 armed men** and a company of artillery guarded the Expedition.

Lamar's Santa Fe Expedition was **foolish in many ways.** The man of Mexican ancestry who knew the best route, with water supplies, to Santa Fe would quit just as soon as the going got tough. Finding fresh water would prove difficult; supplies to feed the men would prove to be insufficient. And Native American attacks would slow progress. Furthermore, the Expedition was almost sure to fail! More of the fate of these men later, but some background is helpful:

After two years under President Lamar, the Republic was in terrible financial shape. So, to fund his Santa Fe Expedition, Lamar had simply directed a printer in New Orleans to print $500,000 in Texas paper money, even though the treasury had nothing of value to back the paper. Existing Texas money was worth 20 cents on the dollar. Millions of dollars had been added to the public debt and government credit was gone. Lamar, an impractical dreamer, had advocated his Santa Fe Expedition to divert attention away from the Republic's real problems and, hopefully, give him a win that might help him get elected to a second term. When Lamar had pitched his Santa Fe Expedition to the Texas Congress, Congressman Sam Houston and a majority had refused to endorse the scheme or to provide money to finance it. President Lamar had ignored Congress and proceeded to promote the Expedition among Texans and to fund and organize it.

By Mid-September, 1841, President Lamar's Santa Fe Expedition was near its destination, Santa Fe. As expected, Mexican officials were in control of the region. However, a strong detachment from the Mexican Army had come north and it confronted them right away. The Texans, 320 men strong, were no match for the 1,500-man Mexican Army detachment. **The Texans surrendered.** They were not allowed to depart for home. Instead, the Texas militiamen were forced to march under guard for 2,000 miles south to near Mexico City. All were imprisoned at the Perote Prison in the Mexican State of Veracruz. They would remain imprisoned for a long, long time.

Back East, the Whig Party finally elects a President, but its Vice President, John Tyler, of Virginia, would serve for all but one month of the 4-year term

In the United States, on March 4, 1841, William Henry Harrison, a Whig from Indiana with ancestral ties to Virginia, replaced President Martin Van Buren, Democrat of New York State, as American President. So, American politicians in opposition to the Democratic Party had finally, yes, finally, managed to defeat Democrats in a presidential election contest!

But President Harrison would hold office only one month. After appointing his Cabinet and getting his administration in order, Harrison delivered his inaugural address outdoors on a cold, windy, March Day. He caught pneumonia and died soon afterward, having **served only 31 days as president.**

John Tyler, Whig of Virginia had been elected Vice President. **So, he immediately assumed the office of President**. Again, the United States was headed by a Virginian, a man from the Mother State. John's great-grandfather had come to Virginia Colony from England in 1653. John's father had been a Virginia governor. John had served in the Virginia House of Delegates, as Governor of Virginia, as a Federal Senator. But, when President Jackson, had threatened to use force against the South Carolina Government when it had attempted to nullify a large increase in Federal import taxes, Senator Tyler broke with Jackson and drifted into the faltering Whig Party. Tyler's time in the Senate ended soon afterward. Running as a Whig, Tyler had won a seat in the Virginia House of Delegates and had become Speaker of that state body in 1839.

President Tyler would favor a merger treaty between the United States and the Republic of Texas, but getting Senate approval of a merger treaty would be difficult.

Chapter 23: The Republic of Texas under Sam Houston's Second Term as President, 1841 – 1844

On December 13, 1841, Sam Houston assumed the leadership of the mess that former President Mirabeau Lamar had made of the Republic in three short years. While Margaret remained back home in Houston City, President Houston took command of the Republic in the new Hall of Congress in Austin, the Republic's new capital. The government financial records were a mess, and, in fact, **the Republic was bankrupt**. Monthly receipts were $33,550 and expenditures were three times that. Commerce in the Republic had ground to a halt. Houston immediately cut his salary in half and reduced others likewise. He consolidated the War and Navy departments and streamlined the Post Office Department. In all, Houston reduced payroll from $174,000 to $32,800. He appointed Anson Jones to the office of Secretary of State. Houston worked directly with leaders in Washington D. C. seeking a merger between the two nations while Anson Jones worked at improving relations with Great Britain and France.

At the time of Sam's inauguration, leaders in Austin had not heard any news about **former President Lamar's Santa Fe Expedition**, that is, until four weeks after that day, when news arrived that all militiamen were, under excessive brutality, being marched south into Mexico, prisoners of war. Figuring out a way to free the surviving 320 Texas militiamen in that prison in Veracruz would have to wait.

But the Republic Congress immediately focused on fighting Mexico in response to the capture of those 320 militiamen. Congressmen went crazy. The Texas Congress adopted a resolution seizing all Mexican land to the west, out to the Pacific Ocean. President Houston, realizing the inappropriateness of the resolution, vetoed it. Congress overrode the veto. **News arrived reporting that Mexican ruler Santa Anna had gathered an army and was marching north to conquer the Republic of Texas**. Sam Houston put his wife, Margaret, on a boat at Galveston bound for Mobile, Alabama. The situation was very serious.

Sam Houston did not like managing the Republic at the partly completed Austin, Texas capital that former President Mirabeau Lamar had instigated. It was not a good place for Margaret and he felt a strong need to be a fine husband. So, during the spring and summer of 1842, Sam moved his presidential office to Houston, Texas, where he and Margaret had their home. He tried to relocate the Republic archives from Austin to his Houston office, but met strong resistance. Oh, well, later perhaps.

In the fall of 1842, President Houston moved his office from Houston to a small town on the Brazos River, 60 miles to the northwest. A great hostess, Margaret was happy in Washington.

About the same time, during September, 1842, **Santa Anna's army under Woll raided San Antonio in the Southwest part of the Republic of Texas**. The Mexican force captured and carried back into Mexico a number of Texans, including the personnel of the Texas District Court, which happened to be in session. Judge James W. Robinson was among Woll's captives. President Houston responded by organizing 1,200 men into sort of an "army," delivered a public "warlike speech" and saw his "army" off in a south direction. These 1,200 men were not equipped to launch a military campaign, but the public display quieted concerned citizens and gave Houston time to exercise diplomacy. Houston sent letters to heads of state in America, Great Britain and France accusing Mexico of an illegal invasion of the independent Republic of Texas at San Antonio, capturing citizens and court officials, and carryings them off to Mexico.

When Houston's "army" of 1,200 men reached the Mexican border at the Rio Grande River most argued against invading and left for home, **but 300, under former Secretary of War William Fisher, crossed the river and entered Mexico.** Fisher knew that he was violating President Houston's orders, but apparently, he was seeking some military glory or something. When news arrived, Houston alerted citizens at home and officials in America, Great Britain and France that **Fisher's entrance into Mexico had violated his, the President's, orders**.

On December 26-27, 1842, Fisher's militia captured a Mexican town, Cuidad Mier, but a larger Mexican army of 2,700 men soon arrived, **captured Fisher's men and marched them toward Mexico City**. During the march south, most of Fisher's men overwhelmed their guards and escaped, only to be recaptured again. The unfortunate escapes were forced to draw beans from a jar containing nine tenths white beans and one tenth black beans. Texans who drew a black bean from the jar were lined up and killed by a firing squad. Remaining captives were marched to Mexico City and imprisoned. Sam Houston would be attempting to free these Texas men, who had violated his orders to not invade Mexico.

Sam Houston's spirits heightened: Elizabeth gave birth to a baby boy, Sam Houston, Jr. on May 25, 1843.

By this time, President Houston was redoubling his diplomatic efforts to encourage America, Great Britain and France to pressure Mexico into seeking peace. England and France applied diplomatic pressure on Santa Anna. The English pressure was the more effective. A big day arrived:

Her Majesty's sloop, Scylla, "raced into Galveston harbor with word that the British Chargé at Mexico City had induced General Santa Anna to request an armistice pending a meeting of peace commissioners. A truce was agreed to, and Lieutenant Galan, of the Mexican Army, arrived in Washington, Texas with proposals for **a peace conference at Laredo**," Texas, near the Mexican border.

Sam Houston appointed George Hockley and other delegates to represent Texas at Laredo. This wonderful event brought joy to Sam, Elizabeth and all Texans. Sam, Jr. was 10 weeks old. Good news would follow: the 1843 grain harvest was the largest in the history of the Republic. Peace and a recovering economy. Sam Houston had accomplished amazing results since he had picked up the mess handed over to him by former President Mirabeau Lamar!

President John Tyler's Merger Treaty

Through secret negotiations with Houston's officials, United States President John Tyler, of Virginia, by April 12, 1844, secured the language of a **treaty to merge all Texas Republic land into the United States**, the heart of the land to become a new American State of Texas and the remainder of the land to be donated as new American national territory land. On April 22, 1844, Tyler submitted a treaty to the United States Senate defining a merger of The Republic of Texas into the United States. Tyler's **Secretary of State, John C. Calhoun**, of South Carolina, having recently assumed that office, **was strongly supporting Tyler's merger**

treaty, arguing that the Southern States would be forever angry if the North succeeded in blocking the merger treaty.

The United States Senate deferred immediate treaty approval. In fact, <u>from May through to the United States Election Day in early November, the Texas merger treaty question became a major issue during the 1844 presidential contest between Southern Democrats and Northern political leaders.</u> Southerners, being Nation Builders, favored the Texas Merger Treaty. Many in the North were against giving Southerners more political power.

Back in America, James K. Polk, of Tennessee is elected President

Meanwhile, in the United States, in November, 1844, James K. Polk, Democrat of Tennessee, defeated Henry Clay, Whig of Kentucky, in the country's presidential election. In March, 1845, Polk would take the office that President John Tyler, Whig of Virginia, had held one month shy of 4 years. Polk was a close friend of a political associate of former President Andrew Jackson, also of Tennessee. Descended from Scots who had lived in Northern Ireland, and born near the North Carolina-South Carolina border, Polk had left North Carolina for Tennessee as a young man, where he became a lawyer. In Tennessee, Polk had served as a representative in the Tennessee House, as a Representative in the Federal House and as Speaker from 1835 to 1839. Polk had been Tennessee Governor from 1839 to 1841, but had failed reelection.

The Democratic National Convention in Baltimore, held back in May 1844 to nominate the party's candidate for president, had been an unusual contest. Polk had lost political luster since losing twice to win re-election to a second term as Tennessee Governor. But, none of the serious contenders for the Democrat nomination had been able to gain enough votes to win the nomination. <u>Eventually, the convention had turned to "dark horse" candidate James K. Polk and the Tennessean had thereby won the Democratic Party nomination.</u>

The Whig Party convention had refused to nominate John Tyler, of Virginia, for a second term as President of the United States, because, as President, he had abandoned several traditional Whig Party principles. <u>Whigs had nominated Henry Clay, of Kentucky.</u>

Twelve days after the Democratic Party nominated James K. Polk, the Senate voted to reject the Texas-United States merger treaty that President Tyler had submitted. The treaty would lie dormant throughout the election campaign. <u>But Tyler continued to seek treaty approval. To assure Texans of eventual treaty success, Tyler sent Andrew Jackson's nephew, Andrew Jackson Donelson, to represent, in Texas, the office of the American President as chargé d'affaires.</u>

A major issue among voters had been whether to approve or not approve a treaty to merge the Republic of Texas and the United States. Clay and Whig Party politicians had argued against the Texas merger, telling voters that America should not add a big state where bonded African Americans lived. Of course, many Whigs were using slavery as an excuse for not allowing Southern Families to Build America any further. James K. Polk and Democrats had favored approval of a treaty to merge the Republic of Texas into the United States. Polk won the presidency with 49.5 percent of the popular vote and 170 of the 275 electoral votes. **Democrats would control the Senate with 31 votes versus the Whig's 25 seats. Democrats would control the House with a huge majority of 143 seats versus 83 opposition seats**.

Approval of a Republic of Texas and United States merger in 1845 in Washington, D. C. seemed assured.

Out West it was campaign time in the Republic of Texas

It was also campaign time in the Republic of Texas. President Houston's second term would conclude on December 31 and, constitutionally, he could not seek a third term. But Sam let it be known that he favored his Secretary of State, Dr. Anson Jones, to assume his office. And Jones would win election

Chapter 24: The Republic of Texas under Dr. Anson Jones's Term as President, 1844 – 1846

On December 9, 1844, Sam Houston concluded his second term as President of the Republic and turned the office over to the newly elected President, **Dr. Anson Jones**. Dr. Jones, who had begun his career as a country surgeon in western Massachusetts, had been serving as President Houston's Secretary of State. But, at the time that Jones assumed the office of President, he and Houston differed on the desired future of the Republic. Houston favored a merger with the United States and Jones wanted Texas to remain an independent Republic and, eventually, capture Mexican land out to the Pacific.

Sam Houston and Margaret left Washington, Texas for a new home to be built on a large plantation 14 miles from Huntsville, Texas. Here, the hills resembled those in Virginia and portrayed happy times to come. Sam would name the place "Raven Hill," in remembrance of his pleasant youth with friends in the Cherokee Nation. Sam was happy. Margaret was happy, too. Margaret asked her husband to join the Baptist Church and he did.

The Northern Culture Knew it was beaten: Three Days before James K. Polk takes office, the Merger Treaty is approved in Washington, D. C.

Outgoing President John Tyler and Whig member of the Federal Senate and House knew that the merger treaty was soon to be passed as the first item on James K. Polk's agenda. **Well, Tyler and the Senate and House went ahead and approved the draft treaty three days prior to the day that James K. Polk assumed the office of President**. The approved draft treaty would soon be on its way to the Republic of Texas capital for approval there.

At the Hermitage, Andrew Jackson, "greatly afflicted and debilitated," congratulates his friend, Sam Houston

On March 12, 1845, from the Hermitage near Nashville, Tennessee, Andrew Jackson wrote his final letter to Sam Houston, addressed to him in Texas:

"My Dear General,

"This will be handed to you by our mutual friend Major A. J. Donelson who returns to Texas, to take you by the hand and to welcome you into our glorious union. I congratulate you, I congratulate Texas, and the United States on this glorious result, on which depended the safety and prosperity of both Texas and the United States . . . I now behold the great American Eagle with her stars and stripes hovering over the lone Star of Texas, with cheering wave welcoming it into our glorious union and proclaiming to Mexico and all foreign governments in stentorian voice, you must not attempt to tread upon Texas – that the United Stars and stripes now defend her – Glorious result, in which General you have acted a noble part, and your name is now recorded among the heroes, the patriots, and the philanthropists.

"You have yet more to do – you have now to lay the basis by proper legislation and remodeling your constitution for the future greatness, wealth, and prosperity of your state.

"...**I am greatly afflicted and debilitated and write with much pain** . . . If providence spares me, to next summer of which I have great doubts, I hope to see you, your noble lady and charming boy at the Hermitage, where you will receive a hearty welcome, not on your way only to see your relatives, but on your way to the senate of the states to take your seat with the sages of our Union representing, in part, the sovereignty of the noble state of Texas. Accept the tender of the friend, salutation of myself and household to you and yours.

"Believe me your friend,

"Andrew Jackson"

President Anson Jones and the Texas Congress consider Tyler's Merger Treaty

Reluctantly, Texas President Anson Jones called the Texas Congress together to consider the merger treaty that had arrived from the United States capital. This discussion among Republic of Texas leaders would take many months.

By this time, Sam Houston, Margaret and little Sam were heading east toward Tennessee and Andrew Jackson's home, the Hermitage, near Nashville. They knew they must hurry because Jackson's illness was advancing and death was near. Former President/General Houston so wanted to see former President/General Jackson one more time. **But sadly, they arrived too late to see the great American Nation Builder alive.** He had died at 6 o'clock in the evening of June 8, 1845. Biographer Marquis James describes the Houston family's arrival that night, well after sunset:

"At nine o'clock, a coach driven at a gallop whirled through the gate. Mrs. John H. Eaton – Peggy – opened the door and admitted General Houston and his family. For several minutes the towering, travel-stained figure stood perfectly motionless before the candle-lit couch of death. **Then, Sam Houston fell on his knees, and sobbing, buried his head upon the breast of his friend. He drew little Sam to his side. "My son, try to remember that you have looked upon the face of Andrew Jackson."**

The formal procedures related to preparing the Republic of Texas to remake itself into a State within the United States would require about nine months. In the process, a State House of Representatives and a State Senate was created and representatives and senators elected. A governor of the future State of Texas was elected. The elected State of Texas Governor was **James Pinckney Henderson**, a North Carolina Lawyer who had arrived in Texas in June 1836 and who had been the Minister to England and France for the Republic of Texas from 1837 to 1840. Two senators were elected to represent the new State of Texas in the United States Senate. **Sam Houston was elected a senator**. He recommended Thomas J. Rusk to be his companion senator. Thomas J. Rusk was elected senator, too. Houston and Rusk would be going to Washington, D. C. and Dr. Anson Jones would feel slighted.

The Two Nations Merge

On February 16, 1846, Texas State officials-elect and Republic of Texas officials stood at Austin before the flying Lone Star Flag of the outgoing Republic to participate in a momentous ceremony.

Addressing the crowd as he closed the era of the Republic of Texas and ushered in the era of the State of Texas, **President Anson Jones said, in part:**

"A government is changed both in its officers and in its organization – not by violence and disorder, but by the deliberate and free consent of its citizens; and amid perfect and universal peace and tranquility, the sovereignty of the [Republic of Texas] is surrendered, and incorporated with that of another. . . The Lone Star of Texas, which 10 years since arose amid clouds, over fields of carnage, and obscurely seen for a while, has culminated, and following an inscrutable destiny, has passed on and become fixed forever in that glorious constellation, which all freemen and lovers of freedom in the world must reverence and adore – The [United States of America]. Blending its rays with its sister States, long may it continue to shine, and may generous Heaven smile upon this consummation of the wishes of the two Republics, now joined in one. May the United States of America be perpetual, and may it be the means of conferring benefits and blessings upon the people of all the States, is my ardent prayer. The first act in the great drama is now performed. The Republic of Texas is no more."

Then President Anson Jones, "with his own hands, struck the tricolor of the Lone Star. United States Senator Sam Houston's arms reached to receive the folds lest they brush the ground." The flag of the State of Texas was raised. The Republic of Texas was thereby merged into the United States.

It became the State of Texas, assured, as much as politically possible, that the Federal Constitution would forever ensure a limited Federal Government and a substantial degree of State Sovereignty. Hopeful of that pledge, Sam Houston and Thomas Rusk would be traveling to the Federal Senate to represent the new State in Washington D. C.

The population at statehood was about 125,000, about 30,000 being bonded African Americans. Two important features of the merger agreement with the United States are noteworthy:

1. The Republic of Texas had controlled 389,200 square miles. The State of Texas controlled 268,697 square miles. Therefore, the Republic of Texas donated 120,503 square miles to the National Territories of the United States, destined to become new states. Yes, as part of the merger agreement, the Republic gave to the Federal Government rights to considerable land to the west and northwest.

2. New York State has 54,556 square miles. So, if, at some future time when population grow justified it, the State of Texas would be divided into five states, each would have an average of 53,739 square miles, each close to the size of New York State. The Merger Agreement between the two nations considered this calculation and promised the people of the new State of Texas that they could divide their original state into as many as five states when population growth justified it. With division, Texans would, therefore, enjoy the political benefits of ten Senators in the Federal Senate. **Of course, that would never happen, because, following the North's conquest of the Confederate States, the Northern States Republican Party would never allow it**. Treaties between nations are often violated. Likewise, the U. S.-Texas treaty!

Chapter 25 — President James K. Polk and Southern Nation Builder's Manifest Destiny

Observers watching the ceremony in Austin on that February day in 1846 would not know the future. That's always the difficulty — mankind never knows the future, just some of the past and some of the present. But we Southerners living today do know their future, which followed that remarkable day. We know 177 years of their future. So, let us review brief summations of that future history while pretending that we were standing beside those Texans who watched the old flag come down and the new flag go up.

America's greatest tragedy — which would result in the needless deaths of one million Americans, White and Black, and result in the destruction of much of the South, from Virginia to Texas — would begin only fifteen years (15 years) into the future, in 1861. At that time, boys and girls born during the year of the Republic of Texas-United States merger, would just be in the middle of their teenage years – growing from 15 to 18 while war raged across their land.

President Polk, of Tennessee, was a Nation Builder with one more job to accomplish. Yes, only three months after lowering the Republic of Texas flag and raising the State of Texas flag, on May 13, 1846, immediately after a contrived minor border clash between a few American soldiers and a few Mexican solders, the United States Congress declared war on Mexico. Apparently, a majority of Americans decided they wanted far more land than what Texans had won from Mexico. They also wanted all of the remaining Mexican land that lay west of what Texans had previously won – all of it – north to the Oregon Territory boundary and west to the Pacific Ocean. And Americans, led by the Nation Builders, would decide that a war of aggression seemed to be the fastest and surest way of getting it.

Soon after taking office, Polk sent men to Mexico City offering to pay Mexico $25,000,000 for all Mexican land west of Texas. The Mexican government refused. Polk, through his Secretary of War, William Marcy, of New York State, had sent a military force under General Zackary Taylor, of Kentucky, to the area of the Rio Grande River along the south Texas border. Mexican military claimed that land, although north of the river, was their land. A small fight occurred on April 25 between a large Mexican army and a small detachment of Taylor's army. The Americans withdrew, but 11 American soldiers had been killed. Polk learned about this fight on May 9. **That was just want President Polk had hoped for: a little skirmish with Mexican military**.

On May 11, 1846, President Polk delivered to Congress, his message advocating a declaration of war against Mexico. In his message he **claimed that Mexico had "invaded our territory and shed American blood on American soil."**

The House of Representatives quickly appropriated $10 million to finance a war against Mexico and authorized an enlistment of 50,000 American volunteer troops. **The House vote to support war was almost unanimous, only 14 no votes being cast. On May 12, 1846, the Senate voted 40 versus 2 to declare war on Mexico**, Senator Houston among those voting for war. **President Polk signed the War bill on May 13**. Strongest support in Congress came from Southern Representatives and Senators who were of the Southern Families that Made America. Those Southern Families had one last job to finish: to stretch America fully west of Texas to the Pacific Ocean

By January 13, 1847, American forces were in full occupation of the west out to the Pacific. They occupied the land that would become New Mexico, Arizona, Nevada, Utah, Southern California and Northern California. But Americans wanted to force the government in Mexico City to surrender those occupied Mexican lands to the United States. That would take longer. And, in September 1847, American forces would be occupying Mexico City.

On March 10, 1848, the Treaty of Guadalupe Hidalgo was signed securing the Mexican cession to the United States of all the land sensible Nation Builders wished to seize, west to California and the Pacific Ocean. The American Senate approved the treaty by a vote of 38 for versus 14 against.

Southern Families had Made America!

Chapter 26 – In 13 Short Years, Northern Politicians Would Seize Control of the America that Southern Families had Made

During a span of 13 years, America would soon experience rapid political change. Emigrants from Ireland, Great Britain, and Europe, especially from the Germanic States, had already begun arriving into the Northern States in huge numbers, rapidly expanding the future political power of the North.

The 1850 census would reveal to Northern politicians that, if a Northern States political party won all of the Northern seats in the House of Representatives, all of the Northern seats in the Senate, and all of the Northern Electoral votes, that party would control Congress and the office of President – a real possibility by 1856, or 1860, or surely by 1864.

Northern States industrial leaders would be especially excited about achieving control over the Federal Government, because, with such control, tariffs on imports could be raised dramatically. With high protective tariffs and cheap immigrant labor, these industrialists would greatly expand their businesses. Anyway, far more than half, about 80 percent, of tariffs were paid by Southerners – clearly a win-win situation for leading men of the North, especially of the Northeast. You see, in the Northern States, the Industrial Revolution was flourishing.

But, how would ambitious Northern politicians contrive a unifying political movement across such a diverse, wide span of Northern States? There were the six New England States, still remembering their Puritan Separatist origins. There were the two large Eastern States of New York and Pennsylvania, populated by experienced people who felt ideologies less. There were the three developed states north of the Ohio River – Ohio, Indiana and Illinois – where political, economic and cultural ties with the South were, though fading, still significant.

Finally, there were the several States north of Missouri and west of the Mississippi River and the Great Lakes, which were expanding in number and into which so many immigrants were moving. Like the South, these people were farmers. But, so many of them were new to America. Did those people have political ideals? Were they susceptible to being tricked by deceitful Northern politicians?

Slavery! Perhaps ambitious Northern States politicians would assemble a sectional political party that would be dedicated to preventing any bonded African Americans (slaves) from living in any future State carved from all Territories that lay west of Missouri, west of Michigan and west of Texas.

A party of that mindset would appeal to the land-owning dreams of sons and daughters of Northern States families, as well as newly arrived immigrant families. Its politicians would claim, "No matter in which future State you and your descendants choose to live, they will have no bonded African Americans living there." That political argument would appeal to almost every Northern voting man and his family, perhaps as many as 98 percent of them.

And Northern men would also expect that very, very few free Colored people would move into any of those future States. They would recall that the Illinois Constitution had long forbid colored people from moving into that State. And they would understand that the so-called Underground Railroad had sent runaway slaves beyond America, into Canada, mostly because **people of the North did not want Colored people as neighbors**.

In 1848, Americans had no knowledge of future "Bleeding Kansas Territory," or "John Brown," or a series of political debates held in seven Illinois counties during 1858 between that State's much-admired Democrat, Senator Stephen Douglas, and a Springfield lawyer by the name of Abraham Lincoln. Douglas would be up for re-election to the United States Senate and Lincoln would have been endorsed by the new Illinois Republican Party to take the seat away from the incumbent. <u>Before Illinois debate onlookers in 1858, Lincoln would advocate exclusion of bonded African Americans from all future States, claiming that slavery was immoral and Congress could contain it, but Congress could not change it where it already existed.</u> Many Northern Republican politicians had been agreeing with Lincoln, but the unresolvable North-South political conflict would be prohibiting slaves from living in all future States, without even one State being excepted. The Illinois legislature would be voting soon on its choice for Senator. It would choose to return Stephen Douglas to the Senate.

By the middle of that year, **1858, every Northern State would have a very active Northern States Republican Party,** <u>politicians in each of those states advocating exclusion of slaves from living in all future States out west.</u> And, those politicians in those Northern States would accuse Democrat politicians in their respective States of sinful behavior, evidenced by their association with fellow Democrats of the "evil" Southern States. **By accusing Democrats in their respective States of "evil" association with Southern Democrats, Republicans were campaigning to win all local elections, ranging from town offices, to county offices, to State offices, including the office of governor.** <u>Obviously, no significant number of politicians in any Southern State would attempt to organize a Southern States Republican Party where they lived.</u>

The presidential election year of 1860 would be not far away. So, during 1859, Northern States Republicans would intensify their campaigning, relying more and more on inciting hatred within their respective States toward Southern people, folks very, very few had ever met. On the other hand, Southerners would rightly feel that, since they had given to the United States considerable land beyond the Nation of Texas as part of the 1846 merger agreement, and since Southern men constituted a large part of the American army that had invaded Mexico to wrestle away her land out to Mexican Californio, then Southern slaves should be permitted to move west into some of it — surely into the land between the State of Texas and the State of California. Northern Republicans would be saying "No! No new land. <u>Slaves must remain in existing Southern States or be 'colonized' elsewhere.</u> No compromise."

The Southern people would be getting mad!

They would remind people of the North that, after Virginia won her independence, along with the other 12 colonies, she gave away her land between the Ohio River and the western Great Lakes and stipulated that it was to be settled only by families who came without slaves. They would further explain that the donated land became Ohio, Indiana, Illinois and Michigan, States where many northerners live today. That vast land was a gift of Virginia — the Mother Colony, <u>the Mother State, the land that gave America General Washington, President Washington and Presidents Jefferson, Madison and Monroe.</u>

They would further argue: When President Jefferson, of Virginia, arranged the **Louisiana Purchase** and almost all of the money used for payment was money the Federal Government was collecting as tariffs in Southern seaports. <u>A Southern President and Southern money made possible the purchase of vast Louisiana Territory.</u>

Southerners would just be getting warmed up in rebuking the political sectionalism of the Republican Parties of the various Northern States. They would press on, arguing that, while the New England colonies lost their fighting spirit during the Revolutionary War, <u>four Southern colonies, Georgia, South Carolina, North Carolina and Virginia, fought on to win independence for each of the thirteen colonies,</u> **including the five in New England**.

Throughout the 1850's, Northern abolitionists, small in number, but well-funded for political effect, would argue that all slaves in the South should be set free; perhaps over a span of a few years; perhaps to be colonized elsewhere, such as Liberia or other places in Africa; or, perhaps, set free rather far into the future (<u>in 1858, Abraham Lincoln would suggest that,</u> **before 100 years would pass,** <u>no slaves should be living in the South</u>). In reply, Southern leaders of public opinion, such as soil scientist Edmund Ruffin, would counter with explanations that most Colored slaves in the South had become Christians, a great benefit to them; that most, having not been born in Africa, would be strangers if sent there, and that the vast majority of American slaves were living better and longer lives in the Southern States than their distant cousins in West Africa.

Many in the South would puzzle over why arguments such as those tendered by Mr. Ruffin were rejected by most people in the North. There were reasons for it, but many in the South would remain puzzled, remain angry over what they would consider unjust persecution. Republican newspapers would smother Southern arguments, but the real reason the vast majority of people in the North would reject them was because the political fight being waged between Republicans and Democrats was over excluding African Americans from living in all future States to the west. <u>Few in the North would care very much about how soon far-away Southern slaves might become free to make livings independently</u> – **people up there just wanted to be assured that**, if and when made free, **Colored people would not be migrating North to become neighbors**.

In early 1860, the historically-national character of the long-predominant Democrat Party – the party of the people originally founded by Virginian Thomas Jefferson – would be in disarray – **split into a Northern Democrat Faction and a Southern Democrat Faction**, with other spin-offs as well.

Northern States Republicans would gather in a northern states convention in Chicago and nominate as their presidential candidate a Springfield, Illinois lawyer who had been **born illegitimately in North Carolina**, a Southern State, to Southern parents, Abraham Enloe and Nancy Hanks; who had, since age 2, lived with his mother and step-father, Thomas Lincoln, in Kentucky; who had moved with mother and step-father to southern Indiana as a boy; who, as a young adult, had left home to live in central Illinois where he had become a lawyer and later pursued his legal career in that state. **That lawyer was Abraham Lincoln, a man with very little formal education or experience in legislative matters and no experience running anything larger than a two-man law office.**

<u>A short time earlier, Democrats, still attempting to hold themselves together as a national party, would have convened in Charleston, South Carolina. Their attempt to remain a national party would fail because the leading Democrat of the North,</u> **Senator Stephen Douglas of**

Illinois, would demand that Southern Democrats accept a platform which called for excluding African American slaves from living in any future State, even a future State west of Texas through which the Rio Grande ran (this State would become New Mexico; half of it had belonged to the Republic of Texas for ten years until 1846, when Texans had given it to the United States as part of the merger agreement). Southern Democrats would not submit to such a humiliating defeat.

The historic Democrat Party would be split. **Northern Democrats would nominate Stephen Douglas, of Illinois, for President** and run a nationwide campaign. **Southern Democrats would nominate Vice-President John Breckinridge, of Kentucky**, and also run a nationwide campaign.

Since Republicans would seek no votes in the Southern States, they would only win 40 percent of the total vote, but they would sweep the Northern States and carry the Electoral College for the lawyer from Springfield, Illinois.

The United States Constitution did not specifically say that a State under the Federal Government was allowed to secede and go its own way. But, **at that time, nothing in Constitutional language specifically prohibited State Secession**. So, after Lincoln would win election and victorious Republicans would refuse to make political peace with the South — even something small, like agreeing to allow slaves to move into just one future State — **a State Secession movement would surge across the South**.

South Carolina would secede first, on December 20, 1860, arguing that it had voted to create the Federal Government and felt entitled to reverse that vote and leave. By the time Lincoln would take office, six other Southern States would have seceded, and all seven would have joined together in self-defense and have formed a new general government they would call simply the **"Confederate States of America."**

For a few weeks, it would appear that the North might let the seven seceded States go in peace. But that would change when key Republican leaders and Northern money men would begin to realize that Southern seaports were where the vast majority (about 80 percent) of Federal revenue had historically been collected, because tariffs on imports were the major source of it. If the seven seceded States were allowed to go in peace, and Virginia and North Carolina would be joining them, the Federal Government would have to raise most of its revenue by leveling new taxes in the North, perhaps taxing its wealthier people. Republican leaders would begin advocating war.

But war would appear to be difficult. President Lincoln would figure, to succeed, he needed a scheme to rally the North to make war on the South. He knew that, without the support of the governors of all of the Northern States and their state militia, his Northern army would never conquer the land of proud and militarily-experienced Southern men. **Lincoln figured he needed the first shot to be fired by the South**. So, he would devise a scheme to incite Confederates in Charleston, South Carolina to fire shore cannon at a partially completed mid-harbor fortress, called **Fort Sumter**, which would be holding a small garrison of Federal soldiers who had refused to leave the State upon its secession, and would be continuing to refuse to leave. **To incite the artillery attack toward the fort, from around the harbor, Lincoln would send a fleet of Navy warships and troop transports south to Charleston, which, by then, was a city in a foreign country**.

Lincoln's scheme would work as planned. Confederate President Jefferson Davis, preferring to evict the garrison before Lincoln's fleet entered the harbor, would order shore batteries to fire their cannon at Fort Sumter. They would do it. So, while Lincoln's fleet would bob about in the Atlantic, just outside the entrance into the harbor, dramatic cannon fire would be exchanged. Amazingly, no one would be hurt inside the partially completed fort and no one would be hurt on shore. Meanwhile, Lincoln's fleet would watch the fireworks from afar and then depart for the North. The garrison would agree to leave Fort Sumter and board a train for Washington.

That same day, Republican Lincoln would be happy to learn that his scheme had worked beautifully – that the "Rebels" had fired on the American flag. Furthermore, Lincoln would know that every Northern State was headed by a Republican Governor, each of them standing ready, when asked, to call up their respective militia to reinforce the Federal army in a joint invasion of the Confederate States of America. So, the next day, Lincoln would call for troops. **The North's war to conquer the South would be underway.**

Refusing to make war upon Southern people, Virginia, North Carolina, Tennessee and Arkansas would secede and swell the Confederacy from seven to eleven States. Lincoln's first military priority would be to subjugate the remaining Southern States, the so-called "border states:" Delaware, Maryland, Kentucky and Missouri. Upon completing that initial mission, the war against the Confederate States of America would be launched.

The war to conquer the Confederate States would persist almost **four years**. **The death toll, consisting of soldiers, sailors and civilians, would total 1,000,000,000, yes, one millionm, people, White and Black**. The Republican war to conquer the Southern People would result in more deaths than all other wars that had been, or would be, fought by Americans throughout human history.

At the time of State Secession, most, but not all, Southern blacks would have been slaves, owned and supported by another person. After the war, all of them, including those living in Delaware, Maryland, Kentucky and Missouri would be free, free to make their own way through life, earning livings, marrying and raising and supporting their families. That would be good. But, the timing of emancipation would be horrendous. The Southern economy and her land were in shambles. Farms and business would have no money to hire workers. Political reconstruction, by its intent, would encourage discord between Blacks and Whites. The struggles would be immense. **But, old friendships among Southern Whites and Southern Blacks, between the two races, would survive.** Working farms for crop-shares would help jump-start the economy and keep life going.

Immediately following the surrenders, the victorious Republican Party would subject the conquered Southern States to ten years of Political Reconstruction. Those politicians knew that no Southern white man would ever vote Republican, so that meant complete victory required installing a controlling Republican Party in each Southern State. This they would accomplish by denying the vote to white men who had supported secession and its defense while organizing black men into reliable Republican voters. It worked. But not forever! It would take ten years for Southern white men to recover their rights to freely participate in the democracy that their forefathers had brought to America.

Chapter 27: We now fast-forward to Our South as viewed today.

Today, people all over America receive glimpses of her Southern heritage, the foundation upon which our country was built. Those glimpses are heard in **American jazz** music pioneered by African Americans in New Orleans; in gospel music sung with such feeling in the churches of our smaller towns; and in **American country music**, which tells much of our story and calls Nashville its home. Those glimpses are remembered as the land where two American brothers, at Kitty Hawk, North Carolina, perfected their invention of the airplane and showed the world how to fly through the air like a bird. And it was in the South that Americans perfected rockets and flew to the moon and back.

Those glimpses are remembered by Christian people around the world who came to know Jesus and God through attendance at massive crusade events, filled with singing and the preaching of **Billy Graham**, who grew up near my home in Charlotte, North Carolina and, as a boy, attend **Calvary Church**, which still exists and where my wife and I presently attend. Those glimpses are known to Americans as the home of the "**Bible Belt**," where America's strongest feelings of faith are held by both Whites and Blacks. Those glimpses are remembered when recalling the encouragement of **Martin Luther King**, of Georgia, who encouraged Americans everywhere to judge a person by his or her character, without regard to the color of his or her skin.

Furthermore, our South is where the older generation from the North come to retire, where they meet people of a similar age whose great-great grandfathers had bravely defended against invading Northern armies, witnessed one fourth of their compatriots die in the attempt; and then persevered onward to heal their devastated land, to restore the destroyed economy, to heal the discords of ten years of Republican Political Reconstruction, and, along with great-great grandmothers, to raise families of similar toughness and faith – families that worked hard, sought God's help and, over the generations, **made the South rise again**. Many of these southward-bound retirees are being welcomed by friendly Southern personalities. Retirees from the North are seeing something beautiful. **They are seeing a South that has risen.**

If, today, inquisitive Americans will simply scrape away the politically correct façade that hides and distorts perceptions of our country's early history and thereby uncover the truth of it – the truth that lies beneath that façade – they will learn that, beginning at the Atlantic shore and expanding westward to the Pacific over a span of 242 years, **it was truly Southern Families that Made America**.

Chapter 28 — Today, Their Descendants are Trying, yes, Trying to Save America

You have witnessed the history of Southern Families making America.

You have also witnessed a brief history of the Northern Culture going to war against those heroic Southern Families. The result:

One million, 1,000,000, Americans suffered death as a result of that war.

Four million, 4,000,000, bonded African Americans were suddenly declared free, the men, the women, the boys, the girls, the babies and the elderly, and required to make livings on their won in a devastated, bankrupt South. The timing of achieving freedom could not have been worse.

Furthermore, the African American men among those four million were organized into Republican Party voters to enable the conquering Northern States Republican Party to dominate the governments of the conquered Southern States, cities, counties and towns.

But, let us now advance the calendar to today. **Yes, today. What is the political, social and cultural situation in America today**?

The political, social and cultural situation today threatens to destroy what is left of the America that Southern Families made.

Today's extremely liberal Democrat Party, which seems to be controlling the decisions of President Joe Biden, is turning America toward a socialistic country.

America can no longer control **the inflow of immigrant migrants** who are coming in through our border with Mexico.

2022   2.76 million walked in.

2021   1.72 million walked in.

In 2020, the U. S. census showed that 26 percent of the American population consisted of immigrants and their children. And many of these immigrants who are here today have come into our nation by simply walking across our border with Mexico. As of the day that I am writing this sentence, Saturday, June 24, 2023, the United States population is calculated to be 336,761,423. Of today's population, 1.33 percent simply walked across our border with Mexico in 2021 and 2022 as illegal migrants. **A nation that cannot control its immigration is a nation destined to lose its heritage, a heritage that began with those Southern Families that made America.**

Today's Republican Party, generally conservative, is trying to slow the nation's destructive advance toward extreme liberalism and socialism. And, as a whole, the Republican Party receives overwhelming support from the voters in the Southern States and the States of Ohio and Indiana, which had experienced strong Southern family settlement in the early years. The following table provides the present numbers of Representatives in the U. S. House for each listed State:

State	Republican	Democrat
Alabama	6	1

Arkansas	4	0
Florida	20	8
Georgia	9	5
Kentucky	5	1
Louisiana	5	1
Mississippi	3	1
Missouri	6	2
North Carolina	7	7
South Carolina	6	1
Tennessee	8	1
Texas	24	13
Virginia and West Virginia	7	6
Southern Total	**110**	**47**
Percentage	**70%**	**30%**
Indiana	7	2
Ohio	10	5
Eastern Midwest Total	**17**	**7**
Percentage	**71%**	**29%**

Today, far too many Americans are being paid by governments (states and Federal) to avoid work; I am referring to those who are able bodied, but just do not want to hold down a job. They prefer to live off of government handouts. This government policy is primarily supported by those members of today's Democrat Party who are in positions to help enable said hand-outs. In April 2023, for example, America had 10.1 million job-openings, positions seeking an employee. That is equal to 3.0 percent of our total population. In May, we had 134.58 million Americans working at jobs. **So, today we have a job opening**, **seeking an employee**, **for every 13 Americans who are working**. Republicans, in general are opposed to flagrant laziness among so many living in America today. I assure you that this culture of handouts to the lazy did not spring from the Southern Families who made America.

Another very troubling political agitation we suffer today is the **widespread homosexual-acceptance-and-celebration-campaign** we normal descendants of the Southern Families that made America are expected to be embracing. God made Adam and Eve and all humans today are descended from that couple. **You should read my book, "God's Humans, from Adam to Today."** It is a wonderful and satisfying presentation that facilitates an understanding that encompasses both the teachings of the Bible and the science we are aware of today. I further explain:

All mammals on earth are two sexes: male and female. Politicians and political agitators cannot alter this basic truth. Clearly, the Holy Bible declares that homosexual behavior is a serious sin. **Americans should not be coerced into celebrating sinful behavior**. Boys in elementary school should not be quizzed, "Child, do you feel like a boy or a girl?" Girls in elementary school should not be quizzed, "Child, do you feel like a girl or a boy?" Young boys and girls are obviously the sex they were born into. For goodness' sake, young boys and girls have not yet experienced puberty! Christian churches should not be coerced into accepting self-proclaiming homosexuals into leadership positions or even positions of Church Pastor. Sinful behavior should never be on display at the pulpit!

I assure you that the people of the Republic of Texas would never have voted to give much of their land to the United States and retain the rest as their new State of Texas, if they had known about the cultural mess our nation is in today, 177 years later.

Let us look at politicians advocating "Reparations." The concept has gone crazy in California. There, in 2022, the legislature founded a **California Reparations Task Force**. It has tabulated a listing of the many ways people of African ancestry living in California have attained less wealth than White people or Asian people living there. If you total the Task force's wealth disadvantage numbers you see that, to even the score, every Californian of noticeable African ancestry should be paid $1,200,000 by the state government. With a population of 2,240,000 people of some African ancestry living there, the state would need to come up with a lot of money for a payout like that. **But, let me suggest a better idea!** Pay California African Americans a bunch of money, perhaps $50,000, to immigrate to Africa, the home of their distant cousins. This gives them a clear choice: **if you do not like being an American,** then take the money and join your cousins in Africa. **Kill Reparation thought**!

Only 620,000 people of African ancestry were brought into the colonies that would become the eastern United States and sold as slaves. **Amazing Story here!** Those purchased slaves, decade after decade, were really well cared for and **enjoyed large families and a far longer and more productive life, when compared to their cousins who remained back in Africa.** Today, the population of people of discernable African ancestry is **49,000,000**. Therefore, on average, every slave sold to a person in the land that would become America has produced **79 descendants living today**. Compare that to today's Native American population, which is much less than the population that was in North America before Columbus started bringing European diseases to the New World.

President Joe Biden is making great strides in **forgiving payment on college student loan debt**. To qualifying for forgiveness, it helps to not be making a big salary. He is pledged to **cancel a total of $66,000,000,000** that is owed to the Federal Government in student loan payments. Rich people do not qualify for debt relief. My son and his wife paid for their son and daughter to go to college. He is angry about missing out on Biden's free college scheme. This debt forgiveness is a ploy designed to win more Americans to vote for Democrat Party candidates! By the way, more high school graduates should skip college and learn a trade, or start a business like another of my sons did.

And let us not forget how Democrats have been real nasty about using the FBI, false stories and legal harassment to destroy the voter appeal of Republican candidates. You know, stuff like accusing a Republican candidate of receiving financial backing from the Russian Government – a big lie.

And, the story of America today goes on and on.

Thanks for reading "Southern Families Made America." It is an **amazing history** about how my ancestors, my wife's ancestors and millions more Americans who are descended from those Southern Families **can be proud**.

Help others learn this history. Toss out the rubbish. Embrace the truthful history of who made America.

And, by the way, those men in Massachusetts who dressed up like Indians and tossed all of that cheap tea into the water did not, repeat, did not, make America.

Let's join together and try to save America, save the democrat principles that our Southern ancestors fought for and handed down to us.

References Relevant to Southern Families Made America

R2   ***The Complete Book of U. S. Presidents***, William A. DeGregorio, Wing, 1984, 1989, 1991, 1993

R23   *Cherokee Tragedy, The Ridge Family and the Decimation of a People*, Thurman Wilkins, Second Edition, Revised, University of Oklahoma Press, Norman, OK, 1970, 1986

R24   *Trail of Tears, The Rise and Fall of the Cherokee Nation*, John Ehle, Anchor, New York, 1988

R25   *The Cherokees, A Population History*, Russell Thornton, U. of Nebraska Press, Lincoln, NE, (first printing 1942), 1990

R27   *The Federalist, a Commentary on the Constitution of the United States*, Alexander Hamilton, John Jay and James Madison, reprint by The Modern Library, New York

R36   ***The Chronological History of the Negro in America***, Peter M. Bergman, Harper & Row, New York, 1969

R37   *The Glorious Cause, The American Revolution, 1763-1789*, Robert Middlekauff, Oxford U. Press, New York, 1982, paperback

R41   ***The Southeastern Indians***, Charles Hudson, The U. of Tennessee Press, (first printing, 1976, cloth) 1994

R43   ***The Life of Andrew Jackson***, Marquis James, (Complete in one Volume; Part One: The Border Captain, copyright 1933; and Part two: Portrait of a President, copyright 1933) The Bobbs-Merrill Company, Indianapolis, 1938

R46   *The Civil and Political History of the State of Tennessee*, John Haywood, (Originally published 1823), Publishing House of the Methodist Episcopal Church, South, Nashville, 1891

R53   *The New Century History of the United States*, Edward Eggleston, American Book Company, New York, 1904, 1907, 1919, 1923

R66   ***Redcoats and Rebels, The American Revolution through British Eyes***, Christopher Hibbert, 1990, Avon Books paperback edition, 1991

R75   ***Edmund Ruffin, Southerner:*** *A Study in Secession*, Avery Craven, copyright 1932, 1991 printing by Louisiana U. Press, paperback

R80   ***Nativism and Slavery, The Northern Know Nothings and the Politics of the 1850s***, Tyler Anbinder, Oxford U. Press, 1992, 1994 paperback edition

R84   *The Anti-Federalist Papers and the Constitutional Convention Debates*, Edited by Ralph Ketcham, Mentor paperback, 1986

R87   *The Know-Nothing Party in Massachusetts, The Rise and Fall of a People's Movement*, John R. Mulkern, Northeastern U. Press, Boston, 1990

R89   *Yankees and God, A History of New England Culture and the Four Phases of Puritanism from the Seventeenth to the Twentieth Century*, Chard Powers Smith, George J. McLeod, 1954

R99   ***The Nat Turner Slave Insurrection,*** F. Roy Johnson, Johnson Publishing Co., 1966

R117 *A History of the American People,* Volume I: The Creation of a New Occidental Power, 1500-1850, Nathaniel Wright Stephenson, Charles Scribner's Sons, New York, 1934

R118 *The Growth of American Nationality, 1492 – 1865*, Fred W. Wellborn, The Macmillan Co., New York, 1943

R119 *The Growth of the United States*, Ralph Volney Harlow, Henry Holt and Co., 1925, revised 1934 edition

R121 *The United States, Experiment in Democracy*, Avery Craven and Walter Johnson, Ginn and Co., Boston and others, 1947.

R131 *The Liberator, William Lloyd Garrison, a Biography*, John L. Thomas, Little Brown and Co., Boston, 1963, first edition

R138 *The Constitution of the United States of America*, Washington, D. C.

R150 ***The Raven, A Biography of Sam Houston,*** Marquis James, University of Texas Press, Austin, paperback reprint from 1929 first edition, 1999 (Winner of Pulitzer Prize)

R152 *A New History of Texas*, Anna J. Hardwicke Pennybacker, Tyler Texas, 1888

R160 *Bloodstains, An Epic History of the Politics that Produced and Sustained the American Civil War*, Volume 1, *The Nation Builders*, by Howard Ray White, Amazon, 2002

R161 *Bloodstains, An Epic History of the Politics that Produced and Sustained the American Civil War*, Volume 2, *The Demagogues*, by Howard Ray White, Amazon, 2003

R162 *Bloodstains, An Epic History of the Politics that Produced and Sustained the American Civil War*, Volume 3, *The Bleeding*, by Howard Ray White, Amazon, 2007

R163 *Bloodstains, An Epic History of the Politics that Produced and Sustained the American Civil War*, Volume 4, *Political Reconstruction and the Struggle for Healing*, by Howard Ray White, Amazon, 2012

R164 ***Understanding the War Between the States***, by Howard Ray White and 15 other writers within The Society of Independent Southern Historians, Amazon, paperback, e-book and audiobook, 2015

Index

Adams, John

   Elected President, 162

   Lawyer, 58

   Peace Commissioner, 109

   Retirement, 175

   Summation, 164

   Suppressing Freedoms, 167

   Vice President, 134

Adams, John Quincy

   Failed Reelection, 255

   President, 246

   Secretary of State, 230, 236, 239

   Summation, 246

   War against British, 222

Adams, Samuel, 58, 61

African American History

   1689-1793, 136

   1793-1797, 152

   1797-1801, 166

   1801-1805, 174

   1805-1809, 186

   1809-1813, 196

   1813-1817, 205

   1817-1821, 231

   1821-1825, 240

   1825-1829, 249

   1829-1833, 258

   1833-1837, 278

   Nat Turner's impact, 1831, 270

African Slavery, 15, 31

Albany Congress, 43

Albany, New York, 18

Alexander, Abraham, 66

Alien Act of 1798, 167, 169, 177

Allen, Brothers Ethan, Ira and Levi, 79

American Colonization Society. *See* American
   Deportation Society

American Deportation Society, 240, 252, 262

American Independence Movement, 49, 50

Boston Area Revolt, 65

Boston Laborer Riot, 57

Boston Riot over Tea Imports, 60

Boston Siege, 65, 67, 68, 71

Boston Stamp Tax Riot, 54

British Evacuate Boston, 71

Bunker Hill, 68

Charleston, First Attack, 73

Declaration of Independence all 13 Colonies, 74

Declaration of Independence, Mecklenburg, 66

Declaration of Rights and Grievances, 55

First Continental Congress, 62

Gaspee, Destruction of, 59

King's Proclamation Line, 50

Loyalists, 71

Quebec City Siege, 72

Stamp Act Congress, 55

Tea Tax, 59

Tea, glass, etc. Tax, 56

Virginia Becomes Independent, 68

Andros, Edmund, 29

Anti-Mason Party. *See* Open-Leagues Party

Arbuthnot, Alexander, 235

Arbuthnot, Marriot, 91

Armstrong, John, 195, 204, 217

Arnold, Benedict, 70, 77, 102

Austin, Moses, 274

Austin, Stephen, 275, 281, 289

Bacon, Nathaniel, 27

Baltimore, Lord. *See* Calvert, George

Banking and Finance, 144

   Boston, 118

   First Bank of the United States, 145

   Second Bank of the United States, 227, 228

Baptist Church, 177

Barbary Pirates, 177, 187

Barbour, James, 249

Barry, William, 258, 278

Benton, Jesse, 209

Benton, Thomas, 209

Berkeley, William, 20, 24, 27

Berrien, John, 258

Biden, President Joe, 311

Billy Graham, 308

Biloxi, Mississippi, 32

Blair, Henry, 279

Blair, John, 116

Blount, William, 143, 159, 161, 167, 202, 211

Bonaparte, Napoleon. *See* French Government Leaders

Bonded African Americans. *See* African American History, *See* African Slavery

   Georgia Colony, 35

   Haiti, 148

   Importation, 31, 39, 64

   Making Independent, 279, 280

   Marine Shippers, 32

   Northwest Ordinance, 117

   Virginia Colony, 38

Boone, Daniel, 51

Booth, John Wilkes, 273

Booth, Junius, 272, 282

Bowie, James, 286

Braddock, Edward, 44

Branch, John, 258

Brazil, 10

Breckenridge, John, 186

British Government Leaders

   Atkin, Edmund, 45

   Carleton, Guy, 155

   Chatham, William, 82

   Dorchester, Lord. *See* Carleton, Guy

   Fox, Charles, 72, 82, 106

   Germain, George, 72, 89, 106

   Grenville, George, 53

   Johnson, William, 45

   North, Frederick, 61, 83, 106

   Pitt, William, 46

British Kings

George III, 53, 61, 83, 106

British Parliament, 106

British Taxes

   Molasses, 53

   Stamps on Documents, 53

   Tea, 60

Brock, Isaac, 201

Buford, Abraham, 93

Burgoyne, John, 68, 77, 79

Burleson, Edward, 284

Burnet, David, 289

Burr, Aaron, 172, 183, 186, 194

Butler, Anthony, 275

Butler, Benjamin, 278

Calhoun, John, 227, 230, 232, 239, 248, 257

Calvert, George, 20

Cammeron, Alexander, 73

Campbell, Archibald, 86

Campbell, Arthur, 87

Campbell, William, 96

Canada, 47

   Boundary with U. S., 158, 226

Carolina Colony, 24, 34

Carroll, Billy, 244, 251, 259

Carroll, William, 221

Carteret, George, 24

Carteret, John, 34

Cass, Lewis, 257, 278

Catawba Nation, 45

Catholic Church, 10

Champlain, Samuel de, 13

Charleston, South Carolina, 25, 73

Charlotte, North Carolina, 36

Cherokee Leaders

   Atta-culla-culla, 66

   Benge, 158

   Black Fox, 207

   Bloodyfellow, 134

   Dragging Canoe, 87, 134

   John Jolly. *See* Oo-loo-te-ka

John Rogers, 265

John Watts, 107, 139, 156

Little Turkey, 134

Oconostota, 66

Oo-loo-te-ka, 207, 232, 260

Sequoyah, 207

Tah-lhon-tusky, 207, 232

Talotiskee, 139

The Bloody Fellow, 139, 156

The Bowl, 285

The Glass, 207

The Ridge, 207, 213

Cherokee Nation, 45, 60, 113, 154

Alliance with British, 73, 87

In Support of British, 76, 102, 107

Nickajack, 156

Raids and Counterraids, 139, 154, 156

Chickasaw Leaders

Piomingo, 155

Chickasaw Nation, 153, 160

Choctaw Nation, 149, 262

Chouteau, Auguste, 261

Church of England, 18

Clarendon, Earl of. See Hyde, Edward

Clark, Lewis, 183

Clay, Henry, 222, 227, 244, 246, 248, 263, 277

Clinton, DeWitt, 204

Clinton, George, 185, 194

Clinton, Henry, 68, 84, 88, 90, 93, 105, 107

Cocke, William, 161

Cod Fishing, 21, 32

Coffee, John, 210, 217, 221

Confederate States of America, 306

Congress, Confederation, 110, 117

Congress, Federal. See Federal House, See Federal Senate

Connecticut Colony, 21

Cooper, Anthony Ashley, 24

Cornwallis, Charles, 93, 94, 95, 97, 99, 101, 102, 104

Cos, Martin, 283, 284

Cotesworth, Charles, 172

Cotton, 137, 152, 225, 233, 236

Crawford, William, 204, 230, 239, 246

Creek Leaders

McGillivray, Alexander, 111, 130, 134, 143

Red Eagle. See Weatherford, William

Weatherford, William, 208, 210, 213

Creek Nation, 87, 111, 153, 160, 235, 262

Fort Mims massacre, 208

Raids and Counterraids, 118, 130, 140, 154, 157

Crockett, David, 244, 286

Crowninshield, Benjamin, 204, 230

Cumberland Settlement, 91

Dallas, Alexander, 204

Davis, Jeff

Ancestry, 73

Davis, Samuel, 73

Deane, Silas, 75

Dearborn, Henry, 186, 201

Defense of Independence. See Treaties, Paris, 1783

Alliance with France, 75, 83, 108

Alliance with Spain, 88, 108

British Peace Offer, 84

British Withdrawal, 106, 109, 111

Camden, South Carolina, 95

Charleston, South Carolina, 90, 92, 105

Charlotte, North Carolina, 97

Continental Congress, 78, 100

Economy, 89

French Alliance, 85, 93, 103

French Canadians, 89

Frontier War, 87, 94, 95, 98

Georgia, Invasion of, 88

Guilford County, 101

Hannah's Cowpens, 100

Kings Mountain, 97

Lake Champlain, 77, 79

Louisiana, 108

New York City, 77, 88

Over the Mountain Men, 96, 98

Penobscot Bay, 89

Philadelphia, fall of, 80, 84

Rhode Island, 85, 93

Saratoga, New York, 81

Savannah, Georgia, 86, 89

South Carolina, Invasion of, 90, 102, 103

State Constitutions, 74

Surrender of Burgoyne's British Army, 81

Trenton, New Jersey, 78

Waxhaw, 93, 99

Yorktown, 102, 104

Delaware Colony, 22, 29

Democratic Party

Precusor, 147, 149, 172

Deportationism, 263, 266

d'Estaing, Comte, 85, 88, 89

Detroit, 155

Dickerson, Mahlon, 278

Dickinson, Charles, 187, 189

Dinwiddie, Robert, 43

District of Columbia. *See* Washington City

Donaldson, John, 90, 91

Donaldson, Rachel, 91

Dougles, Senator Stephen, 305

East Florida Colony, 52, 109, 179, 234, 242

Federal purchase, 1819, 237

East India Company, 60

Eaton, John, 244, 257

Elbridge, Gerry, 167

Embargo Act of 1808, 192

English Civil War, 23

English Kings

Charles I, 18

Charles II, 29

Cromwell, Oliver (Emperor), 19

Henry II, 11

James I, 12, 17

William III, 30

English Parliament, 18

Eustis, William, 195, 202

Faneuil, Peter, 32

Fannin, James, 286

Federal Capitol Building, 176

Federal Constitution

Amendment 11, 151

Amendment 12, 173

Amendments 1-10, 140

Creation of, 115, 120

Ratification of, 129, 131, 132

Text of, 120

The Federalist, 131

Federal Navy, 168, 177, 203

Federal Supreme Court

Cohen vs. Virginia, 241

Establishment, 140

Federalist Powerbase, 174

Gibbons vs. Ogden, 245

John Marshall Era, 175, 237, 241, 245

Marbury vs Madison, 178

Principle of Judicial Review, 179

Second Bank of the United States, 245

Federalist Party, 147, 149, 247

Fenno, John, 148

Ferguson, Patrick, 72, 91, 94, 95, 97

Flood, John, 14, 17, 20

Florida Colony, 34, 47

Forsyth, John, 278

Fort Cumberland, 42

Fort Detroit, 48

Fort Duquesne, 43, 46

Fort Fort Oswego, 80

Fort Gibson, 261

Fort Greenville, 158

Fort Louisburg, 33, 39, 46

Fort Malden, 201

Fort Miamis, 155

Fort Stanwix, 80

Fort Stoddert, 183

Fort Ticonderoga, 67, 79

Franklin, Benjamin, 75, 109, 116

French Government Leaders

Bonaparte, Napoleon, 169, 176, 178, 180, 182, 188, 191, 197, 200, 215

Genet, Edmund, 152

Talleyrand, Charles Maurice de, 167, 169, 180

French Revolution, 152

Freneau, Philip, 148

Fulton, Robert, 244

Fur Trade, 18, 26, 33, 35, 42, 161

Gage, Thomas, 61

Gaines, Edmund, 235

Gallatin, Albert, 186, 195

Gaona, Antonio, 286, 288

Garrison, William Lloyd, 252, 262, 264, 265

Gates, Horatio, 70, 80, 94

Georgia Colony, 35

Germans, 36

Graham, Billy, 308

Grasse, Marquis de, 103

Graves, Thomas, 103

Green, Abner, 142, 146

Green, Thomas, 142

Greene, Nathanael, 100, 101, 103, 110

Haiti, 148, 163, 176, 178, 182

Halifax, 71

Hamilton, Alexander, 116, 131, 141, 144, 157

    Killed by Aaron Burr in Duel, 183

Hamilton, Paul, 195

Hampton, Wade, 210

Hancock, John, 56, 61

Harrison, William

    Indiana Territory, 198

Hoban, James, 176

Houston, Eliza Allen, 254, 259

Houston, Elizabeth, 207

Houston, Sam

    Ancestry, 207

    Battle of San Jacinto, 286

    Cherokee Territory, 260, 261, 264, 265

    Commander-in-Chief Texas Army, 285

    Federal Army Career, 232

    Federal House, 249

    Federal Senate, 300

    Governor of Tennessee, 251, 254, 259

    Mexican Texas, 274, 280, 281

    Nashville Lawyer, 236, 244

    President of Texas, 289

    Texas Independence Movement, 242, 273, 285

    Visits Washington City, 281

    War against Britain, 212

    War for Texas Independence, 283, 284

    Youth, 206

Houston, Tiana Rogers, 265

Howe, Robert, 86

Howe, William, 68, 71, 80, 84

Hudson's Bay Company, 26

Hull, William, 200

Hutchinson, Anne, 20

Hutchinson, Thomas, 55, 60

Hyde, Edward, 24

Impressment of Seamen, 191

Indentured Servants, 37

Indiana Territory, 182

Indigo, 41

Ingham, Samuel, 257

Irish, 36

Iron Smelting, 41

Iroquois League, 18, 26, 33, 43, 69

Jackson, Andrew

    Against Creeks, 138

    Ancestry, 54

    Attorney General, Cumberland, 143

    Burr and Wilkinson, 189

    Campaign for President, 1824, 243, 246

    Campaign for President, 1828, 249

    Crawford, Uncle James, 94, 97

    Cumberland Arrival, 133

    Declaration of Independence, 67

    Defeat of Creeks, 210

    Defense of Independence, 74, 94, 95, 99, 101

    Duel with Dickinson, 189

Duel, Benton vs. Carroll, 208

Elizabeth (mother), 101, 105

Farming, 184, 243

Federal Senate, 167, 244

Fight with Jesse and Thomas Benton, 209

Florida Territory, 242

Judge, 167

Lousiana Purchase, 181

Marriage to Rachel Donelson, 146

Natchez, 142, 146, 206

New Orleans, Defense of, 223

News of San Jacinto victory, 289

Pensacola, 235

President, 255

Racehorses, 186, 188, 197, 200, 236

Reelected President, 277

Salisbury, NC, 119

Spanish East Florida, 234, 236

Summation, 255

Tennessee Statehood, 161

War against Britain, 202, 214, 223

Young Adulthood, 119

Jackson, Andrew (President's Father), 57

Jackson, Rachel Donelson, 133, 146

Jackson, Robert (brother), 101

Jamestown, 12, 17

Jay, John, 109, 131, 155, 157, 158

Jefferson, Thomas

Candidate for President, 162, 164

Defense of Independence, 109

Democratic Party (Precusor to), 147

Elected Vice President, 164

Federal Supreme Court, 241

Lewis and Clark Expedition, 183

Lousiana Purchase, 179

President, 172

Reelection, 185

Retirement, 194

Secretary of State, 142, 153

Summation, 172

Jews, 37

Johnson, Samuel, 63

Joliet, Louis, 26

Jones, Anson, 299

Jones, Dr. Anson, 298

Jones, John, 88

Jones, Richard, 204

Jones, William, 195

Keane, John, 221, 224

Kendall, Amos, 278

Kentucky County, Virginia, 42

Key, Francis, 216, 272

King, Rufus, 116, 185, 229

King's Proclamation Line, 50, 78

Knox, Henry, 70

La Salle, Sieur de, 32

Lafayette, Marie-Joseph du Motier, Marquis de, 76, 102, 105

Lafitte, Jean, 216, 220

Land Cessions

Alabama (1789), 137

Alabama (1814), 214

Georgia (1814), 214

Mississippi (1789), 137

Mississippi (1792), 149

Ohio (1785), 112

Ohio (1795), 158

Tennessee (by North Carolina, 1784), 112

Land Ownership, 38, 50, 62, 108, 112, 117, 159, 162, 168

Leclerc, V. F., 178

Lee, Arthur, 75

Lee, Charles, 70

Lee, Light Horse Harry, 89, 157

L'Efant, Charles, 176

Lewis, Meriwether, 183

Lexington, Massachusetts, 65

Liberator, The. See William Lloyd Garrison

Liberia, 240, 263

Lincoln, Benjamin, 81, 88, 90, 105

Livingston, Robert, 177, 179

Livingston, Susannah Carmack, 158

London Company, 12, 14

Louisiana Colony, 46, 47, 109, 170

Louisiana Purchase, 179, 181

Louisiana Territory, 182

L'Ouverture, Francois Dominique Toussaint, 148, 163, 176, 182

Lowndes, William, 227

Lundy, Benjamin, 252, 262, 264, 266

Macdonough, Thomas, 215

Madison, James

    Declaration of Independence, 116

    Declaration of War, 199

    Federal Constitution, 131

    Marbury vs Madison, 178

    Nonintercourse Act, 197

    President, 194

    Secretary of State, 186

    Summation, 194, 204

Maine, 18

Marbury, William, 178

Marion, Francis, 94, 99

Maritime Trade, 22, 137, 154, 157, 158, 178, 191, 196, 197, 227

Marquette, Father Jacques, 26

Marshall, John, 167, 175, 178, 237

Maryland Colony, 20

Mason, George, 116

Masons, Free and Accepted, 250

Massachusetts Church-State Government, 22, 29, 40, 114

Massachusetts Colony, 18, 33

Massachusetts Secesionists, 219

Masschusetts Bay Company, 18

Mather, Cotton, 40

Mather, Increase, 40

McBury, Leonard, 77

McDowell, Charles, 94, 96

McLane, Louis, 257, 278

McMillan, Alexander, 70, 96

McMillan, William, 96

Methodist Church, 177

Mexican Government Leaders

    Bustamante, Anastasio, 275, 280

    Guerrero, Vicente, 274

    Hidalgo, Miguel, 274

    Iturbide, 274

    Morelos, Jose, 274

    Poinsett, Joel, 275

    Santa Anna, Antonio Lopez de, 275, 280, 283, 284, 286

    Victoria, Guadalupe, 275

Mexican Texas, 280

Milam, Ben, 284

Mississippi, Settlement of, 168

Mobile Bay, 182, 199

Mobile, Alabama, 208, 215

Money, 149

Monroe, James, 195

    Louisiana Purchase, 179

    Minister to France, 153

    President, 239

    Secretary of State, 204

    Secretary of War, 217

    Summation, 229

Montagu, John, 61

Montcalm, Louis-Joseph de, 45

Montgomery, John, 87

Montgomery, Richard, 70

Montreal, Canada, 26, 70

Morgan, Daniel, 100

Morgan, William, 250

Murfreesboro, Tennessee, 251

Murray, John, 68

Murray, William Van, 168

Narragansett Bay, 20

Nashville, Tennessee, 91, 251

National Territories

    Control Over, 100

Nelson, Horatio, 188

New Amsterdam Colony, 18, 25

New England Company, 18

New England, Dominion of, 29

New England, United Colonies of, 23

New France Colony, 13, 25

New Hampshire Colony, 18

New Jersey Colony, 24, 28

New Orleans, 32, 47, 179

New Sweden Colony, 22, 23

New York City, 18

New York Colony, 23, 24

Newspapers

    The Liberator, Lloyd Garrison, editor, 265

North Carolina Colony, 34

Northern States Republican Party, 304

Northwest Territory (Ohio etc.), 117, 143

Northwest Territory (Ohio, etc.), 100

Nova Scotia, 33

Nullification of Federal Law, 170, 192

Oglethorpe, John, 34

Ohio Company, The, 42

Ohio, Settlement of, 148, 153, 155

Open-Leagues Party, 250, 253

    Election Campaign of 1838, 277

Orleans Territory, 182

Osage Nation, 262

Overton, John, 133, 189

Penn, William, 27

Pennsylvania Colony, 28

Pequot Nation, 21

Perry, Oliver, 203, 209

Philadelphia, 69

Pickering, Timothy, 183

Pickings, Andrew, 94

Pinckney, Charles, 116, 177, 185, 194

Pinckney, Charles C., 116, 167

Pinckney, Thomas, 159

Pinckney, William, 195, 204

Plymouth Colony, 16, 20

Plymouth Company, 12

Pocahontas, 13, *See* Powhatan Nation

Polk, James K., 301

Population Statistics

    1775, 39

    1790, 136

    1800, 166

    1810, 196

    1820, 231

    1830, 259

Porter, Peter, 249

Portsmouth, 20

Powhatan Nation, 14, 17

Presbyterian Church, 36, 177

Prevost, George, 215

Provincetown, Massachusetts Colony, 16

Puritan Separatists, 15, 18, 22, 30, 40

Puritans, 18, 40

Quakers, 27

Quebec City, 13, 70, 72

Quebec Colony, 52

Quincy, Josiah, 58

Randolph, Edmund, 116

Raven, The. *See* Houston, Sam

Rawdon, Francis, 102

Religious Leaders

    Edwards, Jonathan, 40

    Whitefield, George, 40

Renssalaer, Stephen Van, 201

Revere, Paul, 61, 65

Rhode Island Colony, 20, 24, 32

Rice, 31

Roanoke Island, North Carolina, 12

Robards, Lewis, 146

Robertson, James, 59, 87, 90, 91, 108, 119, 130, 143, 160

Rochambeau, Jean Compte de, 93, 103

Rockingham, Charles, 107

Rodney, Ceasar, 186, 195

Rolfe, John, 14

Ross, Robert, 215

Royal African Company, 31

Ruffin, Edmund, 233

Rush, Richard, 204, 230, 249

Rutherford, Griffin, 76

Rutledge, John, 116

Sailing Leaders

    Cabot, John, 11

    Columbus, Christopher, 10

    Diaz, Bartholomew, 10

    Gama, Vasco da, 10

    Henry, Portuguese Prince, 10

    Hudson, Henry, 18

    Magellan, Ferdinand, 11

    Newport, Christopher, 12

    Raleigh, Walter, 12

Salem Witch Hysterics, 40

Savannah, Georgia, 35

Schools, 40

Science and Technology

    Cotton Gin, 152

    Iron, 41

Scots, 36, 51

Secession. *See* State Secession

Sectionalism. *See* State Secession

    Campaign of 1824, 247

    Massachusetts Secession Movement, 1804, 183

    Opposition to Lousiana Purchase, 180

Sedition Act of 1798, 168, 169, 170, 177

Seminole Nation, 235

Sevier, John, 87, 94, 96, 102, 107, 113, 115, 149, 154, 161

Shawnee Leaders

    Tecumseh, 198, 201, 208, 209

Shawnee Nation, 63, 198

Shelby, Evan, 87

Shelby, Isaac, 87, 92, 95, 96, 105

Shelby, John, 94

Smith, John, 13

Smith, Robert, 186, 195

Smugglers, 192

South Carolina Colony, 31, 34, *See* also Carolina Colony

Southard, Samuel, 239, 249

Southwest Territory, 143, 160

Spanish Government Leaders

Callava, Don Jose, 242

Gardoqui, Don Diego, 160

Lemos, Manuel Gayoso de, 142, 149

Miro, Don Esteban, 110, 111, 133, 138, 142

Navarro, Don, 111

Onis, Don Louis de, 236

Vives, Francisco Dionisio, 242

Spanish Kings

    Ferdinand, 10

Spanish Queens

    Isabella, 10

St. Clair, Arthur, 79, 118, 143, 148, 153

St. Louis, Missouri, 26

Stanbery, William, 271

State of Texas, 300

State Rights, 120, 132, 169

State Secession

    Massachusetts (1804), 185

    Massachusetts (1813), 209

    Right to Secede, 132

State Sovereignty, 169

Statehood

    Alabama, 1819, 230

    Arkansas, 1836, 278

    Illinois, 1818, 230

    Indiana, 205

    Kentucky, 1792, 136, 149

    Louisiana, 1812, 195

    Maine, 1820, 230

    Michigan, 1837, 278

    Mississippi, 1817, 230

    Missouri, 1821, 239

    Ohio, 1803, 174

    Tennessee, 162

    Tennessee, 1796, 151, 159, 161

    Vermont, 1791, 136, 144

Stone's River, 56

Stuart, James, 24

Stuyvesant, Peter, 23, 25

Sumter, Thomas, 94, 95, 99

Swiss, 37

Taney, Roger, 258

Tappan, Arthur, 266

Tar and Pitch, 34

Tarleton, Banastre, 91, 93, 99, 100

Tax on Whiskey, 144, 156, 177

Taxes on Imports, 137, 227

Tennessee
  Settlement of, 59, 87, 90, 91, 99, 106, 107, 109, 115, 134, 138, 149

Texas, Republic of. *See* Houston, Sam

Thompson, Smith, 230, 239

Tobacco, 14

Tompkins, Daniel, 229

Travis, William, 285

Treaties
  Aix-la-Chapelle, 1748, 39

  Ghent, 1815. *See*

  Hopewell, 1785, 113

  King's Proclamation Line, 1766, 55

  Line of Demarcation, 1495, 10

  Paris, 1763, 47

  Paris, 1783, 109

  Paris, 1800, 170

  Pensacola, 1784, 111

  San Ildefonso, 1800, 176

  Tripoli, 1805, 187

  Tyswick, 1697, 31

  Union of England and Scotland, 1707, 34

  Utrecht, 1713, 33

  With Britain, 1795 (Jay's), 158

  With Spain 1795, 160

Turner, Nat, 259, 266

United States Confederation Government
  Articles of Confederation, 81, 100, 114

  Establishment, 101

United States Constitution. *See* Federal Constitution

United States Federal Government. *See* Federal Government

Universities

Brown, 41

Dartmouth, 41

Harvard College, 40

Princeton, 41

Rutgers, 41

William and Mary College, 40

Yale College, 40

Urrea, Jose, 286, 288

Van Buren, Martin
  Secretary of State, 257

  Vice President, 278

Vergennes, Comte de, 75

Vermont, Republic of, 79

Vesey, Denmark, 241

Virginia Charter, 12

Virginia Colony, 19, 27

Virginia Company, 14, 17

Voting Rights
  Immigrant Waiting Time, 167

Wampanoag Nation, 26

War against Britain
  Baltimore, 215

  Barataria Bay Pirates, 216

  British Escalation (1814), 215

  Canadian Front, 201, 203

  Creek-British alliance, 208

  Declaration of War (1812), 198, 199

  Defeat of Creek Nation, 210, 211

  Effect on American Politics, 226

  Lake Champlain, 215

  Lake Erie (1813), 209

  Marine Commerce, 225

  Massachusetts Secessionists, 209, 215, 223, 225, 226

  Mobile, 218

  Montreal (1813), 210

  Navy Battles, 201

  New Orleans, 216, 218, 223

  Peace Treaty, 222

  Pensacola, 217

  Shawnee-British Alliance, 209

324

Washington City, 215

War against Mexico, 301

Wars

    Against France, 31, 32, 39, 44

    Against France and Native American Nations, 44

    Texas Independence, 284

Wars, Major Battles, Battlefields

    Alamo, 1834, 286

    Alamo, 1836, 284

    Cullonden Moor, 1746, 36

    Horseshoe Bend, Alabama, 1814, 211

    New Orleans, 1814, 220, 223

    San Jacinto, 1836, 286

Washington City, 142, 176

Washington, Bushrod, 263

Washington, George

    Boston Siege, 69

    Boston, British Evacuation of, 71

    Federal Constitution, 114

    Philadelphia, 80

    President, 134

    Reelection, 150

    Retirement, 162

    Southwest Territory, 160

    Summation, 135, 151

    Trenton, New Jersey, 78

    War against France, 43

Whiskey Rebellion, 156

Yorktown, 103

Watauga Settlements, 51, 57, 59, 63, 65, 73, 76, 79, 94, 96, 154

    Frankland, 113, 115

Wayne, Anthony, 79, 89, 153, 154

Webster, Daniel, 219

West Florida Colony, 52, 109, 111, 138, 160, 179, 199, 208, 242

West Louisiana Colony, 160

Western Confederation, 69

Western Frontier, 51, 78

White House, 176

Whitney, Eli, 152

Wilkinson, James, 202, 207, 210, 214, 216

Williams, Roger, 20

Williamson, Andrew, 76

Wilmington, Delaware, 29

Winthrop, John, 19

Wirt, William, 230, 249, 277

Wiseman, William, 51

Woodbury, Levi, 278

Wythe, George, 116

Yamasee Nation, 34

York, Duke of. *See* Stuart, James

You, Dominique, 224

Zavala, Lorenzo de, 283

A listing of Published Books Authored by Howard Ray White, all available on Amazon as print books, most as e-books, some as audio-books.

Now eighty-five years old, the author, Howard Ray White, continues to write, drawing on extensive historical research to build the foundation of his upcoming books. The most important book that Howard Ray White will ever publish is the one you have read.

A listing of Howard Ray White's published books follows.

Wartime Struggles of a Virginia Farm Slave Family. In this amazing historical novel, readers experience the immense difficulties people of color, suffered during the Northern States Republican Party's military invasion of the Seceded Southern States, a war that resulted in the unnecessary death of one million Americans, black and white.

Musk, Ford and Wrights, Amazing Americans Who Fundamentally Advanced Human Travel. The 2023 book is the First Edition. Since the story of Elon's accomplishments continues beyond where the First Edition concluded, you should look forward to the Second Edition, Third Edition, etc.

God's Humans, from Adam to today. This is a Christian book that helps readers understand how the history of humankind, as God revealed to us through his Prophets and eventually was recorded in the first book of the Holy Bible, and today's scientific and geographic knowledge can be rationalized as not in conflict, but as complementary. School teachers and college professors too often scoff at the idea that God created humans, arguing that we just evolved from apes and monkeys. This book should be most helpful to people who are still relatively young.

Bloodstains, an Epic History of the Politics that Produced and Sustained the American Civil War and the Political Reconstruction that Followed. A history in four volumes. Vol. 1, *The Nation Builders.* Vol. 2, *The Demagogues.* Vol. 3, *The Bleeding.* Vol 4, *The Struggle for Healing.* This is a vastly detailed reference that should be in your library.

Understanding Abe Lincoln's First Shot Strategy (Inciting Confederates to Fire First at Fort Sumter). This is a fast read, telling well this critical history.

Understanding "Uncle Tom's Cabin" and "The Battle Hymn of the Republic;" How Novelist Harriet Beecher Stowe and Poet Julia Ward Howe Influenced the Northern Mind. A quick read; important story.

How to Study History when Seeking Truthfulness and Understanding; Lessons Learned from Outside Academia. A brief and compelling guide for all readers of history who seek truth instead of passing a school exam. Good for parents and grandparents, too

Southern Families Made America: Colonization, Revolution and Expansion, from Virginia Colony, to the Republic of Texas, to the Pacific, 1607 to 1848. Southern families were the Nation Builders. This is a thorough documentation that tells their history and amazing stories of Andrew Jackson and Sam Houston.

The CSA Trilogy, An Alternate History/Historical Novel in three volumes about Our Vast and Beautiful Confederate States of America — A Happy Story in Three Parts of What Might Have Been — 1861 to 2011. I suggest you don a dreamer's cap and enjoy a happy story concluding with celebrating the 150th Anniversary of the large, successful Confederate States of America:

> Book 1: *How We Confederates Won Our Independence, 1861 to 1862.*

> Book 2: *How We Confederates Invited Cuba, Northern Mexico, Russian America and Hawaii to Join Our Federation of States, 1862 to 1877.*

> Book 3: *How We Confederates Preserved Our Values while Developing the World's Greatest Economy, 1878 to 2011.*

Rebirthing Lincoln, how an Illinois Lawyer Kept Secret His Illegitimate Birth and Won the 1860 Presidential Nomination of the Northern States Republican Party. This is the most truthful biography ever written about President Abraham Lincoln. It is highly unlikely that Kentuckian Thomas Lincoln was the biological father of baby Abraham. Instead, the boy's father was likely Abraham Enloe a prominent western North Carolinian. When little Abe was about two years old, his mother, Nancy Hanks of western North Carolina, married Thomas Lincoln in Kentucky and the couple raised little Abraham in that state. How did politically ambitious Abraham Lincoln keep his true-birth secret? That is the underlining story in *Rebirthing Lincoln,* which presents a Lincoln biography from birth to 1) his becoming President, 2) to his refusing to seek peace and, 3) instead, to his launching a war of conquest, which lasted four years and resulted in one million unnecessary American deaths. This is truthful history, not an alternate history, not a novel, a MUST-READ biography!

Why and How the North Conquered the South. An essential quick read. "Please just devote 3 or 4 hours to reading this concise, yet complete, history so you will know the truth of America's most horrific catastrophe, a tragedy that resulted in one million unnecessary American deaths."

Three Books Edited by Howard Ray White follow:

Advancing American Reading Achievement During the Great Depression: a 1939 Comparative Study of Seventh Grade White and African American Children in Segregated Nashville, Tennessee Schools, based on a PhD thesis by Dr. Larry Jordan Willis, my father-in-law.

Understanding Granddad Through His Poetry, the Poetry of Tennessean John Andrew White (1874-1951), with story and editing by grandson, Howard Ray White. Jr. I dropped the "Jr." after Dad died.

Springfield Girl, a Memoir, by Martha Frances Bell White, with additions by son Howard Ray White. My mother wrote this and I published it. Following her death, I completed her story and created this, the second edition.

One book that my wife and I jointly authored:

Remembering While We Still Can, the Memoir of Judith and Howard White's Southern Family. We both wrote this for our 60th wedding anniversary.

One book written by my wife, Judith Willis White, about her Hunt family of Easley, South Carolina:

Memories of Easley, South Carolina, My Wonderful Grandparents, Leigh and Camella Hendricks Hunt and Their Descendants, by granddaughter Judith Willis White. This is a wonderful book about Judith's grandparent's family and visits while growing up.

Two books authored by sixteen members of the Society of Independent Southern Historians, a group that I co-founded (I was an editor and contributing author here):

Understanding the War Between the States, A Supplemental Booklet by 16 Writers that Enables a More Complete and Truthful Study of American History (Middle School, High School, College and Beyond), by the Society of Independent Southern Historians, Howard Ray White, co-editor.

American History for Home Schools, 1607 to 1885, with a Focus on Our Civil War, also by the Society. This is very similar to the book above.

Howard Ray White's TV Shows

To view any of my 80, 30-minute TV shows, from the Series titled "True American History," go to www.vimeo.com and query "Howard Ray White" on your computer or query Vimeo on your smart streaming television.

My Close

I feel blessed when Americans, who seek truthful history, turn to my books for enlightenment. It is so easy. Just go to www.amazon.com and query "Howard Ray White." A complete list of my books will appear for your review.

Thank you for reading *Southern Families Made America*. Yes, our ancestors did it!

And God bless every one of you. If of Southern ancestry, be proud!

And, finally, please join in efforts to Save America.

Howard Ray White

www.ingramcontent.com/pod-product-compliance
Lightning Source LLC
Chambersburg PA
CBHW080509090426
42734CB00015B/3015